W9-BYQ-605

The
Love of Learning
and the
Desire for God

THE LOVE OF LEARNING
AND
THE DESIRE FOR GOD

A Study of Monastic Culture

JEAN LECLERCQ, O.S.B.

Translated by
Catharine Misrahi

1907

New York
Fordham University Press
1982

PRINTING HISTORY:
First edition, 1961
Mentor Omega paperback, 1962
Second edition, 1974
Reprinted, 1977
Third edition, 1982

A translation of
*L'Amour des lettres et le désir de Dieu:
Initiation aux auteurs monastiques du moyen âge*
(Paris: Les Éditions du Cerf, 1957)

Printed in the United States of America

Contents

Abbreviations

CCL	*Corpus Christianorum: Series Latina*
CSEL	*Corpus scriptorum ecclesiasticorum latinorum*
DHGE	*Dictionnaire d'histoire et de géographie ecclésiastique*
Du Cange	Du Cange, Favre, Henschel, *Glossarium mediae et infimae latinitatis*
MGH	*Monumenta Germaniae historica*
PG	Migne, *Patrologia graeca*
PL	Migne, *Patrologia latina*
RB	*Revue bénédictine*
RHE	*Revue d'histoire ecclésiastique*
RTAM	*Revue de théologie ancienne et médiévale*
TLL	*Thesaurus linguae latinae*
ZKT	*Zeitschrift für Kirche und Theologie*

Preface

THIS BOOK IS COMPOSED of a series of lectures given to young monks at the Institute of Monastic Studies at Sant'Anselmo in Rome during the winter of 1955–56. It is published at their request and dedicated to them. It is an introductory work and therefore not intended for specialists, for already well-informed scholars. They would, with justice, find fault with it for generalizations which can hardly be avoided in a comprehensive work. Hence, it is desirable at the very beginning that its scope be defined.

Its purpose is not to offer a synthesis that would be premature, nor to provide a bibliography which can be found elsewhere, but to draw attention to subjects for further investigation and to suggest partial and provisional solutions. The sources used will be, primarily, written documents, particularly those of doctrinal or spiritual character; treatises on geography, medicine, or law will not be under consideration. In fact, religious writings are the most numerous and most fully represented in the manuscripts. No complete listing will be given nor will all those which have been used be mentioned. Those which are, will be cited merely as examples. They will rarely be taken from authors later than the beginning of the thirteenth century.

Within these limits and with such reservations, the work will still necessarily involve simplifications and broad generalizations which would call for supporting arguments, shading, and further definition. This has occasionally been done in special studies where evidence is supplied which is not provided in this exposition. We shall not here attempt to shed any new light on the subject but in the main to summarize works whose results have not been brought together in focus. Scholars such as C. H. Haskins, J. de Ghellinck, Paul Lehmann, Bernhard Bischoff, and others have undertaken patient and fruithful research on medieval culture in general. In relation to their findings, perhaps the time has come to ask whether monastic culture has its own identifying characteristics and what they are. This is difficult to decide: there are certain aspects of monastic history to which non-monastic scholars may not have paid enough attention and to which a monk risks paying too much. A margin of error will therefore always exist in evaluations and even in the findings themselves and it is best to admit this at the outset. Accordingly, the point here is less to pass judgment than to understand. Judgment is God's province; the historian must be satisfied to learn why men and events were what the texts tell him they were. No doubt it is an illusion to think that men can be known—the throngs of men, of monks who have lived over the centuries—by means of written documents or pictures, and yet *they* are the only sources we have. These are the work of only a few of their number and cannot show them to us completely even if the testimony of ordinary and often unknown men is enlisted to round out the testimony of the great authors and exceptional geniuses. There were weaknesses in monasticism; there are lies and falsifications in its literature. But that is not all there was. And, after all, the monks' truest self, the self they wished to be, is what was best in them.

The
Love of Learning
and the
Desire for God

Introduction

During the past few years "monastic" theology has become a subject for discussion. Is there any reality behind this expression? Is there any form of intellectuality which is a theology on the one hand, and monastic and nothing but monastic on the other? In order to introduce the subject, and to postulate the existence of a monastic theology, let us consider it at its height, at the time when, having reached its culmination, it is most distinct from any other theology: that is to say, in the twelfth century.

The importance of the twelfth century in the doctrinal history of the Middle Ages need no longer be established. That was discovered fairly recently, in the present century, during the years which preceded the First World War, by C. Baeumker, J. de Ghellinck, M. Grabmann, and others, and has attracted more and more attention through the efforts of masters like E. Gilson, A. Landgraf, P. Lottin, and many more. It is now generally accepted that this period played a capital role in laying the foundations for the scholastic theology of the thirteenth century. The term pre-scholastic (in German *Vorscholastik* or *Frühscholastik*) is given to all doctrinal writings of the period immediately preceding the great expansion of the thirteenth century, the "great scholasticism" (*Hochscholastik*) which in turn preceded "late scholasticism" (*Spätscholastik*). And it is true that all the twelfth-century writings paved the way for those of the thirteenth century. This they did in different ways, since they were themselves different in character. Some were scholastic in character and entitled, on this account, to be called pre-scholastic. Others were not at all scholastic; and it is these that will be treated here. They exist and deserve to be taken into account in the doctrinal and literary history of the twelfth century. Their individuality should be respected and they should not be confused with scholastic writings. These are the "non-scholastic" (*ausserscholastische*) texts.

Here, of course, a dispute over terminology may arise. Some would say that, first, a definition of scholasticism would have to be agreed upon. It happens that on this point there is a difference of opinion; no definite agreement has been reached. For de Wulf, for example, "scholastic" meant a body of doctrine—orthodox doctrine.[1] Consequently, Siger of Brabant and the Latin Averroists could not carry this title. De Wulf later abandoned this interpretation. Grabmann, on the contrary, held that "scholastic" should be applied, not to a doctrine, but to a method, and for that reason he entitled his great work *History of the Scholastic Method.*[2] For some, however, the scholastic method itself consists in the adoption of Aristotle's theses—in which case there is no scholasticism, really, before the thirteenth century. For others, it lay in the use of Aristotle's logic as transmitted to the Middle Ages through writings like Boethius'—and according to this view St. Anselm or Abailard can be described as already scholastics. Today, it is more generally agreed that the scholastic method is characterized not by the use of Aristotle but by the teaching procedures, principally the *quaestio* applied to the *sacra pagina*; in this sense the writings of the school of Laon at the beginning of the twelfth century were already scholastic, as were, even earlier, the *quaestiones* on sacred doctrine which were deliberated from the time of the renaissance of ancient pedagogy beginning with the Carolingian age.[3]

It is in this sense that scholasticism will be used in this work. For it alone corresponds to the obvious meaning of the word, and besides, it makes possible a clear distinction between what is "scholastic" and what is not. As a matter of fact, a "scholastic" is, by etymology, a schoolmaster, a man who teaches in a school. Now—to touch on a point which will later be made more precise—in the twelfth century, there were two types of schools: a school for monks and a school for clerics. The former were called "interior" if they were open only to boys destined for the monastic life; the latter, "exterior" if they were accustomed to admit other students. The curriculum of these exterior schools was exclusively the *trivium* and the *quadrivium*—the Seven Liberal Arts—and only by way of rare exception did they include the study of theology.

In general, the monks did not acquire their religious formation in a school, under a scholastic, by means of the *quaestio*, but individually, under the guidance of an abbot, a spiritual father, through the reading of the Bible and the Fathers, within the liturgical framework of the monastic life. Hence, there arose a type of Christian culture with marked characteristics: a disinterested culture which was "contemplative" in bent. Very different from this are the schools for clerics. Situated in cities, near cathedrals, they are attended by clerics who had already received a Liberal Arts formation in rural, parochial, or monastic schools, one intended to prepare them for pastoral activity, for "the active life." It is in these schools for clerics that "scholastic theology" is born, the theology of the schools, that which is taught in the schools. When men of the twelfth century speak of "schools," of going to schools (*ad scholas ire*), they mean urban, not monastic schools.

Does that imply that the monks have no theology? They do have one, but it is not scholastic; it is the theology of the monasteries, "monastic theology." The men of the twelfth century were clearly aware of this distinction. Here an example may be borrowed from the *Microcosmos* of Godfrey of St. Victor, written about 1185. After having mentioned an opinion given by Simon of Tournai, the Victorine adds: "In any case, let us [monks] leave this question, which holds very little interest for us, to the disputations of the scholastics, and devote our attention to other things."[4] The attitude taken by this regular canon is quite revealing. He makes a clear distinction between what concerns scholastics and what concerns cloistered religious, the *claustrales*.

Let us note carefully that the monastic and the scholastic milieux are not in constant opposition; they form a contrast but are also interrelated and they owe much to each other. In order to recall the truth of this statement we need only refer to St. Bernard, abbot of Clairvaux, and Peter Lombard, master of the *Sentences*; though very different from each other, they were friends. Here we may well illustrate the differences between these two milieux of Christian culture, and, to avoid lengthy generalizations, present two texts taken from the two theologians just mentioned.

Peter Lombard's Prologue on St. Paul

The first is a recently discovered version of Lombard's prologue to his commentary on the Epistles of St. Paul.[5] It differs from the Prologue as known and edited up until now,[6] though its content is substantially the same. It is more in the "oral style," closer to the real teaching given by Peter Lombard to the pupils in his school, and consequently more revealing of the "method" of which we are speaking.

To begin with, a clear distinction is introduced in absolutely impersonal terms, followed, as each term is defined and new divisions are proposed, by a series of other distinctions. The purpose of the procedure is indicated; the aim is to acquire knowledge: *Sciendum quod* . . . , and the way to obtain it is the *quaestio*: *Quaeritur quare*. . . . St. Paul's epistles are subjected to the same type of investigation as might be applied to any other historical document. Problems of authenticity, of dating, of situation and form are examined in succession. For each problem, the solutions of preceding authors (*auctoritates*) are presented first, and then from among these the teacher chooses one solution. Thus the purpose of the commentary and of its Prologue is to resolve the problems which arise in objective history. The sources used are the ancient commentators, particularly Pelagius, known through St. Jerome, Haymo, and, among Lombard's contemporaries, Gilbert of la Porrée. This text, of one of the greatest of the twelfth-century scholastics, has little that is personal, but this is precisely what made it valuable and explains its influence in the tradition of the school.

PROLOGUE OF ST. BERNARD TO HIS
Sermons on the Canticle of Canticles

Let us now compare this text with another example of how Scripture was taught, but this time in a monastic milieu. In order to have a parallel text whose topic is the same and which is also an introduction to a commentary, let us read the first of St. Bernard's *Sermons on the Canticle*. From the very first words, a totally different note is sounded: "To you, my brother, I must say something different from what I say to others, to those in the world, or, in any case, I must say it in a different way. . . ." And what follows enlarges on the same theme. This is no mere impersonal discourse. A man, speaking in the first person, is addressing his readers or a specially selected audience and giving them instruction aimed directly at them. And who are they? They are not laymen destined to receive instruction in the faith of the Apostles such as is required for all; they are spiritual men who must have the *doctrina spiritus*. They are the "perfect" to whom, according to St. Paul, words of wisdom must be spoken: *sapientiam loquimur*. They are men who, "for a long time, have been concerned with celestial realities" and who "make these the object of their meditations by day and by night"; in a word, they are contemplatives. They have both the right and the need to receive instruction in doctrine, an authentic sacred doctrine—in other words, a theology, but a theology closely related to the monastic experience which is, simply, a life of faith led in the monastery. This theology assumes on the part of the teacher, and on the part of his audience, a special way of life, a rigorous asceticism, or as they say today a "commitment." Rather than speculative insights, it gives them a certain appreciation, of savoring and clinging to the truth and, what is everything, to the love of God.

CONTEMPLATION, THEOLOGY, AND POETRY

St. Bernard uses poetic imagery taken from Holy Scripture to define the method and the object of this contemplative discourse, *theoricus sermo*. It is oriented not toward learning but toward spirituality. He insists that one must go beyond the rational methods which may be properly applied to matters of faith. He is therefore assuming that the teacher and his pupils have received a God-given gift and personal grace. It is God really who does the teaching; consequently it is to Him that we must pray. In this light, just as there is no theology without moral life and asceticism, so there is no theology without prayer. Its effect will be the establishment of a certain contact with God, a profound attachment to Him because these shades of meaning as well as others are implied in the word *affectus*, which Bernard uses here; to this he adds expressions which convey the ideas of attraction (*allicit*), of joy, and of sweetness. This "labor" will not be exempt from hardship; it will be a real quest (*investigare*), and a difficult quest (*inquirendi difficultas*). But the experience of the sweetness of God will give rise to enthusiasm, it will blossom in the form of poetry and hymn. The Canticle of Canticles is the expression of both desire and fulfillment; it is a song and a love-song, a song one listens to with one's whole being and a song that one sings in one's heart. In this way it accompanies and sustains the progress of faith, from grace to grace, from vocation, conversion to monastic life, until one's entrance into the life of the blessed. Bernard evokes the labors, the "daily wars," but also the joy of hope, the promised treasures, future rewards, which are just so many ways to say God. For the Lord is there at the beginning. He is there at every stage, He is at the close, He is the End. The important word is no longer *quaeritur*, but *desideratur*; no longer *sciendum*, but *experiendum*. Bernard never tires of emphasizing this in musical, rhythmical, consistently beautiful expressions whose depth cannot be rendered in translation:

> A canticle of this kind, fervor alone can teach; it can be learned only through experience. Those who have experienced it will recognize this. Those who have not experienced it, may they burn with desire not so much *to know* as *to experience*.

At this high point of his exposition Bernard brings us to the frontiers of poetry. But he must bring his discourse to an end, and he does so with still another allusion to monastic observance. For in the writing of this ardent and undoubtedly sincere elevation, he makes use of a literary form and conforms to its laws. He is a theologian; but through the perfection of his style and careful composition, he shows he is, as well, a man of letters. The literary form he employs here is essentially Christian, traditional with the Fathers and in monasticism: the sermon. Now, every well-made sermon contains an exordium, a development, and a conclusion; Bernard bows to its restrictions. And within the rules which he has set for himself, he gives proof of a flexibility and a freedom in strong contrast to the divisions and subdivisions which mark the structure of the Prologue of Peter Lombard. Like the style, the teaching is personal; it is not subjective, it is universal, it has value for all, insofar as each person is unique, engaged in a spiritual experience which is his very own. Finally to the extent that Bernard makes use of sources (or, in any case, models), they are no longer Pelagius, Haymo, Gilbert of la Porrée; they are two great mystical doctors, Origen and St. Gregory the Great.

LITERATURE AND ETERNAL LIFE

Although this simple comparison of two contemporary texts gives rise to certain problems, it also offers a hint for their solution. That there is a theology in Peter Lombard, no one will deny. But is one to be found in St. Bernard, and what are its characteristics? His text itself suggests the answer: it consists in the reconciliation of two elements which seem opposed, but which are to be found in almost all monastic literature. They will be reconciled in different ways by different authors and at various periods. Within monasticism there appear different currents and different milieux—Benedictine and Cistercian, to cite only the most important—as there are different "schools" in scholasticism—that of Laon differs from that of Chartres—and different periods. But these two elements, differing but slightly in proportion, are the constants which guarantee the continuity and the homogeneity of monastic culture. They are, on the one hand, the "literary" character of monastic writings; on the other, their mystical orientation. A written rather than an oral teaching, but well written in conformity with the art of writing (*grammatica*), it is directed to personal union with the Lord here below and later in beatitude; it is marked by intense desire and by a longing for ultimate consummation. That is why it is difficult to describe in one word both this literature and the studies based on it.

Theology, spirituality, cultural history: these three realities were not separated in the real life of the monks, and they can never be dissociated. Thus the plan which seems to be imposed on the study undertaken here consists in describing in a concrete way, with the aid of a few examples, the genesis, the development, and the constants in the cultural current which links St. Benedict to St. Bernard and to his sons. And the only purpose of these pages is to awaken a desire for the reading of the monastic authors.

NOTES

1. This definition is not found in the 6th edition of his *Histoire de la philosophie médiévale*.

2. *Die Geschichte der scholastischen Methode* (Freiburg-im-B., 1911).

3. See p. 203 *infra*.

4. Book 3, Ch. 189 (ed. P. Delhaye [Lille, 1951], 210).

5. "Les deux rédactions du prologue de Pierre Lombard sur les épîtres de S. Paul," *Miscellanea Lombardiana* (Novara, 1957) 109-12.

6. PL 191.1297.

THE FORMATION OF
MONASTIC CULTURE

1

The Conversion of
St. Benedict

Two SERIES OF TEXTS have exercised a decisive, constant, and universal influence on the origin and development of medieval monastic culture in the West, and they contain in germ the two essential components of this culture: grammar and spirituality. These two groups of texts are those connected with St. Benedict, and those of a Doctor of the Church who was very close to him in all respects, St. Gregory the Great. These texts must be examined in succession and they will afford an opportunity to define terms and to recall ideas which are essential to an understanding of all that follows. We begin to follow the sublime path pointed out by St. Bernard in a humble and austere fashion: *angusto initio*.

THE LIFE OF ST. BENEDICT: STUDIES

The monastic tradition of the Middle Ages in the West, taken as a whole, is founded principally on two texts which make of it a "Benedictine" tradition: the Life of Saint Benedict in Book II of the *Dialogues* of Saint Gregory, and the *Rule for Monks*, traditionally attributed to St. Benedict. The first is a document rich in historical and spiritual data. No attempt will be made here to try to distinguish in the stories in the Dialogue between facts and the traditional themes in the Lives of the Saints, since the present investigation is concerned less with the story of St. Benedict than with the history of his influence in the specific province of cultural orientation. Now, on this point, at the beginning of the *Life*, St. Gregory has left an interesting piece of evidence; it was often to be invoked by tradition and has become something of a symbol of St. Benedict. This text is the one in which, in the Prologue of Book II of the *Dialogues*, St. Gregory recounts that the young Benedict left Rome and school to go and lead in solitude a life entirely consecrated to God.[1] A certain number of facts are brought out in this story. To begin with, there is the conversion of St. Benedict. It is no less important for our understanding of his life, or less significant for our understanding of his work and influence, than is the conversion of St. Augustine. Like St. Augustine, St. Benedict began by taking up studies, and then abandoned them. Two questions which may arise here are: What studies did he undertake? Why did he give them up?

What did he study? The subjects then being taught to "freemen": as St. Gregory says, the *liberalia studia*; for the young Romans of the times, this expression meant grammar, rhetoric, and law.[2] Many suppositions have been made as to how old the young Benedict may have been, and consequently what he studied.[3] Did he get as far as the study of law? There is nothing to prove that he did. He is still a child (*puer*); he has scarcely "taken a step in the world." Probably he had studied at least grammar, the *grammatica* of which more will be said later. It is of little consequence here since what interests us is the symbolic meaning of the story. What does happen is that soon, disgusted with what he sees and hears in the school milieu, Benedict leaves everything and escapes from school. Why? Not because he was doing poorly in his studies—that is not implied at all—but because student life, school life, is full of danger to morals.[4] All the rest of St. Benedict's life was to be subordinated to the search for God, and lived out under the best conditions for reaching that goal—that is to say, in separation from this dangerous world. Thus in the life of St. Benedict we find in germ the two components of monastic culture: studies undertaken, and then, not precisely scorned, but renounced and transcended, for the sake of the kingdom of God. Benedict's conduct is no exception: it is typical of the monks of antiquity. The same attitude can be seen, for example, in the life of St. Caesarius of Arles: occasionally leaving the monastery of Lérins, he would go to live with a family who introduced him to Julian Pomerius, "who was famous in the region for his extraordinary knowledge of grammatical art."

They wanted "secular learning to add polish to his monastic simplicity." But very soon Caesarius renounced the instruction of this grammarian who was, incidentally, the author of a work of high order *On the Contemplative Life*.[5] All Benedictine tradition was to be made in the image of St. Benedict's life: *scienter nescius et sapienter indoctus*. It was to embrace the teaching of learned ignorance, to be nurtured by it and to transmit, recall, and keep it alive face to face with the cultural activity of the Church, as an inevitable paradox.

THE *Rule* OF ST. BENEDICT SUPPOSES LEARNED MONKS

Let us now go on to the *Rule* of St. Benedict, with regard to which two problems may arise: What is the culture of its author; What is the culture that he either expects his disciples to have or prescribes for them? It is difficult to estimate what the author of the *Rule* must have known to write it, but there is no need to exaggerate his learning, or to minimize it. As was done with regard to his conversion, historians here too have yielded to one or the other of these temptations. Similar divergences come to light concerning almost every problem of monastic culture, a fact not without some significance. To cast light on St. Benedict's culture, one could search for the sources of his *Rule*. But since he often quotes at second hand, using earlier rules, this criterion does not reveal very much. To sum up, the author of the *Rule* is distinguished less by the breadth of his knowledge than by the intelligence with which he uses it, by his understanding of the monastic life, and by the characteristics he impressed upon it.

It is scarcely any easier to offer a precise and certain answer for the second question: What culture does St. Benedict expect or demand of the monk? On this point again—that is to say, on St. Benedict's attitude toward learning and toward study—varying judgments have been expressed. Some see in the monastery a sort of academy. Others advance the opinion that St. Benedict makes little if any provision for intellectual work. It is true that he makes no legislation on it, no doubt because he takes it for granted, while he regulates manual work according to what is allowed or required by the established daily order of time. Here again there is disagreement among even the well-informed because reasons can be found in the *Rule* to justify different interpretations. In the *Rule* itself the "studies problem" exists; let us try to state it first according to the *Rule* itself, and then by comparison with the teaching of a contemporary of Benedict, Cassiodorus.

In the *Rule* we can distinguish the two elements which we have seen in the life of St. Benedict: the knowledge of letters and the search for God. The fundamental fact that stands out in this domain is that one of the principal occupations of the monk is the *lectio divina*, which includes meditation: *meditari aut legere.* Consequently one must, in the monastery, possess books, know how to write them and read them, and, therefore, if it be necessary, learn how to read.[6] It is not certain that St. Benedict is speaking of a library since the word *bibliotheca*, which he uses in referring to books read in Lent, can mean, for him, the Bible.[7] But St. Benedict evidently takes for granted the existence of a library, and a fairly extensive one at that, since each monk is supposed to receive a *codex* in Lent. Toward the end of the *Rule*, it is suggested that all read the Scripture, Cassian, and St. Basil; they should be able to read in the refectory, in choir, and before guests.

Naturally, in order to possess books, it eventually becomes necessary to know how to write them. All the monks, as a matter of course and without exception, are supposed to know how to write. The abbot and the cellarer must keep accounts of what is expended and what is received.[8] Written documents are kept in the archives.[9] One of the things exacted of the monks is that they ask permission to write each other letters; another is that they possess no writing materials without permission;[10] furthermore, each one is to receive writing equipment.[11] Some at least are expected to know how to make books—that is to say, to copy, bind, and even decorate them, and this with two different purposes in mind. On this point the lack of precision in the *Rule* is clarified by reference to other contemporary rules. Books must be made, first of all, for the monastery; no doubt, books might be received through endowment—such cases are known—but usually they were copied in the monastery. This fact is attested explicitly in several rules of the same period, and it is assumed by St. Benedict, as is the following fact: books were also copied and sold outside the monastery. This is also mentioned in very old rules, in terms identical with those used in St. Benedict,[12] where they can scarcely have any other meaning.

Likewise, St. Benedict assumes that the monks are not illiterate; a few only are judged unable to read and to study. As a whole, in order to do the public and private reading prescribed by the *Rule*, they must know how to read, and this implies a school where reading and writing are learned. As a matter of fact, it cannot be supposed that in the sixth century all who entered the monastery were literate. St. Benedict prescribes that "one shall read [*legatur ei*] the *Rule* to the novice"[13] as if it could have happened that he was not able, on coming to the monastery, to read it for himself, not having yet learned how to read. Besides, the word "read" in this context can also mean "comment": the *Rule* will be read to him, and at the same time explained. It is not said that he will be taught to read during his novitiate. But since children are offered to the monastery and destined to remain there as monks who will therefore eventually have to know how to read and write, there must be for them—and for them only—a school and also books. It has been conjectured that, in all likelihood, the library must have contained, besides Scripture and the Fathers, elementary works on grammar, a Donatus, a Priscian, a Quintilian, and a few of the classical authors. The tablets and the stylus referred to in Chapter 55 are materials which would be used at least as much in school as in a scriptorium.

Lectio AND *Meditatio*

If then it is necessary to know how to read, it is primarily in order to be able to participate in the *lectio divina*. What does this consist of? How is this reading done? To understand this, one must recall the meaning that the words *legere* and *meditari* have for St. Benedict, and which they are to keep throughout the whole of the Middle Ages; what they express will explain one of the characteristic features of monastic literature of the Middle Ages: the phenomenon of reminiscence, of which more must be said later. With regard to literature, a fundamental observation must be made here: in the Middle Ages, as in antiquity, they read usually, not as today, principally with the eyes, but with the lips, pronouncing what they saw, and with the ears, listening to the words pronounced, hearing what is called the "voices of the pages." It is a real acoustical reading; *legere* means at the same time *audire*. One understands only what one hears, as we still say in French: "entendre le latin," which means to "comprehend" it. No doubt, silent reading, or reading in a low voice, was not unknown; in that case it is designated by expressions like those of St. Benedict: *tacite legere* or *legere sibi*, and according to St. Augustine: *legere in silentio*, as opposed to the *clara lectio*. But most frequently, when *legere* and *lectio* are used without further explanation, they mean an activity which, like chant and writing, requires the participation of the whole body and the whole mind. Doctors of ancient times used to recommend reading to their patients as a physical exercise on an equal level with walking, running, or ball-playing.[14] The fact that the text which was being composed or copied was often written to dictation given aloud, either to oneself or to a secretary, satisfactorily explains the errors apparently due to hearing in medieval manuscripts:[15] the use of the dictaphone today produces similar mistakes. The references made in classical, biblical, and patristic antiquity to reading aloud are well known,[16] but it will suffice here if we present evidence furnished by monastic tradition.

Thus, when St. Benedict recommends that, during the time when the monks "are resting on their beds in silence," the one who wants to read should do so in such a way that he does not disturb the others, he clearly considers reading disruptive to silence.[17] When Peter the Venerable was suffering from catarrh, not only was he no longer able to speak in public, but he could no longer perform his *lectio*.[18] And Nicholas of Clairvaux noticed that after being bled he lacked the strength to read.[19] This proves how true it was that the act of verbalizing was not divorced from the visual. The latter was accompanied spontaneously by the movement of the lips, and the *lectio divina* was necessarily an active reading.

In this way reading is very close to the *meditatio*. This latter term is important since the practice it describes will determine, in large measure, the application of monastic psychology to Sacred Scripture and to the Fathers. The words *meditari* and *meditatio* are rich in meaning. In monastic tradition they keep both the profane meanings they had in classical Latin and the sacred meanings they had received from the Bible. These different meanings complement each other; for if the word *meditatio* was preferred to others in biblical versions and in spiritual tradition, it was because it was, in virtue of its original meaning, suited to the framing of the spiritual realities that they desired to express.

In secular usage, *meditari* means, in a general way, to think, to reflect, as does *cogitare* or *considerare*; but, more than these, it often implies an affinity with the practical or even moral order. It implies thinking of a thing with the intent to do it; in other words, to prepare oneself for it, to prefigure it in the mind, to desire it, in a way, to do it in advance— briefly, to practice it.[20] The word is also applied to physical exercises and sports, to those of military life, of the school world, to rhetoric, poetry, music, and, finally, to moral practices. To practice a thing by thinking of it, is to fix it in the memory, to learn it. All these shades of meaning are encountered in the language of the Christians; but they generally use the word in referring to a text. The reality it describes is used on a text, and this, the text *par excellence*, the Scripture *par excellence*, is the Bible and its commentaries. Indeed, it is mainly through the intermediary of ancient biblical versions and through the Vulgate that the word (meditation) has been introduced into the Christian vocabulary, particularly into monastic tradition, where it was to continue to retain the new shade of meaning given it by the Bible.[21] There, it is used generally to translate the Hebrew *hāgā*, and like the latter it means, fundamentally, to learn the Torah and the words of the Sages, while pronouncing them usually in a low tone, in reciting them to oneself, in murmuring them with the mouth. This is what we call "learning by heart," what ought rather to be called, according to the ancients, "learning by mouth" since the mouth "meditates wisdom": *Os justi meditabitur sapientiam*. In certain texts, that will mean only a "murmur" reduced to the minimum, an inner murmur, purely spiritual. But always the original meaning is at least intended: to pronounce the sacred words in order to retain them; both the audible reading and the exercise of memory and reflection which it precedes are involved. To speak, to think, to remember, are the three necessary phases of the same activity.

To express what one is thinking and to repeat it enables one to imprint it on one's mind. In Christian as well as rabbinical tradition, one cannot meditate anything else but a text, and since this text is the word of God, meditation is the necessary complement, almost the equivalent, of the *lectio divina*. In conformity with the modern vocabulary, one can meditate "in the abstract," so to speak. Let us consider the *Meditations* of Descartes, or such books of devotion where "to meditate on the Divine attributes" means to reflect on them, to awaken in the self ideas concerning them. For the ancients, to meditate is to read a text and to learn it "by heart" in the fullest sense of this expression, that is, with one's whole being: with the body, since the mouth pronounced it, with the memory which fixes it, with the intelligence which understands its meaning, and with the will which desires to put it into practice.

As can be seen, this fundamental activity of monastic life is based on literature. For the monks in general, the foremost aid to good works is a text which makes possible the meditated reading of the word of God. This will greatly affect the domain of monastic exegesis, entirely oriented toward life, and not toward abstract knowledge. This point will be taken up later. But from now on can be seen the importance of letters, and of the psychological activities which it has brought about through reading and meditation, since the beginning of the Benedictine tradition. There is no Benedictine life without literature. Not that literature is an end, even a secondary end, of monastic life; but it is a conditioning factor. In order to undertake one of the principal occupations of the monk, it is necessary to know, to learn, and, for some, to teach *grammatica*.

THE STUDY OF GRAMMAR IN ST. BENEDICT

And what does *grammatica* mean? To recall what it meant to the ancients themselves we need quote only two sources, one pagan and the other Christian.[22] Quintilian said that this word, of Greek origin, has as its Latin equivalent the term *litteratura*, and Marius Victorinus, quoting Varro, gave this definition: "The art of grammar, which we call literature, is the science of the things said by poets, historians, and orators; its principal functions are: to write, to read, to understand, and to prove." Thus grammar is the first stage and the foundation of general culture, and the two synonomous terms *grammaticus* and *litteratus* designate a man "who knows how to read"—that is, not only how to decipher the letters, but how to understand the texts. For the Romans of the classical period, as Marrou has demonstrated, grammar is "a truly logical analysis of the cate-

gories of the understanding."[23] The procedure is used in connection with
the texts of the great writers. The analysis and the explanation of the
authors, above all of poets, is done in connection with and by means of a
prepared and, so to speak, "expressive reading selection." To express a
text, to make it give up its full meaning by reciting it to oneself, is to prove
that it has been well understood. No doubt, in St. Benedict's time, this
method was elementary; its aim is to satisfy immediate needs. It is concerned less with reading the great authors and writing in their style than
learning the Bible or at least the psalter, if possible, by heart. During the
Merovingian period, this teaching program was reduced practically to
the psalms: and instead of beginning by the grammatical analysis of letters, then of syllables, words, and finally of sentences, the child is immediately put in contact with the psalter, in which he learns to read first
verses, and then whole psalms.[24] But nothing proves that such was already
the case when the *Rule* of St. Benedict was written, and the fact remains
that for St. Benedict, as for all monastic legislators of his time, the monk
was expected to have some knowledge of letters and a certain proficiency
in doctrine. In the secular schools the *auctores* studied, particularly the
poets, are full of mythology; hence the danger which these studies, however necessary, present for Christians. In the monastic school, teaching is
concerned mainly—but not exclusively—with Scripture and its commentaries. Thus the monastic school resembles at once the classical school,
because of the traditional method of *grammatica*, and the rabbinical school,
because of the nature of the text to which this method is applied. Furthermore, education is not separated from spiritual effort; even from this viewpoint, the monastery is truly a "school for the service of the Lord"—*dominici schola servitii.*

Indeed the one end of monastic life is the search for God. It is clear to
anyone who is acquainted with the *Rule* of St. Benedict that monastic
life has no other purpose than *quaerere Deum*. In order to obtain eternal
life, of which St. Benedict speaks so often as the only end which has any
importance, one must become detached from all immediate interests, devoting oneself in silence and in withdrawal from the world to prayer and
asceticism. All of the monk's activities, including his literary activity, can
have no motivation other than spiritual, and spiritual motives are always
called upon to justify all his actions. If, for example, the monk obeys, it is
"because he wishes to make progress toward eternal life." According to
St. Benedict, monastic life is entirely disinterested; its reason for existing
is to further the salvation of the monk, his search for God, and not for any

practical or social end—which, incidentally, is never even mentioned. The *conversatio* of the monk is presumed to be a *conversio* similar to St. Benedict's which entails total renunciation with the intention of pleasing God alone. The whole organization of monastic life is dominated by the solicitude for safeguarding a certain spiritual leisure, a certain freedom in the interests of prayer in all its forms, and, above all, authentic contemplative peace.[25]

STUDIES ACCORDING TO CASSIODORUS

All this may appear to be self-evident, but the better to appreciate this monastic conception inherited from a former monastic tradition, the only one destined to shape later history, it may be worthwhile to compare it with that of one of Benedict's contemporaries: Cassiodorus. Of course an exact parallel cannot be drawn between the *Rule* of St. Benedict and the *Institutiones* of Cassiodorus, as if they were the same kind of text. One is a monastic rule, the other a program of studies for monks. But each, although from a different viewpoint, informs us sufficiently about the life and preoccupations of monks to permit a valid comparison. It is quite true that Cassiodorus' monastery at Vivarium is not merely a learned academy: it is a monastery devoted to prayer and work.[26] Although the endowment received from the founder makes it unnecessary to assure the monks' livelihood, provision is made for manual labor. It consists mostly of the *artes* and, among these, the most important is copying. On this point, Cassiodorus' monastery may be not so different from Benedict's. But one can easily see that the director of Vivarium, although he shares the life of the monks, organizes and even directs it, is not a monk and does not think as a monk. He never received the vocation, and lacks that experience. He never underwent the radical conversion described by St. Gregory as having been experienced by St. Benedict, and his entire work shows this. To be convinced of this all one need do is to leaf through the *Institutiones* which he wrote for his monks.[27] He wanted this work to serve as an introduction to the study of Holy Scripture and, secondarily, to that of the liberal arts. Thus the work is divided into two books, the first of which treats of "divine letters," the second of "secular letters." The treatise *On Grammar* is intended to complement them, and Cassiodorus urges that it be read.

In the preface he states that his monastery will carry out his plan for a *schola christiana* which the wars had until then prevented him from realizing. In this school two things are to be learned: "how to win eternal life" (which is also the basis for monastic life in St. Benedict's *Rule*) and, in addition, to teach the faithful to speak well. Of the latter St. Benedict says nothing whatsoever. In the course of the treatise these two elements are constantly associated: Cassiodorus mentions, for example, "the Holy Scripture *and* secular writings"; elsewhere he says: "*both* the salvation of the soul *and* secular learning." This *and* is very revealing: studies are placed second in order of importance but are given almost as much consideration as spiritual life. In still other places reference is made to one or the other as subjects for study: *utrasque doctrinas*. It would seem that this "worldly knowledge" is acquired through the reading of correct texts, and therefore requires that such be written, and that those which are erroneous be corrected. An extensive knowledge of spelling and grammar is a prime necessity. Hence the whole program of religious and secular studies in which both are considered inseparable. For the latter, Cassiodorus, inspired by the pagan master Ammonius of Alexandria, lays the foundation for the medieval distinction between the *trivium*, which was to include all the literary studies, and the *quadrivium*, which is the cycle of scientific studies.[28] Cassiodorus tells how to correct the texts; he cites Virgil and the grammarians, and Aristotle's *Perihermeniae* (the *De interpretatione*). No doubt he stresses spiritual values on more than one occasion. He praises the *lectio divina*, which he describes in the same terms as does St. Benedict, and the Fathers, who are the commentators *par excellence* of Scripture. But unlike St. Benedict, he emphasizes learning, the correction of texts, and the literary aspect of sacred studies.[29] For him meditation seems to take on a more intellectual tone than it does in St. Benedict; it should be done with "an attention full of curiosity."[30] He counsels monks to read Hippocrates and Galen in order to learn how to take care of their health. All of this is legitimate and useful, but at the same time totally foreign to St. Benedict.

At the beginning of the second book he declares that he is about to take up secular studies, the preceding book having dealt with sacred studies, even though much is already found in it on grammar and other disciplines. While St. Benedict is satisfied to take the existence of a scriptorium for granted, Cassiodorus talks about it; he inventories the library; it contains many biblical commentaries and relatively few profane works. But St. Benedict had not felt obliged to enumerate either. One of the ends of the monastery of Vivarium is to serve Christian learning. In it Cassiodorus wishes to form professional teachers (*professos doctores*) able to spread, through the written word, the true doctrine. Nothing of the kind receives St. Benedict's slightest attention. These two founders of monasteries accent different realities and different ends. St. Benedict's monastery is a school for the service of the Lord, and it is nothing else. No doubt it is this essential and always valid orientation, this absence of precise prescription as to subject matter, this breadth of vision, this allowance made for discrimination and adaptation, which has made the *Rule* of St. Benedict so enduring; a program of studies like that of Cassiodorus is inevitably, and fairly soon, out-dated.

At the present stage of research, it is difficult to measure Cassiodorus' influence. It seems that in the catalogues of medieval libraries his commentaries on the Psalms are found more frequently than his *Institutiones*, though they are not often cited in the texts themselves. Alcuin owes to them a large part of his treatise *On Orthography*.[31] But the Anglo-Saxon monks who were responsible for the pedagogical renaissance of the Carolingian period preferred, on the whole, to go directly to the sources, as if this program which consisted in knowing a little about everything seemed to them insufficient. Later, when Peter the Venerable uses, without identifying it, a passage from the *Institutiones*, he does not quote Cassiodorus as an "authority" either on monastic life or on studies.[32] Cassiodorus did not become part of monastic tradition as had St. Anthony, Origen, St. Jerome, or Cassian; he has remained an isolated figure, never proposed as a model, nor even mentioned by name. No inspiration is sought in his monastic doctrine; he is asked for ideas, but not for directives; his knowledge is called upon, but not his ideals.

Vivarium is a "monastery school." St. Benedict's monastery is exclusively a monastery; it does possess a school, but it is never spoken of and in no way modifies the monastic ideal. It is not a part of this ideal, but of its realization; it is a means which can be modified, can become more or less important without the ideal's being affected. Cassiodorus enters into details on the organization of studies as well as of everything else in the life of his monastery. St. Benedict gives directives which will retain their value regardless of time or place, in the realm of culture as well as in others, and within which great variations remain possible. He insists only that the following constants be maintained: on the one hand, letters are necessary and ordinarily the monk's life would include them; on the other, they form no part of his vocation, nor of his nor his monastery's ideal. They are but a necessary and accepted means, always subordinated to the search for God.[33]

The Problem of Monastic Studies

We are now able to draw conclusions. No judgment either favorable or unfavorable on the worth of learning or of the study of letters is to be found in the *Rule* of St. Benedict. The only values stressed are those of eternal life, the only reality upon which unfavorable judgment is passed is sin. Study is ranked as one means, within a framework of others, to the end, which is eternal life. St. Benedict does not consider it his task to introduce his monks to such study; that is no part of his role. In this area, as well as in others, the means for intellectual development, the *instrumenta studiorum*, already existing in each country and in each period, will be adopted. There is no Benedictine *ratio studiorum*, there is a spiritual program, and that is why monastic studies have sometimes presented a problem. It is therefore to be expected that in one way or another this problem should arise wherever monastic values retain their vitality. In other forms of religious life this problem is not encountered; it is obviated by a *ratio studiorum* perfected at the time of the foundation of the Order and revised from time to time. In monasticism, however, if the problem exists, it is because there is no one simple solution which has been devised once for all and need only be applied in conformity with a legislative rule. This solution must be continually rediscovered, re-invented, rejuvenated in a living and spontaneous manner, for each period and each milieu, for each monastery, and almost for each monk.

And if there is a problem, it is because the difficulty takes the shape of a tension between two elements whose reconciliation is always precarious and between which an equilibrium must be constantly re-established. There is always the risk of weighting the balance too heavily on one side or the other. These two elements are the two constants of Western monastic culture: on the one hand, the study of letters; on the other, the exclusive search for God, the love of eternal life, and the consequent detachment from all else, including the study of letters. When St. Bernard and Abailard, Rancé and Mabillon differed on the subject of studies, each was defending values which in reality belonged to tradition, but each, from a different point of view, laid stress on one of the two aspects of the problem. There is no ideal synthesis which can be expressed in a speculative formula, as there might be if the solution were of the intellectual order; the conflict can be transcended only by raising it to the spiritual order. It remains therefore for us to examine how this reconciliation has been effected in the history of monastic culture, and what its fruits have been in the two realms of letters and the spiritual life.

NOTES

1. *Dialogus* (ed. U. Moricca; Rome, 1924), pp. 71–72.

2. Cf. H. I. Marrou, *History of Education in Antiquity* (New York, 1956), p. 346.

3. The most perceptive study of this point is that of Suso Brechter, "Benedikt und die Antike," in *Benedictus der Vater des Abendlandes* (Munich, 1947), p. 141. On schools in Rome in the 6th century, cf. F. Ermini, "La scuola in Roma nel secolo VI," in *Medio evo latino* (Modena, 1938), 54–64.

4. This point has been stressed by J. Winandy, "Benoît l'homme de Dieu. Considérations sur l'hagiographie ancienne et moderne," *La Vie Spirituelle* (March 1952) 279–86.

5. *Vita* 9 (ed. G. Morin, *S. Caesarii Arelatensis opera*, II [Maredsous, 1942] 299–300).

6. M. van Assche ("Divinae vacare lectioni," *Sacris Erudiri* 1 [1948] 13–14), in a very suggestive study, has assembled the texts of St. Benedict on this matter, clarifying them by means of contemporary witnesses.

7. A. Mundo, "*Bibliotheca*: Bible et lecture de carême d'après S. Benoît," RB 60 (1950) 65–92.

8. *Rule of St. Benedict*, Ch. 32, 35.

9. Ibid., Ch. 32, 58.

10. Ibid., Ch. 33.

11. Ibid., Ch. 55.

12. Ibid., Ch. 52.

13. Ibid., Ch. 58.

14. F. di Capua, "Osservazioni sulla lettura e sulla preghiera ad alta voce presso gli antichi," *Rendiconti della Accademia di archeologia, lettere e belle arti di Napoli*, N.S. 28 (1953) 59–62.

15. A. J. Chaytor, "The Mediaeval Reader and Textual Criticism," *Bulletin of the John Rylands Library* (1941) 49.

16. J. Balogh, "Voces paginarum. Beiträge zur Geschichte des lauten Lesens und Schreibens," *Philologus* (1927) 83–202.

17. *Rule of St. Benedict*, Ch. 48.

18. *Pierre le Vénérable* (Saint-Wandrille, 1947), p. 27.

19. PL 202.491.

20. Texts in TLL, *s.v.* See also *infra* p. 73.

21. E. von Severus, "Das Wort 'Meditari' im Sprachgebrauch der Heiligen Schrift," *Geist und Leben* (1935) 365. "Das Wesen der Meditation und der Mensch der Gegenwart," ibid. (1956) 109–13. H. Bacht, "Meditation in den ältesten Mönchsquellen," ibid. (1955) 360–73.

22. These and other texts are quoted in TLL, *s.v.*

23. *Hist. of Educ. in Antiquity*, p. 276. Cf. M. P. Cunningham, " 'Ars grammatica' and 'enarratio'," *Proc. of American Philosophical Society*, 101 (1953) 486–89.

24. P. Riché, "Le Psautier, livre de lecture élémentaire, d'après les Vies de Saints mérovingiens," *Études mérovingiens* (Paris, 1953), pp. 253–56. On the teaching of Scripture, cf. B. Bischoff, "Elementarunterricht und *probationes pennae* in der ersten Hälfte des Mittelalters," *Classical and Mediaeval Studies in Honor of E. K. Rand* (New York, 1938), pp. 9–20.

25. See the rather subtle exposition of H. Dedler, "Vom Sinn der Arbeit nach der Regel des heiligen Benedikt," *Benedictus der Vater des Abendlandes*, pp. 103–18.

26. This has been properly emphasized by M. Cappuyns, "Cassiodore," DHGE, XI (1949) 1359–60.

27. *Cassiodori Senatoris Institutiones*, ed. R. A. B. Mynors (Oxford, 1937); trans. L. W. Jones, *An Introduction to Divine and Human Readings, by Cassiodorus Senator* (New York, 1946).

28. P. Courcelle, *Les lettres grecques en Occident de Macrobe à Cassiodore* (Paris, 1943), pp. 326, 340.

29. M. Cappuyns (n. 26), 1404.

30. I, xvi, 3: "Curiosa vobis intentione meditandi sunt" (Jones, 114); on meditation as a school exercise, I, praef. 7 (Jones, 70–71).

31. A. Marsili, *Alcuini de othographia* (Pisa, 1952), pp. 14–77.

32. See *infra* p. 123.

33. A similar conclusion has been thus expressed by David Knowles: "St. Benedict wished his monks to work because he knew that the normal man could not always be either reading or praying, but to attribute to him any purpose of using his institute as a great economic or social or intellectual or even apostolic force would be neither spiritually nor historically true." *The Benedictines* (New York, 1930), p. 13, quoted by L. Megher, *The Benedictine Review* (1956) 29. Cf. also E. von Severus, "Hrabanus und die Fuldaer Schultradition," *Fuldaer Geschichtsblätter* (1957) 88–89.

2

St. Gregory,
Doctor of Desire

AFTER HAVING SPOKEN of St. Benedict's conversion and its importance for the orientation of monastic studies, and of the part allotted to learning in his *Rule*, we must now turn to the man who exercised a decisive influence on the share given in monastic culture to the spiritual tendency, St. Gregory the Great.

St. Gregory the Great, Theologian

St. Gregory was a great pope, a great man of action; his *Pastoral Care* and his Letters have become sources of moral theology, canon law, and medieval pastoral theology. But he was also a great contemplative, a great doctor of the life of prayer, and it is through the writings in which he has given his spiritual doctrine that he has had the most influence on monastic culture. His mystical theology is as yet little known; so far is it from having been studied adequately that Marrou seemed to have made a novel discovery when he called St. Gregory "one of our greatest mystical doctors."[1]

As a matter of fact, there can be found in St. Gregory a full and authentic theology of the Christian experience, a doctrine of Christian life and prayer which, as in Origen and St. Augustine, is marked by continual recourse to experience. For this reason, St. Gregory bridges the gap between the patristic age and the monastic culture of the Middle Ages. His teaching is much more than a simple empiricism; he devotes a profound and, as we would say today, structured reflection to the subject of Christian experience. In order to formulate it, he uses terms which are both constant and precise: the dialectics of presence and absence, possession and non-possession, certainty and uncertainty, light and darkness, faith and eternal life.

A short introduction to this vast doctrine seems essential for anyone who wants to become informed on monastic literature of the Middle Ages.

Almost all its vocabulary comes from Gregory the Great; we find in him a whole sacred philology which we might be tempted to think of as purely symbolic, and which indeed does arise from poetic expression, but which is not, for all of that, any the less rich in content. It is important, then, to call attention at this point to a certain number of these terms which St. Gregory used, and which were subsequently handed on and endlessly enriched by the monastic tradition.

GREGORY'S INFLUENCE

Everyone, in fact, had read him and lived by him. We have several kinds of proof of this fact. Manuscripts of his works are innumerable.[2] In every period, centos were composed, made up of more or less elaborated excerpts from characteristic texts.[3] We have explicit information about his being constantly read at Cluny[4] and elsewhere.[5] All the authors quote him or are dependent on him. Isidore, in his *Sententiae*, borrows much from him as does Defensor of Ligugé[6] in his *Liber scintillarum*, which was to become so widespread; in the eighth century, Bede, Ambrosius Autpertus, then the authors of the Carolingian period, later John of Fécamp, St. Anselm, St. Bernard, all owe a great deal to him. In the East, he was one of the most read of the Latin Fathers. If in the East his reputation entitled him to be called simply *Dialogos* from the title of one of his works, as we say Climacus when we mean the author of the *Ladder of Paradise*, it is because his doctrine on compunction harmonized so well with theirs.[7] In the West, after the monastic centuries, he continued to exert great influence. After Aristotle and St. Augustine, he is the most quoted author in the *Summa* of St. Thomas;[8] he is apparent in the work of Gerson; St. Teresa annotated his *Moralia*; St. John of the Cross was certainly inspired by him. In the seventeenth century, Bossuet as well as Fénélon and Nicole were to use him. In our time, a Redemptorist has published a book entitled *S. Grégoire le Grand: Méthode de vie spirituelle tirée de ses écrits.*[9] More recently, a collection of parallel extracts from St. Gregory and from St. John of the Cross has shed light on the kinship and the modernity of these two mystical authors.[10] The legacy left by St. Gregory has been handed down even to our own times, and his ideas and expressions have passed into the doctrine and language of countless spiritual writings generally after having lost any connection with their original context. Without knowing it, we are living, in great measure, on his modes of expression and on his thoughts, and for that very reason they no longer seem new to us. However, there had to be a first time when they were invented and experienced. Let us try then to discount the familiarity we have with them, and rediscover them at their source. They have perhaps still more value today than in the past. In spite of the sometimes disconcerting character of his style and exegesis, St. Gregory is a doctor one would be tempted to call, in some respects, fairly modern. He has elaborated, not only a theology, but a psychology of the spiritual life; one might go so far as to call it a phenomenology of the states of prayer. He has described these in concrete terms with a very human accent, which explains his lasting fruitfulness. Let us therefore consider in succession the formation of his doctrine and then the doctrine itself.

Gregory's Education and Character

Before being pope from 590 to 604, St. Gregory had been a monk. He spent five years in the monastery of St. Andrew, which he founded on the Caelian Hill in Rome, before being sent to Constantinople as apocrisiary. It is there that from 579 to 586 he gave the monks lectures which were to become the *Moralia in Job*. He was also to write *Homilies* on Ezechiel, on Kings, on the Gospels, a commentary on the Canticle of Canticles of which we have an abridged version, four books of *Dialogues*, and a great quantity of letters.

His vast literary output[11] may sometimes give the impression of being unorganized and overly diffuse; but, to be truly appreciated, his works must be understood and savored, a state perhaps rarely achieved in our times. They demand a certain leisure, the *otium* of which he so often spoke. Nevertheless, the rather unsystematic character of his writings has this one notable advantage—we can profitably read, beginning at any point and stopping where we will.

St. Gregory could hardly have frequented the monastic milieux in Byzantium for six years without acquiring a certain knowledge of the spiritual traditions of the East—not necessarily book knowledge, however, since he knew scarcely any Greek. But he did have living contact with the Greek monks of his times. Besides, he had read, as a matter of course, the *Lives of the Fathers* and Origen, translated by Rufinus and others. Sometimes he follows Cassian very closely and yet differs from him deliberately. He does not propose, as Cassian does, the ideal of an ἀπάθεια accessible only to those monks in possession, so to speak, of specialized spiritual technique. His doctrine is more general, more broadly human. From St. Augustine he takes a few Neoplatonic ideas and the terms for expressing them; but he retains Augustine's moral and religious doctrine more than his philosophic speculation.[12] One may well imagine that he was acquainted with the *Rule* of St. Benedict;[13] but in any case, through his *Life* of Benedict of Cassino, he belongs to the Benedictine tradition whose progress he was to guide for the future.

What is original about his contribution? Above all, his personal experience, that experience in the spiritual life and in sanctity which itself reflects his character and the circumstances of his life: a monk's experience, as has been seen, and the experience of a cultivated man. And though Gregory is not an intellectual, he is a man of learning as cultivated as any Latin who lived in sixth-century Rome could be: Rome at the time may have been decadent, but it was still Rome. Because of his extreme sensitivity, he experiences spiritual states which others had in fact known, although they did not analyze them with the same degree of precision as he did. Thanks to the flexibility of his Latin style, he describes them with great subtlety. It was the experience of an ailing man, too: his body's infirmity gives him a strong sense of human suffering, of the effects of Original Sin, but also of the value of weakness and temptation for spiritual progress. More than once, he speaks of the discomforts he is feeling, and in moving terms.[14] Gregory's poor health is one of the great events in the history of spirituality, since to some degree it determines his doctrine. It gives it those qualities of humanity and discretion and the ring of conviction which explain his influence. For him, man's suffering is by no means a theoretical notion; he knew it from the inside at the cost of a sensitivity that was sharpened and increased by the difficulties of each day. Finally, his experience is that of a contemplative condemned to action. His ideal is the calm of monastic life: that is, the life he wanted to lead, and was able to lead for only a few years. External circumstances and the call from God obliged him to serve and then to govern the Church, to live, as he says, in the "agitations of the world," and this during a time which was particularly troubled in Rome and in all Italy. He will unite action and contemplation; but he will always have a nostalgia for the latter. The supreme pontificate will be a burden to him, and the suffering he will undergo from being so divided will arouse in his soul an ardent longing for peace.

GREGORY'S CONCEPTION OF THE CHRISTIAN LIFE AND PRAYER

His spiritual teaching is neither a system nor a method. But his doctrine of prayer is linked to his general conception of the Christian life. Therefore we must first examine the Christian life according to St. Gregory, and then the role which prayer plays in it. The Christian life is conceived of as, above all, a life of detachment and desire: detachment from the world and from sin, and an intense desire for God. This attitude is already a prayer in itself, a life of prayer. It is only for clarity in exposition that the *life of prayer* may here be distinguished from the *act of prayer* itself.

REALIZATION OF MAN'S MISERY

At the root of this concept of the Christian life is found a lively awareness of man's misery: a lived consciousness, an experienced knowledge. It is very often expressed in texts of compelling truth. This awareness is basic, and it is always close to the surface in St. Gregory's vocabulary, in his modes of expression and in the themes habitual with him.[15] Man's wretchedness comes from his physical nature, from Original Sin, from the egoism which harries each one of us, which is always on the watch, and which tends to vitiate all our actions, even the good ones. It must be put to rout constantly: not only at the outset of our actions, by purifying our intentions, but also during our actions, and again at the end, for it is always a menace to us. With regard to this, St. Gregory recalls the "weight" which attracts us to earth; the weight which is proper to what is changing and mortal, the "gravity" which is the sign of corruption, the particular attribute of sin, the reason why we speak of "grave sins."[16] He also describes agitation, the *inquietudo*—that is to say, the lack of tranquillity and peace. The last manifestation of this mutability, the ultimate change, will be death. But once it has started, our entire life will be led under the sign of this mortal instability.

COMPUNCTION, DETACHMENT, AND DESIRE

The first result of experiencing man's condition, for the Christian who knows how to interpret it, is humility, in other words detachment from the world, from ourselves, and from our sins, and the consciousness of our need for God. Such is compunction under its double aspect: compunction of fear, compunction of desire. In its original profane use, the word "compunction" is a medical term,[17] designating attacks of acute pain, of physical illness. But it has been used especially in the Christian vocabulary in a sense which, without losing contact with its origins, is nevertheless richer and loftier. Compunction becomes pain of the spirit, a suffering resulting simultaneously from two causes: the existence of sin and our own tendency toward sin—*compunctio paenitentiae, timoris, formidinis*

—and the existence of our desire for God and even our very possession of God. St. Gregory, more than others, accentuated this last aspect: an obscure possession, awareness of which does not last, and consequently gives rise to regret at seeing it disappear and to a desire to find it again. The "compunction of the heart," "of the soul"—*compunctio cordis, animi*—always tends to become a "compunction of love," "of delectation" and "of contemplation"—*compunctio amoris, dilectionis, contemplationis*. Compunction is an act of God in us, an act by which God awakens us, a shock, a blow, a "sting," a sort of burn.[18] God goads us as if with a spear; He "presses" us with insistence (*cum-pungere*), as if to pierce us. The love of the world lulls us; but, as if by a thunderclap, the attention of the soul is recalled to God.[19]

How is this action of God accomplished in us? By what means, through what intermediaries, and on what occasions? By all kinds of trials: tribulation, the *flagella Dei*, the thousandfold sufferings of life, sin itself,[20] and, above all, temptation.[21] Permission to tempt man is given by God to the demon for reasons of wise providence (*dispensatio*), because of the benefit resulting from temptation. The latter is necessary and becomes more frequent and more violent as one progresses in the life of prayer. It encourages the purification of intentions, it humbles, and it is a cure for pride. This is why God accepts the risk involved; temptation, and even sin, are less grave than pride.[22] But all this is merely an occasion, and not a cause. It is God Himself who is working in us by His mysterious action; compunction is a gift beyond our power to understand.[23] It induces, therefore, a purification which can be called passive: the Lord accomplishes it in us; our part is to consent to it.[24] One must above all, and first of all, make oneself sensitive to this invisible action of God, to this subtle intervention which can be captured only by new senses, the five "spiritual senses" previously outlined in theory by Origen, and which explain St. Gregory's expressions like *palatum cordis* or *in aure cordis*, which, it is to be remembered, are to become part of later tradition.[25] An inner song, a slight murmur, a silent word[26]—Gregory loves this poetic vocabulary, this paradoxical language, so suitable for expressing the realities of the mystical life. The ultimate role of compunction is to bring to the soul a longing for Heaven, and it is understandable that this theme is related to the theme of tears. Two kinds of tears symbolize the two forms of compunction: the lower stream, *irriguum inferius*, is the stream of repentance; the higher flood, *irriguum superius*, that of desire. Tears of love always accompany those of penitence; but more and more these are dominated by tears of joy.[27]

With humility there grows the desire for Him who alone can fill our inner emptiness. Compunction hollows us and thereby increases our capacity for God. St. Gregory is the doctor of desire; he constantly uses terms like *anhelare, aspirare, suspirare*,[28] which express a tendency toward transcendence, "sublimation." Another of his preferred themes is that of the spiritual flight which counteracts our heaviness; on wings, and with the plumage of an eagle, one must rise, must thrust oneself up toward God, seek Him, and hasten toward Him.[29]

But what motive prompts this journey to the beyond? The desire to avoid the pains of this life? Not at all: they are but an occasion for desire. One must surmount them, rise above them up to God who is speaking to us through them and who is calling us to Him. "Detachment," in the original meaning of this figurative word, must also be exercised with regard to prosperity which binds so many men to earth.[30] The only desire which is legitimate is to possess God here below and forever: here below, in the very midst of sorrow, and because of it; later, in Heaven, since celestial realities (*caelestia*) are but another name for God. It is in order to reach God that one must love, desire, and wish for death, which does not eliminate the suffering or fear of death. It must be accepted, consented to, at the hour when God sends it, as the means for being united to Him.

Furthermore, if desire for God is ardent, it is also patient. It grows under the trial of time. One must learn to wait for God in order to love Him the more and to take advantage of the passage of time to become ever more open to His infinite plenitude.[31] The importance given to desire confers on St. Gregory's doctrine an extremely dynamic quality. It is concerned with constant progress, for desire, as it becomes more intense, is rewarded by a certain possession of God which increases it still more. The result of this desire is peace rediscovered in God, since desire is itself a possession in which fear and love are reconciled. In the desire which, here below, is the very shape of love, the Christian finds God's joy, and union with the glorified Lord.[32] "He who with his whole soul desires God, certainly already possesses the One he loves."[33] Love gives unity to all, and resolves all contradictions. *Quies in labore, fatigatio in requie*, these and other paradoxes explain this reconciliation of opposites. The force of love intensifies the spiritual quest. A new weight carries the soul toward God, the "weight of love" which is greater than that of mutability.[34] It is to the love of God that we should cling.[35] The power of love is like a "machine" which raises us.[36] The soul hardened (*durata*) by egoism becomes tender (*emollitur*);[37] the cold soul is warmed and cleansed of its rust.[38] Returned, brought back to its true center of gravity, "converted," it is simplified,[39] rectified,[40] freed.[41] At peace, it enjoys tranquillity.[42] Not that it has become indifferent or unfeeling;[43] it is only reconciled with itself and with God. It consents to its condition, which it understands better; it consents to God who causes Himself to be loved through expectation; it accepts its tasks.[44] It grows in stature, and as it were is "dilated": the soul becomes fruitful in the service of God.[45]

KNOWLEDGE THROUGH LOVE

In such a conception of the Christian life, prayer is all-pervading. Gregory took pleasure in describing its most varied, and particularly its highest, forms. According to him, man tends toward the "light without limits."[46] And at the same time he is "blind" to this light.[47] He is so by nature, since he thinks by means of images which are necessarily material and consequently limited; while God, a spirit, is without limits. Man is unstable, while the eternal is immutable. He is also blind because of his sins which constantly turn his eyes back upon himself and on what is least good in him. But he can be raised (sublevari) above himself by the Spirit of God. It is through the Holy Spirit, this "finger of God," that the hand of the All High touches us, and gives us His gifts, His gift, which is Himself.[48] Man cannot help but desire this, prepare himself for it through detachment, asceticism; in other words, by the "active life," through the reading of Scripture and meditation on the mysteries of Christ, the objects par excellence of Christian contemplation. Then, sometimes, under the divine breath, the soul is elevated above its function of animating the body, and the mind beyond its customary modes of knowing. The intelligence, which is but one aspect of the mind, is "transcended." From a distance (de longe), we contemplate the beauty of our Creator in the knowledge of love: per amorem agnoscimus.[49] This adhesion of the spirit is not the result of striving; it is a taste, a relish, a wisdom, and not a science.[50] Contemplative understanding is understanding through love, which enriches the faith from which it proceeds. "You know, I say, not through faith, but through love. . . ."[51] "When we love supracelestial realities, we begin to know what we already love, since love itself is knowledge."[52] The soul cannot, however, remain long on these heights. It is, as it were, dazzled by what it perceives of God; the light of God repels it, and it falls back upon itself, wearied and as if struck by lightning, by a sort of violent blow (re-verberatio).[53] It takes up again its life of desire in the midst of temptations, all the stronger and more numerous for its having been admitted to a higher plane. It is in a deeper, stronger state of humility,

humility born of the knowledge of God: *in contemplatione Dei homo sibi vilescit.*[54] Active humility (*vilescit*) is not the acquisition of a scientific principle, it is an experience, a personal growth in real awareness. It is a humility which effects a change in being, not in one's possessions. The gifts of God cannot be the end of such elevation, and even less the gifts of Nature. "Do not take thought in yourself of what *you have* but of what *you are.*"[55] The soul, illuminated by God's light, the soul which knows God, perceives in itself all that is impure and contrary to God. Thus it is confirmed in humility, in the same attitude which had been the point of departure and the fundamental reason for its initial flight toward God.

PEACE

The Christian life, according to St. Gregory, is, one might say, a progress from one humility to another; from acquired humility to infused humility, humility nourished by the desire for God in a life of temptation and detachment, deepened and confirmed through loving knowledge in contemplation. Gregory recalls these successive stages in descriptions which are constantly renewed. He does not analyze them in abstract, philosophical terms; rather he borrows from the Bible concrete images which enable each one to recognize in these experiences the story of his own life. And because of this, his teaching filled the need of generations born into a barbarous world after the invasions. To these simple and new souls he offered a description of the Christian life which was comforting and accessible to all. This doctrine, a very human one, was founded on a knowledge of man as he is, body and soul, flesh and spirit. Without either illusions or despair, it was animated by insight which came from faith in God, and by real confidence in man in whom God dwells and whom God fashions through trial. The reading of his work communicates a feeling of peace through the calm of his writing. This man who constantly describes man's inner conflict does so with soothing words. On every page one finds, alternately, suffering and experience but also their reconciliation, their synthesis in charity.

Finally, this doctrine is a real theology. It implies a dogmatic theology; it develops a theology of the moral and mystical life, for these, as well, belong to the province of theology. Although scattered through long commentaries, this theology is nonetheless explicit. Would anyone dare say that there is no philosophy in Plato because it is dispersed in dialogues, and that there is philosophy in Wolff just because it is systematically presented? Gregory reflects on the realities of faith, the better to understand them; he does not confine himself to drawing up practical directives as to the way to live in conformity with these realities. He seeks and offers a deep knowledge of them. The search for God and union with God are explained in Gregory in the form of a generalized doctrine of the relationship of man to God. The monastic Middle Ages in turn never ceased to reflect on this doctrine and the texts which express it. They enriched it, without renewing it. Péguy used to say: "Plato has never been surpassed." It seems that in the realm of theological analysis of the Christian experience, nothing essential has been added to Gregory the Great. But if the great ideas of the past are to remain young and vital, each generation must, in turn, think them through and rediscover them in their pristine newness. This is a duty which, in the Benedictine tradition, has not been neglected.

NOTES

1. "S. Grégoire le Grand," *La Vie Spirituelle* (1943) 442. Dom B. Capelle (RB [1929] 210) described St. Gregory as "Doctor of Contemplation." C. Butler, *Western Mysticism* (London, 1927), showed the importance of Gregory in the spiritual tradition of the West.

2. H. Rochais, "Contribution à l'histoire des florilèges ascétiques du haut moyen âge latin," RB (1953) 256.

3. "Un centon de Fleury sur les devoirs des moines," *Analecta monastica* I (Rome, 1948) 75–89.

4. Peter the Venerable, PL 189.839. *Pierre le Vénérable*, p. 261. J. Laporte, "Odon disciple de S. Grégoire le Grand," *A Cluny: Congrès Scientifique* (Dijon, 1950), pp. 138–43.

5. E. Bertaud, "Une traduction en vers latin des Dialogues de S. Grégoire," *Jumièges: Congrès Scientifique du XIIIe centenaire* (Rouen, 1955), pp. 625–35.

6. He cites Gregory three hundred times, according to H. Rochais, "Pour une nouvelle édition du 'Liber scintillarum'," *Études mérovingiens* (Paris, 1953) 260.

7. I. Hausherr, *Penthos* (Rome, 1944), p. 23; F. Halkin, "Le pape Grégoire le Grand dans l'hagiographie byzantine," *Miscellanea Georg Hoffmann, S.J. Orientalia Christiana periodica* (1955) 109–14.

8. Cf. Indices in *Summa theologiae* and *Summa contra gentiles* (Rome, 1948), pp. 213–15.

9. F. Bouchage (Paris, 1930).

10. G. Lefèvre, *Prière pure et pureté de cœur. Textes de S. Grégoire le Grand et de S. Jean de la Croix* (Paris, 1953). He pointed out to the author the texts of St. John of the Cross which bear so close a resemblance to those of St. Gregory as to suggest direct dependence. Compare *Moralia* 5.56 and *Dark Night of the Soul* I II ch. 13; *Moralia* 30.39 and *The Ascent of Carmel* I 10; *In Ezech.* I II 9 and *Canticle*, strophe 27. In this last instance, both commentaries suppose the translation of *Surge* (Aquilo) by "depart" and not by "come."

11. PL 75–79.

12. On this point, see the fine introduction of R. Gillet to *Morales sur Job* (Sources Chrétiennes; Paris, 1950), pp. 81–109. The portion of the *Moralia* which appears in this volume, the beginning, does not perhaps find Gregory at his best as a doctor of mysticism. There he spends rather more time than usual on the explanation of the literal meaning of the text of Job.

13. O. Porcel, *La doctrina monastica de S. Gregorio Magno y la Regula monasteriorum* (Madrid, 1950), pp. 129–55.

14. *Epistolae XI* 30. (MGH *Epist.* II XI 18). Only a few texts will be cited here, merely as examples.

15. For example, *Moralia* 8.8–9; 8.53–54.

16. Corruptionis gravitas . . ., mutabilitatis pondus . . . *In Ezech.* II, I, 17; *Moralia* 8, 19, 53; 11, 68; 12, 17.

17. TLL, *s.v.*

18. *Moralia* 32.1.

19. Ibid. 6.40–43; 27.42.

20. Ibid. 2.79.

21. Ibid. 2.70, 83; 9.20.

22. Ibid. 33.25; 22.31–34.

23. Ibid. 27.40–41.

24. Ibid. 6.40–46.

25. The texts are quoted in *Un maître de la vie spirituelle au XIe siècle, Jean de Fécamp* (Paris, 1946), p. 99. "Aurem cordis" ("The ear of the heart") occurs in the first sentence of the *Rule* of St. Benedict.

26. *Moralia* 30.20; 27.42; 5.52.

27. *Dialogus* III 34; *In Ezech.* II 10, 20–21; *Epist.* VII 26.

28. "Termes de S. Grégoire exprimant le désir céleste," *Analecta monastica*, I 90.

29. *Alae spirituales* . . ., *aquilae pennae* . . ., texts indicated in *Un Maître*, 90n4.

30. *Moralia* 5.2; 7.49.

31. Ibid. 26.34.

32. Ibid. 10.13; 22.48–51; *In Ezech* II 1 18.

33. *In Evangelia* 30.1.

34. Ibid. 25.1–2.

35. *In Ezech.* II 7, 5.

36. *Moralia* 6.58.

37. Ibid. 18.45.

38. *In Evangelia* 25.2.10.

39. Ibid. 30.5; *Moralia* 10.48; 12.44.

40. *Moralia* 9.64, 80.

41. Ibid. 4.71; *In Ezech.* I 4, 13.

42. *Moralia* 33.63; 4.58.

43. Ibid. 2.28–29.

44. Ibid. 18.70.

45. *In Ezech.* II 2, 8–15; II 3, 8–13.

46. *Moralia* 10.13.

47. Ibid. 8.49–50; *In Evangelia* 1.1.

48. *In Ezech.* I 10, 26. "Le doigt de Dieu," *La vie spirituelle* (May 1948) 492–507.

49. *Moralia* 10.13; 31.101.
50. Ibid. 23.43; 28.1–9; *In Ezech.* II 6, 1–2; II 3, 14.
51. *In Evangelia* 14.4.
52. Ibid. 27.4.
53. *Moralia* 23.10–12. Other texts are studied in Gillet (n. 12) 50–54.
54. *In Ezech.* I 8, 11, 17–18; II 1, 18; II 2, 1.
55. *In Evangelia* 28.3.

3

Cult and Culture

Now THAT WE HAVE SEEN in St. Benedict and in St. Gregory the essential elements of monastic culture and the decisive factors which guided it, we must consider the period in which it took shape. It is the custom to call this the Carolingian period, that is to say, the hundred or so years embracing the second half of the eighth century and the first half of the ninth. It was at this time that this culture took on substance and acquired distinct and definitive characteristics.

MONASTIC LANGUAGE AND CULTURE: FRUIT OF THE CAROLINGIAN RENAISSANCE

Much has been written on the definition of the words "culture" and "civilization," and it seems clear that, from a very general point of view, culture includes an overall conception of the world and of life, and the means for expressing it—that is to say, language and the arts. Precisely, language is the foremost of the arts, the art of speaking well, writing well, and of expressing thought well. Thus, language is always the symbol of a culture, and it shows the level of a culture. Therefore, to witness the birth of a homogeneous monastic culture means witnessing the formation of its language as well. Thus we will see the language of the Middle Ages come into being, the one which is to be used by the monastic Middle Ages. It will be, because of its origins, an essentially religious language, that is to say, a language intended to express a religion, and this in the very highest act of any religion: worship. To understand this, one must first of all recall how Western monasticism had paved the way for the Carolingian reform, and then emphasize the liturgical character of this cultural renaissance, and the part the monks played in it, in order to gauge its results on monastic literature.

We need not add that no attempt will be made here to exalt the "civilizing role" of the monks. We shall try only to understand why, and from what period on, medieval monastic culture became what it was.

Missionaries: Grammarians

St. Gregory the Great as Pope had sent monks to England where they planted the culture of the Latin Church. The Anglo-Saxon monks who brought to fruition the seed received from Rome were obliged to forge their own mode of expression. They needed one for the observances of the cult which inspired so many of their poems, and for the apostolate; an Aelfric had to be at the same time a "maker of sermons and a grammarian."[1] During and after the long period when invasions were devastating the Continent, Latin culture was preserved primarily in England; a work like the *Ars grammatica* of St. Julian of Toledo was known to Aldhelm and later to the Venerable Bede.[2] Bede himself is an admirable product of all this effort. It is remarkable that, less than one hundred years after the arrival of St. Augustine of Canterbury, this grandchild of pagans should become a Doctor of the Church, and one of the classics of our Christian literature. This child of barbarians knew and quoted Pliny and other authors of classical antiquity, particularly the poets: Ovid, Lucan, Statius, Lucretius, and above all Virgil, whom he even tried to imitate. He was very well acquainted with the Fathers of the Church, especially St. Augustine, and, to an even greater degree, with St. Gregory, and he unites all these treasures in an harmonious synthesis. In his treatise on meter, his models are the classics, as well as Christian authors and liturgical hymns. He defends as legitimate certain liberties taken by Sedulius with regard to the classical rules, the better to sing the glory of the Trinity[3] or to translate more exactly the truth of the words of the Lord.[4]

St. Boniface

From England this Latin culture was to be taken back to a large part of the Continent. The missionaries carried across the Channel, not only the sacred books, but also the literary models left by the profane authors: there is a manuscript of Livy, copied in Italy in the fifth century, brought to England in the seventh or eighth century, that was soon carried back to the Utrecht region by one of the Anglo-Saxon missionaries.[5] Nor did their efforts stop there; they further elaborated the theory of this literary art. Characteristically, the Apostle of Germany, the reformer of the Frankish Church, St. Boniface, was a grammarian and wrote a handbook on meter and a treatise on grammar, an aspect of his work that has scarcely been studied. And yet, one of the instruments of his apostolate, one of his means, and not the least of them, by which he was able to implant in the regions he evangelized the faith and the culture of the Church, was this grammar he considered necessary to teach through the written word. The texts he used in it are extremely revealing. Certainly his *Ars grammatica* resembles many others,[6] and this is, no doubt, the reason why it did not detain the attention of the historians of St. Boniface and of monastic culture. In it, he gives the rules for declension and for the different parts of speech and he illustrates them with examples taken from the classical authors of antiquity. But the original feature of this conception of grammar lies in the brief preface where he explains why and how these rules were established and his examples chosen.[7] He addresses a pupil, an adolescent, with the latter's religious formation in mind. This formation will require him to study the *auctores* and the Latin grammarians of antiquity. But Boniface is a Christian master, he is a Christian grammarian, and he teaches Christian grammar; he is a churchman, and his teaching, in all domains, is ecclesiastical. Indeed, this Latin tongue which his disciple is to learn is henceforth a traditional language tested over centuries of Christianity. The authors and the grammarians of antiquity must, then, be studied—but their works must be integrated into the life of the Church. What is not in conformity with Catholic tradition must be eliminated; what the latter has introduced into the expression of religious ideas must be added.[8] The norm is the Latin inherited from the Church and from the doctors who were read every day. But the knowledge of grammar is absolutely necessary for the understanding of this reading, for Holy Scripture has its subtleties which are a hazard which could prevent its contents being understood.[9] As he brings this prologue to an end, St. Boniface explains why he placed at the head of his treatise, in a circle, a cross and the name of the Lord Jesus: just as the whole Old Testament led to Christ and already contained, under veiled images, the realities of the mysteries of salvation, all the good that can be found in reading and "scrutinizing" the grammarians, poets, historians, and the writings of both Testaments must be referred to Christ, in accordance with the advice of St. Paul: "Try everything, keep what is good." All of that should be placed, as in a safe fortress, within the circle of the faith, outside of which the mind has no right to wander. To understand things is to realize the relationship they have to Christ. It is at this price alone that one can see, with the eyes of the spirit, the growth of the temple of the love of God.[10] And this invitation to the study of grammar ends in a highly spiritual hymn: through virtue the citizen of Jerusalem should aspire to Heaven, where, with the angels, he shall see the Christ eternally.[11]

Such is the true character of the culture which had paved the way for the Carolingian reform: a humanism wholly inspired by classical antiquity, but a humanism whose touchstone is Christ crucified, risen from the dead, who by His example and His grace makes us renounce evil in order to lead us to the heavenly city.

An expert has written: "The quality of the Latin in the Middle Ages is the best test of the intellectual level of the time. It so happens that ninth-century Latin is scarcely at all inferior to what was to be the Latin of the sixteenth-century humanists."[12] Consequently, there really was a Carolingian renaissance.[13]

But how did it happen that Charlemagne should have instigated this revival of learning? His purpose was a religious one, and toward 780 he had undertaken to restore order to everything in the West: to the political, economic, and ecclesiastical life of his times. During his religious reform, he attacked disorder in every domain: doctrine, morality, worship, and monastic observance. Among the many reforms which he set in motion were two which resulted in the literary renaissance: those intended to revitalize the liturgy and monastic life.

At this period, the great controversies which had agitated the Church from the fourth to the sixth century had died down in the West; the faith was practically no longer menaced by heresy; the survival of Priscillianism and Adoptianism in Spain did not extend to the mass of the faithful. But if the faith was not under attack, it was undergoing a kind of deterioration. It was but little known, and since it was practiced just the same—because man, particularly in primitive societies, is religious—it often degenerated into superstition and remained without much influence on the moral life of the people. From the sixth to the eighth century, Councils continually forbade idolatry and practices which exploit the credulity of simple people and the memories which paganism had left in their minds. To safeguard faith and morals, it was necessary to substitute for these practices the authentic cult of the Church, with the doctrinal safeguards which it possesses. In other terms, the liturgy had to be restored, and, it was thought, closer contact with Roman liturgy had to be renewed.

RESTORATION OF THE LITURGY AND THE RENEWAL OF CLASSICAL STUDIES

But in order that that be possible, it was important first of all for the clergy to know Latin. It happened, however, that Latin was not being spoken or even understood. The Romance languages, then barely taking form, and the Germanic languages lent themselves but poorly to expressing Catholic dogma, already so developed and rich in nuances, molded into formulae, and with so precise a vocabulary. To think Christian doctrine otherwise than in Latin involved the danger of introducing into it inexactitudes, or even errors. The liturgical texts themselves were written in a very incorrect Latin whose spelling varied and whose punctuation was defective. Men knew neither how to read nor how to transcribe Latin; the copies were so poor that Charlemagne had almost all the manuscripts destroyed and ordered that only the best be kept. And even those—we can judge from the very few, rare ones which have come down to us—swarm with mistakes. To preserve orthodoxy and to assure the service an expression worthy of it, a double restoration was necessary: that of the Roman liturgy and that of literary culture. Charlemagne saw to it that trained copyists were charged with transcribing the liturgical books correctly. Clerics were, all too often, *idiotae*, that is to say, men who knew only their own language. If they knew neither how to write nor how to speak Latin, how then could they understand the Gospel? If Charlemagne wanted to promote classical studies, his reason was that they were supposed to make available to the pastors and their flocks an understanding of the Sacred Scriptures.[14]

PAUL THE DEACON AND ALCUIN

The principal teachers who were to carry out this project were Paul the Deacon and Alcuin. The first was a monk of Monte Cassino. Now, it is a fact that culture had taken refuge at the two extremities of the Europe that remained Christian after the Arab invasion: England and the south of Italy. Italy was the home of Ambrosius Autpertus, "monk and theologian."[15] Paul the Deacon played an important role in the revision of the liturgical books and we also know that he wrote a treatise on grammar,[16] in which, in addition to examples from the classical grammarians, Donatus, Charisius, Diomedes, and others, he added some borrowed from the Bible and Christian poets, such as Juvencus. Side by side with the names of Jupiter, of Priam, and of Orpheus, his pen evokes those of Adam, Abraham, David, and that of the Lord Jesus, which gives him the opportunity to make a touching profession of faith: "Jesus, the name of our Redeemer, which we venerate, we love to render in accordance with Latin usage."[17]

Alcuin, on the other hand, had received his formation at the monastery of York. It is not certain that he was a monk, and an historian has described him very well when he wrote: "It is not known whether he was a professed monk or a cleric who did not make a monastic profession:

there are reasons in favor of both opinions, perhaps better reasons for considering him as a monk who did not lead a strictly monastic life, but a *via media*. Certainly the stability of the Benedictine monk, so remarkable in Bede's life and work, plays a lesser role in Alcuin's career, and he confesses his vain attempts to reach *ad portum stabilitatis.*"[18] As a matter of fact, in order to carry out his mission in the Church, he had to travel a great deal. He understood that incorrect speech was caused by the lack of books and schools. Manuscripts had to be sent for, in particular those of the classical authors, and schools had to be founded. We are in possession of a most beautiful letter in which he informs the Emperor of his project: "In order to nourish the pupils with the fruits of grammatical subtlety" it was essential to have at one's disposal choice books, "the most erudite among those of scholarly erudition. We must bring the flowers of England to France in order that the school of York be no longer merely garden enclosed: the fruits of Paradise will also be able to be plucked in the school of Tours."[19] Alcuin himself composed a grammar and a treatise on orthography; in it, he takes his examples, not only from the secular classics, but from the Vulgate and the Fathers of the Church as well.[20] He organized the royal palace school at Aachen, and later the school of St. Martin of Tours. The pupils formed there were to carry culture throughout Europe. These were, for example, at the palace Angilbert, future abbot of St. Riquier, Adalhard, who was to become abbot of Corbie; at Tours, Rhabanus Maurus, abbot of Fulda, Amalarius of Metz, and Adalbert of Ferrara, and many amongst them later created schools at their own monasteries. The result was what had been hoped for, and a capitulary of 816 observes that, in the monasteries, the pupils spoke among themselves, not the vulgar tongue, but Latin: *"Usum latinitatis potius quam rusticitatis. . . ."*[21]

St. Benedict of Aniane and Notker

Another personality, this time an authentic monk, played a decisive role, if not, like Alcuin, in the general renewal of cult and culture, at least in the renovation of the monastic life: this was St. Benedict of Aniane. His role as reformer is well known; he was guided and sustained by a culture whose main features he has left us in a document which established definitively the intellectual attitude which was to be retained by the monks of the Middle Ages.[22] In it he describes the "form" which faith must acquire in order to be precise, harmoniously developed, or, in other words, adult. Using, but at the same time transcending, grammar and reasoning, the spirit should seek a certain understanding of the mysteries of faith in order to achieve divine friendship. It should endeavor especially to reflect on the dogmatic teaching of the "orthodox Fathers." Benedict of Aniane lays stress on the Trinity, and on the doctrine of the image of God in man, which was to occupy such a large place in the spiritual writings of the monks; he is the first to outline a study on friendship which others after him were to bring to perfection. He proposes as an example Ammonius, Origen's master, and recommends the reading of the two outstanding monks, St. Jerome and St. Gregory,[23] and of all those who taught the search for wisdom by means of renunciation and spiritual leisure: "An acutely sensed experience alone makes one a friend of God; it is through this wisdom that one becomes a friend of God and obeys Him."[24] In this manner, faith will remain pure and it will grow until faith's content is revealed.[25] Thus at the dawn of the great monastic centuries of the Middle Ages, he who has been sometimes considered the second founder of Benedictine monasticism gives the deciding impetus to a kind of theological research, but the theology in question is oriented toward love as monastic theology always will be.

There are abundant examples to illustrate the effects of the Carolingian renewal on monastic culture. We have only to think of their need to sing and their aptitude for making Latin verses to which we are indebted for innumerable poems—liturgical and otherwise—which fill so many volumes.[26] The need to versify produced masterpieces when true poets appeared, like Notker of St. Gall. With regard to this remarkable man, a demanding critic, having observed that his poems "seem to have been composed not very far from Attica," wonders why Notker and so many others wrote in Latin, and not in the mother tongue, German. It is, he answers, because Latin was not foreign to them. They learned it in the grammarians like a foreign language, but they learned it because it was the language of their true homeland, the Church. It was the language of the Latin culture which nourished them spiritually, the language of all Latin tradition before them, which means both classical antiquity and Christian antiquity, the Bible and the Fathers. It was the language of their religion, their only means for Christian expression, the only one adequate for communicating the realities and the experiences they wished to express.[27] Notker wrote poems not for a public, whether German- or Latin-speaking, but "for his Lord." As it was, the Lord gave His word to him in Latin; this language alone allowed him to express that additional life, culture, and experience that was *the contribution* of Christianity. The Holy Scripture, the hymns of the Church, everything which touched his soul deeply, and raised it above itself, he received in Latin. To transcribe so many new realities, he had no words except in that language. When he wanted to shout his joy, give vent to his enthusiasm, what he wanted to chant was too beautiful, too sublime for any other tongue than Latin. He sang to the Church, for the Church, the mysteries of the Church; and these were impressed on his soul in Latin; it was in this language as well that he had to express them. He in turn, by using it, enriched the Latinity he had received from the ancient tradition.

Smaragdus of St. Mihiel:
Christian Learning and Monastic Spirituality

Another example of the monastic culture inspired by the Carolingian revival is Smaragdus, abbot of Saint Mihiel in the first half of the ninth century. He left a work on grammar in which he teaches, as he does in his treatises on the spiritual life, a way to reach Heaven. It is through Latinity that the elect have been admitted to the knowledge of the Trinity; therefore it is through it that they must win an eternal crown.[28] How does grammar help one get to Heaven? By making possible the reading of the Scripture and the Fathers, it becomes a means for salvation and takes on sublime dignity. It is a gift of God, like His word itself, from which it cannot be separated since it furnishes the key to it. Smaragdus sings the praises of grammar in a poem like the one he was to place at the head of his commentary on another means of salvation, the *Rule* of Saint Benedict:

> Here you will find that measure of gold which comes from Heaven and which we have been accorded by the Holy Spirit Himself. In this book, he relates the great deeds of the Patriarchs; in it the lyricism of the Psalms resounds. This little book is full of holy gifts; it contains Scripture and it is seasoned with grammar. Scripture teaches us to seek after the kingdom of God, to detach the self from the earth, to rise above the self. It promises the blessed these heavenly boons: to live with the Lord, to dwell always with Him. Grammar then, through the goodness of God, confers great benefits on those who read it with care.[29]

The Latin which Smaragdus teaches is, like St. Boniface's, Church Latin. He makes no effort to hide this fact; on the contrary, he is proud of it. Just as the psychology and the erroneous beliefs of the pagans explain characteristics of secular Latin, the Christian faith has added new riches and greater flexibility to the language of Virgil. Far from being reduced to making excuses for the language of the Church, he admires it, he reveals its spiritual scope and its literary quality. Christianity gave the Latin tongue an opportunity to free itself, by making possible a new use of certain words which the rules did not exclude, but which common usage did not include, since the occasion for the introduction of such usage had not arisen. It has been pointed out that Smaragdus gives recognition to a "prophetic imperative" unknown in classic usage. Again, at times, this usage was mysterious, and the key to it was to be given only by faith. Thus, in the examples cited by Smaragdus, meanings used in the Scripture and the Fathers are added legitimately to those of classical antiquity.[30]

Such an exposition was no idle amusement. If Bede, Boniface, Alcuin, and so many others have written on Donatus, it was because concrete necessities had to be faced. We have a proof of this, for example, in one of the oldest manuscripts of Smaragdus' grammar. It contains Celtic glosses which philologists have studied for themselves, independent of the Latin texts which they surround; from the point of view of culture and religious psychology, they are worth being considered in their relationship to the text. They would no doubt reveal the difficulties experienced and the methods followed by some monk whose mother dialect was not a romance language, and who wanted to learn Latin.[31] Again in the same manuscript, we see Smaragdus' grammatical principles applied to what was their main objective, the liturgical cult. We refer to a series of benedictions and absolutions for the Office which are cadenced in accord with the laws of meter.[32] It is this same Latin language, made of the double legacy received from classical antiquity and Christian tradition, which Smaragdus has here used in his spiritual writings: his *Diadema monachorum*—from which the *Royal Road* has been taken and arranged for the laity[33]—and his *Commentary on the Rule*.[34] The latter, among the older commentaries, is at once the richest in ideas, most documented from traditional sources, most precise as to philological content, and the most beautiful. It is the one which is written in the most graceful and harmonious language, best adapted to interpret the realities of the spiritual life: a Latin already "mystical," and which anticipates that of the great monastic authors of the following centuries. As he did in beginning his grammar, Smaragdus puts at the head of his *Commentary* a poem which proclaims its purpose. Here again the winning of eternal life is the only consideration. The way for the monks to rise above themselves as far as the "heavenly kingdoms" is the *Rule*. This he says in verse, then in prose: "By observing the letter of the *Rule*, they hope one day to enjoy eternal happiness."[35] And he immediately employs his grammatical knowledge to further this end. The spelling *Obsculta* of the first word of the Rule is justified grammatically; the *O*, which is the second word, is an interjection, and so on for the remainder. Farther along, Smaragdus defends a phrasing of St. Benedict's by referring to the usage of the schoolmasters. And whose example does he choose? None other than that of St. Gregory the Great.[36] By exercising his grammarian's competence on each word of the *Rule*, the Abbot of St. Mihiel is merely conforming to one of the prescriptions of the great monastic capitulary of 817: "Let the abbots scrutinize the *Rule*, word for word, in order to understand it well, and, with their monks, let them endeavor to practice it."[37]

Pagan Literature and the Biblical and Patristic Tradition

Only a few examples have been cited here, and they would give an incorrect idea of the renewal in the Carolingian period if they were to create the impression that that movement was the privilege of a few great centers. As historians have remarked, the preservation and diffusion of classical texts were not confined to a few great abbeys like Fulda, Lorsch, or Corvey; Virgil, Statius, and other ancient writers were studied in very many less important, less famous, monasteries, if not always with deep understanding or with the aid of numerous and complete texts, at least with perseverance.[38] The same was true of patristic works. In this vast movement of cultural renewal different currents became apparent according to regions, and periods, or influences exerted by a master with an original mind or a faculty for organization. What matters here is for us to emphasize the general character of monastic culture in the Carolingian period.

To begin with, it can be said that in this culture literature assumes a place of unparalleled importance. In other words, everything is governed by the art of writing whether in verse or in prose. Everything is taught according to the *artes*, which are inspired by the best models, and to which all production must conform. An art, in the classical and medieval acceptance of the term, is a collection of precise rules; "grammar" includes all those which serve written expression. In conformity with the principle dictated by St. Augustine, and which Isidore had transmitted to the Middle Ages, "grammar, as its name indicates, is the study of letters [*litterae*] and that is why in Latin it is called literature [*litteratura*]. Everything which does not deserve to pass into oblivion and has been entrusted to writing, belongs necessarily to the province of grammar."[39]

At the same time, the sort of grammar upon which Christian expression depends must be understood. Carolingian grammar is actually a reflection of the whole culture of the times and is primarily the reason why this period appears to be a renaissance. But since the latter term has been much abused it is important to define the meaning it is to be given here. Rather than an original or a creative period, the Carolingian era is a time when the literary heritage of antiquity, whose continuity had been interrupted in many regions by invasions, was rediscovered and assimilated. However, it was truly a "re-nascence," for this new contact with antiquity gave a powerful impetus to creative effort. A period of transition—and in this sense a real middle age—between the patristic era and the literary expansion of the tenth and following centuries, the Carolingian era was, at a later time, to seem like an age of enlightenment after a time of darkness: *hoc tempore fuit claritas doctrinae.*[40]

The culture resulting from this renaissance is rich in the possession of a twofold treasure, each portion of which is transmitted. It consists, on the one hand, of the classical legacy, and on the other, of the Christian heritage inseparably biblical and patristic. Not only does the idea of a purely classical renaissance seem unthinkable, but the Christian, or rather Christianized, character of the new Latinity becomes more and more evident as the renewed culture develops. The norm for a living, evolving Christian Latin had been furnished by the Fathers. St. Gregory, among others, had said, "I consider as entirely unworthy the confinement of the words of celestial truth within the rules of Donatus."[41] Although barely formulated by Bede, the same conviction is very clearly expressed by Smaragdus. In the eyes of all men, the whole ancient heritage belongs to the Christians who are guiding it at last toward its true destiny: the worship of God in the Church. A figurative way of describing this humanism is often borrowed from the theme of the pagan woman taken prisoner (*captiva gentilis*). According to Deuteronomy,[42] an Israelite could, under certain conditions, marry a pagan woman taken in time of war. And Rhabanus Maurus, for example, comments:[43]

> That is what we customarily do, and what we ought to do, when we read pagan poets, when the books of worldly wisdom fall into our hands. If we meet therein with something useful, we convert it to our own dogma: *ad nostrum dogma convertimus.*

A real conversion thus takes place, thanks to which these cultural values return to their real end. "But if," adds Rhabanus Maurus, "we find superfluous things, concerning idols, love, preoccupation with the things of the world, we eliminate them." These words explain the character of the language and literature which resulted from the Carolingian renaissance, and which expressed its culture, a language and literature consciously indebted to the classical tradition, but which willed to be religious and serve religious ends. A new language appears, a sort of "mixed" language, and, this time, deliberately so. There had arisen, spontaneously, a patristic Latin, when the doctors of the first Christin centuries began to translate into Latin the message of the Church. From that time on, there was a Christian grammar.

MEDIEVAL LATIN LITERATURE

Following this there was forged that Christian medieval Latin which was to be developed and further enriched during the following centuries. Less vigorous perhaps than that of the classics and the Fathers, this simple and easy, flexible and clear, musical and rhythmical language was the one needed by these new people. It has been said of Christian Latin in general that it was in comparison with that of Horace "what Notre Dame is to the Parthenon."[44] There is even more reason for seeing in the Latin written in the centuries when the sober Romanesque churches were being built the continuation as well as the renewal of the Latin which had been spoken in the Pantheon and in the basilicas of Augustan Rome. Medieval culture will always remain divided by the two tendencies which correspond to the double inheritance which has been its wealth from the beginning: classical literature considered as necessary and admirable, and yet perilous; patristic literature, beneficial and legitimate. Some, however, will occasionally feel the need to find excuses for it because it will seem to them less beautiful in expression than that of the pagans. Because of this, a sort of dualism will result in medieval culture and in its very language. It remains to be seen what attitude monasticism will adopt in this evolution.

NOTES

1. This expression forms the suggestive title of the book by M. Dubois, *Aelfric, sermonnaire et grammairien* (Paris, 1942).

2. W. Levison, *England and the Continent in the Eighth Century* (Oxford, 1946), p. 148.

3. "But, the poet chose to neglect some of the rules of grammar in order to sing more clearly the glory of the holy and undivided Trinity." Cf. Keil, *Grammatici latini,* 8.1 (1878) 252. In St. Cyprian "lectio divina" means a passage of the Bible read during a liturgical function; cf. C. Dumont, "La lecture de la parole de Dieu," *Bible et vie chrétienne,* 22 (1958) 23–33.

4. "He changed the rules of a secular discipline, that he might more clearly state the truth of the divine word." Ibid.

5. P. Lehmann, "The Benedictine Order and the Transmission of the Literature

of Ancient Rome in the Middle Ages," *Downside Review* (1953) 408, who points out (ibid. 409) that the influence of Ireland and its missionaries was, in this domain, rather less than that of the Anglo-Saxon monks.

6. Ed. A. Mai, *Auctores Classici* (Rome, 1828–1838) VII 475.

7. The preface to this work is a dedicatory letter, the beginning of which is published anonymously in MGH, *Epist.* IV 564–65; a final fragment was rediscovered and published by P. Lehmann, *Historische Vierteljahrsschrift* (1951) 754. Various publications have established the fact of St. Boniface as author. Cf. Levison (n. 2), 145.

8. "I have only touched briefly on the grammatical precepts of the ancients whom we know to have followed quite different rules of style from those which we accept in modern times; this I have done so that you may properly understand whenever you come across something in Scripture that does not agree with modern usage. . . . In general, I have always tried to select that rule which I have found to be most often used in the works of ecclesiastical writers, in the sacred treatises, and with which we are familiar from our daily reading." Cf. Lehmann (n. 2), 754 and MGH, *Epist.* IV 564–65. In two other works, entitled *De caesuris verborum* and *De metris* (Cod. Pal. 1719, fols. 114–15), St. Boniface writes: "St. Jerome tells us that the Book of Deuteronomy was written in hexameters which, it is certain, were used by Moses long before Pherecides and Homer. Hence it appears that the study and practice of verse was older among the Hebrews than among the pagans. The psalms of David, also, are written in trimeters and hexameters." On the attribution of this text to St. Boniface see A. Willmanns, "Der Katalog der Lorscher Klosterbibliothek aus dem zehnten Jahrhundert," *Rh. Museum* (1868) 403–404.

9. "A knowledge of the art of grammar is extremely useful to those who wish to come to a knowledge of the more subtle meanings that are often to be found in Scripture because a reader who is ignorant of these rules will often fail to grasp the full meaning." Ibid.

10. The full text is given in Lehmann (n. 7), 755.

11.
> Vale Christo veraciter
> ut et vivas pereniter,
> sanctae matris in sinibus
> sacris nitens virtutibus,
> Hierusalem agricola,
> post et mortem caelicula,
> et supernis in sedibus
> angelorum cum milibus
> Christum laudes per ethera
> saeculorum in saecula.   (Ibid.)

12. J. Calmette, *Le monde féodal* (Paris, 1934), p. 349.

13. On the application of the word "renaissance" to the pre-Carolingian period, some useful corrections have been presented by P. Lehmann, A. Monteverdi, C. G. Mor, and others in *I problemi della civiltà carolingia* (Spoleto, 1954), pp. 309–82; some texts and authors of the Carolingian period have been gathered by F. Heer, "Die 'Renaissance' Ideologie im frühen Mittelalter," *Mitt. des Inst. f. Öster. Geschichtsforschung* (1949) 30–40.

14. *Admonitio generalis* of 789; MGH *Capit.* I 6–12; *Epistola de litteris colendis*: ibid. 79; *Epistola generalis*: ibid. 80.

15. J. Winandy, *Ambroise Autpert moine et théologien* (Paris, 1953).

16. Ed. A. Amelli (Monte Cassino, 1899).

17. "Ihesus quoque nomen nobis venerabile nostri Redemptoris, quod ad latinitatem placet inflectere." Ibid. 10.8.

18. Levison (n. 2), 153. On Alcuin, there are some suggestive pages in R. R. Bolgar, *The Classical Heritage and its Beneficiaries* (Cambridge, 1954), pp. 110–17.

19. MGH, *Epist*. IV 106.

20. Ed. A. Marsili (Pisa, 1952). In his Introduction, Marsili has noted the essentially religious character of the culture of Alcuin and the Carolingians; as a matter of fact, in the sources and examples quoted by Alcuin (ibid., pp. 83–85), pagan and Christian authors appear in just about the same proportion; and, if we recall that Virgil was considered as a Christian, because in the Fourth Eclogue he had foretold the coming of Christ, we could say that Alcuin quotes more Christians than pagans.

21. *Statuta Murbacensia*, ed. B. Albers, *Consuetudines Monasticae*, III (Monte Cassino, 1907) 93.

22. "Les Munimenta fidei de S. Benoît d'Aniane," *Analecta Monastica* 1.1–74.

23. Ibid. 62.10–20.

24. Ibid. 63.33–34.

25. Ibid. 64.75–76.

26. MGH, *PLAC* 4 vols.; Dreves–Blume, *Analecta Hymnica Medii Aevi*, 55 vols. (Leipzig, 1886–1922), *passim*. Still other texts have been published by Bischoff and others, for example in *Studien zur lateinischen Dichtung des Mittelalters, Ehrengabe K. Strecker* (Dresden, 1951), *passim*.

27. W. von den Steinen, *Notker der Dichter und seine geistige Welt* (Bern, 1948), pp. 79, 80, and *passim*. Bolgar, *Classical Heritage*, p. 103.

28. "Smaragde et la grammaire chrétien," *Revue du moyen âge latin* 4 (1948) 16.

29. This prologue is found in MGH, *PLAC* I 607.

30. "Smaragde et la grammaire chrétien," 15–21.

31. Ibid. 22n36. Interlinear glosses are especially frequent in the 8th–10th centuries and in the High-German regions; a list is given by W. Stack, "Mitteilungen zur mittelalterlichen Glossographie," *Liber Floridus, Festschrift P. Lehmann* (St. Ottilien, 1950), pp. 12–16.

32. "Bénédictions pour les lectures de l'office de Noël," *Miscellanea G. Mercati*, II (Vatican City, 1946) 477.

33. *Smaragde et son œuvre. Introduction à la voie royale. Le diadème des moines* (La Pierre-qui-Vire, n. d.), pp. 3–23.

34. PL 102.689–932.

35. Ibid. 691.

36. Ibid. 694.

37. Capitula Aquisgranensia I, *Consuetudines Monasticae*, III (Monte Cassino, 1907) 116.

38. Lehmann, "The Benedictine Order . . ." (n. 5) 420–21.

39. Idem, 141–42.

40. St. Bonaventure, quoted by Gilson, *The Spirit of Medieval Philosophy* (New York, 1940), p. 396.

41. Preface to *Moralia in Job*, MGH *Epist*. I 1, 357.

42. Deut. 21.10–13.

43. *De clericorum institutione*, III 18 (PL 107.396). On the sources of this theme, J. de Ghellinck, *Le mouvement théologique du XIIe siècle* (Bruges, 1948), p. 94.

44. R. de Gourmont, *Le latin mystique* (Paris, 1892), p. 15.

THE SOURCES OF
MONASTIC CULTURE

4

Devotion to Heaven

MONASTIC CULTURE OF THE MIDDLE AGES has two kinds of sources. Some are of a literary nature: written texts whose content must be assimilated through meditative reading or through study. Others belong to the domain of religious experience. Of these latter, the most important, the one which enables all the others to be combined in the harmony of a synthesis, is the one which induces the desire to reach the culmination of this experience. The content of monastic culture has seemed to be symbolized, synthesized, by these two words: grammar and spirituality. On the one hand, learning is necessary if one is to approach God and to express what is perceived of Him; on the other hand, literature must be continually transcended and elevated in the striving to attain eternal life.

A LITERATURE OF TRANSCENDENCE

Actually, the strongest and most frequently occurring description of this transcendence was to be found joined to considerations on eternal life. Thus, in order to complete the presentation of the essential components of monastic culture, and after having emphasized the place that *grammatica* held in it since St. Benedict and particularly since the Carolingian reform, we must speak of its dominant orientations, of what keeps it faithful to St. Gregory's influence: its eschatological tendency, which is but another name for compunction.

THE SYMBOLS OF ELEVATION

The first, the most important, of the themes to which the monks of the Middle Ages applied literary art is what could be called devotion to Heaven. The monks delighted in using the new language they created to translate the desire for Heaven, so dear to the heart of every contemplative that it becomes the characteristic feature of monastic life. Let us listen, for example, to an anonymous witness, who represents, so to speak, the general opinion, and who, not being a monk, is free from any prejudice. After having defined, in a commentary on the Canticles, "practical life" or "active life," he adds: "The theoretical life, with which this book of Scripture is concerned, is the contemplative life in which one aspires only to the celestial realities, as do monks and hermits."[1] To speak of this longing for Heaven will then mean evoking the spiritual atmosphere in which monastic culture flourishes. To do this in connection with the use the monks will make of the sources of their culture, we need no longer adhere to the chronological order of events. Henceforth unchanging principles common to all periods will be under consideration. Once the fact has been established that devotion to Heaven was much practiced in medieval monasticism, its importance for the culture and theology of the monks will follow as a natural conclusion.

THE HEAVENLY JERUSALEM

Without doubt, medieval men thought about Hell. Monks describe it in "visions" into which they project the images and ideas they have of the other world. But their adventures beyond the grave, like Dante's later, almost all end in Paradise.[2] And, in the texts they used for prayer, meditation on Heaven is more frequently met with than meditation on Hell. In their spiritual works, there are not only chapters but entire treatises with titles like *On Celestial Desire;*[3] *For the Contemplation and Love of the Celestial Homeland, Accessible only to those who Despise the World;*[4] *Praise of the Celestial Jerusalem;*[5] *On the Happiness of the Celestial Homeland.*[6] Sometimes these texts are exhortations or elevations in verse or in prose; sometimes verses of psalms alternate with subjects for meditation and with prayers. As people today occasionally make the exercise for a good death, then they used to make the exercise of Jerusalem: they reflected on Heaven, they cultivated the desire to go there one day, and they asked for the grace to do so. In order to understand monastic psychology, let us take from writings which crystallized it a few revealing themes. The word "theme" is the one most suited to this subject. For the topic we are discussing differs from speculative science, where theses are stated, followed by proofs. It belongs to the realm of symbolic expression. Its intent is to arouse desire for an indescribable experience. And, just as in music and in poetry, art consists in making "variations" on simple yet rich themes, so the true worth of monastic language lies in its evocative powers. This could not be otherwise, since it is a biblical language, concrete, full of imagery, and consequently poetic in essence. But, although not abstract, these modes of expression must not be taken any the less seriously.

All the themes used are biblical in origin. This in no way excludes, in certain cases, calling upon classical literary reminiscences: thus, in speaking of celestial happiness, by referring to the *locus amoenus*, the Golden Age, the Elysium whose description by Pindar and Aristophanes had left traces in St. Augustine's Neoplatonism, and, through him in particular as intermediary, in medieval literature. But the primary inspiration always comes from Sacred Scripture. The fact is that in all monastic literature, even in writings not specifically intended to treat of heavenly beatitude, Heaven is continually mentioned. Many themes embody the same realities under different forms: no logical connection can be established between them. The following are the principal ones.

First of all, there is the theme of Jerusalem. St. Bernard defines the monk as a dweller in Jerusalem: *monachus et Ierosolymita*. Not that he must be bodily in the city where Jesus died, on the mountain where, it is said, He is supposed to return. For the monk, this might be anywhere. It is particularly in a place where, far from the world and from sin, one draws close to God, the angels, and the saints who surround Him. The monastery shares Sion's dignity; it confers on all its inhabitants the spiritual benefits which are proper to the places sanctified by the life of the Lord, by His Passion and Ascension, and which will one day see His return in glory.

The mountain of the return is the symbol of the monastic mystery, and for every Christian who becomes a monk, it is as if he always lived in this blessed spot. It is there that he can be united to the real Holy City. St. Bernard adds: "Jerusalem means those who, in this world, lead the religious life; they imitate, according to their powers, by a virtuous and orderly life, the way of life of the Jerusalem above."[7] Speaking of one of his novices, he said that the latter had found the way to accomplish the words of St. Paul: *conversatio nostra in caelis est*,[8] and he adds:

> He has become not a visitor who admired the city as a traveler, but as one of its devoted inhabitants, one of its authentic citizens, not of the earthly Jerusalem comparable to Mount Sinai in Arabia which is, with all its children, in slavery, but of the one above, the free Jerusalem, our mother. And if you must know, I am speaking of Clairvaux. There one can find a Jerusalem associated with the heavenly one through the heart's complete devotion, through the imitation of its life, and through real spiritual kinship. There, henceforth, he will find rest, according to the

promise of the Lord, for ever and ever; he wanted to dwell there, because there is to be found, if not as yet the vision, at least the expectation,
in all security, of the true peace, of which it is said: "The peace of God
surpasseth all understanding."[9]

The monastery is then a Jerusalem in anticipation, a place of waiting and
of desire, of preparation for that holy city toward which we look with
joy. His biographer wrote of a disciple of St. Bernard, the Blessed David
of Himmerod, who was always smiling: "He had, like the Saints, a face
shining with joy; he had the face of one going toward Jerusalem."[10]

Actually, one of the favorite themes of monastic mysticism in the Middle Ages is the contemplation of the glory which God enjoys and which
He shares with His elect in heaven. This final reality, which, in prospect,
is the goal of our present existence, is frequently described by a symbol:
that of a city, Jerusalem. Most frequently it is not said that this city is in
Heaven, as if to distinguish it from another which is not in Heaven.
Occasionally it is even called "the land of the living." What matters is
not its location—the human images we are forced to use in speaking of it
are only analogies—it is the life that is led there, that is to say, God's own
life. Thus those who participate in God are all citizens of one and the
same Church, in Heaven and on earth. The "type" which serves to evoke it
is, not the Jerusalem of the flesh whose Temple was material, but the
spiritual Jerusalem of which St. Paul spoke to the Galatians and of which
the earthly Jerusalem was merely a figure. Those who are united with
God form a single community: Heaven and the Church. It is simply
given one name; to it is applied what the Bible said of the Holy City,
in the description of the Prophets or of Revelation.

Often linked to the theme of Jerusalem are those of the Temple and the
Tabernacle. From Bede to Peter of Celle, more than one author has written
of these symbols for the presence of God and the life led eternally in his
dwelling place.[11]

ASCENT INTO HEAVEN

The Jerusalem above is the end the monk strives for. He will rise toward
it through everything which calls to mind—and gives reality to—an ascension, and this introduces a whole series of themes. First that of the Ascension *par excellence*—of Christ Our Lord: This is one of the Mysteries of
Christ on which St. Bernard left the greatest number of sermons, more
even than on the Passion.[12] The monk leaves the world. Like every Chris-

tian, he detaches himself from it. But even more, because of special vocation, he separates himself from it. He goes away into solitude, often onto a
mountain, the better to fulfill the precept that the Church, on the feast of
the Ascension, gives to all the faithful: "To live in the celestial regions"
(in caelestibus habitemus). When the Lord had disappeared in the cloud
of His glory, the Apostles kept their eyes raised to Heaven. Two angels
came to tell them that they would not see Him again until such time as
He would return. Soon would come the time for them to spread out over
the whole world, to sow the seeds of the Gospel, to plant the Church.
Monks, however, have the privilege of continuing the watch. They know
that they will not see the Lord; they will live by faith. Nevertheless, there
they will remain. Their cross will be to love without seeing, and yet to
watch constantly, to keep their eyes on nothing but God, invisible yet
present. Their testimony before the world will be to show, by their existence alone, the direction in which one must look. It will be to hasten, by
prayer and desires, the fulfillment of the kingdom of God.

The Transfiguration foreshadowed the Ascension, and hence, they loved
to think of this mystery. Peter the Venerable introduced to Cluny and to
monasticism this Eastern feast, which entered the calendar of the universal
Church only some three centuries later. He composed an office for it and
wrote on this mystery a long treatise as beautiful as it is rich in doctrine.[13]

THE FELLOWSHIP OF THE ANGELS

Still another theme is borrowed from the angels; all sorts of comparisons
suggest connections, points of resemblance, between the life of the monks
and the vita angelica. On this point, there are innumerable texts.[14] What
is their significance? Did they propose escaping from our world of the
senses, becoming disincarnated, "playing the angel"? By no means. But
the adoration the angels render God in Heaven helps us understand the
important place given to prayer in the life of the monks. When angelic
life is spoken of, the being of the angels receives less consideration than
the function of praise which they perform. It has been correctly stated
that this mode of expression is not a

> hyperbole full of ambiguities which a sound theology, with a liking
> for exact terms, would have to distrust. . . . What is being sought, first
> and foremost, is an equivalence for the expression of eschatological values.
> It is in Heaven that man will be "like unto angels."[15] But since we are
> already on the threshold of the Kingdom and are participating in the

initial benefits of eternal life, it is altogether natural that this present life
be described in terms of angelic life.[16]

This theme and all those which encourage us to think of Heaven are valid
for every Christian, and they are by no means restricted to the monk. It
is only that they are so much more developed in monastic literature—the
literature written by the monks and the literature which is of interest to
them—because monks seek after the perfection of Christian life in a certain way, which more than for others has eschatological meaning. Its role
is to recall to all men that, after all, they are not made for this world.

The symbolism of flight is also frequent in the texts. Generally it is based
on this verse of Psalm 54: "Had I but wings, I cry, as a dove has wings, to
fly away, and find rest." From Origen to St. Teresa of the Child Jesus,
mystical authors have liked to express their desire for God by means of
this image.[17] St. Gregory was not the first to make use of this idea,[18] but
the importance which he gave to the symbolism of weight, and of flight
which overcomes it, contributed much to the penetration of this vocabulary into medieval monastic literature. Long lists of references can be found
in St. Bernard as well as in all the others.

The contrast between what may be called the two concupiscences likewise helped Smaragdus, for example, to express his desire for celestial life.
The task we face is, really, to substitute the concupiscence of the spirit for
that of the flesh. A parallel is established between them in which the role
of spiritual concupiscence is to comfort the weary soul with hope of future
glory.[19] But instead of placing emphasis on the negative aspect of asceticism, that is to say on suppression of desire, this mode of expression accen-
tuates the positive side: the soaring toward God, the inclination toward
the End of man which is God possessed fully and eternally.

The Gift of Tears

Finally, the desire for Heaven inspires many texts on tears. The tears of
desire, born of the compunction of love, are a gift from Our Lord; they
are asked for and their meaning is interpreted. In a chapter *On the Grace
of Tears*, Smaragdus has gathered together references taken from Holy
Scripture, from the Lives of the Fathers, and from St. Gregory. Others
have developed the theme in a more original manner. Such a one was, in
particular, John of Fécamp whose works were to have great influence on
all later spiritual literature. These "tears of charity," these "suave tears,"
engendered by the perception of God's sweetness, by the desire to enjoy
it eternally, are accompanied by sighs, which are not signs of sadness, but

of hopeful desire.[20] In the Middle Ages, monasticism has a whole literature of *suspiria*.[21]

THE GLORY OF PARADISE

We have thus seen in a rapid survey the principal themes which served to express the monk's longing for Heaven. The texts that will illustrate them are almost countless, and often extremely beautiful. Sometimes they are accompanied, in the manuscripts, by pious illustrations of very high quality, which picture for the eyes what the Bible describes for us concerning the City above. The iconography of the desire for Heaven is no less artistic, no less rich in poetry than the literary texts. One of the best known, most frequently copied, and edited texts is St. Peter Damian's *On the Glory of Paradise*.[22] Its stanzas have a profundity of vocabulary, a musical rhythm which makes them all but untranslatable. The poem opens with twenty stanzas which state the theme: the parched soul thirsts for the fountain of eternal life; imprisoned, it longs soon to see the walls within which the flesh keeps it captive break down; exiled, it aspires to enjoy at last its native land.

This is the happiness which it had lost through sin. The soul wants to recover possession of it, and that is why it loves to contemplate its glory. Its present suffering awakens the memory of Paradise lost. All the most beautiful things, the most pleasing to the senses, to be found in Scripture are called upon to give an idea of this total happiness: fruits, flowers, springtime, sunlit meadows, the glory of the saints, the splendor of the Lamb, the recovered harmony between flesh and spirit, health, inexhaustible youth, understanding and mutual love among the elect, unalterable union—nothing is lacking of all that the Christian could desire to receive from God upon entering the heavenly joys. But this happiness is not static, fixed once for all within a boundary that cannot be crossed. Happiness grows to the degree that it receives satisfaction, and is satisfied in the proportion that it grows. Endlessly, desire and possession cause each other to increase, because God is inexhaustible—and this consideration is, no doubt, the one which best helps us acquire a certain picture of what eternity really is. What Gregory of Nyssa had analyzed under the name of ἐπέκτασις, St. Peter Damian has also described: "Always eager and always satisfied, the elect have what they desire: satiety never becomes wearisome, and hunger, kept alive by desire, never bcomes painful. Desiring, they eat constantly, and, eating, they never cease to desire."[23] The joys which more than satisfy the senses and the spirit seem to renew themselves, because the Lord gives of Himself more and more. This long poem ends with a plea for entrance into Heaven. But the expressed request is given less place than the contemplation of the desired happiness. To think of the glories of Paradise is to prove that we love the One we hope to possess there, who already gives Himself to us when He gives us the capacity to desire Him.

Another example of this literature of desire is the *Epithalamium between Christ and the Virgins*, which is probably by a monk of Hirsau of the twelfth century and which has come down to us through Cistercian manuscripts.[24] The text contains no fewer than one hundred and twenty-nine double strophes. They describe the entrance of the virgins into the Kingdom of Christ, and then the happiness which they find there. Here again, the garden of Paradise supplies all the images: flowers and perfume, enchantment for the senses and the spirit—such is the setting where love is to bloom. The wedding procession comes forward, and Christ is at last revealed. His glory, which up to now has remained hidden, appears in its full light: "How great is the intimate love which devours the soul when faith produces its full effect: to unite members to their true leader!" The bride is decked with all the ornaments described in Psalm 44, and this happiness belongs to all united by the same love of God. This time which shall have no end—*tempus interminabile*—is a Sabbath, a Passover, a summer; there, there will be no old age, no death, or any change. It is repose which consists in knowing God as He is, in looking at Him with a glance which is absolutely pure. Again it is a city, Jerusalem, adorned with all the precious stones, each of them symbolizing a virtue and the joy which is its reward. And here it is the hymn *Urbs Jerusalem beata* which fires the poet's imagination. But the five spiritual senses, fully satisfied, are but means for speaking about the one true happiness, the one real reward, which is God Himself, and the description of this holy City provides the opportunity for a paean of thanks in anticipation of the promised and expected glory, complete union with Christ. It is an exhortation to detachment from all that is not God, to the exclusive pursuit of God; it is a prayer for help and perseverance in this obscure and unrelenting quest: "We seek you Lord, sighing; raise us to You, Yourself." Several times there recurs the word *interminabilis*, used to qualify both celestial joy and the poem which sings of it. The soul joins in the happiness of the Virgin and the Blessed, happiness described in symbols which are always new. In searching for means to express it the soul begins to sing the canticle of the Lamb. The singing is kept up so that it may give an idea of the happiness which is its object, and in order to obtain it by means of repeated prayer.

John of Fécamp

No author has developed the theme of desire of Heaven more than has John of Fécamp. It can be said that his whole work is an aspiration toward God. This work is important first of all because it is very beautiful, and—on that very account—because it had an immense influence, an influence which cannot be measured. Under the names of Cassian, St. Ambrose, Alcuin, St. Anselm, St. Bernard, above all under the title of *Meditations of St. Augustine*, the writings of John of Fécamp were the most widely read spiritual texts before the *Imitation of Christ*. St. Bernard was well acquainted with John of Fécamp—reminiscences may be discerned in his writings—and he is akin to him in quality of style, and in the intensity of his mystical élan. We wish that we could here quote long passages from these lofty songs. The heading itself of the longest portion of the *Confessio theologica* will suffice to give an idea of its contents:

> Here begins the third part in which the soul, full of devotion, animated by extreme love of Christ, inclined toward Christ, sighing for Him, desiring to see Him who is its only love, finds nothing sweeter than to groan and weep, unless it is to flee, to remain silent, and to rest, saying: "Had I but wings, I cry, as a dove has wings, to fly away, and find rest." [25]

Finally, there is a long elevation on the glories of Jerusalem.[26] Its author, whose name is unknown to us, was probably a religious of the Benedictine Abbey of Bèze, at the beginning of the twelfth century; in any case, he is clearly a disciple of Gregory the Great and of John of Fécamp. His words pour out like a torrent in the enthusiasm of his fervor. As he says, he "heard within him God speaking to him of Himself"; he belongs to those in whose hearts "there flows already a little of the dew that falls from Heaven." He attempts no abstract treatise on beatitude. He wnts to provoke, to prepare the way for a certain contact with God, a sort of union, entirely spiritual, which he is obliged to describe by means of sensory comparisons: sight and touch. He sings the litanies of the Glorified Lord, surrounded by His court.

The inhabitants of the City, inseparable from one another, are angels and men. Their happiness comes from being with God; He penetrates their entire being and even the body is given its share of bliss.

From this contemplation of the City of God there is born the desire to be there, an active desire; it is both expectation and inclination; properly, it is hope.

The duties of asceticism flow from this mythical view; detachment is only the reverse of attachment to Christ; it is, henceforth, the condition and the proof of love. He who wishes to fly to his God bends toward Him: he stretches forth his arms, he prays, and his eyes stream with tears of joy.

THE CITY OF GOD

The text, in the manuscript, has no divisions. But, in reality, it is a kind of poem in prose. The biblical flavor and the vitality which account for the charm of this poetry, the rhythm and assonance of the very musical language at once so sober and so powerful, give to these burning stanzas a movement and a freedom which reflect the inner life of a truly spiritual man, one who is already participating in the happiness he is describing.

Necessarily translation will weaken a text of this quality, but it can at least give an idea of it. Here then is this admirable prayer which reveals so well the inner attitude of so many other nameless monks:

> The frequent recollection of the city of Jerusalem and of its King is to us a sweet consolation, a pleasing occasion for meditation and a necessary lightening of our heavy burden. I shall say something briefly—and, I hope, usefully!—on the city of Jerusalem for its edification; and for the glory of the reign of its King I shall speak and I shall listen to what the Lord within me tells of Himself and of His city. May my words be as a drop of oil on the fire which God has enkindled in your hearts, so that your souls, burning with both the fire of charity and the oil of this exhortation, may rise up stronger, burn with greater fervor, and mount ever higher. May your soul leave this world, traverse the heavens themselves, and pass beyond the stars until you reach God. Seeing Him in spirit and loving Him, may you breathe a gentle sigh and come to rest in Him. . . .
> Therefore, as the Catholic faith believes, and as Sacred Scripture teaches us, the Father is the ultimate origin of all things, the Son is the archetype of perfect beauty, and the Holy Spirit is the perfection of all joy; the Father is the cause of the established universe, the Son is the light by which we perceive the truth, the Spirit is the fountain whence we drink of the waters of felicity. The Father has mightily created all from out of nothing, the Son has wisely ordered this mighty creation, and the Holy Spirit has multiplied with benignity the things thus created and ordered. On our way, the Son makes us disciples, the Holy Spirit con-

soles us as He would grieving friends; arrived in our true home, the Father makes us victors and covers us with glory. Comprehensible to itself is the all high and all holy Trinity, but incomprehensible to angels and men; and what here we believe, there do we see: how one is divisibly Three, and the Three are indivisibly one.

The city of Jerusalem is built upon the heights. Its builder is God. There is but one foundation of this city: it is God. There is but one founder: it is He, Himself, the All High, who has established it. One is the life of all those who live in it, one is the light of those who see, one is the peace of those who rest, one is the bread which quenches the hunger of all; one is the spring whence all may drink, happy without end. And all that is God Himself, who is all in all: honor, glory, strength, abundance, peace, and all good things. One alone is sufficient unto all.

This firm and stable city remains forever. Through the Father, it shines with a dazzling light; through the Son, splendor of the Father, it rejoices, loves; through the Holy Spirit, the Love of the Father and the Son, subsisting, it changes; contemplating, it is enlightened; uniting, it rejoices. It is, it sees, it loves.

It is, because its strength is the power of the Father; it sees, because it shines with the wisdom of God; it loves, because its joy is in the goodness of God. Blessed is this land which fears no adversity and which knows nothing but the joys of the full knowledge of God.

Now, each has his own garment; but in the eighth age, the armies of the blessed will bear a double palm. All will know. All words will be hushed and only hearts will speak. Bodies will be spiritual and invisible, bright as the sun, quick and pliant as could be desired, with strength to carry out any command.

Then will be the month of months, and the most glorious of sabbaths. Then will the light of the moon be like to the light of the sun, and the light of the sun will shine with seven-fold brilliance, and every saint's face will shine like the sun in the kingdom of his Father.

This city will have no need of the sun's light; but God the all-Powerful will illumine it. His torch is the Lamb: the Lamb of God, the Lamb without spot whom the Father sent into the world as a saving victim, who, living without sin, dying for sinners, took away the sin of the world, loosed the pains of hell, and liberated the prisoners from the lake without water, triumphant before them, and reinstating them in His kingdom by His side.

He is most beautiful in countenance, very desirable to see, He upon whom the Angels desire to gaze, He is the King of peace, He whose countenance is desired by all the world. He is the propitiator of sinners, the friend of the poor, the consoler of the afflicted, the guardian of the little ones, the teacher of the childlike, the guide of pilgrims, redeemer of those who have died, the courageous helper of warriors, the generous rewarder of victors.

He is the golden altar of the Holy of Holies, the place of rest of sons, the spectacle pleasing to the angels. He is the sublime throne of the supreme Trinity, raised above all, He who is blessed of the ages. He is the crown of the saints, the light of all, the light of angels.

O what will we give Him in return for all He has given us? When shall we be delivered from the body of this death? When shall we be filled with the abundance of the house of God, seeing the light in His light? When then will the Christ appear, our life, and shall we be with Him in Glory? When shall we see the Lord God in the lamb of the living, the kindly rewards, the man of peace, the dweller in repose, the consoler of the afflicted, the first-born of the dead, the joy of the Resurrection, the man of the right hand of God, He whom the Father has established. He is the Son of God, chosen from among thousands. Let us hear Him, run to Him, thirst for Him; may our eyes stream with tears of desire, until we be taken away from this valley of tears and rest in the bosom of Abraham.

But what is Abraham's bosom? What do they possess, what do they do, those who rest in Abraham's bosom? Who will understand by his intelligence, who will explain in words, who will experience through love what strength and beauty, glory, honor, delight and peace there are in Abraham's bosom? Abraham's bosom is the Father's repose. There are revealed openly the power of the Father, the splendor of the Son, the sweetness of the Spirit. There the saints feast and leap with joy in the presence of God, there are luminous dwellings, there the souls of the Saints rest and take their fill of the abundance of Divine praise: in them is found joy and gladness, thanksgiving and words of praise.

There is magnificent solemnity, opulent repose, inaccessible light, interminable peace. There are the great and the humble, and the slave set free from his master. There dwells Lazarus, who once sat covered by ulcers by the door of the rich man, now forever happy in the glory of the Father. There is enjoyment for the choirs of angels and saints.

O how broad and pleasing is Abraham's bosom! O how calm and secret! How free and clear! O Israel how good is Abraham's bosom, not for those who glory in themselves but for those whose hearts are good principally for those it embraces and makes anew. Without your help, O God, eye has not seen what has been prepared in the bosom of Abraham for those who await you. Man does not know this secret, which does not appear upon earth to those who live in pleasure. This secret is one which the eye has not seen, nor ear heard, nor has it entered into the heart of man; it is what is promised to the faithful fighting for

Christ, and what is given to the victorious who reign with Christ in glory.

What do we have still in common with perishable things, we to whom so much is promised in Heaven? What could we enjoy on earth in the company of sinners, we who are called to the court of the heavenly host? What are the pleasures of the flesh to us who ought to bear the image of the celestial? What do we have to do with the concupiscence of the eyes, we who long to gaze upon the spectacle which is pleasing to the angels? With wordly ambition, we to whom is promised the possession of Heaven?

Thus, while like all our fathers we are guests and strangers, while our days pass by like a shadow over the earth and there is no respite, while the avenging angel, the blinding cloud, the wind of the tempest, and the enveloping fire pass over the earth, let us flee from the darkness of Egypt to the shadow of the wings of God, and stay there until iniquity has passed away, until the day breathes and the shadows bow low, in order to merit being placed in Abraham's bosom.

There are the true riches, there are the treasures of wisdom, length and joy of life. There is full force where nothing is weakness, where nothing courageous is lacking. There is full wisdom where there is no ignorance, where no true understanding is lacking. There is utmost felicity where there is no adversity, where no goodness is lacking. There is full health because there is full charity, there is full beatitude because there is full vision of God. Vision, I say, is in knowledge, knowledge is found in love, love is with praise, and praise finds security and all this is without end.

Who will give us wings like the dove, and we shall fly across all the kingdoms of this world, and we shall penetrate the depths of the eastern sky? Who then will conduct us to the city of the great king in order that what we now read in these pages and see only as in a glass, darkly, we may then look upon the face of God present before us, and so rejoice?

City of God! What glorious things have they not said of thee! In thee is the home of those who are joyous, in thee is the light, and the life of all. Thy foundation is a single stone, a living corner-stone, uniquely precious. Thy gates will shine with splendid diamonds. They will be opened wide. Thy walls will be of precious stones, thy towers gleaming with jewels. Thy streets, O Jerusalem, will be paved with gems and with a pure gold like transparent crystal, and in thee will be seen the vision of glory, in thee will be sung the songs of gladness, and all will hear the sweet concert of Heaven, the symphony, the choir, and all will utter a single word: Alleluia!

A word without peer, word of all sweetness, word full of praise! In this city dwell our parents and dearest friends ready to call upon God on our behalf; they await our coming, and so far as they are able, they hasten our journey.

Let us lift up our hearts to them in our hands, let us rise above all transitory things. Let our eyes stream constantly with tears toward the joys which are promised us. Let us be happy because of what has already been accomplished in the faithful who, yesterday, were fighting for Christ, and today reign with Him in glory. Let us be happy because of what has been told us in truth: We shall go into the land of the living.

Most illustrious of lands, celebrated land which the Lord has blessed, land flowing with milk and honey, desirable land which carnal Israel counted as nothing but for which every true Israelite will struggle until death. Blessed is the hour when we shall enter into this land, where the Lord as He passes will minister unto us, while the angels rejoice and the saints enjoy bliss everlasting.

On that day, God will manifest Himself to us and to all our friends, He will wipe away every tear from the eyes of the saints. He will give back great things in return for small; for perishable things, bliss. Then all will become clear to us, everything will belong to all; then, visibly, shall we see how God is three and one, all in all, and above all. Then will our hearts rejoice with the fullness of joy, and our joy no one shall take from us: for what we are now in expectation, then shall we be in reality: sons of the kingdom, united to the angels, eternal inheritors of God, co-heirs with Christ, by the same Christ, Our Lord who with the Father and the Spirit, liveth and reigneth, world without end. Amen!

THEMES OF ANTICIPATION

It is true then: medieval monastic literature is, in large part, a literature of compunction, whose aim is to possess, to increase, and to communicate the desire for God. And this fact opens up to us a whole conception of monastic culture and of monastic life. The latter is considered as an anticipation of celestial life; it is a real beginning of eternal life. Everything is judged according to its relationship with the final consummation of the whole of reality. The present is a mere interlude. This conception is often expressed by means of two themes which can merely be indicated here. The first is that of the pre-libation, which again calls upon the vocabulary borrowed from the senses, notably the sense of taste;[27] this foretaste engenders in the soul a joy, an exaltation, a sort of intoxication, but an intoxication within the bounds of faith and asceticism. It owes nothing to purely natural stimulant; it is a "sober inebriation."[28]

Rest and Leisure

The second theme is that of leisure. Because it anticipates eternal rest, monastic life, the life in the "cloistered paradise,"[29] is a life of leisure. That is the definition most frequently found and in this case it is expressed in terms like *otium, quies, vacatio, sabbatum*, which are occasionally used to reinforce each other: *otium quietis, vacatio sabbati*.[30] These terms must be understood properly; the reality they describe is as different from quietism as the traditional ἡσυχία is from hesychasm. *Otium* lies midway between the two perils *otiositas* and *negotium*, which is the very denial of *otium*. *Otium* is the major ocupation of the monk. It is a very busy leisure, *negotiosissimum otium*, as St. Bernard and so many others have repeated. This theme, like all the others, is of biblical inspiration. There is, to be sure, a classical tradition of *otium*. But when William of St. Thierry, for example, takes from Seneca and Pliny the expression *otium pingue*, he gives it an entirely new meaning,[31] the one used by Ecclesiastes in an expression often repeated by monastic writers: *sapientia scribae in tempore otii*.[32] The symbol of the bed, and even of the "little bed," is grafted on the theme of leisure: *lectulus noster floridus*.[33] The bed is monastic life; the *lectulus* is contemplation.[34] Hence a whole symbolism of "waking sleep."[35] Mystical language constantly uses paradoxes like these to evoke, without exhausting their meaning, realities too complex to be contained within abstract definitions. It is always a question of the reconciliation, on the level of spiritual experience, of ideas which, in appearance and on the natural level, are contradictory.

Desire: Possession of Love

This conception of the foretaste of Heaven gives direction and also its form to the monks' culture and theology. Because it belongs to the eschatological order—anticipated but still imperfect participation in the sight of God—contemplation is essentially an act of faith, hope, and love. It is not, therefore, the end result of a discursive activity of the intelligence, it is not the reward of learning acquired through study, and it does not result in an increase of speculative knowledge. It tends to foster love under the forms love takes on while awaiting celestial beatitude: a vague possession, the possession of desire. Since contemplation in its full meaning means possession in perfect knowledge, it will be attained only in Heaven; it is impossible here on earth. But one can obtain from God the gift of real anticipation which is the desire itself.[36] To desire Heaven is to want God and to love Him with a love the monks sometimes call impatient.[37] The greater desire becomes, the more the soul rests in God. Possession increases in the same proportion as desire.[38] But just as death is the condition upon which full satisfaction depends, so this foretaste demands that we must die to the world. There is no contemplation without mystical death, without mortification.[39] This obligation is incumbent upon all Christians; all the faithful are called upon to detach themselves from the world and to cling to God who is symbolized by Heaven. St. Anselm, at the end of the *Proslogion* where he tries, in his own words, "to elevate his spirit unto God," engages in a long contemplation of the happiness of God and those who enjoy it in Heaven, as if that were the end to which all his striving to understand revelation was directed.[40] He considers this same contemplation the aim of all moral exhortation. In a letter to Hugh the Hermit, in which he sketches the outline of a sermon which could be given to seculars, he emphasizes in closing the necessity of stimulating them to long for Heaven, and he refers to what he had written at the end of the *Proslogion*.[41] In reality, devotion to Heaven cannot remain a monopoly of the monks. They, however, did practice it more than others, since in the cloistered life their attention was less distracted from the God who gives Himself in creating the desire for Him. An anonymous monastic author of the twelfth century showed very clearly how union with God is realized in desire and becomes inseparable from it:

> He who wishes to merit reaching the threshold of eternal life, God asks of him only a holy desire. In other words, if we are unable to make the efforts which merit eternity, we are, in spite of being so base and so slow, through our desire at least for eternal realities already hastening toward it. We want to eat in proportion to our hunger, to sleep in proportion to our weariness; in the same way it is by virtue of a holy desire that we search for Christ, that we are united with Him and love Him.[42]

NOTES

1. Cod. Paris BN 568, fol. 2, recension A of the Commentary of Anselm of Laon. "Le commentaire du Cantique des cantiques attribué à Anselme de Laon," RTAM (1949) 29–39.

2. "Visions monastiques d'outre-tombe," *Analecta Monastica*, 5.

3. Smaragdus, *Diadema monachorum*, PL 102.620.

4. Ps.-Alcuin, *De Psalmorum usu* I 5 (PL 101.474). Likewise, *De varietate librorum sive de amore caelestis patriae*, written by Haymo for Abbot William of Gellone (†812); PL 118.875–958.

5. Eadmer, *S. Anselmi liber de similitudinibus*, 44 (PL 159.624).

6. Eadmer, PL 159.587–606. Other titles will be mentioned later. A collection of very beautiful texts with reproductions of medieval representations of the heavenly Jerusalem will be found in: S. A. Hurlbut, *The Picture of the Heavenly Jerusalem in the Writings of Jean de Fécamp's De contemplativa vita and in the Elizabethan Hymns* (Washington, 1943).

7. St. Bernard, *Super Cantica*, 55.2 (PL 183.1045).

8. Philippians, 3.20.

9. St. Bernard, *Epist*. 64 (PL 182.169).

10. A. Schneider, "Vita B. Davidis monachi Hemmerodensis," *Analecta S. Ord. Cist.* (1955) 35. Cf. also Giles Constable, in RB (1956) 106.

11. *La spiritualité de Pierre de Celle (1115–1182)* (Paris, 1946), pp. 33–36.

12. "Le mystère de l'Ascension dans les sermons de S. Bernard," *Collectanea Ord. Cist. Ref.* (1953) 81–88.

13. *Pierre le Vénérable* (Saint-Wandrille, 1946), pp. 326–32: "La lumière du Thabor"; pp. 379–90: "L'office de la Transfiguration."

14. *La vie parfaite: Points de vue sur l'essence de la vie religieuse* (Paris–Turnhout, 1948), pp. 19–56: Ch. I "La vie angélique."

15. Luke 20.30; Matt. 22.30.

16. J. C. Didier, "Angélisme ou perspectives eschatologiques?" in *Mélanges de sc. relig.* (1954) 31–48.

17. "Technique et redemption: La mystique du vol," *La revue nouvelle*, 162–64.

18. M. Walther, "Pondus, dispensatio, dispositio," *Werthistorische Untersuchungen zur Frömmigkeit Papst Gregors des Grossen* (Lucerne, 1941).

19. "Concupiscentia vero spiritus mentem lassam, ne deficiat, spe futurae gloriae corroborat." *Diadema monachorum*, Ch. 94 (PL 102.684). *Smaragde et son œuvre*, p. 22.

20. *Un maître de la vie spirituelle au XIᵉ siècle: Jean de Fécamp*, pp. 89–93: "Suavité de Dieu," "Les larmes," and *passim*.

21. "Écrits spirituels de l'école de Jean de Fécamp. II. Une 'aspiration' inédite," *Analecta Monastica*, I 108–14 (list of MSS and edition of a sample).

22. *Rhythmus de gloria paradisi*, PL 145.980.

23. Ibid. 982.

24. Dreves, *Analecta Hymnica* 50 (1907) 499–506.

25. *Un maître*, p. 142.

26. "Une élévation sur les gloires de Jérusalem," *Mélanges J. Lebreton, Rech. de sc. relig.* (1952) 326–34.

27. *La spiritualité de Pierre de Celle*, pp. 75–81; "La prélibation du ciel," *Un maître*, p. 83 and *passim*.

28. "Jours d'ivresse," *La vie spirituelle* (April 1947) 576–91.

29. *La vie parfaite*, pp. 161–69: "Le paradis."

30. *La spiritualité de Pierre de Celle*, pp. 82–90: "Otium quietis." "Les deux compilations de Thomas de Perseigne," *Mediaeval Studies* (1948) 206–207. Winandy, *Ambroise Autpert*, pp. 71–82: "Vacatio sabbati."

31. J. M. Dechanet, *Guillaume de Saint Thierry, L'homme et son œuvre* (Bruges, 1942), pp. 58–65: "Pingue otium." Dom Dechanet indicates the sources in Seneca, *Guillaume de Saint Thierry, Lettre d'or* (Paris, 1956), p. 168. The word *pingue* is,

in Pliny, connected with *otium* and *secessus* in the meaning of "comfortable leisure"; William is speaking of a "leisure fruitful and well-filled" by exercises of contemplation. Cf. ibid. 35.

32. Eccles. 38.25; in place of *otii* the Vulgate reads *vacuitatis*.

33. *Cant*. 1.15. Thomas of Perseigne, PL 206.157, 325, 361.

34. "Sermon ancien sur la persévérance des moines," *Analecta Monastica* II 25, 135–38 and 20n3. St. Bernard, *Super Cantica* 426. Geoffrey of Auxerre, "Le témoignage de Geoffrey d'Auxerre sur la vie cistercienne," *Analecta Monastica* II 178. Cf. also *Analecta S. Ord. Cist.* (1955) 117–18.

35. For example, St. Bernard, *Sup. Cant.* 52.

36. "Contemplation et vie contemplative du vie au xiie siècle," *Dict. de spiritualité*, II (1953) 1946–1948.

37. A. Schneider (n. 10), 39. Peter of Celle, *Epist.* 46.

38. "Repausat anima sponsi, sui desiderio inflammata, tot deliciis fluens, quot caelestibus studiis studens, tanta beati fructus ubertate se satians, quanta fuerit in appetitu facultas." *Speculum virginum* (an anonymous monastic work of the twelfth century), ed. M. Bernards, *Speculum virginum: Geistigkeit und Seelenleben der Frau im Hochmittelalter* (Cologne–Graz, 1955), p. 193.

39. "The soul contemplates, in desire, the immense and unchangeable unity of the Godhead and it grasps the Trinity in a way that the intellect of faith cannot. Out of love of God, the soul withdraws itself from the contact of earthly things and the distractions of desire, in order to see God, as much as He can be known by those who have died to this world. For, one can come to this knowledge only if he has died to earthly things. He sees, as in a glass, darkly, as I say, but more certainly because the image of the light begins to appear to him more pleasant." Paschasius Radbertus, *In Matt.* 3.5 (PL 120.223). *Dict. de spiritualité*: "Contemplation and the Contemplative Life," col. 1938–39 and *passim*.

40. *Proslogion*, c. 25–26, ed. F. S. Schmidt, *S. Anselmi opera* I (1938) 118–22.

41. *Epist.* 112, III (1946) 246. The purpose of every exhortation contained in this letter is indicated from the beginning: "In order that they may glow more ardently with the love of their heavenly home."

42. *Speculum virginum*, 193 (n. 38). A similar formula is found in St. Bernard, *Sermo de S. Andrea* II 5 (PL 183.511). Cf. J. Nicolas, "S. Bernardo e il desiderio di Dio," *Camaldoli* (1953) 119–27.

5

Sacred Learning

THE PRINCIPAL LITERARY SOURCES of monastic culture may be reduced to three: Holy Scripture, the patristic tradition, and classical literature. The liturgy, which will be treated later, is the medium through which the Bible and the patristic tradition are received, and it is the liturgy that gives unity to all the manifestations of monastic culture. In the first place, then, we must attempt to supply an introduction to the study of monastic exegesis. "Attempt" and "introduction": these two terms are justified by the fact that this domain has been, till now, but very little studied. What has been studied most are the classical sources, probably because these problems of medieval culture have been approached more often by medievalists than by theologians and patrologists. However, it is now perceived that the monastic Middle Ages in general and St. Bernard in particular must be understood from the point of view of what preceded them—the patristic tradition whose principal task was to transmit and explain the Bible. A general study of the medieval monastic commentators is still lacking.[1] The groundwork for this study will have to be prepared for by editions of individual works, a task which still remains to be done. If, therefore, solutions cannot be proposed, at least attention may be drawn to some of the problems which are encountered.

To begin with, one fact is certain: there really is a monastic literature on Scripture, and it is abundant, more abundant than the few studies dedicated to it would lead us to believe. To verify this fact, we have an elementary method, that of statistics. If this is applied to the *Biblical Repertory of the Middle Ages*, it is seen that, for the period which extends from the ninth century to the beginning of the thirteenth, monastic authors are nearly three times more numerous in it than others.[2] Moreover, this list is far from complete.[3] It can even be said that up to and during the twelfth century, monastic authors are so numerous that they set the tone. Then, little by little, scholastic commentaries become more numerous.

If we wish to understand monastic exegesis from the inside, so to speak, it would seem that we must begin with the genesis of the biblical experience from which this exegesis proceeds. The characteristics of monastic exegesis will then become apparent and will embody our conclusions.

GRAMMAR: INTRODUCTION TO SCRIPTURE

emiss held by all who work with Holy Scripture is that grammar
....essary introduction to it. Since Scripture is a book, one must know
how to read it, and learn how to read it just as one learns how to read any
other book. In the first place, a verbal analysis must be made, using the
same philological methods Smaragdus used in connection with the *Rule*
of St. Benedict. That grammar is considered as the "introduction to Sacred
Scripture" is clearly stated in the life of St. Hugh of Cluny, for example,[4]
and this application of grammatical analysis to Scripture resulted in a
certain attachment to the written word itself, and great importance being
given to the texts and to the words.

However, this application of grammar to Scripture has been practiced
in monasticism in a way which is entirely its own because it is linked with
the fundamental observances of monastic life. The basic method is different
from that of non-monastic circles where Scripture is read—namely, the
schools. Originally, *lectio divina* and *sacra pagina* are equivalent expressions. For St. Jerome as for St. Benedict, the *lectio divina* is the text itself
which is being read, a selected passage or a "lesson" taken from Scripture.
During the Middle Ages, this expression was to be reserved more and
more for the act of reading, "the reading of Holy Scripture." In the school
it refers most often to the page itself, the text which is under study, taken
objectively. Scripture is studied for its own sake. In the cloister, however,
it is rather the reader and the benefit that he derives from Holy Scripture
which are given consideration. In both instances an activity is meant which
is "holy," *sacra, divina*; but in the two milieux, the accent is put on two
different aspects of the same activity. The orientation differs, and, consequently, so does the procedure. The scholastic *lectio* takes the direction of
the *quaestio* and the *disputatio*. The reader puts questions to the text and
then questions himself on the subject matter: *quaeri solet*. The monastic
lectio is oriented toward the *meditatio* and the *oratio*. The objective of the
first is science and knowledge; of the second, wisdom and appreciation. In
the monastery, the *lectio divina*, which begins with grammar, terminates
in compunction, in desire of heaven.

"ACTIVE" READING

It has already been mentioned that in the Middle Ages the reader usually
pronounced the words with his lips, at least in a low tone, and consequently he hears the sentence seen by the eyes—just as today, in order to

learn a language or a text, we pronounce the words. This results in more than a visual memory of the written words. What results is a muscular memory of the words pronounced and an aural memory of the words heard. The *meditatio* consists in applying oneself with attention to this exercise in total memorization; it is, therefore, inseparable from the *lectio*. It is what inscribes, so to speak, the sacred text in the body and in the soul.

This repeated mastication of the divine words is sometimes described by use of the theme of spiritual nutrition. In this case the vocabulary is borrowed from eating, from digestion, and from the particular form of digestion belonging to ruminants. For this reason, reading and meditation are sometimes described by the very expressive word *ruminatio*. For example, in praising a monk who prayed constantly Peter the Venerable cried: "Without resting, his mouth ruminated the sacred words."[5] Of John of Gorze it was claimed that the mumur of his lips pronouncing the Psalms resembled the buzzing of a bee.[6] To meditate is to attach oneself closely to the sentence being recited and weigh all its words in order to sound the depths of their full meaning. It means assimilating the content of a text by means of a kind of mastication which releases its full flavor. It means, as St. Augustine, St. Gregory, John of Fécamp, and others say in an untranslatable expression, to taste it with the *palatum cordis* or *in ore cordis*.[7] All this activity is, necessarily, a prayer; the *lectio divina* is a prayerful reading.[8] Thus, the Cistercian Arnoul of Bohériss will give this advice:

> When he reads, let him seek for savor, not science. The Holy Scripture is the well of Jacob from which the waters are drawn which will be poured out later in prayer. Thus there will be no need to go to the oratory to begin to pray; but in reading itself, means will be found for prayer and contemplation.[9]

Meditative Prayer and Reminiscence

This way of uniting reading, meditation, and prayer, this "meditative prayer" as William of St. Thierry calls it, had great influence on religious psychology. It occupies and engages the whole person in whom the Scripture takes root, later on to bear fruit. It is this deep impregnation with the words of Scripture that explains the extremely important phenomenon of reminiscence whereby the verbal echoes so excite the memory that a mere allusion will spontaneously evoke whole quotations and, in turn, a scriptural phrase will suggest quite naturally allusions elsewhere in the sacred books. Each word is like a hook, so to speak; it catches hold of one or several others which become linked together and make up the fabric of the exposé. This accounts for the difficulty of what we call research into sources: are the monks quoting older versions of Scripture or are they modifying them? Most frequently, it would seem, they are quoting from memory; quotations by means of the "hook-words" group themselves together in their minds and under their pen, like variations on the same theme. It happens that the same context is found several times in the same author and in others. Not that the one is necessarily referring to what he has already said or is citing another author who is using the same series of texts. Quite simply, the same words evoke similar quotations.

As it had for the Fathers, reminiscence on the part of the monastic authors of the Middle Ages had a profound effect on their literary composition. The mere fact of hearing certain words, which happen to be similar in sound to certain other words, sets up a kind of chain reaction of associations which will bring together words that have no more than a chance connection, purely external, with one another. But since the verse or passage which contains this word comes to mind, why not comment on it here? In such a case an author may turn away from his original subject which he had started to treat, and apparently lose the thread of his discourse. It was said of St. Augustine: "He composes 'poorly'," that is to say, not after our fashion.[10] This is true of many monastic authors; they do not always compose after a logical pattern which has been definitely fixed upon in advance. Within the literary form chosen, they make use of the utmost freedom. The plan really follows a psychological development, determined by the plan of associations, and one digression may lead to another or even to several others. Thus, in the *Sermons on the Canticles*, in connection with these words of the second verse of the Canticle: "Thy very name spoken soothes the heart like flow of oil," Bernard speaks at length on the perfumes of the bride when suddenly he pauses to insert a discourse in praise of humility. Had he lost the trend of his sermon? By no means. He realizes that he has gotten away from the Canticle and he does not regret it. He takes up again the verse where he had left off. But now Psalm 75 proclaims "that in Israel the name of God is extolled" and Bernard introduces a discourse on the Synagogue and the Church, devoting an entire sermon to it. In the following sermon, he sings the praises of the name of Jesus, and, while on the subject of the individuals of the Old Testament who bore a cognate name, he expounds the Prophets. He compares them to the staff which Elisha sends to the son of the Sunamite before coming to raise him from the dead. Coming back to life, the child yawns *seven* times; thereupon, after a long introduction on the meaning of the allegories of the Old Testament, Bernard gives a sermon on the *seven* phases of conversion, and this makes him think of the gifts of the Holy Spirit: a new direction in which he willingly follows. This brings his mind back, little by little, to the second verse of the Canticle. Now, this series of digressions has taken up six complete sermons.[11]

BIBLICAL IMAGINATION

Another important factor explained by rumination and reminiscence is the power of imagination of the medieval man. Exuberant as this faculty is, it nevertheless possesses a vigor and a preciseness which we find difficult to understand. We are used to seeing, almost without looking at them unless with a distracted eye, printed or moving pictures. We are fond of abstract ideas. Our imagination, having become lazy, seldom allows us to do anything but dream. But in the men of the Middle Ages it was vigorous and active. It permitted them to picture, to "make present," to see beings with all the details provided by the texts: the colors and dimensions of things, the clothing, bearing, and actions of the people, the complex environment in which they move. They liked to describe them and, so to speak, re-create them, giving very sharp relief to images and feelings. The words of the sacred text never failed to produce a strong impression on the mind. The biblical words did not become trite; people never got used to them. Scripture, which they liked to compare to a river or a well, remained a fountain that was always fresh. The spiritual men of those days counsel the renunciation of carnal images; but this is in order to substitute for them a holy imagination. The sanctification of the imagination results in their attachment to the slightest particulars of the text, and not merely to the ideas it contains.[12] This strength of imagination had great consequences in the field of iconography, and in literary expression as well. The memory, fashioned wholly by the Bible and nurtured entirely by biblical words and the images they evoke, causes them to express themselves spontaneously in a biblical vocabulary. Reminiscences are not quotations, elements of phrases borrowed from another. They are the words of the person using them; they belong to him. Perhaps he is not even conscious of owing them to a source. Moreover, this biblical vocabulary is twofold in character. In the first place, it is often poetic in essence. Sometimes it has greater value because of its power of suggestion than because of its clarity or precision; it hints at much more than it says. But for that very reason it is the better suited to express spiritual experience which is completely impregnated with a mysterious light impossible to analyze. Furthermore, though lacking in precision, this vocabulary is endowed with a great wealth of content, as the following example will show.

In monastic literature, the most important source for the study of the virtues is the Bible itself. Now, in the Bible, the names of the virtues take on a meaning that they do not have anywhere else. Thus, for example, fear is very often the same thing as charity; it is not at all like fright, or terror. There is a biblical conception of the fear or dread of God which is in no wise fright of God or terror of punishment. This word "fear" is a biblical Hebraism. It continues to be used, therefore, in a sense completely different from that given to it by secular authors. This loving fear is rather reverence, or respect. It is accompanied by confidence; it engenders peace; it is on a par with charity and with the desire for Heaven. What the Bible calls "fear of God" is a way of referring to charity under its somewhat negative aspect. The only true fear is that of losing the presence of the God one loves and whom one wishes to enjoy eternally. Understood in this way, fear is, like charity, the root of all virtues: *Initium sapientiae timor Domini*. This singularly rich conception of the fear of God comes from the Old Testament, and it is repeated in the New. St. Benedict takes it as his inspiration in speaking of humility, the first degree of which is fear of God: that is to say, the feeling of the presence of God. And all monastic authors are in line with this tradition. The doctrine they counsel is not based on abstract concepts, or invented *a priori*; all their ideas come to them from Scripture. From this point of view, all the virtues are synonymous; whether they are called fear, wisdom, or prudence, they have the same origin and the same end. All are gifts of God; they are directed to eternal life and awaken desire for it. The ancients felt no need at all to try to define the special object of each one of them. Christian life is one, and, when one has differentiated amongst the virtues, one has to admit that they are connected and condition each other mutually.

As in Scripture itself, everything that is said of virtue is said of each one of the virtues. One is distinguished from another only because the Bible, during its long history and on different occasions, used different words in speaking of the same moral life. Unity is born of a higher order than logic —that of supernatural reality, by which all virtues come from God, and all, likewise, lead to Him.[13]

EXEGESIS BY CONCORDANCE

Finally, the phenomenon of reminiscence has weighty consequences in the field of exegesis. For there is an exegesis that is specifically monastic.[14]

However, it is largely an exegesis through reminiscence, and for this reason it approaches rabbinical exegesis. It consists in explaining one verse by another verse in which the same word occurs. From this point of view, it is not so different, as has sometimes been believed, from a certain procedure used in exegesis today, the one which consists in making wide use of the concordance. As it was, thanks to the medieval mastication of the words, the Bible came to be learned "by heart." In this way, one can spontaneously supply a text or a word which corresponds to the situation described in each text, and which explains each separate word. One becomes a sort of living concordance, a living library, in the sense that the latter term implies the Bible. The monastic Middle Ages made little use of the written concordance; the spontaneous play of associations, similarities, and comparisons are sufficient for exegesis. In scholasticism, on the contrary, much use is made of these *Distinctiones* where, in alphabetical order, each word is placed opposite references to all the texts in which it is used;[15] these written concordances can be used to replace, but only in a bookish and artificial manner, the spontaneous phenomenon of reminiscence.

All monastic exegesis is not to be explained, however, by reminiscences which are, so to speak, automatic. There is no refusal to make use of certain working tools and certain books which had themselves been so assimilated that reference can often be made to them from memory. These working tools are kinds of repertories—we would call them lexicons— where the meaning of words is given, the total meaning, not merely the philological meaning. They are mostly of two sorts. Some are collections of *nomina sacra*. St. Jerome, followed by Isidore and numerous other compilers, had explained the etymology of place names and of the names of persons.[16] In addition, some etymologies were also found through reminiscence, when the sound of one word sufficed to evoke another.[17] Consequently the interpretation of names could not be arbitrary, left to the invention of each commentator. There existed, in this field, a tradition from which no departure could be made, and which, in part, went back to the Old Testament itself.

USE OF PROFANE LEARNING

Another source of information was made up of the writings of ancient naturalists who had explained the meanings of animals, stones, plants, and colors. Thus they consulted bestiaries and lapidaries, or simply what they could learn of the ancient naturalists, as much as was preserved in the writings of Isidore and Bede. In reading a medieval author one is tempted to believe he is inventing his allegories, but when several are compared, one finds that they agree on details which appear fanciful to us. In reality, they depend as do etymologies on a literary tradition that was then thought to be scientific. Thus, "nard" is an herb unknown to the medieval West, but all the commentators give the same description of it, attribute to it the same properties, and, in scarcely differing terms, confer on it the same spiritual significance. This testifies to the existence of a traditional and unanimous interpretation. The most honest of these commentators and also the cleverest, St. Bernard, says that on this point he relies on the competence of those who have studied plants. And the fact is that all the information upon which the interpretation of nard was founded was furnished by Pliny in his *Natural Histories*.[18]

It is the same with the colors that the Sacred Books attribute to the precious stones and metals which adorn the vestments of the high priest, and the cloth from which the curtains of the tabernacle were made. The interpretation of all these is based on traditional data. At the outset, there is always an affirmation. It may be connected with the obvious meaning of the words, such as: gold is the most precious of all metals, and it will therefore signify the greatest riches. These will be, depending on the context, either wisdom, or faith, or God. Sometimes, a passage from Scripture gives, as it were, the authentic interpretation of a word, as when the words of God are likened to silver in a verse from Psalm 11.[19] To God's words, then, will be applied the virtues of silver, particularly the luster which is its greatest beauty. Again, symbolism may sometimes be based on natural properties. Here two cases must be considered. Sometimes, the symbolism is so simple that the whole tradition has to accept it. The hyacinth, for example, is blue; the ancient naturalists cited by Bede had all recorded this fact. But blue is the color of the sky, and so the hyacinth will therefore stand for celestial life. Or again, the symbolism may be complex, in which case it then lends itself to different possibilities. In the case, for example, of the scarlet cloth which was twice dyed (*coccus bistinctus*), the interpretation can be based either on the color of the cloth, that of blood, or on the fact that it was dyed twice—if the latter is chosen, one will be obliged to think of the two inseparable commandments of charity toward God and toward one's neighbor—or on the combination of both the color and the fact of its being dyed twice which evokes the passions of the body and of the heart. All these interpretations may appear far-fetched in a period when the symbolism of colors and precious stones is scarcely used except by poets. But for the ancients they were founded on reality. It is natural then to find them, with very slight variations, in all the patristic and medieval commentators. Many of them, besides, had already been proposed, at least summarily, by Origen.[20]

The monastic Middle Ages were not lacking in representatives of what we would call scientific exegesis. Hervé of Bourg-Dieu of the Benedictines and Nicholas Maniacoria of the Cistercians chose to correct certain errors or inexactnesses of the Latin text.[21] But most, being ignorant of Greek and Hebrew, and relying on the authority of St. Jerome, accepted the text as it is. The Vulgate is the basis of all their biblical experience, and almost all their commentaries came from this experience. They were not the outcome of academic training but were written to fill the personal, spiritual needs of the author himself or his public—that is to say, a reader or a community.[22] To find illustrations of this experience, which was practiced by all, one can read the treatises in which it is spoken of explicitly. Two of the most characteristic are by Peter of Celle[23] and William Firmat.[24] In treating of Holy Scripture and the way to read it, they make use of almost all the themes which, since Origen and St. Gregory, had been animating spiritual literature and fostering desire for heaven. Since they were not among the greatest, such authors afford us the opportunity to learn about the biblical experience of the average monk. Even St. Bernard made scarcely any innovations in the realm of thought-processes and modes of expression. Because he was a genius, he had new ideas, but they were produced in an environment and in conformity with a psychology which he shared with the whole ensemble of monasticism and its past, and without this living context, neither his style nor his influence could be understood.[25]

THE OLD TESTAMENT

These observations now make it possible for us to define more clearly the characteristics of monastic exegesis. It can be said that it is at one and the same time inseparably literal and mystical. It is literal because of the importance it gives to words (the fact that grammar is applied to them), because of the auditory memory of them (the reminiscences which follow), and because of the repertories which explain the words. It interprets Scripture by Scripture itself, the letter by the letter itself. It is mystical because of the monks' conception of Scripture. The latter is not primarily a source of knowledge, of scientific information; it is a means for salvation, its gift is the "science of salvation": *salutaris scientia*.[26] This is true of Scripture in its entirety. Each word it contains is thought of as a word addressed by God to each reader for his salvation. Everything then has a personal, immediate value for present life and for the obtaining of eternal life. In Scripture are found both truths to believe and precepts to practice. According to a comparison which the medieval monks owe to St. Augustine who was himself indebted for it to Plato, Holy Scripture is a mirror. In it one sees the picture one should reproduce. As one reads, one can compare oneself with what one ought to be, and try to acquire what the picture needs so that it can resemble the model.[27]

One of the consequences of this essentially and uniquely religious conception of Scripture is the importance accorded the Old Testament. If the latter was more frequently commented than the New, it is because they had definite and fertile ideas on the relationship between the two.[28] Such continuity does indeed exist between them that one cannot be understood without the other. Both must therefore be studied, not separately, but always in conjunction. It is clear that many facts, ideas, and expressions found in the New Testament writings cannot be studied independently of their antecedents in the Old Testament. But it is equally certain that the Old Testament itself can be neither read nor explained without constant reference to the New, as if it constituted an historical document relating to a closed past whose meaning alone it conveys. The Bible is concerned with the whole mystery of salvation: what God is, what He does for man from the beginning until the end of the world. The son of God made flesh is at the center of the whole great work of the creation and sanctification of the world. It is in relation to Christ that all that preceded His coming in time, all that accompanied it, all that has followed it must be understood and correlated. This principle is applied in many different ways. But the creative principle underlying all medieval exegesis is the evolutionary character of all Sacred History, the conception of the Church as a growing body, and this body being the total Christ.

OLD AND NEW TESTAMENT:
SYMBOL AND REALITY

For the Middle Ages as well as for the patristic era, the Old and the New Testament taken as a whole tell the same story of the same people of God. The story told by the Old Testament is not the history of Israel, it is already the history of the Church which begins with Israel. Thus the Old and New Testaments are considered in the Middle Ages, not as two collections of "books," but as two periods, two "times" which echo each other. The time of the law (*tempus legis*) and the time of grace (*tempus gratiae*) are different stages of one and the same salvation, and each of them includes, over and above the scriptural texts, the sum of the realities told us in these texts.

Between the Old and the New Testament, progress is made not through accretion but thanks to an evolution which brings forth the "perfect" from the "imperfect." The first period of the history of salvation leads to the second, not only because it lays the foundation for it, but because it already contains it, although in an imperfect, incomplete fashion. The New Testament perfects the Old; but the Old began the New. The Word of God was already at work before the Incarnation. All of the Old Testament participated in the Redemption which is clearly revealed in the New, and in reality inaugurated it. It is the sign and the figure of the New Testament whose image it is. The perfect gives the imperfect its form, its value, and its efficacy. The Old Testament is a typical anticipation of the New Testament because it shares in the work accomplished therein.

In consequence, the New Testament is the norm by which we must interpret the Old, which cannot be explained fully without reference to the New, or as if the New did not exist. On the other hand, the New Testament itself is much better understood if we recall what came before it. The figure contained the truth while concealing it; truth unveils the figure and shows forth its meaning; once revealed, the figure in turn illuminates the Truth. This turning back again to the figures is not without value, for they are a means by which the truth may be better seen and better appreciated. Thus, preoccupation with studying the Old Testament as if it were an historical document, for the information it gives us on the "history of the Hebrew people," is foreign to the Middle Ages. The texts of the Old Testament must have a figurative meaning, and often have no other. At times, then, they may have a double meaning, historical and figurative, and at others only a figurative meaning, but never a meaning which is purely historical.

Old Testament texts can always be used for expressing the loftiest realities of the New Testament. Rupert of Deutz, in his treatise *On the Works of the Holy Spirit*, speaks first of those which were accomplished under the Old Law; but when he gets up to the time of the New Testament, he still takes his texts from the Old Testament. He puts into the mouth of Christ speaking to His Father the words that Job said to God. What interests Rupert is not Job's historicity. He sees Job as the symbol of man face to face with God, and first of all as the perfect man. Job is the Christ, the just, expressing his thoughts on redemption. Thus what is demanded of the Old Testament is light on religious problems, not historical problems, not even problems in the history of religions.

These considerations can be illustrated by an example taken from the treatise by Baldwin of Ford, a Cistercian of the end of the twelfth century, *On the Sacrament of the Altar*.[29] In writing on the Eucharist, Baldwin takes the Last Supper as his point of departure, but to explain it he puts together a chain of texts borrowed largely from the Old Testament, and comments on each of them in succession. What takes place on the altar is the summit, the résumé, the recapitulation of what had taken place on all the altars men have raised since their creation, of all that God has done for them and continues to do. The passage of time is only a divine pedagogical method by which humanity is taught progressively to take part in the Mass. Genesis tells us of Melchisedech's offering bread and wine; later on, Psalm 109 says that the Messiah is to be a priest in the line of Melchisedech; Jesus, fulfilling the prophecy, consecrates the bread and wine, and the Epistle to the Hebrews interprets authentically both the figure and its accomplishment. The eucharistic sacrifice is, therefore, the "perfection," that is to say the completion, of all that preceded it. The reality of salvation is given wholly but under different forms, in each of its phases. Exegesis tries to understand each of these phases in the light of all the others and inseparably from them. The eucharistic supper was inserted in the celebration of the Passover; it is the culmination of the cult of the Old Law; it is the center and the core of history. It cannot be understood without reference to the Old Testament. Biblical teaching is given us according to the historical method, and dogma is revealed progressively in the course of time and through events. Baldwin's treatise follows the same procedure. Its form resembles, as it were, two sloping lines: the first rises from the Creation to the Last Supper of Holy Thursday; the second descends to the figures in the Old Testament and sheds on them the light of Christ. From the Supper, which is the peak, the exegete can cast his glance downward on the entire past of the Hebrew people, on the whole ancient history of the Church.

The Old Testament. The Desire for God

But the Old Testament takes on still another value. In it is seen, not only the past of the Church, but also its future. The people of God are still, in relation to the Parousia, in a stage of imperfection and incompletion, like the stage they were in, in relation to the Incarnation, before the coming of the Messiah. The two phases of sacred history already completed are preparatory to a third. Several trilogies are used to express this gradation: *praeparatio–reparatio–consummatio*; *figura–gratia–gloria*.[30] In the present state of the Church, the reality of salvation is already given completely; it is not as yet fully manifest, but is communicated only in the sacraments. The condition of Christians has consequently this in common with that of the just of the old Law, that all must have faith in a revelation to come. The history of the chosen people is therefore instructive for us, and the spiritual interpretation of the Old Testament is the beginning of what will one day be vision. It keeps alive in us eschatological desire and nourishes in us not only faith but hope and love as well.

For the very reason that the Old Testament is prophetic in nature, desire is perhaps the sentiment most frequently found in it: desire for the Promised Land or desire for the Messiah interpreted spontaneously by the medieval monks as desire for Heaven and for Jesus contemplated in His glory.[31]

Thus, we are always being brought back to eschatology. The grandeur of this exegesis lies in the fact that it sheds full light on the unity of Scripture, in its being a religious, mystical exegesis. But its weakness lies in what could be called, however paradoxically, an excess of literalism. The Law and the Gospel are like two interlocutors of the same dialogue. They complete and explain each other mutually; each approving and confirming the other's testimony. For each text in the Old Testament there is always another in the New, answering it like an echo. To perceive this we have no need at all to resort to difficult procedures. All that is needed is attention to similarities of words, sentences, and ideas, and the transposition to the Old Testament of the meanings these expressions have in the New Testament. Concentration is therefore placed on the words, parallel passages are collated, the meaning of each expression minutely examined, the meaning of one clarifying another. As we have seen, the Bible itself is the commentary on the Bible. Because of this same concentration on words, and for all the reasons we have already recalled, the Middle Ages did not limit itself to applying the traditional conception of the harmony between the two Testaments to great religious themes or great historical movements, but applied this conception to individual texts as well. In this way, it was sometimes led into establishing a purely artificial connection between two texts. In exegesis of this type what remains valid is not explanation in detail but rather its general concept of the essentially religious, soteriological nature of Holy Scripture, its profound conception of the evolutionary character of Scripture, from the Old Testament to eschatology. One need hardly emphasize, then, the profound influence such exegetical studies must have had on the interior life of these authors and the deep understanding they had of God's message to man.

THE CANTICLE OF CANTICLES

Finally, in order to complete these few remarks on monastic exegesis, we must remember the book which was most read and most frequently commented in the medieval cloister, a book of the Old Testament: the Canticle of Canticles. The fact that they loved to read it, and commentaries on it, is sufficiently attested by the ancient catalogues of the monastic libraries. It will be sufficient at this point to cite two examples. Cluny, in the time of Peter the Venerable, possessed fifteen commentaries on the Canticle, among which were three copies of Origen and two of St. Gregory.[32] Likewise, among some seventy manuscripts of Orval which have been preserved, there are no fewer than seven commentaries on the Canticle, which is a tenth of the total number.[33] As early as St. Benedict's time, Cassiodorus had gathered a corpus of commentaries on the Canticle including Origen's.[34] Later, Alcuin, praising the Canticle, sees it as an antidote to Virgil's frivolities, and as the song which teaches the true commandments, those conducive to eternal life.[35] It is not by chance that the masterpiece of medieval monastic literature is a commentary on the Canticle. In the sermons he devoted to it, St. Bernard has simply given a very superior expression to a tendency, a pursuit, and a love which were widespread and shared by all. These commentaries on the Canticle, particularly St. Bernard's, were very widely read in the twelfth century, in monasteries of all observances.[36]

In order to appreciate the manner in which these commentaries were conceived, a comparison must be made between them and the way the Canticle was commented on in scholastic milieux.[37] No doubt, the history of the interpretation of the Canticle in medieval monasticism is still to be studied,[38] but certain differences between the two types may be discerned.[39] The scholastic commentary is, in some ways, collective; it speaks mostly of God's relations with the entire Church, it emphasizes the revelation of divine truth, which man must possess through faith and the knowledge of the mysteries, and the presence of God in the world through the Incarnation. On the other hand, the monastic commentary's object is rather God's relations with each soul, Christ's presence in it, the spiritual union realized through charity. The commentary on the Canticle, especially for the Cistercians, is the equivalent of a treatise on the love of God. Scholastic commentary furnishes, in a clear, generally concise style, a doctrine addressed to the intelligence. Monastic commentary is addressed to the whole being; its aim is to touch the heart rather than to instruct the mind. It is often written in a fervent style which expresses an inner rhythm which the author wants to communicate to his readers. Scholastic commentary is almost always complete; it explains the entire "letter" of the sacred text. Monastic commentary is often incomplete; St. Bernard, in eighty-six sermons composed over a period of eighteen years, had reached only the beginning of the third chapter. And that is understandable. When the spiritual man has told what he feels, what he thinks of the love of God—and he may be able to do so in a few verses—he has the right to lay down his pen.

What is the significance of the interest that the medieval monks took in the Canticle of Canticles? The question is worth the asking since certain historians have too ready an answer. For them the dialogue of the bridegroom and the bride corresponds with what is called today depth psychology. But in reality, what we know of eschatological desire in milieux consecrated to a life of prayer sufficiently explains their special affection for the Canticle of Canticles. What they saw in it above all is the expression of that desire. The Canticle is the poem of the pursuit which is the basis for the whole program of monastic life: *quaerere Deum*, a pursuit which will reach its end only in eternity but which already obtains fulfillment here in an obscure possession; and the latter increases desire which is the form love takes here below. The Canticle is the dialogue between the bridegroom and the bride who are seeking each other, calling to each other, growing nearer to each other, and who find they are separated just when they believe they are finally about to be united. St. Gregory had given perfect expression to this alternating intimacy and separation in his *Moralia in Job*—for he spoke of the Canticle in works other than the commentary he had devoted to it: "The bridegroom hides when he is being sought so that, not finding him, the bride will search for him with renewed ardor; and the bride's search is prolonged so that the delay will increase her capacity for God, and she will eventually find in a fuller measure what she had been seeking."[40] St. Bernard often spoke along the same lines;[41] his whole Sermon 84 on the Canticle—one of the last texts he wrote—once more treats this theme which was to be used as well in the *Spiritual Canticle* of St. John of the Cross.

The Canticle of Canticles is a contemplative text: *theoricus sermo*, as St. Bernard would say. It is not pastoral in nature; it does not teach morality, prescribe good works to perform or precepts to observe; nor even purvey exhortations to wisdom. But with its ardent language and its dialogue of praise, it was more attuned than any other book in Sacred Scripture to loving, disinterested contemplation. One can understand why Origen commented it twice, why St. Gregory, St. Bernard, and so many others preferred it over other parts of the Old and the New Testament.[42] Now, the particular virtue of contemplation is to foster the desire for the heavenly life. When John the Grammarian composes a commentary on the Canticle for Countess Mathilda, he wishes her, in the dedicatory letter accompanying it, "the grace of contemplation." And immediately afterward he defines the book he is about to explicate: "The Canticle of Canticles is a doctrine of contemplation."[43] Then he adds: "'The man who is possessed by the sweetness of contemplation is already participating in heavenly life."[44] Later on, the scholastic masters were to prefer to explicate the Sapiential Books: "They will examine Solomon's wisdom in Proverbs and in Ecclesiastes."[45] The monks, for their part, have associated themselves with the canticle of love. An anonymous commentator on the *Rule* of St. Benedict sees the Canticle of Canticles as the complement of the monks' rule: it is, he says, the rule of love.[46]

NOTES

1. "We need a general study of the twelfth-century monastic commentators." B. Smalley, *The Study of the Bible in the Middle Ages* (Oxford, 1952), p. 72.

2. F. Stegmüller, *Repertorium Biblicum*, vols. 2–5, "Auctores" (Madrid 1950–1955). I have verified this fact for the names beginning with the letter A.

3. "Écrits monastiques sur la Bible aux xiᵉ-xiiiᵉ siècles," *Mediaeval Studies* (1953) 95–106.

4. "In this town, he had his first taste of Grammar, by which he was introduced to the profundity of the Scriptures." Life by Hildebert of Le Mans, I 2 (PL 159.861). The couplet of Matthew of Rievaulx was also applied to Sacred Scripture:

> Grammatica pueros sapiens prius imbuit heros:
> Haec iter est menti scripturas scire volenti.

Ed. A. Wilmart, "Les mélanges de Mathieu, préchantre de Rievaulx au début du xiiiᵉ siècle," RB (1940) 59.

5. *De Miraculis* I 20 (PL 189.887).

6. John of St. Arnulf, Life of John of Gorze (†976) n. 80 (PL 137.280).

7. Texts will be found in *Un maître*, p. 99n3.

8. "Lecture et oraison," *La Vie Spirituelle* (May 1944) 392–402; "La lecture divine," *La Maison-Dieu*, 5 (1946) 21–33; "Lecture spirituelle et vie mystique," *Un maître*, pp. 97–103; "De la lecture à la contemplation," *La spiritualité de Pierre de Celle*, pp. 99–107; "Bernard, homme de prière: Études sur S. Bernard et le texte de ses écrits," *Analecta S. Ord. Cist.* IX, I–II (Rome, 1953) 180–82. Among texts gathered by Martène (PL 66.413–414) we find *meditatio* as a synonym for reading, for study, for singing the psalms in private, as well as for contemplation. An ancient translation, cited there, renders *meditari* by "to say the Psalter." Cf. *supra*, Ch. 1, at n. 14.

9. *Speculum monachorum* I (PL 184.1175).

10. H. I. Marrou, *S. Augustin et la fin de la culture antique* (Paris, 1949), pp. 59–76.

11. *Super Cantica*, Serm. 12–17.

12. *La spiritualité de Pierre de Celle*, pp. 52–58: "Le Langage mystique"; pp. 59–69, "La poésie biblique."

13. *Smaragde et son œuvre*, pp. 14–16: "Vertus bibliques."

14. Although some disagree, this fact has been affirmed in connection with St. Bernard by E. Kleineidam, *Wissen, Wissenschaft, Theologie bei Bernhard von Clairvaux* (Leipzig, 1955), p. 44n129.

15. A collection of this kind, edited by Wilmart, "Un répertoire d'exégèse composé en Angleterre vers le début du xiiiᵉ siècle," *Mémorial Lagrange* (Paris, 1940), pp. 307–35, is undoubtedly monastic, but it is late. R. W. Hunt, "Notes on the Distinctiones monasticae et morales," in *Liber Floridus, Festschrift P. Lehmann*, pp. 355–62, thinks it is Cistercian. The other known collections are, at the earliest, of the end of the twelfth century, and Dom Wilmart could write, at the end of his "Note sur les plus anciens recueils de distinctions bibliques" (pp. 355–46), that "These alphabetical collections, originally made for purposes of study and then applied to pastoral use . . . dominated the thirteenth century and, in large part, continued to be copied in the next two centuries."

16. Ed. P. de Lagarde, *Onomastica Sacra* (Göttingen, 1870).

17. R. Baron, "Hugonis de Sancto Victore epitome Dindimi in Philosophiam," *Traditio* 11 (1955) 136 makes some very judicious remarks, with examples, on this matter.

18. "Études sur S. Bernard" (n. 8) 118n1; to the testimonies quoted there, we may add that of the anonymous monk of Clairvaux who wrote the *Vita S. Mariae Magdalenae*, XVII (PL 112.1456c). (On this author, cf. V. Saxer, *Mélanges S. Bernard* [Dijon, 1953], pp. 408–21, Hugo of Fouilloy, *De bestiis et aliis rebus*, IV 12 [PL 177.153], and others.)

19. "Eloquia Domini, eloquia casta: argentum igne examinatum. . . ."

20. These applications can be illustrated by an analysis of the *De tabernaculo Moysi* of Peter of Celle (cf. *La spiritualité*, pp. 147–67) and of his sources and the parallels in other authors. Compare, for example, Arnold of Bonneval, *De VII verbis Domini*, PL 189.1719, 1724 and Peter of Celle, *De tabernaculo Moysi*, PL 202.1050A; *De tabernaculo* (ed. J. Leclercq, *La spiritualité*, p. 163) 9ff. with Origen, *In Exod.* IX 3 (ed. Baehrens, 240); Isidore, *Etymologiae*, 18.41.1927; *Quest. in Num.* PL 83.349,25; Bede, *De tabernaculo*, I 3, PL 91.399D; II 2, 425–28; *In Exod.* XXVII, PL 91.324B.

21. G. Morin, "Un critique en liturgie au xiiᵉ siècle: Le traité inédit d'Hervé du Bourg-Dieu '*De correctione quorundam lectionum,*'" RB (1907) 36–61. R. Weber, "Deux préfaces au Psautier dues à Nicolas Maniacoria," ibid. (1953) 3–17.

22. On the elements that distinguish the monastic and the scholastic literature on the Bible, I have given some indications in a review of *Esquisse d'une histoire de l'exégèse latine au moyen âge*, by A. Spicq, *Bulletin Thomiste* (1942–1945) 59–67.

23. "De afflictione et lectione," in *La spiritualité*, pp. 231–39.

24. *Exhortatio ad amorem claustri et desiderium lectionis divinae*, ed. in *Analecta monastica* II 28–44.

25. "S. Bernard et le xiiᵉ siècle monastique," *Dict. de Spiritualité* IV (Paris, 1958) 187–94.

26. *Exhortatio* 32.

27. *Un maître*, pp. 56–60: "La Bible, miroir de l'âme." *La spirtualité*, p. 67. Other

texts are gathered by Sister Ritamary, c.h.m., "Backgrounds of the Title *Speculum* in Mediaeval Literature," *Speculum* 29 (1954) 100–15.

28. "L'exégèse médiévale de l'Ancien Testament," *L'Ancien Testament et les chrétiens* (Paris, 1951), pp. 168–82. See also the important work by Henri de Lubac, *L'exégèse médiévale*, 2 vols. (Paris, 1959).

29. PL 204.641–774. Introduction to the French translation of the *De Sacramento altaris* of Baldwin of Ford.

30. *Loc. cit.* (n. 28), p. 179; E. Kleineidam (n. 14), 44–45.

31. *S. Bernard mystique*, pp. 140–41.

32. L. Delisle, *Inventaire des manuscrits de la bibliothèque nationale: Fonds de Cluni* (Paris, 1884), pp. 240–64.

33. *Analecta monastica* I 208.

34. P. Courcelle, *Les lettres grecques en Occident de Macrobe à Cassiodore* (Paris, 1948), pp. 364–67.

35. "Haec tibi vera canunt vitae praecepta perennis; Auribus ille [Virgilius] tuis male frivola falsa sonabit." MGH, *PLAC* I 239.

36. "Le genre litteraire des Sermones in Cantica," *Études sur S. Bernard*, pp. 121–22. "Recherches sur les Sermons sur les Cantiques de S. Bernard, I: La littérature provoquée par les Sermons sur les Cantiques," RB 64 (1954) 208–22. "Poèmes sur le Cantique des Cantiques," RB 62 (1952) 290–91.

37. "Le commentaire du Cantique des cantiques attribué à Anselme de Laon," RTAM (1949) 29–39.

38. "Les Distinctiones super Cantica de Guillaume de Ramsey," *Sacris erudiri* 10 (1958) 329–52. F. Ohly, *Hohelied-Studien, Grundzüge zur Auslegung einer Geschichte der Hoheliedauslegung des Abendlandes bis um 1200* (Wiesbaden, 1958). H. Riedlinger, *Die Makellosigkeit der Kirche in den lateinischen Hoheliedkommentaren des Mittelalters* (Münster, 1958).

39. "Le commentaire de Gilbert de Stanford sur le Cantique de cantiques, I. Le genre," *Analecta Monastica* I 205–209. "Écrits monastiques," *Med. Studies* (1953) 98–100: II. "Commentaires du Cantique des cantiques."

40. *Moralia in Job* 5.6; PL 75.783. See also the opening of Gregory's commentary on the Canticle, PL 79.478.

41. For example, *Supt. Cant.* 74.2–4 (PL 183.1139–41).

42. As to the Mariological interpretation of the Canticle, if, under the influence of the liturgy, it sometimes appears in the form of casual allusions in sermons, still it is rarely found in the form of an extended commentary in monastic circles, with the exception of Rupert of Deutz; in particular, it is not found in Cistercian commentaries: cf. J. Beumer, "Die marianische Deutung des Hohen Liedes in der Frühscholastik," ZKT (1954) 419–25.

43. Ed. B. Bischoff, "Der Canticumkommentar des Johannes von Mantua," *Lebenskräfte in der abendländischen Geistesgeschichte. Festgabe W. Goetz* (Marburg, 1948), p. 37.

44. "Cantica canticorum, qui est doctrina contemplationis. . . . Iam vitae caeletis particeps efficitur, qui contemplationis dulcedine capitur et eius suavissimo gustu saginatur." Ibid.

45. B. Smalley, "Some Thirteenth-century Commentaries on the Sapiential Books," *Dominican Studies* (1950) 264.

46. See Appendix I: The *Rule* of St. Benedict and the Canticle of Canticles.

6

The Ancient Traditional Spirituality

MEDIEVAL MONASTIC CULTURE is based on the Latin Bible. But the Bible cannot be separated from those who commented it—that is to say, the Fathers. Often called simply the *expositores*, even in their writings which are not commentaries they did little else but explain Holy Scripture. Moreover, monasticism is inclined toward patristics for a very special reason: its basic text and its origins. On the one hand, the *Rule* of St. Benedict itself is, in fact, a patristic document; it assumes, it evokes an entire ancient spiritual milieu. On the other, St. Benedict prescribes the reading in the Divine Office of the *expositiones* written by those he calls the Fathers;[1] in his last chapter, he again urges the monks to read the Fathers. The word occurs four times in this chapter and designates more especially the Fathers of monasticism. The latter are Easterners, and this fact results in something new: Benedictine monasticism is attracted, not only to patristic sources in general, but to Eastern sources in particular.

THE EASTERN MONASTIC TRADITION

This is a fact which must be strongly emphasized, for St. Benedict had no wish to break with ancient monastic tradition, which is largely Eastern.[2] Quite the contrary, in the life of St. Benedict by St. Gregory, in the spirit of his *Rule*, in the reading he recommends and the observances he prescribes, everything betrays his concern for continuity and for fidelity to ancient monasticism. Not that Benedict is "an Easterner who has strayed into the West." He is a Latin; but he respects the Eastern tradition "which is to monasticism what apostolic tradition is to the faith of the Church."[3] Even more, as can be gathered from allusions found in his *Rule*, he feels a certain nostalgia for the monasticism of ancient times.

Consequently, it is not at all surprising that, during all the great periods of Western monasticism, the desire has been felt to renew relations with this authentic tradition. In the Carolingian period, Benedict of Aniane accords great importance to the Eastern rules in his *Codex regularum*. In later periods, the monks were always clearly aware of what they owed to ancient monasticism, and an Italian manuscript of the eleventh century furnishes a revealing example of this. Immediately after the text of St. Benedict's *Rule*, there is appended a list of those who "founded" monastic life. Out of the twenty-six Fathers of monasticism enumerated, there are only four Latins.[4] And even among these we find St. Jerome, who was often considered an Easterner.[5] In fact, monastic observances and the texts which inspire them owe a great deal to the East and to the writings through which it was known: the *Apophthegms* and *Lives* of the Fathers, the *Conferences* of Cassian, the *Rules* of St. Basil. Everything in Benedictine life is ordered according to the ideas, practices, sometimes even the words, which have come down from the monks of antiquity and which link each generation to the origins of monasticism. Furthermore, each renewal of Benedictine life is effected with reference to these same origins. For example, at the beginning of what was to become the Cistercian Order, Ordericus Vitalis, not implausibly, attributes to Robert of Molesme this characteristic speech: "Read the acts of Sts. Anthony, Macarius, Pachomius. . . . We are no longer following in the footsteps of our Fathers, the Egyptian monks, of those who lived in the Holy Land or in the Thebaid."[6] Thus at every period, the monks feel the attraction of the "light which comes from the East," from which they know they have received their ideas and the practices on which their way of life is founded. And William of St. Thierry is speaking for all when he expresses the wish in his *Letter to the Brothers of Mont-Dieu* that they "may implant in the darkness of the West and in the cold of Gaul the light of the East and the ancient fervor of Egyptian religious life."[7]

THE GREEK FATHERS

It is true, it will perhaps be said, that the monks did turn to the patristic age and particularly to the ancient East. But what did they know about it? What could they get from it? Actually, they had not only book knowledge of the patristic age but in addition, and primarily, a special knowledge through a living communion, through a kind of experience and connaturality. From the patristic age monasticism inherited and preserved faithfully, more exclusively than non-monastic milieux, a fourfold treasure: texts, models, ideas and themes, and a vocabulary. Moreover no distinction can be made here amongst these elements except for clarity in exposition, because in reality they are inseparable.

As for the texts first of all, much preliminary work remains to be done before any general view or definite conclusions may be arrived at. But even now some facts relating to the writings of the Greek Fathers and those of the Latin Fathers may be accepted as established. After making some observations of a general nature on the former, we shall illustrate our findings with examples from the Latin tradition of Evagrius and Origen.

For knowledge of the Greek Fathers, the medieval monks were entirely dependent upon the translators of the patristic age. Whereas the period when Cassiodorus was directing his school of translators was still bilingual, the Middle Ages in general, particularly up until nearly the end of the twelfth century, was quite unacquainted with Greek.[8] In the twelfth century, Latin monks took the initiative of having Greek texts translated whenever it was possible. But a considerable part of the patristic legacy inherited from the Greeks had already been translated: it was preserved and handed on, as was all that remained of ancient culture, especially in Italy and in England. In the poem in which he sings the praises of the Church of York, Alcuin says that "traces of the ancient Fathers can be found there, all that Latium gave the Roman world, and all the gifts which luminous Greece had brought to the Latins";[9] and he gives as examples St. Athanasius, St. Basil, and St. John Chrysostom.

Concerning medieval transmission of Greek patristic texts we have a useful work written by Dom Siegmund.[10] Even after this volume much remains to be done,[11] as even its author recognized, but at least this work provides sound documentation and sure orientation. First of all, it makes it possible to draw up a list of the Greek Fathers whose texts have survived in manuscripts or are attested by ancient library catalogues of different collections and *florilegia*. This alphabetical list is long; from Adamantius to Timothy of Alexandria and to the *Verba seniorum*, it includes no fewer than forty-three names. An examination of the documentary material collected during this minute research leads to two conclusions. The first has to do with the provenance of the preserved texts: the great majority of the manuscripts by which they are transmitted are monastic in origin, particularly the most important texts. On this point we can assess the major role played by great cultural centers like the monasteries of Corbie, Fleury, Fulda, Gorze, Lobbes, and so many others. Many of them were located along the valley of the Middle Rhine, around the Lake of Constance, at Bobbio, and above all in the north of France and in present-day Belgium, that region in which there were so many monasteries.[12]

The second conclusion has to do with the nature of the texts that have been preserved. Those that were most often translated and most widely disseminated are, so to speak, the most monastic: those which speak *of* monks or *to* monks. They are, on the one hand, ascetical texts: Basil, Ephrem, Chrysostom; on the other, biblical commentaries:[13] Chrysostom, Hesychius, and above all Origen. He, of all the ancient Greek authors, is the most widely read, and in every domain. To these texts are joined the historical texts of Sozomen, Eusebius, and Josephus. But those which were least often copied, and therefore least often read, are controversial texts directed against the Arians and other heretics. Furthermore, one must take note of the almost complete absence, in monastic tradition, of the pseudo-Dionysius, even though he had been translated by John Scottus Eriugena and was to be the special predilection of Scholasticism. It has been proved that he had little or no influence until the twelfth century.[14]

That he had little influence on Rupert of Deutz[15] and St. Bernard[16] has likewise been established. The few seemingly Dionysian allusions which have been noted in the latter[17] seem to have been acquired at second hand, perhaps simply through Hugh of St. Victor who had commented *The Celestial Hierarchy*; in any case, they are very slight. Perhaps the work of pseudo-Dionysius appeared to the monks—and to Bernard himself who could not have been entirely unacquainted with it—too abstract, too speculative, and even, perhaps, not sufficiently biblical.

In any case, what stands out clearly from the preceding observations is that texts were wanted that could be utilized in monastic life. At every period, for purposes of private reading and for the public reading done at table or elsewhere, they preserved and transmitted texts like the *Rules* of St. Basil, St. Ephrem's exhortations, Evagrius' sentences, the *Lives* of the Fathers, the homilies, letters, and treatises of St. John Chrysostom. These are in no way learned controversial writings, like those that appeared in exegetical *catenae*.[18] The ones they retained are useful, not in the war against heresies, but for the life of the monks. Again, in periods of monastic reform or renewal, more importance was given to certain texts in particular. Thus Benedict of Aniane includes St. Basil and St. Pachomius in his *Codex regularum*, and in his *Concordia regularum* he furnishes numerous Eastern parallels to the *Rule* of St. Benedict. In the tenth century, after the Norman invasions, when Jumièges was rebuilt, copies were made there of Origen, Cassian, and St. Basil.[19] Still later, when the same monastery was restored after being pillaged, the commentaries of Origen were transcribed.[20]

In sum, Western medieval monasticism did not possess enough Eastern texts for a real knowledge of the whole of Greek theology.[21] But the monks wanted to have, and indeed did possess, all those that pertained to religious life, all that could be helpful to it, and all that transmitted the concepts and practices of ancient monasticism. In reality, what was received from Greek antiquity fulfilled William of St. Thierry's desire: to restore the ancient fervor of the religious life of Egypt.

Thus, a certain spontaneous agreement with ancient Greek thought is discernible in the spiritual and theological writings of the monks. In Rupert of Deutz, in Isaac of Stella, as in others, we sense the shadow of the whole archaic Eastern background whose content is hard to define and remains to be studied.[22] No doubt, several of these infiltrations came from Philo through St. Ambrose. Moreover, at every period, the terminology and ideas of Clement of Alexandria and of Irenaeus were universally known through the works of Cassian,[23] but many elements are derived from Origen, known either at first hand or through Evagrius.

EVAGRIUS

The history of Evagrius' *Sentences* for monks gives us an opportunity to observe the life of a text.[24] In fact several successive forms of these *Sentences* have been found in Latin. A first, and very old, version is extremely literal. In it, words are sometimes given in simple phonetic transcription, as for instance: *accidia, dogmata, eremus*. It is so literal that it made possible the rediscovery of a Greek word which, until then, was not to be found in the lexicons.[25] A second version, itself very old, improves somewhat on the Latin of the first. It is transmitted by manuscripts which are divided into three groups corresponding to three geographic areas, for each of which the archetype is known. The available evidence suggests that when it became known in one region that a monastery had a certain text, the other monasteries hastened to have it copied. In this way, beginning with a single copy, we can follow Evagrius' progress across all of twelfth-century Austria. Likewise, in the tenth century, a copy belonging to the Abbey of Silos was copied during the same period at the Monastery of Valvanera, which was not very far away. This second version passed, in the form of more of less elaborated excerpts, into *florilegia* like the *Liber scintillarum* or a *Liber deflorationum* of the Abbey of Clairvaux. Finally there was a composite revision made up of elements taken from the two earlier versions, and which is found in a manuscript belonging to the Abbey of Monte Vergine. Similar phenomena may also be observed with reference to other texts, particularly ancient monastic rules.

Thus, great freedom was exercised in the use of the most respected sources and highest authorities. In compilations whose purpose was practical, not literary or scientific, they felt free to transform, adapt, or gloss documents which were to serve as a rule of life. It is often in such an elaborated—but not always improved—form that the monastic texts of antiquity have come down to us. Furthermore, the manuscripts of these different forms of the same text present variants which are not all due to copyists' gross mistakes. But the very divergency among manuscripts of the same translation proves the changing, and living, character of these ancient monastic texts. Not only was the translation of the *Sentences for Monks* redone twice, but, in the transcriptions of both, the copyists allowed themselves a certain liberty: at times they simply omitted a clause they did not understand, at others they took it upon themselves to change the phrasing. They did not consider the text they were working on as having been established once for all; it continued to live and to change.

The Influence of Origen

Evagrius transmitted ideas and themes of Origen, but Origen himself was also known.[26] If we read the introductions to the different volumes of the critical edition of the Latin Origen, we note that almost all the manuscripts are of monastic origin and that most date from the ninth and the twelfth centuries. Other indications point to the conclusion that in every period or place where there was a monastic renewal, there was a revival of Origen. It is true of the Carolingian reform; it is even more definite, or in any case more readily apparent, in the monastic revival of the twelfth century.

Almost always when an intact twelfth-century library can be examined, or when its collection can be reconstructed by the aid of ancient or modern catalogues, we find that Origen is represented by at least one manuscript. This is particularly true in the case of monastic libraries, as Origen is less frequently represented in the libraries of the cathedral churches.

Just as the Origenist revival of the ninth century coincided with the monastic revival connected with the name of St. Benedict of Aniane, the Origenist revival of the twelfth century coincides with the monastic revival connected with the name of St. Bernard. Hence, one might even wonder if it is not due, at least partially, to St. Bernard's influence. We are in possession of the list of manuscripts which he gathered for the library of Clairvaux. Under the title *Libri Origenis*, eight manuscripts are listed, which is a considerable number for that period; they contain not only the commentaries on the Old and New Testaments, but also the *Periarchon* and even Pamphilus' *Apology* for Origen.[27] A similar statement must be made concerning the Cistercian abbey of Signy; we still possess six folio volumes of Origen's works which came from this monastery.[28] Likewise, the catalogue of Pontigny for the twelfth century lists all of Origen's biblical commentaries, and, in particular, two copies of his commentary on the Canticle of Canticles.[29] Their presence in the Cluny catalogue of the same period proves, moreover, that interest in Origen was not a Cistercian monopoly.[30]

It has been definitely established that St. Bernard was inspired directly —and more than once—by the pages of Origen.[31] He was not merely acquainted with Origenist themes as transmitted by the Latin Fathers or medieval compilations: so much so, that St. Bernard's contemporary, Peter Berengarius, could even accuse him of having plagiarized Origen's commentary on the Canticle in writing his *Sermons on the Canticles*.[32] This accusation is certainly unjust in that Bernard in reality wrote an original work; however, his own general conception of the Canticle and his commentary is close to Origen's. The great bishops of the patristic age—St. Ambrose and St. Gregory of Nyssa—had written interpretations of the Canticle which devoted much attention to pastoral preoccupations, often concerning the sacraments of Christian initiation.[33] As for Origen, his was a less mystical and more psychological interpretation of the Canticle. This is the direction taken by St. Bernard and the twelfth-century monastic commentators. They preach, not as pastors, but as monks; furthermore initiation in their day is conferred upon children, not adults. Besides, their psychology and their peculiar kind of imagination are in harmony with Origen's exegesis; the spiritual needs of both are similar and are satisfied by similar means. From this point of view, Origen's biblical commentaries were akin to monastic literature; they satisfied a need for an inner life that was felt especially in monastic circles.

Actually this fidelity to Origen did them great credit for they knew all the harsh things St. Jerome had said about him. They also knew that errors had been imputed to him on certain precise points, and yet they felt an irresistible attraction for his work in general and for his biblical commentaries in particular. In order to justify their yielding to this feeling and to free readers' consciences from this complex of distrust, they often prefaced Origen's text with passages in which St. Jerome himself praised him, or with various poems affirming his orthodoxy.[34] A curious document reveals the anxiety which was felt not only over the orthodoxy of Origen's doctrine but for his personal salvation as well. The nun Elizabeth of Schönau († 1164) tells that one Christmas night, during a vision, she asked the Virgin Mary about this, at the instigation of her brother Egbert of Schönau, a Benedictine.

In accordance with the counsel I had received from my brother who at that very moment was celebrating the office at our convent, I addressed her in this fashion: "My Lady, I beg of you, kindly reveal to me something concerning the great doctor of the Church, Origen, who in so many places in his works has sung your praises so magnificently. Is he saved or not? For the Catholic Church condemns him because of the many heresies found in his writings." To which she answered in these words: "It is not the Lord's intention that much be revealed to you at this point. Know only that Origen's error did not come from bad will; it came from the excess of fervor with which he plunged into the depths of the Holy Scriptures he loved, and the divine mysteries which he was wont to scrutinize to an excessive degree. For this reason the punishment he is undergoing is not severe. And because of the glory his writings have given to me, he is illuminated by a very special light on each feast commemorating me. As for what will happen to him on the last day, that must not be revealed to you, but must remain hidden among the divine secrets." [35]

Such a text tells a great deal about the psychology of the milieu in which it was written. In monasteries of different observances, sermons under Origen's name were read at divine office, not all of which were his and some of which were in praise of the Virgin. But also, whether in private, in chapter, or refectory, commentaries were read which he had composed on the Scripture "which he loved." Though his reputation remained tainted, it did not prevent him from being read. For what was sought in him was not so much a doctrine as a mentality, and, most of all, a way of interpreting Holy Scripture. Origen, in fact, was admired because of what was known of him, that is to say, particularly because of his biblical commentaries, and they are the ones we almost always find quoted. Origen was considered above all as a biblical doctor. He is, so to speak, the first of the great monastic commentators of the Bible, and he was loved because the Bible was loved and because he had interpreted it with the same psychology, the same contemplative tendency, and to fill the same needs as those felt by the medieval monks. He was loved for his religious feeling, for the "spiritual" significance he had so well known how to find in Sacred Scripture. [36]

Studies in the history of St. Basil and other Greek Fathers in the Middle Ages would no doubt justify some interesting conclusions. For instance, the channels through which certain texts were transmitted to the West are already known. Thus, in twelfth-century Hungary, Latin monks established contact with Eastern monks. One of them, Cerbanus, translated the *Capita de caritate* of Maximus the Confessor; his translation, dedicated to the Benedictine abbot David of Pannonhalma (1131–1150), was brought by Gerhoh of Reichersberg to Paris where Peter Lombard made use of it and introduced it into his *Sentences*, and thereby into scholasticism.[37] These examples are sufficient to show that in the Western Middle Ages monks felt a real attraction for all that came from the East. They knew its writings as extensively as was in their power.[38]

THE LATIN FATHERS:
DEBT TO ST. JEROME AND ST. AUGUSTINE

The legacy that medieval monasticism received from the Latin patristic tradition is extremely vast. Actually, almost all its texts had been preserved and handed down. Some lacunae and the scarcity of texts of certain writings, like those of Tertullian, may be explained perhaps by the care that was taken to read only "orthodox" Fathers. Also, equal importance was not accorded everything that they did preserve. It would be helpful to make a thorough study of what the medieval tradition owes to each of the Latin Fathers. Of St. Ambrose the Middle Ages particularly prized the treatises on the Old Testament which owe so much to Philo's use of allegory. It was St. Jerome they consulted on the philological interpretation of Holy Scripture, though he seems to have exerted influence above all through his letters: here were at the same time models of the art of letter writing and a source for ideas on monastic asceticism.[39] St. Augustine's influence was paramount in the formation of the "monastic style." In his *Sermons* and particularly in his *Confessions*, he had produced a model of artistic prose in which all the procedures used in ancient rhythmical prose were put to the service of his Christian enthusiasm. His biblical commentaries, differing from Origen's but equally allegorical, found great favor. Some of his theological treatises are but seldom quoted, but they were highly valued. For example, when Abbot Jerome of Pomposa took inventory in the eleventh century of that monastery's library, he used, not the alphabetical order, but an order based on the relative importance of the various authors. At the head of his list he placed St. Augustine, represented by as many works as he was able to find; as for the remaining works, he drew up a list according to the *Retractationes* so that he could acquire the texts when they became available.[40] St. Augustine's treatises were also proportionately well represented, along with his other works, in the libraries of St. Aubin of Angers,[41] Nonantola,[42] and many other Benedictine abbeys. St. Augustine also enjoyed great prestige in the first Cîteaux.[43] However, his most frequently copied works were not his works of controversy, but his pastoral treatises, sermons, letters, and biblical commentaries. This proportion is found to have existed already in the library of the Venerable Bede[44] and seems to have been generally maintained.

What has been said of the Greek Fathers must, therefore, be said of the Latin Fathers: what monasticism sought in them primarily was all that could be helpful in leading the monastic life; consequently, during the same period, different milieux would use St. Augustine for different purposes. Whereas the scholastics valued a whole arsenal of metaphysical proofs in the *Confessions*, monasticism's teachers retained only the testimony of the mystic.[45] They separated the essence of the Augustinian confession from all the philosophical developments which, in the *Confessions*, envelop it as with a matrix, very valuable in itself but alien to Augustine's life of prayer. The polemics against the Manichaeans or the Neoplatonists had lost all timeliness for the medieval monks and therefore did not arrest their attention. Augustinianism was, as it were, decanted through St. Gregory, John of Fécamp, and the generations of monks who lived by their writings. The form under which it was to captivate the thirteenth-century scholastics was quite different from that given to it by the great spiritual writers of the monastic age. Here, as elsewhere, the monks studied the past in their own way.

Moreover, like Evagrius' sentences and the ancient rules, Latin patristic texts had not ceased to live. They were not used as if they were dead documents; with adaptations when necessary, they were put into a living context where in every milieu and period they retained their timeliness. A long prayer on the vices and virtues gives us an example of this process. It demonstrates the successive enrichments which the texts receive from Cassian to John of Fécamp, passing through St. Gregory the Great, Ambrosius Autpertus, Alcuin, and Halitgarius.[46]

St. Anthony: Father of Monks

With the texts and through them, but through a living tradition as well, the monastic Middle Ages received from the patristic age still other treasures. First of all, models: all these "founders" of monastic life who were almost always, particularly the earliest ones, Easterners. The greatest had been St. Anthony, "the Father of Monks." He remained truly the Father of all monks; and so in all milieux and in every period of the Western Middle Ages they considered themselves as truly his sons. Everywhere they claimed his support, sometimes even against each other.[47] During each monastic revival, they hark back to ancient Egypt; they want, they say, to revive Egypt, to inaugurate a new Egypt, and they call upon St. Anthony, his example and his writings. This is true in the Carolingian period; later also, in the eleventh century, at Monte Cassino, Cluny, Camaldoli, and in the twelfth century at Cîteaux and Tiron, in England as well as in France and in Italy.

In all controversies between monks, as for example when the Cluniacs are in opposition to Cistercians, each party appeals to St. Anthony and does so legitimately because what is remembered of his discourses is not the attacks against the Arians which were borrowed from him by St. Athanasius: what is recalled of his life is neither its historical circumstances nor the details of his temptations and the diabolic imagery with which the biographer had adorned it; it is rather the spiritual themes and instructions which are valid for all monks, regardless of the observance under which they lived. St. Anthony represents for all an ideal whose essential characteristic is its potential for realization in different ways. St. Anthony's life, then, for the medieval monks is not simply an historical text, a source of information about a definitely dead past. It is a living text, a means of formation of monastic life.

Patristic Terminology and Themes

Finally, the monastic Middle Ages received from the patristic era a terminology and themes and a whole vocabulary whose meaning cannot be grasped if their source is not recognized. Along with the words, it faithfully kept the practices and ideas which they represented. It is well to be informed about this in order to respect their wealth of content. When, for example, Peter the Venerable writes of Matthew of Albano, then Prior of Cluny: *"Non relinquebat partem aliquam theoriae intactam,"*[48] it should not be translated, as has been done: "There was not a single point of theory that he neglected." In this instance, it is not a theory of monastic life which is under discussion. The subject is prayer in the fullest sense of the word, including the mortification on which it rests. The whole context confirms this, and it should be rather translated as: "He never relaxed for one moment from contemplation," or: "He practiced continual asceticism and prayer." In the same way, when St. Bernard calls the Canticle of Canticles *theoricus sermo,* he does not mean a "theoretical discourse" in the modern sense of the word; he is suggesting the idea of an eminently "contemplative" text which gives expression to prayer and induces contemplation. A certain editor of medieval texts, in spite of the fact that all his manuscripts read *spiritualibus theoriis,* did not understand and so felt obliged to correct it to *theoricis.*

Theoria

The persistence in medieval times of the word *theoria,* however, is amply attested.[49] The βίος θεωρητικός of the ancient Greek philosophers and the Neoplatonists had passed, with a modified meaning adapted to the Christian regime, into the terminology of ancient Christian mysticism. Cassian contributed much to the transmitting of this expression and this idea to the West, where the word *theoria* is often accompanied by adjectives which prove that it is understood as a participation, an anticipation of celestial contemplation: *theoria caelestis* or *theoria divina.* It gives rise to the terms *theoricus* and *theoreticus* in expressions like *theorica mysteria, theorica studia,* which must not be translated as "theoretical studies," but as "love of prayer." Herrad of Landsberg, for example, is combining all these ideas when, in her *Garden of Delights,* she counsels: "Constantly finding repose in divine theory, scorning the dust of this earth, hasten toward heaven where you may see the Bridegroom who is now hidden."[50]

Similarly, the repeated genuflections and inclinations practiced at Cluny in the days of Peter the Venerable[51] were like the exercise of prayer and asceticism which the desert Fathers had known as μετάνοια. The term *metania* is sometimes found in medieval Latin texts with the meaning of a bow before the altar[52] or for satisfaction for certain faults made while kneeling.[53] The word does not have, in this case, the primitive meaning assigned to it in the New Testament (repentance), but the derived, restricted meaning it acquired under ancient monasticism. The monastic habit also continued often to be called by the traditional Greek term σχῆμα.[54] Also, the words *theologia, theologus* kept for John of Fécamp and for others all their ancient flavor, and did not have the speculative nuance they were to receive in the West from the time of Abailard onward.[55]

Philosophia

Another Greek term whose ancient meaning is retained is *philosophia.* The Greek Fathers had defined the monk's life as "philosophy according to Christ" and "the only true philosophy," or even simply as "philosophy." This term, meaning the practical discernment of the value of things and of the vanity of the world which must be renounced, is applied to those whose whole existence manifests this renunciation. In the same way, in the monastic Middle Ages as well as in antiquity, *philosophia* designates, not a theory or a way of knowing, but a lived wisdom, a way of living according to reason.[56] There are, in effect, two ways of living according to reason. Either one lives according to worldly wisdom, as taught by the pagan philosophers, and that is the *philosophia saecularis* or *mundialis*, or one lives according to Christian wisdom which is not of this world but already of the world to come, and this is the *philosophia caelestis* or *spiritualis* or *divina*. The philosopher *par excellence*, and philosophy itself, is Christ: *ipsa philosophia Christus*.[57] He was the Wisdom itself of God incarnate; and the Virgin Mary, in whom was accomplished the mystery of the Incarnation, is called "the philosophy of Christians." They must learn from her: *philosophari in Maria*.[58] Those who had heralded the advent of the Lord Jesus or who have transmitted His message are the philosophers the Christians obey; they speak of *philosophia Pauli*, and of "David the philosopher."

Philosophia caelestis

Now, this integral Christianity, this way of life entirely consecrated to God, this *conuersatio caelestis*, is indeed realized in monastic life. That is why the lawgivers and the models of monasticism are considered masters of philosophy. The cloisters are schools of philosophy, "gymnasia" where the "philosophy of St. Benedict" is learned.[59] St. Bernard is praised because he formed the monks of Clairvaux in the "disciplines of celestial philosophy,"[60] and Adam of Perseigne declares he is committed to the "Cistercian philosophy."[61] To lead a monastic life is simply "to philosophize." Du Cange gives no other medieval equivalent for the word *philosophari* than: *monachum agere*. The verb *philosophari* is applied to cenobites living in monasteries as well as to the solitary in his hermit's cell. In monastic literature well into the twelfth century, the expression *christiana philosophia* when employed without commentary or explanation very often stands for monastic life itself.

Disciplina

Akin to the word *philosophia* is the term *disciplina*. During the monastic centuries, it too, kept all its ancient value.[62] It is derived from *discipulus* and, originally, in classical Latin, its general meaning is teaching; soon it is used for the matter taught, and then, for the method of teaching and, consequently, education and formation, like παιδεία. It is applied in particular to military, family, and political life. In these different domains, the accent falls on realities that are social and collective in nature. This meaning of the word is preserved, in the first centuries of the Church, by the writings of the Fathers, biblical versions, the liturgy, and monastic rules. It is enriched with new uses, but they always imply the original meaning of pedagogy. The *Rule* of St. Benedict begins with these characteristic words: *Ausculta, o fili, praecepta magistri.* . . . The monks are "disciples who should listen";[63] the monastery is "a school for the service of the Lord,"[64] an expression which calls to mind both instruction in the school and military service.

In the Middle Ages, in monastic circles, this word stays alive; its meaning continues to evolve, but always as a prolongation of what it had been from the very beginning. In the twelfth century, Peter of Celle was to write a treatise *De disciplina claustrali,* on the way to lead the Christian life in a cloister. He defines and explains it with words (*magister Iesus, cathedra, schola*) associated with the idea of *disciplina* from its origins.[65] St. Bernard speaks of the "magisterium of the celestial discipline" which Christ brought to men,[66] and Guerric of Igny tells his Cistercian brothers: "Blessed are you, my brothers, you who have enlisted in the discipline of wisdom, who have registered in the school of Christian philosophy."[67] The word evokes all its ancient content; the *disciplina spiritualis* or *caelestis* is what the *Verbi discipulus* learns under the magisterium of the Word. The vocabulary of the schools and of military life (*erudire, verbera, exerceri*) fit naturally into this context to which are applied biblical verses in which the word *disciplina* occurs.[68] Beginning with the twelfth century, however, the word *disciplina* ceases to live and acquire new and precise meanings in the realm of spirituality. It continues to evolve in the philosophic vocabulary of scholasticism.[69] But, for the ascetical authors its meaning has been seriously impoverished; it means the way to conduct oneself properly, and signified good deportment. Monastic tradition alone had preserved all the breadth of meaning attributed to it by the patristic age, in continuity with classical antiquity.

Via regia

Finally, another example may be drawn from the theme of the *via regia.*[70] At the origin of this theme, as with almost all, there is found a biblical expression. It comes from Numbers 21.22. There it is related that during the wanderings of the Hebrew people in the desert of Pharan, after the children of Israel had been healed of serpent bites by the sight of the brazen serpent which Moses had made at God's command, they were constrained to undertake an expedition against Sehon, king of the Amorrhites, under the following circumstances: "Israel," says the sacred text, "sent an ambassador to Sehon, king of Amor, to say to him: I beseech thee that I may have leave to pass through thy land; we will not go aside into the fields or the vineyards, we will not drink waters of the wells, we will walk the royal road, till we be past thy borders." Sehon refuses and even decides to attack. He is overcome, and Israel takes possession of his kingdom.

Such is the letter of the sacred text. It presents a problem in historical interpretation. What exactly does the expression "royal road" mean? These words designate a public thoroughfare as opposed to a private road, but mean also a straight, direct road rather than paths which are more or less winding. The expression "royal road" understood in this way corresponds to a precise idea and image which were very widespread in the ancient world, especially in Egypt. The conception implied in this case is that of the state roads which all lead, without detours, to the capital of the kingdom where the king resides; they furnish no communication with the villages which they bypass; they have no turnings; they are comfortable, without danger; they take one unfailingly to one's destination. Generally constructed of basalt, they are kept up at the expense of the sovereign or the State, and are the pride of an empire as well as the guarantee of its prosperity.

It is understandable that Hellenic Egyptian writers from Philo to Clement of Alexandria very naturally made use of such a comparison in describing the ascension of the soul. The principal truths they thus illustrated were that man should go, not to a private individual, but to a great king, *the* great King, who is God, who awaits man at the end of his journey; and again, that all other roads are crooked, long, and dangerous, and consequently to be avoided. This theme, Christianized, was developed at length by Origen who interpreted all the events and all the names of persons spoken of in Numbers,[71] and also by Cassian[72] in a context used as a source by St. Benedict. Through their agency, it passed into the monastic Middle Ages. Rhabanus Maurus summarizes Origen, and others apply the theme to various situations. The royal road becomes the equivalent of the monastic life. Since it consists in avoiding deviations to the right or to the left, its application may vary according to the person being addressed and the circumstances, but the theme remains the same. For example, in an ancient sermon on the perseverance of monks, the symbolism is applied to what is proper to the cloistered life: its contemplative character; the temptation a monk must avoid is to engage in the occupations of the active life.[73]

The abbots, those who are entrusted with guiding the monks, should be the first to set out upon the royal road. Their personal life, first of all, should avoid any swerving and their manner of governing men must be kept at equal distance from all extremes. Smaragdus, in his commentary on the *Rule* of St. Benedict, recommends to the abbot moderation in all his orders: let him be neither too demanding nor too condescending toward human weaknesses; let him see that the precepts are obeyed and ask neither more nor less.[74] Only by so doing will he be truly the head of his army of monks; for the Christian combat of which St. Benedict liked to speak, and which Origen had shown we are committed to at baptism, is not waged alone; it is waged in common and under the leadership of a chief. Therefore sometimes we read in the eulogy of an abbot "that in the days of this excellent general, the soldiers of Christ advanced on the royal road."[75] For St. Bernard, the royal road which bends neither to the right nor to the left is the one on which those march who, wanting to avoid bypaths, detours, and occasions for dissipation resulting from the possession of earthly goods, sell all that they have and devote themselves to God alone.[76]

But after the great monastic centuries, the theme of the royal road loses its precise meaning, because it is used without reference to its biblical origin and its patristic interpretation. However, the use of the theme of the royal road by the Fathers and in monasticism is characteristic of traditional exegesis. The foundation for all this symbolism is, as almost always, taken from the Bible, and, in the Bible, from the Old Testament. The constant interpretation of the tradition remains faithful to the historical premisses based on the literal meaning; but it proceeds from that point of departure and rises to allegory. How, one may ask, does it manage to do so? By resorting to fantasy? By no means. All the *auctores* put philology to the service of typology, and in order that there be a "type," two conditions must be satisfied: first of all, the story has to contain a certain prefiguration of a spiritual reality which is exemplary in nature; at the same time, and necessarily, this story must have effectively laid the foundation for the Christian reality it foreshadowed, and this causality must belong to the order of efficiency.

It is a fact that the entire history of the Hebrew people, and in particular its wanderings, symbolized the march of the Church toward the heavenly Jerusalem which is the true Promised Land, and most certainly paved the way for the coming of Christ and, consequently, of the Church. From this point of view, Israel's whole history is the image of the whole life of the Church. But just how far does each event in this history correspond to a particular activity of the Church and its members? To learn this, are we reduced to conjecture or guesswork, each to his own taste? The example of the royal road proves to us that this is not so. To understand the spiritual significance of a text, two sources of information are called upon: first, ordinary concepts purely natural in content which the sacred text utilizes; in this case, it is the idea of the state highway which sheds light on the letter of the story in Numbers. Subsequently, recourse is had to the etymology of the names. This corresponds to a conviction held by the ancients and the Middle Ages that the name expresses the essence of a person or thing (*Nomen - omen*). Besides, the etymologies were established by the grammarians with an assurance which seemed sufficient to inspire complete confidence in them. With these historical and philological bases, the interpretation of an Old Testament text can be made in the light of the New. This light comes from gospel texts in which the same words are used as in the text under explanation: for example, Christ said: "I am the Way" and "I am King." The light also comes from the sum of the realities which give life to the Church: the sacraments, faith, and Christian practices.

This is the way the Greek Fathers proceeded, and the Middle Ages adopted their methods: it approved them and readily accepted their results. But it also used the traditional method. Not satisfied with handing on the legacy of antiquity, it further enriched it with new developments. There is continuity, but also progress. Within norms established by means of these procedures, there flourished great variety. Unanimity amongst authors comes from the fact that all depend on the Bible, and their originality results from the fact that the basic analogy can have various applications: the royal road is for all the straight way; but straightness can be understood in several senses according to the nature of the deviations to which it is subjected and to the particular aspect of the life of Christ or of the Church explained by the text of the New Testament which is being correlated to the Old. Charity, obedience, chastity, fidelity to the duties of monastic life, governing the community well, are so many ways of practicing rectitude. There is, then, in this exegetical tradition, not uniformity but unity, fidelity to sources, and freedom of the spirit. The monastic authors were able to adapt formulas inherited from antiquity to certain requirements of their observance; there was no need for them to indulge in innovation.

CONTINUITY OF THE PATRISTIC AGE
AND THE MONASTIC MIDDLE AGES

[handwritten margin note: Early patristics appreciated for their literary grammar & spiritual teaching]

From the survey of patristic sources of medieval monastic culture we have just given, two conclusions may be drawn. The first is that there is real continuity between the patristic age and the medieval monastic centuries, and between patristic culture and medieval culture. The monks knew and loved the patristic writings whose literary quality they appreciated—the study of grammar is responsible for this—and whose religious significance satisfied the desire for God which monastic life fostered: that is eschatology's contribution. Nor is their knowledge of the Fathers just bookish learning, limited to the realm of erudition. The part played by what can be called the living tradition in the continuity linking Western monasticism to the past of the whole Church must not be underestimated. It is often affirmed that monasticism maintained tradition by copying, reading, and explaining the works of the Fathers, and that is correct; but it did so also through *living* by what these books contained. This might be called an experiential mode of transmission. Well into the middle of the twelfth century, in the midst of the flowering of scholastic theology, while minds were incurring the risk of getting lost in side issues, the abbeys remained conservatories, as it were, of the great Christian ideas, thanks to the practice of the cult and the diligent reading of the Fathers of the Church. As for the monastic tradition, properly speaking, it can be claimed that from Tabenne to Camaldoli, Cluny, and Cîteaux, from St. Anthony to St. Peter Damian or Peter the Venerable, there had been no interruption. An evolution had taken place but there was no break, and this continuity found expression in a language profoundly marked by the language of the Fathers.[77]

And—this is a second conclusion—it is this continuity which gives medieval monastic culture its specific character: it is a patristic culture, the prolongation of patristic culture in another age and in another civilization. From this point of view, it seems possible to distinguish, from the eighth to the twelfth centuries in the West, something like two Middle Ages.[78] The monastic Middle Ages, while profoundly Western and profoundly Latin, seems closer to the East than to the other, the scholastic Middle Ages which flourished at the same time and on the same soil. Our intention here is by no means to deny that scholasticism represents a legitimate evolution and a real progress in Christian thought, but rather to point out this coexistence of two Middle Ages. To be sure, the culture developed in the monastic Middle Ages differs from that developed in scholastic circles.

The monastic Middle Ages is essentially patristic because it is thoroughly penetrated by ancient sources and, under their influence, centered on the great realities which are at the very heart of Christianity and give it its life. It is not dispersed in the occasionally secondary problems discussed in the schools. Above all, it is based on biblical interpretation similar to the Fathers' and, like theirs, founded on reminiscence, the spontaneous recall of texts taken from Scripture itself with all the consequences which follow from this procedure, notably the use of allegory.

All this is not to say that the monastic Middle Ages are not medieval or that they added nothing to patristic culture. To this assimilation of the Church's past, the monks brought the psychological traits proper to their own time. But the foundations, sources, and the general atmosphere in which their culture grew were patristic. By prolonging patristic culture in a period different from that of the Fathers, they produced a new and original, yet traditional, culture deeply rooted in the culture of the first centuries of Christianity.

St. Bernard, Last of the Fathers

Thus while St. Bernard exemplified the "new sensitivity" of the eleventh and twelfth centuries,[79] and has been called "the first of the great French prose writers,"[80] he was equally the "last of the Fathers." In fact, Pius XII proclaimed him as had the humanists of the sixteenth and seventeenth centuries: *ultimus inter patres, sed primis certe non impar*.[81] For this reason, St. Bernard is the symbol of a whole spiritual world, a whole literature which is a prolongation of the patristic age.[82] Dom Morin very correctly perceived that the patristic age had lasted until the twelfth century when he said that a certain anonymous author of that period was the representative of "patristic literature at its decline."[83] In this case, the word "decline" implies the terminal point of a period; there is nothing pejorative in its meaning since St. Bernard, who belongs to the same period, is not inferior to the ancient Fathers: *primis certe non impar*. Dom Rousseau has shown that, with some new additions and also with some impoverishment, monasticism has, on the whole, faithfully transmitted the values of the patristic age to the medieval Church.[84] In doing so it was not serving the interests of archaeology, nor was it motivated by any devotion to the past as such. For one thing, this turning to the sources of ancient culture had about it nothing artificial or constrained; it was free and spontaneous; it was not even done consciously except in cases where circumstances obliged the monks to confront scholastic culture. For another, the past was considered, not as being definitely over, but as a living reality which continued to animate the present. To attune themselves to it is a spontaneous and, so to speak, vital reaction in monastic circles. It is their life itself, since that life is oriented toward the contemplation of the great mysteries of salvation, and is completely imbued with an intense desire for God which sustains in them the need to recover, through and beyond literary sources, the "ancient fervor," the real source of their Christian life, to get as close as possible to the sources of Christianity, to the apostolic age, to the person of our Lord. It is through fidelity to their vocation that the monks, throughout the scholastic period, maintained the patristic spirit.

NOTES

1. *Rule* of St. Benedict, Ch. 9.

2. This point is made, clearly and strongly, by Winandy, "La spiritualité Bénédictine," *La spiritualité catholique* (gen. ed. J. Gautier; Paris, 1953), pp. 14–18.

3. Ibid., p. 18.

4. The text is found in "S. Antoine dans la tradition monastique médiévale," *Studia Anselmiana* 38 (Rome, 1956) 246.

5. "Illam orientalium ecclesiarum lampadem Hieronymum," as Rupert of Deutz wrote, *Epist. ad Liezelinum*, PL 170.667.

6. *Hist. Eccles.* III, viii (PL 188.656).

7. "Orientale lumen et antiquum illum in religione Aegyptium fervorem tenebris occiduis et gallicanis frigoribus inferendis," PL 184.309.

8. B. Bischoff, "Das griechische Element in der abendländischen Bildung des Mittelalters," *Byzantinische Zeitschrift* (1951) 27–55.

9.   Illic invenies veterum vestigia patrum,
          Quidquid habet pro se Latio Romanus in orbe,
          Graecia vel quidquid transmisit clara Latinis . . .
MGH, *PLAC* I 203–204. The first words are an echo of Ovid, *Ars amatoria*, I. 91, "Illic invenies quod ames. . . ."

10. *Die Überlieferung der griechischen Literatur in der lateinischen Kirche bis zum zwölften Jahrhundert* (Munich, 1959). Cf. also A. Malet, *Personne et Amour dans la théologie trinitaire de S. Thomas d'Aquin* (Paris, 1956), pp. 161ff.

11. B. Altaner, "Der Stand der patrologischen Wissenschaft," *Miscell. G. Mercati* I (Rome, 1946) 519.

12. A. Siegmund (n. 10), 278.

13. P. Chevalier, art. "Denys l'Aréopagite," *Dict. de spiritualité* III (1954) 320.

14. O. Rousseau, "La Bible et les Pères," *Bible et la vie chrétienne*, 14 (1956) 19–22, has shown that the Fathers were primarily the commentators of the Bible for the Middle Ages in the West.

15. J. Beumer, "Rupert von Deutz und seine Vermittlungstheologie," *Münchener theologische Zeitschrift* (1953) 267n60.

16. E. Boissard, "La doctrine des Anges chez S. Bernard," *S. Bernard théologien* (*Anal. S. O. Cist.* IX, iii–iv), 115–34.

17. A. Fracheboud, art. "Denys l'Aréopagite," *Dict. de spir.* III 330.

18. A. Siegmund (n. 10), 169.

19. G. Nortier-Marchand, "La bibliothèque de Jumièges au moyen âge," *Jumièges: Congrès scientifique du XIIIe centenaire* (Rouen, 1955), p. 601.

20. Ibid., p. 611.

21. A. Siegmund (n. 10), 280.

22. Beumer (n. 15), 263–64; E. Mersch, *Le corps mystique du Christ: Études de théologie historique* (Louvain, 1933) II 146.

23. M. Olphe-Gaillard, in *Revue d'ascetique et de mystique* (1935) 273–78, 289–98. But, in Bede, *Hom.* 3 (CCL 15.17–19), the reference to Irenaeus is not justified by any real textual reminiscence.

24. "L'ancienne version latine des sentences d'Évagre pour les moines," *Scriptorium,* 5 (1951) 195–213.

25. M. Muhmolt, "Zu der neuen Übersetzung des Mönchsspiegels des Evagrius," *Vigiliae Christianae* (1954) 101–103.

26. "Origène au xiie siècle," *Irénikon* 24 (1951) 425–39. "Nouveau témoins sur Origène au xiie siècle," *Mediaeval Studies* 15 (1953) 104–106. Apart from the evidence cited in the first of the above studies, add those of Artur Landgraf, in *Theologische Revue* (1955) 348–49.

27. Wilmart, "L'ancienne bibliothèque de Clairvaux," *Coll. Ord. Cist. Ref.* 10 (1949) 117–18.

28. MS Charleville 107.

29. *Cat. gén. des mss. des bibl. publ. de France* (Paris, 1849) I 707–708.

30. L. Delisle, *Inventaires des manuscrits de la Bibliothèque Nationale, Fonds de Cluni* (Paris, 1884), pp. 349–51.

31. J. Daniélou, "S. Bernard et les Pères grecs," *Anal. S. Ord. Cist.* 11 (1953) 45–51. Delhaye, "La conscience morale dans la doctrine de S. Bernard," ibid. 219–22; and cf. Index, 320.

32. *Apologeticus pro Abaelardo,* PL 178.183.

33. J. Daniélou, "Eucharistie et Cantique des cantiques," *Irénikon* 23 (1950) 257–77.

34. Many of these texts are published in "Origène au xiie siècle" (n. 26) 433–36.

35. The Latin text is found in F. W. E. Roth, *Die Visionen der hl. Elisabeth und die Schriften der Äbten Ekbert und Emecho von Schönau* (Brünn, 1884), pp. 62–63. This account is attested with certainty in the manuscript tradition of the visions of Elizabeth, according to K. Koster, "Das visionäre Werk Elisabeths von Schönau," *Archiv für mittelrheinische Kirchengeschichte* (1952) 106.

36. W. Seston, "Remarques sur le rôle de la pensée d'Origène dans les origines du monachisme," *Rev. d'hist. des religions* (1933) 197–213, treats only of Eastern monasticism, and of that, only the beginnings, but, note (201) that the main themes of monastic literature in the East are found already developed in Origen. By this path, Western monasticism in the Middle Ages could meet the ancient East.

37. "Origène au xiie siècle" (n. 26), 433–36.

38. On the ecumenical tendencies of this kind that were traditional in monastic culture, cf. "Médiévisme et unionisme," *Irénikon* 19 (1946) 6–23.

39. "S. Jérôme, docteur de l'ascèse," *Revue d'ascétique et de mystique. Mélanges M. Viller* 29 (1949) 143–45. On St. Jerome in the Middle Ages, see the bibliography in M. Bernard's *Speculum virginum* (1955) 24–25. Cf., for the ninth century especially, M. L. W. Laistner, "The Study of St. Jerome in the Middle Ages," in F. X. Murphy,

A Monument to St. Jerome (New York, 1952), pp. 233–56.

40. G. Mercati, *Opere minore* (Vatican City, 1937) I 373.

41. L. W. Jones, "The Library of St. Aubin's at Angers in the Twelfth Century," *Class. and Med. Studies in Honor of E. K. Rand* (New York, 1938), pp. 143–61.

42. J. Ruysschaert, *Les manuscrits de l'abbaye de Nonantola* (Vatican City, 1956), pp. 20–33.

43. J. de Ghellinck, "Une édition ou une collection médiévale des *opera omnia* de S. Augustin," *Liber Floridus: Festschrift P. Lehmann* (1950), p. 72. On St. Augustine at Clairvaux and Liessies, cf. *Scriptorium* 6 (1952) 52.

44. M. L. W. Laistner, "The Library of the Venerable Bede," *Bede, His Life, Times, and Writings*, ed. A. Hamilton Thomson (Oxford, 1935), p. 263.

45. *Un maître*, pp. 63–68: "S. Augustin et S. Grégoire."

46. "La prière au sujet des vices et des vertus," *Analecta Monastica* II 3–17.

47. "S. Antoine dans la tradition monastique médiévale," *Studia Anselmiana*, 38 (1956) 229–47.

48. *De Miraculis* 2.8 (PL 189).

49. L. Gougaud, "La theorie dans la spiritualité médiévale," *Revue d'ascétique et de mystique* (1922) 381–94.

50. Quoted ibid. 390.

51. *Statuta* 53 (PL 189.1040).

52. "Facit ante altare metanoeam," Bernard of Cluny, *Vetus disciplina monastica*, ed. M. Herrgott (Paris, 1726) I 264.

53. "Metanoeis quae cotidiano usu in capitulo fiunt et quae vulgo veniae nominantur." Peter the Venerable, *Statuta* 4 (PL 189.1027). Other examples in Du Cange, *s.v.*

54. E.g., Ordericus Vitalis, *Hist. eccles.*, ed. A. Le Prévost (Paris, 1838–1855) II 420.

55. *Un maître*, pp. 76–78.

56. "Pour l'histoire de l'expression 'philosophie chrétienne,'" *Mélanges de sc. rel.* (1952) 221–26.

57. H. Rochais, "Ipsa philosophia Christus," *Mediaeval Studies* (1951) 244–47.

58. "Maria Christianorum philosophia," *Mélanges de science religieuse* (1956) 103–106.

59. Bruno of Querfurt, *Vita S. Adalberti* IV 609 (MGH, 55); Peter of Celle, *Epist.* PL 202.522.

60. *Exordium magnum Cist.* PL 185.437.

61. *Epist.* 6 (PL 211.598).

62. "Disciplina," *Dict. de spir.* Fasc. 22–23, 1291–1302.

63. *Rule* of St. Benedict, Ch. 3.

64. Ibid. *Prologue*, cf. C. Mohrmann, in the edition of the *Rule* by P. Schmitz (Maredsous, 1955) 28–33. B. Steidle, "Dominici schola servitii," *Benediktinische Monatsschrift* (1952) 397–506.

65. PL 202.1097–1146.

66. *Sup. Cant.* 27.7.

67. *Sermo in fest. S. Ben.* 4 (PL 185.101).

68. *Epist.* 20 (PL 211.652–53).

69. M.-D. Chenu, "Notes de lexicographie médiévale: Disciplina," *Rev. d. sc. phil. et théol.* (1936) 686–92.

70. "La voie royale," Supplement to *La vie spirituelle* (1948) 339–52.

71. *In Num.* 12.2 (ed. Baehrens, 106).

72. *Conlat.* XXIV 24–26 (ed. Petschenig, CSEL 13.700–704).

73. "Sermon ancien sur la persévérance des moines," *Analecta monastica* II 24, 119–23.

74. II (PL 102.730).

75. Cf. *Vita* of St. Ansegisus, abbot of Fontenelle in the ninth century, Ch. 5 (PL 105.737).

76. *De Diligendo Deo* 21.

77. B. Schmiedler, "Vom patristischen Stil in der Literatur, besonders in der Geschichtsschreibung des Mittelalters," *Geschichtliche Studien: Albert Haucks Festschrift* (1916), pp. 25–33, has insisted particularly on the patristic themes (*loci*); he hoped to see medieval writings studied from this point of view but his call has scarcely been heeded.

78. *Irénikon* (1946) 6–23.

79. "S. Bernard et la devotion médiévale envers Marie," *Revue d'ascétique et de mystique* (1954) 375.

80. C. Mohrmann, "La style de S. Bernard," *San Bernardo* (Milan, 1954), p. 170.

81. O. Rousseau, "S. Bernard le dernier des Pères," *S. Bernard théologien*, pp. 300–308. Add to the texts there cited, the one published in "Recherches sur les Sermons sur les Cantiques de S. Bernard," RB (1954) 222n1.

82. "Aux Sources des Sermons sur les Cantiques de S. Bernard," RB (1959) 237–57. "S. Bernard et la tradition biblique," *Sacris erudiri*, 1959.

83. "Le sermon attribué à l'abbé de Clairvaux," RB (1927) 305. Cf. on this sermon RB (1955) 308.

84. Rousseau (n. 81), 305–306.

7

Liberal Studies

The Monks and the Classics

THIRD IN IMPORTANCE among the sources of medieval monastic culture is classical culture, the word "classical" having in this instance a meaning which requires definition but which, in general acceptance, can be taken to mean the cultural values of pagan antiquity. From the standpoint of the relative worth of its contribution, this source is last in order of importance. But it must be studied; first, because it really does constitute a source, and furthermore because it creates a problem for medievalists and sometimes for readers of the medievalists, as well as for readers of the texts that emanated from medieval monasticism. This problem arises from the diversity of conclusions drawn by historians of medieval literature, a diversity bearing on two issues. On the one hand, as to the knowledge of classical antiquity that the monks actually had: according to some, they were permeated with it; according to others, they possessed merely a superficial acquaintance with it. They knew scarcely more than a few commonplaces, kinds of proverbs or all-purpose quotations such as are found today in the pages of a dictionary. On the other hand, historians are also divided as to how the monks judged the classical authors. According to some, they held them in high esteem, finding in them their masters and their favorite models; according to others, they felt for them only aversion.

What causes this divergence of opinion? First of all it is the general difficulty of finding out what medieval men thought. They scarcely ever spoke of themselves or of what they were doing. They were engaged in living, satisfied to exist and act without telling us why. Theirs was not a time like ours when books are written on contemporary tendencies. These tendencies did exist but they were translated into action, and it is only the final product which has reached us.[1] This factual evidence allows us at least to pose the psychological problems for which solutions had to be found.

Further, the difficulty is only increased by the very complexity of a problem for which the sources furnish contradictory, or apparently contradictory, information. On the one hand, the medieval monks are acquainted with the classics and they use them: that is an undeniable fact. On the other, it often happens that they speak disparagingly of them and advise against reading them. Thus, Alcuin reproaches one of his monastic friends for too great a liking for Virgil and does so by quoting him a verse from the *Aeneid*,[2] and his own writings are full of Virgilian reminiscences. St. Bernard himself, in order to suppress vain learning, was to call on Persius as an authority.[3] Such findings would seem to justify the clever remark which has it that Virgil and the other poets were "the enthusiasm of some, the scandal of others, and everybody's concern."[4] Thus the divergent opinions of historians are founded on partial information, each of them based on but a part of the texts and the facts; whereas, in reality, there are two tendencies and two attitudes seemingly contradictory, but which were reconciled: the use of the classics and a distrust for them.

How can this problem be resolved? There can be no question of passing judgment on the monastic Middle Ages. To do this with fairness would require finding an absolute norm to compare it with, a sort of Golden Age representing perfection. We can perhaps try to ascertain its relative position. Our task will be to establish the facts as objectively as possible and then to try to understand them. The method which seems most likely to ensure some degree of success is to examine first the origin of the classical culture of monks, and then its results. This inquiry will involve St. Bernard and the Cistercians as well as the earlier Benedictine tradition. Gilson, in an observation which has since become famous, said that St. Bernard and the Cistercians had "renounced everything save the art of writing well."[5] Now, the art of writing is an acquired art. We shall attempt to discover how it was done, why and by what methods the monks read the classics, which ones they read, and how extensively.

STUDY OF THE CLASSICS AT SCHOOL

As to the genesis of classical culture in medieval monasticism, two questions are seen to arise: when—that is to say, at what time in their lives— did the monks read these authors; and what method was used?

Certain monks read the classics, more or less all through their monastic life itself. But all, or almost all, had worked on them in school in their youth at the age when memorizing is easy. It is a fact that the classical authors were studied in the cloister schools as well as in the others; even more, as we shall see, than in the others. We have two kinds of proofs for this. First, the existence itself of classical manuscripts which have come down to us. The introductions to critical editions of collections like Teubner or Budé furnish the information that most of the sources given are monastic in origin, and since the Renaissance, humanists have recognized the great value of these manuscripts. But we possess a still more explicit proof, valid even for manuscripts which have not been preserved; it is found in the catalogues of medieval monastic libraries. A great number of names of classical authors appears in them, and this new source furnishes the first precise item of information: these *auctores* are listed generally in the catalogue of the cloister school, not in the catalogue of the community. They are placed, not amongst the *libri divini*, but with the *libri liberales*, or even *saeculares*, or, most frequently, *scholastici*; they are school books, classbooks, and, in the sense we continue to use, they are really "classics." They appear less frequently in the catalogues of the Cistercian abbeys because they did not have schools;[6] but the *auctores* are nonetheless represented in their writings: the Cistercians had become familiar with them before entering the monastery. No doubt the evolution which monasticism had undergone in the course of its long medieval history must also be taken into account, and necessary distinctions must be made. In the Merovingian period, in many regions, *grammatica* was learned in a fairly rudimentary fashion through the use of the psalter alone, but very soon, in the England of the seventh and eighth centuries, the classical authors resumed their role. And from the pedagogical renaissance of the eighth and ninth centuries on, they never again lost it: they were considered as the best models for the learning of Latin.

Who are these *auctores*? They are not just the "classics" in the sense given to this word by today's literary history, that is to say, the authors of the Latin Golden Age. For to the latter were added later writers who were equally considered as authorities on Latinity: secular poets like Lucan, Statius, Persius, and others; Christian poets like Juvencus and Sedulius; and finally grammarians, Quintilian, Donatus, and the others. Accordingly, attention has been drawn to the fact that while it may be permissible to speak of a "twelfth-century humanism" no case at all can be made for a "twelfth-century classicism."[7] In brief, the *scholastici* are *all the ancient authors* who can serve as guides to good expression, the first step in good thinking. To these are joined philosophers, particularly in circles where dialectics plays a greater role than it does in monasticism. Several masters of language, moreover, are masters of reflection as well, like Seneca and Cicero. Depending on the time and the place, the influence of one schoolman or another, preference was given to one author rather than another.

Certain historians of medieval literature have spoken of an *Aetas ovidiana, horatiana*, or *virgiliana*;[8] but nothing must be oversimplified, and today these too sharply defined classifications have been abandoned.[9]

All future monks benefited by this teaching founded on the authors but each student derived more or less benefit, each master performed his task more or less effectively. Furthermore, in the Middle Ages the word "school" embraces a wider range of meaning than in our times. The schools were then, no doubt, places where an elementary, then later, secondary, education was given to young men of all classes; the program of the *trivium* and *quadrivium* included different series of lessons, that is, classes and courses. But the master was far more than a teacher: he was able to pick out the most talented or the most willing workers in the study-group and train them with particular care. This system of selection and specialization favored the rise of a few men of outstanding personality who, in turn, exercised an enriching influence on the environment from which they had come and on a few select disciples. We know, for instance, that Aimoin had received this kind of formation from Abbo at Fleury. In like manner, in the second half of the eleventh century, Albericus of Monte Cassino dedicated a part of his *Breviarium de dictamine* to two of his disciples, Gunfridus and Guido, who, after their elementary studies, wished to brave the difficulties of composition and advance *ad pugnam compositionum*. As a matter of fact, Guido was to become the successor of the Cassinese chronicler, Leo of Ostia.[10]

The *Accessus ad auctores*

How were these authors studied, and what procedures were used? By what channels did they penetrate medieval monastic psychology? There were three principal ways: the introduction to the authors, commentary or explanation of the texts, and, lastly, copying. No author was taken up without preparation. This introduction was effected through preparatory notes on each which were called *accessus ad auctores*. There are many examples of this genre extant dating from the twelfth century, but they derive from an older tradition. The problems of literary history, sources, and psychology raised by the *accessus* have already been studied,[11] and the texts of two of them have recently been edited. The first is an anonymous collection,[12] and of the three manuscripts which have preserved it, we know the origin of two. They come from the Benedictine abbey of Tegernsee. As for the other, it is the work of Conrad, a monk of the abbey of Hirsau, which, under the abbot William, in 1079 had adopted the Cluniac reform.[13] Conrad, William's pupil, was a schoolmaster at this monastery and wrote, in connection with his teaching, a *Dialogue on the Authors* in which the details of the *accessus* are presented in the form of a conversation between a teacher and his pupil. The *accessus* is a short history which takes up for each author the following questions: the life of the author, title of the work, the writer's intention, the subject of the book, the usefulness of its contents, and, finally, the question what branch of philosophy it belongs to. This whole procedure, which was used by the lawyers (both the canonists and the civilians), theologians, rhetoricians, and philosophers, seems to stem from a much more elaborate technique for commentaries on the works of Aristotle. In scholasticism, it was also applied to Holy Scripture; it is practically the same as the one used by Peter Lombard in the prologue to his commentary on St. Paul.[14] But the underlying intention which inspires these texts is patristic in origin. St. Jerome, who did not follow the system of the *accessus* in his Prologues to the different books of the Bible, had, however, shaped the direction it was to follow by framing and applying the two postulates on which all this literature rests: optimism with regard to the pagan authors and the necessity of giving them an allegorical interpretation.

OPTIMISM ABOUT PAGAN AUTHORS

The optimism consists in thinking that everything true or good or simply beautiful that was said, even by pagans, belongs to the Christians. In conformity with this principle, St. Jerome quoted the *auctores*, praised their virtues, compared the Prophets' figures of speech with the hyperboles and apostrophes of Virgil, called attention with evident gratification to the fact that Solomon recommends the study of philosophy and that St. Paul quotes verses by Epimenides, Menander, and Aratus. St. Augustine likewise pointed out that the sacred authors used the same literary methods as the pagan authors of antiquity.[15] All that was valuable in pagan literature was compared by the Fathers and the medieval authors to the treasures of the Egyptians that the Hebrews were authorized to take with them at the time of the Exodus.[16] The *accessus* and the commentary on the *auctores* constitute a real declaration of principle: they place pagan writings in the ranks of the *auctores authentici* who by their nature cannot err, contradict themselves, or deceive. Consequently, every effort is made to find a good intention in each of these works.

Allegorical Interpretation

This optimistic bias produced, in consequence, a method for the interpretation of the classics: allegorism. Since all these authors said nothing but what was good and with good intentions, to discover these in the texts requires forcing and explaining. This is what is called *exponere reverenter* or simply *exponere*. The same allegorical methods will then be applied to them as to the Old Testament, and a Christian refurbishing of the pagan texts will become the normal practice.

The anonymous *Accessus ad auctores* has 29 paragraphs dealing with 19 authors. Ten paragraphs, more than a third of the whole, are devoted to different works of Ovid; he is constantly presented as a moralist: *bonorum morum est instructor, malum vero extirpator.* "His intention is to counsel legitimate love and marriage."[17] He teaches chastity, "lawful love,"[18] and for that reason suffered persecution.[19] Such judgments would have doubtless been a surprise to Ovid, but did they not believe that he had died a Christian? Because of the treatise *De vetula* attributed to him and found, according to a legend, in his tomb, it was thought that toward the end of his life he had become a Christian and had taught the mysteries of Our Lord, and the life and the Assumption of the Virgin Mary.[20] Because of his fourth Eclogue, Virgil was invoked as a witness to the coming of Christ—His second coming in glory, at the end of the world, of His first coming in the Incarnation, according to Lawrence of Durham.[21] Horace was as often presented as a moralist (*ethicus*) as he was as a pagan (*ethnicus*).[22]

Although it was generally recognized that these authors were pagans, it was the important thing for medieval monks that they should make use of them as Christians.

Conrad of Hirsau, after some prefatory remarks on the various literary forms and on the purpose of the *accessus*, begins his study with Donatus, followed by Cato: he finds no difficulty in praising the Censor whom St. Jerome had so much admired. When he comes to Cicero, he devotes himself mostly to the *De amicitia*, and he approves not only the moral doctrine of this treatise but the arguments used in its exposition which are similar to those found in Sacred Scripture: friendship and the virtues which fortify it lead to the highest good.[23] Boethius is congratulated for having taught "the joy of divine grace and the hope of eternal reward."[24] Lucan, in his writings as well as in his private life, gave nothing but examples of virtue.[25] Horace provides the occasion for an exposé on principles: "I shall

explain to you," Conrad promises his disciple, "how the milk with which
the poets nourish you can become for you more solid food, that is to say,
more inspirational reading. For those who seek wisdom, worldly learning
should be looked upon in such a way that, should any exhortations to
ordinary virtue be found in it which could lead to higher wisdom, they
should not be rejected; the mind should endeavor to find what it is seeking."[26] Ovid knew God, even though he did not serve Him.[27] Whatever
he said that was good, he must have received it from the Creator of all
men, and this is the reason why the sacred writers did not refuse to borrow
from the pagans. St. Paul is inspired by Menander and cites Epimenides;
and St. Benedict's *Rule* takes from Terence the *ne quid nimis*, "which had
been applauded in the theater when Calliope recited it," and Augustine
and Jerome made generous use of pagan authorities.[28] St. Jerome, in particular, is the more famous among the Doctors of the Church for having
drawn more on secular literature; he praised Homer, among others,[29] and
Persius had the great merit of having denounced the vices of the Romans.[30]

Toward the end of his *Dialogue*, Conrad of Hirsau sums up the advice
he had given concerning the authors:

> There is no greater happiness in this world than to be nourished by
> God's word; the soul who believes, who hopes for rest after labor, buries
> deep within him, at the beginning of his pilgrimage, the word of God
> as if it were the "repository of his hope," and through that very fact,
> the soul is already drawing close to its homeland. Therefore we should
> continually cultivate the philosophical disciplines, meaning those which
> consist of realities and not merely words. They produce scorn for the
> temporal and love for eternity; they teach us to "walk in the spirit," to
> combat the demands of the flesh; they inculcate divine love, the cult of
> the invisible, hatred of the world, a persevering love of truth, and an
> aversion toward error.

"We are called," says St. Paul, "in liberty": let us serve our King, then,
through liberal studies.[31] It is in our power to orient the arts toward divine
knowledge.[32] The literature of this world can be an ornament of our
souls as well as of our style, if we but know how to direct it to the worship
of God.[33]

All this *accessus* literature is difficult to evaluate, since we can hardly
avoid asking ourselves the question: To what degree were the authors of
the *accessus* serious; to what extent their readers dupes? The men of the
Middle Ages do not appear to have asked themselves these questions.
Once it had been accepted that everything good has come from the hands

of God—and this assumption does not arise from childish naïveté but from a correct theological view—the result naturally follows: allegorical interpretation of the texts could be undertaken, but on condition that it would not become merely literary history. Unlike the practice of today, these texts were not studied solely as evidence of the past or as dead documents. A practical end was sought: to educate young Christians, future monks, to "introduce" them to Sacred Scripture and guide them toward Heaven by way of *grammatica*. To put them in contact with the best models would, at one and the same time, develop their taste for the beautiful, their literary subtlety, as well as their moral sense. To succeed in this they used practical, not scientific, methods: they interpreted. Certainly in the writings of the Fathers and of the medieval monks there is no lack of statements condemning the immorality of certain texts, Ovid's, for example; he was known to be dangerous. But once it had been decided to study him, they wished to make him acceptable. There was no difficulty over the things he had said which were right, but as for the rest, he had to be brought into conformity with Holy Scripture in order to safeguard his prestige and authority.

The result of this kind of pedagogy was to set free the consciences of both teachers and pupils with regard to the pagan authors, and to develop in all a power of enthusiasm and the capacity for admiration. It also made possible an amazing contact with ancient literature. The vital use they made of it is something that we can no longer achieve in our times. Ovid, Virgil, and Horace *belonged* to these men as personal property; they were not an alien possession to which to refer and quote with reverence—and with bibliographical references. Medieval men claimed for themselves the right to make the authors conform to usage, to the actual needs of a living culture. Each of these authors was quoted freely and from memory and even without acknowledgment. The important thing was not what he had said or meant, nor what he was able to say in his own time and place, but what a Christian of the tenth or twelfth century could find in him. Wisdom was sought in the pages of pagan literature and the searcher discovered it because he already possessed it; the texts gave it an added luster. The pagan authors continued to live in their readers, to nurture their desire for wisdom and their moral aspirations. Through the *accessus* method, the writers of antiquity were made comprehensible and useful to men who lived in an environment totally different from their own, but who were not resigned to possessing only a bookish, scholarly knowledge of them. The authors had really, in the words of Rhabanus Maurus, been "converted" to Christianity.

GLOSSES

Another component of the method of initiation into the classics was the commentary. Many of the classical texts have come down to us in manuscripts surrounded by scholia, marginal and particularly interlinear glosses, explaining various words and phrases.[34] While the *accessus* was a general introduction to each author and to each work, the gloss is a special explanation of each word of its text. Conrad of Hirsau defines it, in terms taken from Isidore's *Etymologies,* as a process which consists in clarifying one word by another.[35] To look for and find in this way an equivalent for each word necessitates acquiring not only a general idea of the work through a superficial reading, but a minute, attentive study of all the details. The superior wisdom sought for in the texts is obtained only through *grammatica.* No doubt this procedure was not practiced everywhere or always in the same manner and to the same degree, but it is attested by manuscripts of every period: it was, therefore, a constant of medieval education.

ORAL COMMENTARY

To the gloss, a written commentary, was added the oral commentary. It was given by the teacher at whose feet a child learned to "read," which means, not merely learning the letters of the alphabet—this had already been the subject of elementary instruction—but understanding the words, learning the rules which determined their use, and understanding the meaning of sentences. What was called *legere ab aliquo,* to "read with" a grammar master, was to listen to him read and explain the texts, to receive his "lessons." His oral explanations were concerned not only, as was the written gloss, with the meanings of the words but with their grammatical forms. He taught how to "decline," that is, to produce the "derived" forms of each word subject to varying inflections in the different cases, numbers, moods, and tenses. This *declinatio,* as the ancients understood it, implied what is called today both "declension" and "conjugation."[36] On the use of this method, we fortunately possess a very detailed document. St. Anselm, then prior of Bec, wrote these words to one of his young monks who was staying for a time at Canterbury:

> I have learned that Dom Arnoul is giving you lessons. If this is so, I
> am delighted; as you may have noticed, I always wanted to see you
> make progress, and I now desire it more than ever. I have also heard

that he excels in declensions; now, as you know, it has always been a hard chore for me to decline with children, and I am aware that in this science you made less progress with me than you should have. I send you then, as to my dearest son, this word of advice, this plea, in fact, this order: everything you may read with him, or in any other way, apply yourself to declining it with care. And don't be in the least ashamed to study in this way, even if you think you don't need to, as if you were just a beginner. For, with him, you are consolidating in yourself, as you hear them, the things you already know, so as to remember them the more firmly; and under his instruction, if you do make an error, you will correct it and learn what you do not as yet know.

If he is not reading anything with you, and this through any negligence on your part, I am grieved; I want this done, and wish you to work at it as much as you can, particularly with regard to Virgil and the other authors whom you didn't read with me, avoiding those who contain any obscenity. If for some reason you are prevented from attending his classes, make every effort to decline, as I have told you to do, completely from the beginning to the end with the utmost concentration, and whenever you can, the greatest possible number of the books you have already read. Also, show this letter to my very dear friend in which, as well as asking you in a few words to give him all your affection, I ask him to prove that I can rely on his true friendship, and I assure him that whatever he does for you, it is for my own heart that he will be doing it. It is a long time since we pledged our mutual friendship; I shall never forget it; may he also be kind enough to remember it.

With all the respect in your power, extend our greetings to him and also to the Prior, Dom Gondulphus, and the other fathers and brothers who are with you. God be with you, my dearest child; and above all, do not disdain the advice of one who loves you with all his fatherly affection.[37]

With gifted individuals, this very precise method when practiced under such masters and in such an atmosphere could produce astonishing results: it fixed forever in the pupil's memory the letter of the text studied, and obliged him to make close contact with language at its best; and for that very reason, it taught him not only how to read the ancients but also how to write well. It is on such a basis that we should judge the relative truth of this statement made by Suger's biographer:

Because of his tenacious memory, he was unable to forget the ancient poets, to such a point that he would recite for us from memory twenty and sometimes thirty or more lines from Horace that contained something useful.[38]

A stylist like St. Bernard came from the obscure school of St. Vorles about which we know nothing; we are likewise in ignorance of the names of the teachers of John of Fécamp, Peter the Venerable, and so many other great writers. But, at least, we do know the methods which were universally in use and which, consequently, they must have employed; these explain in part their style and give us some indications as to their psychology.

The Monastic Scriptorium

Finally, if we were to inherit texts and glosses, there obviously had to be, not only teachers and pupils, but also *scriptoria*. This word refers to the whole group who were engaged in book-making: the head of the workshop, the copyists, correctors, rubricators, painters, illuminators, and binders; for a number of monks took part in the making of every book. The task of the copyist was an authentic form of asceticism. Deciphering from an often poorly preserved manuscript a text which was often long and badly written and reproducing it correctly constituted a task which, however noble it was, was also hard and therefore meritorious, and medieval scribes have taken pains to inform us of this fact: the whole body is concentrated on the work of the fingers and constant and precise attention must be exercised. It was work that was both manual and intellectual. Calligraphy is a difficult art as we know only too well. But copying was not the only thing involved. Each text transcribed required very careful revision, correction, collation, and criticism. The best copies had to be procured, and for this purpose an "inter-library loan and exchange system" had to be organized between the different monasteries.

Abbo of Fleury tells us that copying a book was, like prayer and fasting, a means for correcting one's unruly passions. Horace and Virgil as well as Smaragdus or canonical collections were dedicated to St. Benedict and transcribed in his honor. When the book was completed, offering it to God was, at times, a kind of liturgy. *Suscipe, Sancta Trinitas, oblationem huius codicis* . . . reads the heading of an eleventh-century text of Flavius Josephus from Stavelot. The prayer goes on to mention the local patron, St. Remaclus, in whose honor the volume is dedicated to God, and then the two monks who, sinners that they are, prepared the parchment and made the copy, and finally those who will read the book or who will be its owners in the future. For all of them it will be a means of gaining the blessing of God's mercy and of attaining eternal life.[39]

This laborious work was held in high esteem, not only, nor even principally, as an ascetic exercise, but more especially because it was a way for the monks to exercise an apostolate in the Church. Tribute to the scribe and praise for the apostolate of the pen constituted a traditional literary theme which is met with at every period; it had been developed, perhaps for the first time, by Cassiodorus.[40] Alcuin took it up in a poem which was inscribed at the entrance to the scriptorium at Fulda.[41] Peter the Venerable was thinking of it when he spoke of the solitary who devotes to this work the leisure time of his cloistered life:

> He cannot take to the plow? Then let him take up the pen; it is much more useful. In the furrows he traces on the parchment, he will sow the seeds of the divine words. . . . He will preach without opening his mouth; without breaking silence, he will make the Lord's teaching resound in the ears of the nations; and without leaving his cloister, he will journey far over land and sea.[42]

Blessed Goswin, abbot of Anchino in the second half of the twelfth century, had transcribed this whole passage in his treatise *On the Instruction of Novices*.[43] And in the fourteenth century the heading of the catalogue of the library of the Cistercian abbey of Ter Doest was similarly inspired: "Since the monks cannot preach the word of God by word of mouth, let them do so with their hands. The books we transcribe are so many proclamations of the truth."[44]

Moreover, this work, besides commanding respect, fixed in the copyists' and revisers' memories, and not merely in the minds of the students, the texts and the glosses which were copied with so much care and patience. One can, of course, wonder what went on in the imaginations of the monks who slowly copied out Ovid's *Art of Love* or the comedies of Terence. To this question, the *accessus* gives only a partial answer. There still remains an element of mystery that one would perhaps do better to respect. All this work did at least help to keep alive a widespread appreciation for texts which represented so much work and expense. In those days, we must not forget, a manuscript meant a capital investment; a flock of sheep was needed to provide the parchment necessary for copying a book by Seneca or Cicero. And in order to procure the leather and skins required for binding the volumes, abbeys possessed either hunting permits for wild animals—deer, roebuck, boar—or owned the forests where game was to be found.[45] Even in spite of such costs, classical texts were among those that were chosen for purposes of study, and there is little doubt that they were studied because of their beauty. It was commonly agreed that they were the best models of Latin. Even though a whole Christian literature was in existence, still the monks did not content themselves with it, but went to the sources of classical culture.

ADMIRATION FOR AND DISTRUST OF
PAGAN LITERATURE

The results of this classical formation were numerous. The origin of this culture helps us learn the monk's opinion of the classics and what use they made of it. It would seem that in spite of their optimistic bias and the use of the allegorical method, most monks on becoming adult remained divided between a certain distrust of the classics and a sincere admiration for them. Distrust, because the works sometimes contained obscenities or perpetuated pagan mythology, and admiration for texts surrounded with so much prestige: the prestige enjoyed by everything ancient and the prestige of things discovered and loved in youth even if this had been won at the price of a hardy discipline. The temptation—and here asceticism was directly concerned—was that Virgil might outshine Holy Scripture in the monks' esteem because of the perfection of his style. There was the danger that the beauty of the imagery, ideas, human sentiments, and the words in which they were expressed might appear more brilliant than the wholly interior, supernatural, and spiritual charm of the Gospel. For this reason, several authors felt themselves obliged, as St. Jerome and St. Augustine had done, to make excuses for Holy Scripture's having been written in such a humble style; its beauty is entirely from within. Asceticism consisted in establishing a hierarchy, a balance between the sources of culture. This constituted for many a more or less constant problem of conscience that was, in varying degrees, difficult to resolve. This will explain somewhat the often contradictory statements on the subject of the classics which can be found in certain authors. They could the more easily speak ill at times of the classics since they had assimilated them in youth well enough to remember and quote them although they no longer read them. According to Bernard of Cluny's Customary, in the scriptorium where silence was the rule the monk who wanted to ask for a book written by a pagan author made the sign that indicated a book (open hands, palms upward), but in addition, touched a finger to his ear to imitate a dog scratching his ear, for, as the text says, a pagan may rightly be compared to a dog.[46] And yet, in the very same monastery of Cluny, a monk could receive for Lenten reading a work by Livy,[47] and in the abbey of Hirsau where the same sign had been adopted,[48] the schoolman Conrad taught his students to consider these authors with admiration.

Henry of Pomposa seems to have put into words and to have resolved, as many others may have done, the conflict over the classics which troubled the monastic soul. After having drawn up a long inventory of the manuscripts collected by his abbot Jerome, he sees in the latter's desire for books an indication of his whole inner attitude:

> Admirable clemency of God toward His own! It renders their faith so fervent that, famished, it feeds without ever becoming full; thirsty, it drinks and grows thirstier still. In the same way his desire to acquire books knew no bounds. . . .[49]

And since this desire extended even to pagan authors, the cataloguer answers the objection of those who might criticize him: why did he choose to "mingle divine truth and the pages of the Holy Books with pagan texts full of fables and errors? Answer must be made in the words of the Apostle: 'A great house, apart from plate of gold and silver, contains other objects made of wood and earthenware.'"[50] He acted in this manner so that each one, according to his zeal and merit, might have something to delight him and exercise his own intelligence. Does not truth itself say: "In the house of my Father, there are many mansions"?[51] There each will be happy insofar as he has attained sanctification. In like manner, pagan writings, if understood with pure intentions, are a source of edification. What other lesson do they teach than that worldly pomp is as nothing? As the Apostle says again: "We know that to them that love God, all things work together unto good."[52]

Next, we might consider what use they made of pagan literature. Its influence can be seen in every domain of monastic culture: in the monks' works of art, in their writings, and in their personalities.

Interest in Archaeology

Archaeology aroused in the monks the same fascination it held for all cultivated men:[53] the same pains were taken in the study of the artistic monuments of antiquity as in the grammatical analysis of classical literary texts. Their means for learning about ancient art were the same as those we use today: travel, excavations, museums—with this significant difference, that fewer masterpieces had as yet disappeared. They could undertake long journeys to go to see ruins which excited in them an admiration we find echoed by many chroniclers whose testimony is sometimes our only source of information about them. Pilgrims and curiosity-seekers, then as today, were attracted particularly to Rome and Italy, but they went as well to the towns of Provence and to any others where vestiges of Gallo-Roman architecture were to be found. Ravenna was much visited for its mosaics and the Crusades afforded to many the opportunity to see the monuments of Constantinople and Latin Syria and to hear them talked about. When digging foundations or while repairing a pavement, as soon as they discovered engraved stones, tombs, or ancient objects, they hastened to extricate them and decipher the inscriptions. Archaeologists rushed to examine everything at first hand; the learned, using whatever knowledge they had, did not hesitate to perform autopsies on skeletons that were brought to light to see if a trace of some wound would not enable them to identify a hero spoken of by Virgil. In the "treasuries" were kept collections of Greek vases, *stelae*, coins, ivories, intaglios, bas-reliefs, bronzes, and pottery. All that belonged to the past of Greece and Rome enjoyed the prestige which accompanies beauty and the memory of a civilization that was known to have been great.

They had no scruples about using all these works of art in the service of Christianity. St. Gregory the Great had advised the first missionary monks to England not to destroy pagan temples if they were well built but to convert them to use for the worship of the true God, and they continued this practice. From burial urns they made reliquaries; from sarcophagi, altars; emperors' statues could represent none other than the Saints; consuls became bishops; Livia became the Queen of Sheba, and winged victories were recognized as angels. They did not hesitate to incorporate into the iconographic themes supplied by Christian bestiaries, themselves stemming from the Bible, all those marvelous animals—centaurs, sirens, and satyrs—that were seen on ancient monuments and which at present are displayed on the capitals at Fleury, Vézelay and so many other abbey churches. Ancient fables and mythological scenes were sculpted on the columns of cloisters and particular emphasis has been placed on the

> peculiarity, even audacity, of portraying the gods of paganism within the cloister of an abbey, in the very place intended for the monks' meditation and last sleep; even sixteenth-century men themselves would not dare go so far.[54]

It is to an abbot, perhaps St. Hugh of Cluny, that Fulco of Beauvais addressed the poem he wrote when an ancient head was found at Meaux.[55] In connection with this, the remark was made that there is

> a contrast between the interest that these learned men took in the artistic productions of antiquity and the Christian spirit in which they applauded the destruction of temples and statues which aroused their ad-

miration. . . . Their aesthetic sense and religious conviction must have clashed upon occasion and the latter did not always win without a battle.[56]

INFLUENCE OF CLASSICAL TEXTS

The art of bookmaking itself is largely dependent on classical texts: Ovid's *Metamorphoses* inspired the decoration of certain manuscripts; in others the representation of animals owes much to the traditional bestiaries, to the *Physiologus* whose influence was so great, as for example in the Cistercian school. Animals, fantastic or real, painted exactly as described therein, are to be found in the manuscripts of St. Stephen Harding, that is to say, at the first Cîteaux, in those which St. Bernard had had ornamented toward the end of his life, and in many other later ones, and at every period.[57]

The influence of classical authors is even more manifest in the monks' writings. This influence was, in fact, exerted in a variety of ways. There are examples of conscious imitation: for instance, in the tenth century, the nun Hrotswitha composes poems after the manner of Terence—to divert, she says, her sisters from excessive reading of the real Terence;[58] still, the expressions she borrows from the comic author, even when taken out of the obscene context which they cannot fail to evoke, make her blush, as she admits.[59] Again in the tenth century, a monk of Micy, Letaldus, composes in Virgilian hexameters a delightful comic poem,[60] and certain chroniclers imitated Sallust.

There also exist cases of conscious quoting or conscious adaptation of classical texts. Many authors, like St. Bernard, occasionally, though infrequently, quote one or another ancient verse.[61] But there are many who make generous use of the classical writers. William of St. Denis, in his *Apologetic Dialogue*, takes his inspiration from *The Lives of the Caesars* of Suetonius and from many other texts.[62] Dom Wilmart found in this piece of thirty or so pages more than seventy borrowings from twenty-five different works by twelve classical authors. William of St. Thierry, not always citing a reference to his source, uses very freely a work he simply calls *Seneca noster*.[63] Aelred of Rievaulx, as is well known, makes a Christian adaptation of Cicero's *De Amicitia*.[64] Finally Thomas of Perseigne has no qualms at all about inserting in his commentary on the *Canticle* a number of citations of several verses each; in his preface he had already quoted Virgil three times and Ovid once.[65] A painstaking—and judicious —inventory of classical reminiscences ought to be made for all the authors as has been done for Rupert of Deutz.[66] Then the use each author made of the classics would be understood since, in this domain, there is an extraordinary variety. Some, like Suger, seem to handle quotations with ease; others, like Ordericus Vitalis, introduce them awkwardly like ready-made phrases learned in school.[67]

The most commonly found example is that of borrowing from the classical authors, without imitating or quoting precisely, expressions and procedures which are remembered by virtue of the phenomenon of reminiscence which an early education had made both possible and easy. Such classical echoes are found in abundance in some authors and less in others, but they are present in all, even in the most mystical like John of Fécamp and St. Bernard. These implicit and, no doubt, occasionally unconscious borrowings are of two kinds. Sometimes they are allusions, associations of words, rhythmical *clausulae* introduced so naturally in each author's individual style that they are not easily recognized; they are used and assimilated with a freedom and ease which make exact identification of the source uncertain. Sometimes the implicit borrowings are literary themes or devices, *loci communes, colores rhetorici* which, in the West, are part of the literary tradition of all time,[68] and are so often and so widely encountered. This must be taken seriously into account in reading the monastic authors of the Middle Ages. It should not be forgotten that almost anything can become a literary convention, such as protestations of the author's ignorance, disdain for literature, and the extolling of rustic simplicity.

INFLUENCE OF LITERARY THEMES

Not that their sincerity, ordinarily, should be called in question, but it is not always easy to distinguish in their declarations what is spontaneous from what is more or less constrained or imposed by the laws of style or literary form. They considered submission to the rules of art a form of loyalty: accepting the exigencies of art is one way of showing one's sincerity. The fact that St. Bernard gave the traditional panegyric form to the funeral eulogy of his brother Gerard[69] did not exclude sincerity any more than it had for St. Ambrose when his brother Satyrius died.[70] In both cases, the very intensity of the emotion they so truly felt demanded the more literary expression. The panegyric for Gerard by St. Bernard is a sermon on the Canticle, and the literary tradition gives us reason to think it was one of his most carefully prepared sermons. The abbot of Clairvaux put all his artistry into it because the writing of it was a work of love.[71]

With equal love and in similar style, Gilbert of Hoyland was to compose a panegyric for St. Aelred.[72] One of St. Bernard's few adversaries, Peter Berengarius, reproached him for choosing to imitate ancient models when he was composing his brother's eulogy, for quoting Socrates, Plato, Cicero, St. Jerome, and St. Ambrose.[73] And to be sure, St. Bernard did not disregard them. He demonstrated, in the way he used them, the freedom of a man of genius. But, although his intent was to express a real sorrow, a personal grief, he did not permit himself to deviate from a literary tradition which was, itself, also a reality.

Art (τέχνη) implies using means and instruments which are not those of nature in its perfect spontaneity. Today, we try very hard to hide the part played by artifice under the appearance of a sincerity which is sometimes extremely artificial. In the classical periods no one blushed over the pains taken for artistic device, which deceived neither the author nor his readers. For this reason, no doubt, no "diary" existed in ancient literature such as has appeared in our time: this literary form, in which one is supposed to be setting down, for oneself alone, intimate thoughts which would never be committed to writing if they were not intended to be read, would have been considered in those times lacking in sincerity. Literary fiction, on the contrary, was an artistic way to express the truth. It could do this all the better since it was often doing so unconsciously: the devices had become spontaneous. Certainly they had been studied, but during the writer's youth, and they were learned from contact with grammar and the classical authors. From then on, these devices could be used without too obvious a striving for effect. Moreover, every reader was prepared to accept them without undue surprise. The ancients acknowledged more readily than we that the "composition" of a work of art of any description includes a certain amount of fiction; St. Gregory had declared that to "dissemble" and to "compose" are synonyms.[74]

Feeling for Nature

This literary—and fictional, in the sense explained above—character of medieval writings, including those written by monks, becomes clearly apparent when we take as an illustration the "feeling for Nature." What we mean by this expression is, largely, lacking in medieval men. Apart from exceptions, they do not look at Nature itself to admire it as it is; they see it through literary reminiscences coming from the Bible, the Fathers, or classical authors. Texts confirming this can be found in John of Fécamp,[75] Peter the Venerable,[76] St. Bernard,[77] or Otto of Freising.[78]

Descriptions of the celestial Jerusalem furnish further proof.[79] When St. Bernard speaks of the "book of Nature"[80] and of all that can be learned "under the shade of the trees," he is not thinking of the beauty of the surroundings but of the labor that the preparation of a field necessitates, and of the prayer, reflection, and mortification furthered by work in the fields.[81]

Of course, these men admire nature; they praise the beauty of a spot which they sometimes say "delights" them. A founder of a monastery would choose a site because of its pleasantness: *loci iucunditas*; a hermit will prefer for his retreat "a beautiful forest." But their admiration is not aroused, as ours is, by the picturesque. The pleasurable aspect they appreciate is more moral than material: a beautiful forest is above all a forest suited to the solitary life; a "Beaulieu" is a place which has been made fertile.[82] And since eschatology never loses its rights, every garden where spiritual delights are found recalls Paradise and is described in the lush images which, in the Bible, depicted the garden of the Spouse or of the first Adam.[83] The cloister is a "true paradise," and the surrounding countryside shares in its dignity. Nature "in the raw," unembellished by work or art, inspires the learned man with a sort of horror: the abysses and peaks which we like to gaze at are to him an occasion of fear.[84] A wild spot, not hallowed by prayer and asceticism and not the scene of any spiritual life, is, as it were, in the state of original sin. But once it has become fertile and purposeful, it takes on the utmost significance. William of Malmesbury, comparing the land cultivated by the monks of Thorney with the untilled land that surrounded them, writes:

> In the middle of wild swampland where the trees are intertwined in an inextricable thicket, there is a plain with very green vegetation which attracts the eye by reason of its fertility; no obstacle impedes the walker. Not a particle of the soil is left to lie fallow; here the earth bears fruit trees, there grapevines cover the ground or are held on high trellises. In this place cultivation rivals nature; what the latter has forgotten the former brings forth. What can I say of the beauty of the buildings whose unshakable foundations have been built into the marshes? This incomparable solitude has been granted the monks so that they may grow more closely attached to the higher realities for being the more detached from those of mortal life. . . . Truly this isle is the home of chastity, the dwelling place of probity, the school of those who love Divine Wisdom. In short, this is an image of Paradise; it makes one think already of heaven.[85]

The remarks we find as to the behavior of animals and their habits denote occasionally a certain sense of observation.[86] Yet, here again, allegories from the bestiary are often superimposed on the things seen. In Nature, everything is symbolic. The symbols come either from biblical and patristic tradition or from classical tradition, but they all have moral overtones. This is particularly noticeable in the admirable Cistercian toponymy: the symbolic names of almost all the ancient monasteries evoke light, peace, and joy.[87] Place names which were sometimes originally only those of a river or of a landowner are transformed so as to express a spiritual reality: the "Mount of Angil" becomes the Mountain of Angels, *Mons angelorum*, Engelberg.[88] Moonlight is appreciated not because its effect on the scenery provokes admiration but because the moon symbolizes the highest mysteries.[89] Similarly, works like the *Hortus deliciarum*, or a curious treatise addressed to a prospective monk, *monachellus*, are used for teaching all the virtues through the imagery of the flowers that beautify a wholly spiritual garden.[90] The meaning of the flowers and fruits lies less in their beauty than in their organic composition and properties. No doubt few Western monks ever had any opportunity to see mandrake,[91] nard,[92] or pomegranate,[93] but the plants which they did see, they saw through descriptions given by the *auctores*.

LITERARY EXAGGERATION

Another outcome of the medieval monks' classical formation is what might be called literary exaggeration. It accounts for much in the ancients' works and is quite in keeping since these men are, so to speak, "learned primitives." As primitives—and the word in this context has no pejorative connotation—they think one thing at a time, experience one feeling at a time, but they think and feel intensely. They have little in common with those complex individuals whose every psychological reaction interferes immediately with another which tempers and modifies it. Men of God like St. Bernard and Peter the Venerable can, within a few days, express in their letters completely different feelings: the warmest affection and the liveliest, even the most violent, indignation. Each time they are really expressing what they feel about a particular matter. They can do so without contradicting themselves, without their general attitude toward the particular correspondent having changed. It has often been pointed out that during the Crusades the same men who, in the morning, gave full rein to unbridled brutality would, in the evening, follow a procession inspired by true repentance, piety, and the fervent love of God.[94] These contrasts are seen in all aspects of secular life in the Middle Ages.[95] But, in due proportion, neither are they absent from the lives of clerics and monks.[96] Even the most refined and best trained in the control of their instincts retain to some degree this simplicity which lends their inner attitudes a quality that is direct and absolute: on every occasion their soul expresses itself whole and undivided.

They are, at the same time, men of letters and speak as such; to the expression of reactions which in themselves are simple, they devote their talent, their entire classical culture, all their biblical imagination, and the whole vocabulary given to them by the Prophets and the Apocalypse. Thus armed, they cannot resist the joy of writing a fine page, of inventing elegant turns of expression. This explains, for example, the tone of St. Bernard's famous letter to his cousin Robert, of which no one would take all its assertions literally. In some cases, as for instance St. Bernard's invectives in his sermons and treatises against the luxury of prelates, a comparison between them and more precise statements found in the same Bernard's epistles warrants the conclusion that the violence and universality of his reproaches do not correspond to the actual situation.[97] What they do betray is nothing more than burning zeal for Church reform which devours Bernard. An allowance for exaggeration is equally important for understanding St. Peter Damian. The holiest are the ones who exaggerate the most because their zeal is the most ardent (one might dare say the "most violent" in the sense used in the Gospel which says that the violent take the kingdom of God by storm).

In St. Bernard's *Apology*, the Cluniac meals are described with obvious irony. The monk is seen struggling with so many different courses that he must do battle to get the better of them; the combat ends finally because no more adversaries are left, and the monk, worn-out, falls on his bed to do his digesting.[98] This is a real masterpiece of satire, and it makes one think of the Epistle by Horace which, in turn, was to inspire Boileau.

The picture Peter the Venerable drew of the meat-loving Cluniacs is in the same vein. Writing to the priors of the Order to inculcate in them the love of abstinence, he compares the monks to predatory animals, bears and wolves who fling themselves on the carcass of an animal.[99] Literary exaggerations or powerful images illustrate the facts presented, and fiction serves to express an idea that is true. The ancients knew how to discover, under these picturesque and more or less fictitious details, the idea that really matters. Furthermore, in an exchange of correspondence on the subject of their respective observances. St. Bernard and Peter the Venerable agree on the facts but not on the details of expression. They exaggerate as much in praising as in blaming. Peter the Venerable himself justified what was excessive in the praises he bestowed: they served an end which was to give pleasure, to express the intensity of his friendship, and to perform an act of charity.[100] Literary exaggeration is, therefore, only a means, but it is a legitimate means. Exaggerating is not, in such cases, lying; it is using hyperbole to make what one wants to say more unmistakable.

However, since monastic writers are spiritual men, and in so much as they are detached from literature for its own sake, their use of exaggeration is correspondingly less conspicuous. At the very most the art of writing for them consists of a good knowledge of grammar and the acceptance of its demands to which they submit without attaching undue importance to it. In brief, they remain free, supremely free—and this is true of the greatest of them. Literature should not be discounted, but still it is not the ultimate explanation. With these men of God, a liking for invective, or their declarations of admiration or affection, are in proportion to their fervor. They are commensurate with their indignation with regard to sin, and their enthusiasm for God's work. A much more important role than that assigned to grammar is reserved for the desire for God.

Monastic Humanism

One might legitimately suggest that we might admit that the medieval monks were indebted to their classical formation for artistic themes and literary reminiscences and methods, but, in reality, was not all that merely an arsenal of images and quotations which could serve as embellishments, confirmations, and modes of expression but which made no profound impression on their own souls? Or, did familiarity with the classics indeed deeply influence the psychology and the personality of the medieval monks? This problem is none other than the problem of the monks' humanism. It is a very delicate one and must first be properly formulated. The question in reality is: do the monks owe to classical tradition values which are specifically human, with the power to enrich, not only their style and intellectual capital, but also their very being?

This question may be answered if we are permitted to make a distinction. If humanism consists in studying the classics for their own sake, in focusing interest on the type of ancient humanity whose message they transmit, then the medieval monks are not humanists. But if humanism is the study of the classics for the reader's personal good, to enable him to enrich his personality, the monks are in the fullest sense humanists. As has been said, they had in view a useful and personal end: their education. And what, in fact, did they get from the classics? They took the best these authors had to give. Through contact with them, like all who study the humanities in any period, they developed and refined their own human faculties. To begin with, they owed to the classics a certain appreciation of the beautiful; this can be seen in the choice the monks made of texts to be preserved and in the quality of the texts they wrote under this influence. In fact, the relative numbers of manuscripts in the libraries show what criterion was used in assessing the authors and the reason why they were read and used. This criterion is their beauty itself. It is because of this taste for the beautiful that Virgil or, depending on the period, Ovid and Horace were preferred to minor writers. The medieval monks were neither antiquarians nor bibliophiles, theirs was in no sense a collector's mentality; they were looking for the useful. They were not pedants, nor were they aesthetes, but they did live intensely. On the one hand, the liturgy developed their feeling for beauty; on the other, asceticism and the cloistered life forbade the pleasures of the senses either crude or refined. Consequently they delighted in beautiful language and beautiful poetry. Certainly they never kept any text which had not charmed them with its beauty. If they read and copied Ovid, for example, it was because his poetry is admirable. At times they drew moral lessons from these authors, but they were not, thanks be to God, reduced to looking to them for that. Their desire was for the joys of the spirit, and they neglected none that these authors had to offer. So, if they transcribed classical texts it is simply because they loved them. They loved the authors of the past, not simply because they belonged to the past but because they were beautiful, with a beauty which defies time. Their culture has always been timeless—and it is for that reason that it was effectual.

This familiarity with well chosen models explains the monks' intense need for literary expression, and this has been demonstrated in numerous works. No doubt these texts are uneven in quality; still, they are more numerous than is supposed and several remain to be published. Some second-rank authors have left us their names, which no longer have any meaning for us; other writings are anonymous. All these texts imply the existence of teachers, a tradition, and an educated public capable of appreciating them and for which they were copied. They reveal the average cultural level of the monastic milieux.

Monastic Verse

This feeling for literary expression explains, in particular, a certain need to rhyme or versify which is evident in every period and environment. In the ninth century, Paul the Deacon used the lyrical form to refute this imputation: "The Muses flee the austere life and refuse to dwell within cloisters."[101] However, in the cloister there was always a love for celebrating in verse the cloistered life and the Christian mystery. St. Odo of Cluny, to enhance the dignity of the monastic ideal, wrote a long poem of 5,600 Virgilian hexameters.[102] An anonymous Englishman, defending Benedictine tradition against attacks by Master Thibaut of Étampes, adds to his prose answer an invective in verse form.[103] Others paraphrased in verse the whole Bible,[104] or certain of its books.[105] Or again they would sing in verse the memory of their dead brethren,[106] or the ordinary occurrences of their own lives; in line with this practice at the abbey of Hautmont in Hainaut, every copyist would add to the manuscript he had just completed at least one poem in which he described the circumstances under which he had worked.[107] These poems, often animated by genuine lyricism, sometimes contain very fine lines.

This need to rhyme showed itself, as it had elsewhere, at Cîteaux. Toward the end of the twelfth century, a general chapter forbade yielding to this impulse.[108] Still, Thomas of Froidmont was to relate in verse the life of Margaret of Jerusalem; it is true he prefaces it with a long prose prologue in which he explains why only the prologue is in prose.[109] And at the beginning of the thirteenth century, one of the Clairvaux monks, Itier of Vassy, was to compose on the monk's life and the vanity of versification a long piece in verse.[110]

Neither metrics nor verses bring health to the soul.
True restorers are piety, tears, and good works.
Monks chant the psalms: let others make rhymes.
The monk's heart is reserved for the praise of his God.
He abandons poetry to think on Christ's glory;
In his words and his deeds let him honor the Lord!
It is not eloquence that joins one to heavenly beings.
Polished words do not lead to the highest of joys.
These are reached by meritorious actions.
Cast far from you the flowers and the charms of worldly literature. . . .
Its favors can only be displeasing to the seeker for perfection. . . .
If you wish to be of avail, give to the monks a good example,
And do not try to win them by literary embellishments.
The religious life is of greater value than any literature.
If I were myself a true monk, I should weep tears for my sins.
To weep is fitting for a monk, the writing of poetry is not.

MONASTIC HUMOR

A psychological trait for which the monks seem indebted to classical literature is a certain sense of humor. The other sources of their culture are full of gravity and explain the monks' profound seriousness. But literature explains perhaps, at least in part, the pleasing, occasionally ironic way in which they sometimes expressed their thoughts. This humor often appears in monastic works of art. An example of this, to cite only one, may be taken from the Cistercian school. As in the Cluniac and other Benedictine manuscripts, we find in those of Cîteaux, from its origins and down through every period, bizarre chimeras. Now, these fanciful beasts are not only not indispensable in Bibles or liturgical books, but not all of them possess an edifying or symbolic meaning. Very evidently the illuminator's intention in showing these animals devouring each others' tails was to amuse. Since the Statutes forbade the possession of cranes which "incite to vanity,"[111] they were pictured in the initials of the texts.[112] These innocent designs represent an allowance made for fantasy in a life whose austerity did not exclude poetry and the play of the imagination. Humor is characteristic of the spiritual man; it supposes detachment, levity—in the Gregorian sense of the word—joy, and the easy sally.

This same humor appears in many literary productions. In the ninth century the "gently satirical" poems of Paul the Deacon give an idea of the recreations in monastic schools.[113] In the tenth century Letaldus, in a real "literary man's whimsy," endows little people of no importance with epic attitudes and this accompanied by a whole play of classical reminiscences borrowed in the main from Virgil but also from Ovid, Lucan, Statius, and Claudian.[114] St. Bernard could be amusing when, in his intimate and daily preaching, he would invent stories and parables[115] like the one in which he compares the monk to a merchant. His listeners were aware that his words had this delightful quality: *Quam jucunde!*[116] Nor was he averse to using irony in his published works, even in the most sober ones, like the *De Consideratione* he wrote toward the end of his life and addressed to the pope; the pictures he sketches of the highest ranking prelates are no doubt more amusing than true to life. Earlier, in his first treatise, *On the Degrees of Humility*, the twelve portraits, which make up the second part, after the manner of Theophrastus, are full of good sense and the droll things seen by a man who has a knack for observation. An astonishing verve makes them very living portraits. Galland of Rigny dedicated to St. Bernard his curious works, the *Book of Proverbs* and the *Book of Parables*, wherein the most elevated principles are set forth good-naturedly in an often piquant style.[117] Burchard of Bellevaux, a friend of St. Bernard, wrote in an amusing and edifying tone a long *Apology for Beards*. In it his biblical imagination is allowed full play. In this "barbilogy" as he calls it, he defines in two different places the correct way to laugh: the joyous laugh, *cum jucunditate*, which does honor to wisdom because it originates in the enthusiasm aroused by wisdom, differing from vain laughter, *cum jocositate*, which engenders nothing but foolishness.[118] It finds everything an occasion for joyous thought, *jucunda consideratio*; thus the chapter *On the difference between the razor and tweezers taken in the moral sense* is a good-humored exhortation to the renunciation taught by the Lord and the Apostles: to forsake the world, poor in spirit and in goods, and detached from all that is superfluous.[119] Many obscure monks and modest writers spoke in this vein of the realities of their religious life, with a charm which in no way diminished the seriousness of their lives and their teachings. A certain anonymous, probably Cistercian, epigram is, in its own way, a masterpiece of conciseness and cheerful gravity. Five lines suffice to express the four characters' opinions of the monk who falls asleep during the night office:

The abbot says: My son, bow your head at the *Gloria Patri*.

The Devil says: He will not bow before he has broken his fetters.

The abbot continues: Lord, so that this lamb shall not perish, deliver him from his bonds and from his enemy.

God declares: I free the captive, it is up to you to chastise the negligent.

The monk concludes: Sooner would I have my head cut off than fall asleep again.[120]

The Classics: A Source of Wisdom

Finally, the medieval monks could not come into contact with classical tradition without profiting from its accumulation of wisdom and truth. They found in it quantities of verses and sayings—from which they made proverbs—in which the ancients had condensed human experience, and some of those were very salutary.[121] They came upon examples of true greatness and were not afraid to find inspiration in them, once they had transposed them—they did so spontaneously—to the plane of Christian virtue.

In order to defend the ideal life as described by St. Benedict, a Cluniac quotes Phaedrus, Terence, Plautus, Statius, Virgil, Juvenal, Persius, Cicero, and the historian Josephus. Recollections from the satires and comedies are blended in his writings as they are in his mind with those coming from the desert Fathers, St. Basil, St. Jerome, St. Ephrem, St. Gregory, and Cassian.[122] Does not this imply that he not only loved the beauty of the classical texts but also thought highly of their content?

Another delightful example of the same attitude is found in the *Dialogue* of William of St. Denis.[123] Suger had been a man of very strong personality, and it was difficult to replace him as head of his monastery, or even simply to be his successor. At his death, the monks of St. Denis almost unanimously elected Odo of Deuil as abbot. Shortly after, they found themselves thinking he did not possess all the qualities Suger had accustomed them to expect, and some of them complained. The monk William had been Suger's confidant and secretary. When he learned of the criticisms leveled at the incumbent, he undertook to avenge him against his detractors. This he did very subtly in the form of a long dialogue. In a conversation carried on between a fictitious character named Geoffrey and himself, William assumes the distasteful role of the accuser. The account of himself being convinced he had been wrong and should change his opinion affords him an opportunity to exercise humility. This device also enables him to avoid giving to another the unpleasant task of denouncing the administrative errors of the abbot of the monastery. William himself intimates these accusations with great frankness and, at the same time, with exquisite delicacy he exploits, for the rehabilitation of his superior, all the resources of ancient wisdom, and of the spirit of the Gospel.

Along with quotations from Holy Scripture, St. Benedict's *Rule*, the liturgy, and the Fathers, he employs others from classical authors: philosophers like Plato, Socrates, Cicero, and particularly Seneca, whose letters and different treatises are widely utilized; or historians like Valerius Maximus, Justin, and, oddly, Suetonius, whose Lives of the Emperors Augustus, Tiberius, Domitian, and Vespasian provide ideas on government and examples of personal virtue. This moral lesson is embellished throughout by aids enlisted from the poets: Horace, Macrobius, Terence, Lucan, and especially Ovid, and this is done without the slightest pedantry. William makes no display of his erudition, which is vast, and, like so many other writers of his time, he gives scarcely any references. He does not quote to show off what he knows; it is enough for him if what he is saying is true and is well put. It is to the secular authors of classical antiquity that he owes a practical philosophy full of good sense and Stoic in derivation: the principal lesson he teaches is that of disregard for riches. The two monks of the *Dialogue* converse on the subject of the search for the "happy life" just as had so many Greek and Roman sages. This "felicity" resides in contemplation. Solitude and silence had been prescribed by Seneca and Cicero as requisite for peace of soul and for the joy of understanding. This conception, far from contradicting, coincides with the ascetic prescriptions inherited from monastic tradition. William here extols studious leisure in terms taken from Cicero and Seneca but to which a Christian or a monk could not fail to subscribe. Happiness is also the reward of constancy in adversity and opposition. In this light, the criticisms Odo of Deuil is undergoing become supremely valuable: they provide the opportunity to practice those virtues for which we can find so many examples in the lives of the men of antiquity. William refers to the patience and resolution of Cato and the clemency of Caesar. Augustus, the godlike Titus, and the other Roman emperors are proposed to an abbot as model executives. Antiquity is endowed with a prestige which William makes no attempt to disguise; the examples it furnishes are the ones he most admires. The human virtues it offers for our consideration edify him. How much he loves natural virtues! Truly, he is incapable of reading Suetonius with indifference, and this spiritual reading always does him good. The deeds and sayings of Vespasian are particularly admirable. Demetrius, Cato, and Attalus the Stoic abound in excellent advice. Agreeing with Seneca but not with Horace, William undertakes the defense of Epicurus as not being the sensualist he was sometimes claimed to be. The wars of Xerxes aid in the understanding of the wars of Louis IV of France, and the election of an Indian king, as related by Pliny, is the ideal model for the election of an abbot.

All of this culture is used to further aims dictated by a compelling charity. William loves his abbot and understands how to secure appreciation for his deeds and his administration. Without any painful sermonizing, he preaches wittily, in a style that is lively and pleasing. He excuses Odo's faults, but first he begins by enumerating them, and he does not hesitate to recall the complaints lodged against him. We must admit that in a text addressed to Odo himself this course of action presupposes genuine humility on the part of both the author and the person addressed. The freedom of language enjoyed by these virtuous and discriminating men was so great that they could say anything to each other, providing it was done with taste. The only requirement was that it be done for each other's benefit. And, to ensure this, each one took his material wherever he found it. In the secular authors, William discovered good counsel and examples to imitate, and he shares them with his reader. But neither did he reject the treasures of Christian tradition: quite the contrary. He is familiar with the Bible, and what a thorough knowledge he has of it! The ethics he describes is very much more elevated than that of the Stoics. Adversity, for the Christian, is not merely an occasion for affirming his personality, for overcoming his craving for revenge, for being greater than the enemies who criticize us; it is an opportunity to imitate Jesus Christ and, in imitation of the saints, all of whom were persecuted, to participate in the merits of the Passion and contribute efficaciously to the salvation of this world. William here recalls in moving words the calumnies of which Christ was the butt, and the crimes which were only recently attributed to St. Bernard and to Suger. If he speaks of the "fortune" which has favored Odo in all his enterprises from the beginning of his abbacy, he knows its real name is Providence, and that the "felicity" he praises in his abbot which is on a par with his religious zeal is a grace and an effect of divine protection.

In this continuous passing from the secular vocabulary, which William had assimilated, to the vocabulary of Scripture, there is no artificiality or affectation. These borrowings from antiquity are not just pedantic display. They are not merely echoes or literary modes of expression. William of St. Denis admires the ancients' ways of thinking and living. Could the humanism of a monk be pushed further than this imitation of pagan virtues?

Did the men of letters of the sixteenth-century Renaissance often practice to the same degree this type of fidelity to their models? All that is beautiful, true, and good in humanity's past should be put at the service of the lives of the members of the Church. To allow the pagans in this way to bring beauty into our lives and to render us service, is that not a way of giving them a means for survival in us in the light of Christ?

INTEGRAL HUMANISM

For Christians, integral humanism consists in increasing in man the influence of Him who alone is "perfect Man," the Christ, the Son of God who is to return in His glory. This eschatological humanism does not exclude the historical humanism which seeks in the writings of the past lessons capable of contributing to man's harmonious development. The medieval monks have proved that the two can be reconciled.[124]

THE MONASTIC STYLE

As the time comes for drawing conclusions as to the sources of monastic culture, it is important not to neglect certain nuances in the interests of brevity. The influence of the classical tradition on the monastic culture of the Middle Ages should be neither minimized nor unduly exaggerated. Nothing must be oversimplified or excessively generalized. At every period, from the eighth to the twelfth century, the monks received the education given children in the schools of their times. And almost everywhere and almost always, it was based largely on classical culture. The monks were not obliged either to reject or to further this culture. They assimilated it in different ways, but in every milieu they welcomed it. Consequently, it would be a distortion of history to draw a distinction between a "monasticism of worship" (*Kultmönchtum*) supposedly that of Cluny, Fleury, and other French monasteries and a "monasticism of culture" (*Kulturmönchtum*) presumably that of the countries of the Empire, on the pretext that, from the eleventh century on, Cluny chose not to have in the monastery itself any other school but one for the formation of its own monks.[125] But there is no need to insist here on the weakness of such misconceptions.[126]

In order to avoid attributing to classical sources either too great or too small an influence as a component of monastic culture, we must situate them in their relative position among all of the sources which nourish this culture. They are not the only or the most important component, but they are a very real one nonetheless, and, in conjunction with the others, they contributed to the development of a homogeneous culture.[127] Its foundation was Christian, it was based on Holy Scripture, and this was apparent in the domain of thought and imagination as well as in verbal expression. Monastic language is, first of all, a biblical language, fashioned entirely by the Vulgate. Monastic culture was also based on patristics, as is revealed in the topics for reflection, in the allegorical method of exegesis, in the vocabulary and even more so in the general "style" of literary works. But this fundamentally Christian culture avails itself, in the realm of expression as well as in the realm of the inner life, of antiquity's human experiences—but only of the most beautiful, or of those which it took it upon itself to embellish. From this blend of various influences was born an original culture which was neither purely and simply the culture of the patristic age nor a neo-classical culture after the manner of certain humanists of the fifteenth and sixteenth centuries. The relative proportions of its component elements varied with the environment and the individuals concerned. But, on the whole, this blending confers on monastic culture its own particular quality which grows more and more marked as the twelfth century approaches. Just as ancient monasticism gave birth to a vocabulary and a language,[128] so, in turn, does medieval monasticism;

and insofar as it remains faithful to ancient monasticism, it preserves its language. But it enriches it with elements which come from classical tradition; the latter continues to enter more and more fully into the fabric woven by the Bible and the Fathers, and all these threads are inextricably interwoven in the new sensibility of medieval men. This results in a continuously increasing variety of patterns worked on a changeless background, whose color is monasticism's own. The Carolingian period had been rather a bookish return to ancient sources; in the eleventh and twelfth centuries culture becomes increasingly personal and creative, producing original work without losing the Carolingian legacy: it too had been assimilated in its turn.

This culture, however, does remain profoundly impregnated by literature. It is more literary than speculative. This characteristic differentiates monastic humanism from another, different but no less legitimate, known as scholastic humanism.[129] In the schools, one of the seven liberal arts, dialectics, tends to take precedence over the others to the detriment of grammar, music, and rhetoric; clarity of thought was more sought after than artistry in expression, and this preoccupation is reflected in a language which, by contrast, allows us all the better to appreciate the nature of a non-scholastic language, that of monasticism. Stripped of ornamentation and abstract, the scholastic language accepts words originating in a sort of unaesthetic jargon, provided only that they be specific. Under these conditions, as has been observed, "the language of orators and poets gives place to that of metaphysicians and logicians. . . . Certain pages of Abailard might have come from the facile pen of one of our classic rationalists, when compared with the warm but very carefully formed effusions of St. Bernard."[130] Instead of assimilating the inheritance from tradition as the monks do, and turning spontaneously toward the past, scholastic milieux are oriented toward the investigation of new problems and the search for new solutions. Clarity, rather than experience or mystery, is their concern, and it is attained through the "distinctions." No doubt the monks have no monopoly on grammar, any more than the scholastics have on dialectics; but in the two different milieux the accent falls on different disciplines.

On the other hand, through all it owes to sources which are properly Christian—biblical and patristic—monastic culture differs from still another contemporary form of humanism: the humanism of purely literary writers like Hildebert, Marbod, Peter of Blois, worldly clerics, to say nothing of the Goliards.[131] These stylists easily become precious. Their linguistic artifices very often are not placed at the service of any spiritual message or

Christian instruction. However, they also occasionally produce master-pieces. One of the best representatives of this classic humanism is John of Salisbury, so full of Petronius and Horace—to whom "he refers constantly"[132]—and other secular authors. Belonging neither to scholasticism nor to monasticism, this observer who had friends in both milieux saw their distinguishing traits very clearly, and he was able to keep his affection for St. Bernard as well as for Gilbert of la Porrée.[133] His letters were not widely disseminated; there are very few manuscripts of them in existence. They are, however, very beautiful, as are other writings of the same type.[134]

Monastic style keeps equally distant from the clear but graceless style of the scholastic *quaestiones* and the neo-classic style of these humanists. St. Bernard was able to achieve with perfection the synthesis of all the elements transmitted by the cultural tradition of the West while still according predominance to the Christian content.[135] The same conclusion is reached after a thorough analysis of the style of Ordericus Vitalis.[136] In this sense, one can rightly speak, with regard to the most representative types of monastic culture—a John of Fécamp, an Ordericus Vitalis, a St. Bernard, and still others—of a "monastic style." The literary heritage of all of antiquity, secular and patristic, can be found in it, yet less under the form of imitation or reminiscences of ancient authors than in a certain resonance which discloses a familiarity, acquired by long association, with their literary practices. Much of the wealth of classical tradition had been handed down, already assimilated, in the writings of the Fathers. Let us reflect, for example, on all that the *De officiis* of St. Ambrose or St. Jerome's letters owed to Cicero. This was both a way of thinking and a way of expressing oneself. Thus the *lectio divina* complemented harmoniously the grammar that was learned in school. And when the monks wrote, their literary technique showed no "bookish" traits. Their imitation of literary models became spontaneous, and, for that very reason, often scarcely discernible. Under these conditions, grammar was no obstacle to the longing for heaven; literature was not a screen between the soul and its God, but rather, it was transcended. The purpose of liberal studies had been attained. The most dangerous author had been "converted," and in the very mind of the student of literature. Learned once and then forgotten, perhaps even denied, they remained present in the deepest recesses of the soul. The monastic humanists are not like those of the Renaissance,[137] torn between two cultures. They are not partially pagan. They are wholly Christian, and in that sense are in possession of the *sancta simplicitas*.

NOTES

1. A number of facts have been gathered with a fine bibliography by P. Schmitz, *Histoire de l'Ordre de S. Benoît*, II (Maredsous, 1942) 52–203. E. de Bruyne, *Études d'esthétique médiévale*, 3 vols. (Bruges, 1946) is equally rich in ideas on many of the problems to be treated here.

2. MGH, *Epist.* VI 39, quoting *Aeneid* 4.657. The index of sources in the MGH edition of the poems and letters of Alcuin shows how frequently he made use of Virgilian echoes.

3. *Sup. Cant.* 36.3 (PL 183.968) quotes Persius, *Saturae* 1.27.

4. Dom J. Perez de Urbel, *Historia de la Orden benedictina* (Madrid, 1941), p. 145.

5. E. Gilson, *The Mystical Theology of St. Bernard* (New York, 1940), p. 63: "These Cistercians have renounced everything save the art of good writing; each and all of these hardy ascetics carried in his bosom a humanist who by no means wanted to die."

6. *"On teaching Grammar to boys.* Let no boy be taught grammar within the monastery or on the property of the monstery unless he is a monk or has been received into probation as a novice; they may be so occupied during the time assigned for reading. It is further to be noted that we are not permitted to receive any boys into probation before their fifteenth birthday." *Super instituta generalis capituli apud Cistercium* XLI, ed. C. Noschitzka, *Anal. S. Ord. Cist.* (1950) 37.

7. E. R. Curtius, *European Literature and the Latin Middle Ages* (trans. W. R. Trask; New York, 1953), p. 53*n*54.

8. L. Traube, *Vorlesungen und Abhandlungen*, II (Munich, 1911) 113.

9. P. Renucci, *L'aventure et l'humanisme Européen au moyen âge, IVe–XIVe siècle* (Clermont-Ferrand, 1953), p. 114*n*147.

10. M. Inguanez–H. M. Willard, *Alberici Casinensis Flores rhetorici* (Monte Cassino, 1938), p. 14.

11. Edwin A. Quain, s.j., "The Medieval *Accessus ad auctores,*" *Traditio* 3 (1945) 215–64.

12. R. B. C. Huygens, *Accessus ad Auctores* (Collection Latomus XV, 1954).

13. R. B. C. Huygens, *Conrad de Hirsau: Dialogus super Auctores* (Collection Latomus XVII, 1955)

14. See *supra*, at n. 6.

15. Curtius (n. 7), p. 40.

16. On the theme of *Spoliatio Aegyptiorum* and its sources, cf. Quain (n. 11), 223–24. Another theme used in the same sense is that of the *Captiva gentilis* (cf. Ch. 3, n. 51 *supra*). On the sources of both, J. de Ghellinck, *Le mouvement théologique du XIIe siècle*, pp. 94–95.

17. Ed. Huygens, p. 25.

18. Ibid. 27.

19. Ibid., p. 29. J. Engels, *Études sur l'Ovide moralisé* (Groningen, 1945), studied the texts of the thirteenth and fourteenth centuries but he gives (pp. 65–81) an ample bibliography on Ovid in the Middle Ages.

20. "Ad ultimum ponit fidem suam, tractans egregissime de incarnatione Iesu Christi, et de passione, de resurrectione, de ascensione, et de vita B. Mariae Virginis et de assumptione eius," in a medieval preface quoted by Quain, 222–23. On the

De vetula of pseudo-Ovid, cf. P. Lehmann, *Pseudo-antike Literatur des Mittelalters* (Berlin–Leipzig, 1927), pp. 13ff.

21. Quoted, with other examples, by F. J. E. Raby, "Some Notes on Virgil, mainly in English authors," *Studi Medievali* (1932) 368ff.

22. Cf. M.-D. Chenu, "Horace chez les théologiens," *Rev. des sc. philos. et théol.* (1935) 462–65, and H. Silvestre, "Les citations et réminiscences classiques dans l'œuvre de Rupert de Deutz," RHE (1950) 172–73.

23. *Dialogus super auctores* (ed. Huygens), p. 39.

24. Ibid., p. 45.

25. Ibid., p. 47.

26. Ibid., p. 49.

27. Ibid., p. 51.

28. Ibid., p. 53.

29. Ibid., p. 54.

30. Ibid., p. 55.

31. Ibid., p. 58.

32. Ibid., p. 59.

33. Ibid., p. 65.

34. We get an idea of these glosses in the manuscripts of Virgil as reproduced by E. A. Lowe, "Virgil in South Italy: Fascimiles of Eight Manuscripts of Virgil in Beneventan Script," *Studi Medievali* (1932) 43–51.

35. "When we clarify the meaning of one word by another word, it is called 'glosa' in Greek, 'lingua' in Latin" (ed. Huygens), p. 19. This definition is developed and illustrated by some examples: "Le *de grammatica* de Hugues de Saint Victor," *Arch. d'hist. doctr. et litt. du moyen âge*, 14 (1943–45) 299.

36. Texts are found in TLL, *s.v.* "*declinare.*" H. I. Marrou, *History of Education in Antiquity*, p. 276.

37. *Epist.* 64, *S. Anselmi opera* (ed. F. S. Schmitt; 1946) III 180–81.

38. *Life of Suger* by William of St. Denis, PL 136.1194. *Suger: comment fut construit Saint-Denis* (Paris, 1945).

39. The text is found in C. Gaspar–F. Lyna, *Les principaux mss. à peinture de la bibliothèque royale de Belgique* (Paris, 1937) II 67.

40. *Institutiones* I 30 (ed. Jones, 133).

41. "It is more meritorious to copy books than to tend the vines." MGH, *PLAC* I 320. Cf. F. Milkau, *Handbuch der Bibliothekswissenschaft* (Wiesbaden, 1955) III 1.355.

42. *Epist.* I 20 (PL 189.98) where this theme is developed. The full text is quoted in *Pierre le vénérable*, p. 268.

43. "Deux traités sur la formation des jeunes moines," *Revue d'ascétique et de mystique* 33 (1957) 397–99.

44. Ed. A. de Poorter, *Catalogue des mss. de la Bibl. publ. de la Ville de Bruges* (Gembloux–Paris, 1934), p. 10. A text of Guiges the Carthusian is quoted by L. Gougaud, "Muta praedicatio," RB (1930) 170. Cf. also Matthew of Rievaulx in RB (1940) 78.

45. B. van Regemorter, "La reliure des manuscrits à Clairmarais aux xiie et xiiie siècles," *Scriptorium* 5 (1951) 99–100. Cf. J. W. Clark, *The Care of Books* (Cambridge, 1901).

46. "If he wants a school book written by a pagan, he should make the usual sign

for a book [palms open before him] and then he should touch his ear with a finger, just as a dog scratches with his foot, since the infidel may well be compared to an animal." *Ordo Cluniacensis per Bernardum* I 27, ed. Herrgott, *Vetus disciplina monastica* (Paris, 1726), p. 172.

47. A. Wilmart, "Le couvent et la bibliothèque de Cluny vers le milieu du xie s.," *Revue Mabillon* (1921) 94n54.

48. *S. Wilhelmi Constitutiones Hirsaugiensis* I 21 (ed. Herrgott [n. 46] 397). Cf. G. van Rijnberk, *Le langage par signes chez les moines* (Amsterdam, 1954), p. 84. Even Paul the Deacon, who made copious use of the pagan poets in his own verse, could write of them: "Potius sed istos conparabo canibus" (MGH, *PLAC* I 49).

49. Ed. G. Mercati, *Opere minori* I 388.

50. 2 Tim. 2.20.

51. John 14.2.

52. Romans 8.28.

53. A number of facts have been assembled on this point by J. Adhémar, *Les influences antiques dans l'art du moyen âge français* (London, 1937). J. B. Ross, "A Study of Twelfth-century Interest in the Antiquities of Rome," *Medieval and Historiographical Essays in Honor of J. W. Thompson* (Chicago, 1938), pp. 302–21, has shown that the interest in the ancient ruins was closely allied to the interest in literary texts.

54. Adhémar (n. 53), p. 265.

55. A. Boutemy–F. Vercauteren, "Foulcoie de Beauvais et l'intérêt pour l'archéologie antique au xie et au xiie siècle," *Latomus* (1937) 173–86.

56. Ibid. 186n3.

57. "Les peintures de la Bible de Morimondo," *Scriptorium* 10 (1956) 22–26. J. Morson, "The English Cistercians and the Bestiary," *Bulletin of the John Rylands Library* (1956) 146–70.

58. *Hrotsvithae Opera*, Liber II *Praefatio* (ed. Strecker; Leipzig, 1930), p. 113. Cf. E. Franceschini, *Rotsvita di Gandersheim* (Milan, 1944).

59. Ibid. Cf. E. Franceschini, "Il teatro post-carolingio," *I problemi comuni dell' Europa post-carolingia* (Spoleto, 1955), p. 306.

60. J. P. Bonnes, "Un lettré du xe siècle: Introduction au poème de Létald," *Revue Mabillon* (1943) 23–47.

61. While we wait for someone to do a complete study of the classical quotations and reminiscences in St. Bernard, it would be well to consider the judicious remarks of E. Franceschini in *Aevum* (1954) 572–73 in his review of *Bernard de Clairvaux* (Paris, 1953).

62. A. Wilmart, "Le dialogue apologétique du moine Guillaume, biographe de Suger," *Revue Mabillon* (1924) 80–118.

63. J. M. Dechanet, "Seneca noster: Des lettres à Lucilius à la Lettre aux frères du Mont-Dieu," *Mélanges J. de Ghellinck* (Gembloux, 1951), pp. 753–66.

64. P. Delhaye, "Deux adaptations du *De Amicitia* de Cicéron au xiie siècle, RTAM (1948) 304–31.

65. PL 206.17. As to its authenticity, cf. "Les deux compilations de Thomas de Perseigne," *Mediaeval Studies* (1948) 204–209; the poets most frequently quoted (listed, 206) are Ovid, Lucan, Homer, and Juvenal. The sources have been studied by B. Griesser, "Dichterzitaten in des Thomas Cisterciensis Kommentar zum Hohenlied," *Cistercienser Chronik* (1938) 11–14, 118–22; (1939) 73–80.

66. H. Silvestre, "Les citations et reminiscences dans l'œuvre de Rupert de Deutz," *RHE* (1950), 140–74. The same scholar has undertaken a similar inquiry on the *Vita Eracli* of Rainier of St. Laurence, RHE (1949) 65–86.

67. H. Woltjer, *Ordericus Vitalis: Ein Beitrag zur kluniazensischen Geschichtsschreibung* (Wiesbaden, 1955), p. 225.

68. E. R. Curtius (n. 7), *passim*. L. Arbusow, *Colores rhetorici* (Göttingen, 1948).

69. *Super Cantica* 26.

70. *De Excessu fratris sui Satyri* 1.1 (PL 16.1289–1316).

71. "Recherches sur les Sermons sur les Cantiques de S. Bernard," RB (1955) 80.

72. *Sermo* 41.4–7 (PL 184.216–18).

73. *Apologeticus pro Petro Abaelardo*, PL 178.1806.

74. "Fingere namque componere dicimus; unde et compositores luti figulos vocamus." *In Evang.* 23.1 (PL 76.1282). Cf. TLL, *s.v.* "fingo."

75. *Un maître*, pp. 47–49.

76. *Pierre le Vén.* pp. 23–24.

77. P. Sinz, "Die Naturbetrachtung des hl. Bernhard," *Anima* (1953) I 30–51.

78. L. Arbusow, *Liturgie und Geschichtsschreibung* (1951) 32–33.

79. See Ch. 4 *supra*. Other texts in E. Faye Wilson, "Pastoral and Epithalamium in Latin Literature," *Speculum* (1948) 35–57.

80. "Études sur S. Bernard," *Anal. S. Ord. Cist.* 184n2.

81. E. Gilson, "Sub umbris arborum," *Mediaeval Studies* (1952) 149–51. The contrast between the "shady vales" and the calm so much loved by the Cistercians and the cities symbolizes the difference between manual labor and "the schools of cultivated men" (*scurrarum scholis*) in the anonymous poem, *De Mauro et Zoilo* (ed. Thomas Wright, *Latin Poems Commonly Attributed to Walter Mapes* [London, 1841], p. 245). See the picture reproduced under the title "Une peinture des origines cisterciennes," *Anal. S. Ord. Cist.* (1956) 305 and ibid. Pl. III.

82. Texts will be found in L. Zoepf, *Das Heiligenleben im 10. Jahrhundert* (Leipzig, 1908), pp. 219–28.

83. Texts in *La Vie parfaite*, pp. 166–68: "Le paradis."

84. *Pierre le Vén.* p. 23.

85. *De gestis pontificum Angliae* IV (PL 179.1612–13).

86. E. Faral, "Les conditions générales de la production littéraire en Europe occidentale pendant les IXe et Xe siècles," *I problemi communi dell' Europa post Carolingia* (Spoleto, 1955), pp. 288–89, has recalled that the influence of Phaedrus was joined to that of *Physiologus* but that the *Ecbasis captivi*, "the prototype of the famous story of the fox," appeared in the tenth century at the monastery of St. Evre in Lorraine.

87. A. Dimier, *Clarté, paix, joie. Les beaux noms des monastères de Cîteaux en France* (1944).

88. *La vie parfaite*, pp. 46–47.

89. "Symbolique chrétienne de la lune," in *Lunaires, Carte du Ciel*. Cahiers de poesie (Paris, 1947), pp. 133–48.

90. "Deux opuscules sur la formation des jeunes moines," *Revue d'ascétique et de mystique* 33 (1957) 387–99.

91. For example, Thomas of Perseigne, *In Cant.* VI (PL 206.759). The sources in Pliny and the Fathers are indicated by H. Lauretus, *Silva allegoriarum* (Lyon, 1622) *s.v.* On the symbolism of mandrake, see H. Rahner, "Die seelenheilende

Blume, II. Mandragore, die ewige Menschenwurzel," *Eranos Jahrbuch* (1945) 202–39.

92. See p. 78 *supra*.

93. On its symbolism, see "Les deux compilations de Thomas de Perseigne" (n. 65) 207n65.

94. R. Grousset, *L'épopée des croisades* (Paris, 1939), p. 45.

95. *Pierre le Vén*. pp. 31–37: "Le vrai moyen âge."

96. Ibid., pp. 37–40: "Contrastes monastiques."

97. E. Vacandard, *Vie de S. Bernard* (Paris, 1895) I 210–11; *Histoire générale de l'Eglise* XI (Paris, 1948), pp. 142–43. J. Stiennon, "Cluny et S. Trond au xiie siècle," *Anciens pays et assemblées d'états* 8 (Louvain, 1955) 65, has stressed the part that exaggeration played in the "Reformrhetorik," and from known facts it is clear that we should not be deceived.

98. *Apologia* 20–22 (PL 182.910–11). "Aspects littéraires de l'œuvre de S. Bernard, Un modèle du genre satirique," *Cahiers de la civilisation médiévale* (1958) 444–50.

99. *Epist*. VI 15 (PL 189.422).

100. *Carmina*, PL 189.1005.

101.   Angustae vitae fugiunt consortia Musae,
                  Claustrorum septis nec habitare volunt,
in Adalbert of Corbie, MGH, *PLAC* I 43.

102. Ed. Swoboda (1900); some extracts in "L'idéal monastique de S. Odon d'après ses œuvres," *A Cluny. Congrès scientifique* (Dijon, 1950), pp. 227–30. In the time of Peter the Venerable, Rodulfus Tostarius devoted one of his many poems to a eulogy of Cluny. Edd. M. B. Doyle and D. M. Schullian, *Rodulfi Tostarii carmina* (Rome, 1933), pp. 448–53. On another Cluniac poet, Peter of Poitiers, cf. *Pierre le Vén*. p. 276 and *passim*.

103. "Un débat sur le sacerdoce des moines au xiie siècle." *Analecta monastica* IV (in collaboration with Mlle R. Foreville).

104. For example, the *Hypognosticon* of Lawrence of Durham, of which selections have been published by J. Raine, *Dialogi Laurentii Dunelmensis* (Durham, 1880), pp. 62–71.

105. A. Boutemy, "Fragments d'une œuvre perdue de Sigebert de Gembloux," *Latomus* (1938) 196–220; Sigebert here gives a description of creation which is an adaptation of that of Ovid in the *Metamorphoses*, ibid. 203.

106. "Documents sur la mort des moines. IV. Epitaphes et poèmes divers," *Revue Mabillon* (1956) 70–81.

107. "Les manuscrits de l'abbaye d'Hautmont," *Scriptorium* 7 (1953) 59–67. "Un nouveau manuscrit d'Hautmont," ibid. 107–109.

108. "Monachi qui rhythmos fecerint ad domos alias mittantur, non redituri nisi per generale Capitulum," *Statuta Capit. gen. Ord. Cist.* I (ed. J. M. Canivez, 1933) 232 ad an. 1199, n. 1.

109. "Manuscrits cisterciens à la Bibliothèque Vaticane," *Anal. S. Ord. Cist.* Other Cistercian examples: J. H. Mozley, "The Collection of Mediaeval Latin Verses in MS Cotton Titus D. XXIV," *Medium Aevum* (1942) 1–45 (poems of a monk of Rufford in the twelfth century); A. Wilmart, "Les mélanges de Matthieu préchantre de Rievaulx au début du xiiie siècle," RB (1940) 15–84. Quite differently from Itier de Vassy, Matthew of Rievaulx does not take his verses very seriously. Ibid. 68, 15:
              Haec metra, mi fili, tu noli pendere vili.

110. "Les divertissements poétiques d'Itier de Vassy," *Anal. S. Ord. Cist.* (1956) 296–304. We translate here only a few extracts.

111. "Quod animalia vitium levitatis ministrantia non nutrientur," "Super instituta generalis capituli apud Cistercium XXII," ed. C. Noschitzka, *Anal. S. Ord. Cist.* (1950) 26. Cf. ibid. ch. 5, 23–24. Aelred of Rievaulx, *Speculum caritatis* II 24 (PL 195.572), does not approve of the same animals.

112. "Les peintures de la Bible de Morimondo," *Scriptorium* 10 (1956) 22–26.

113. F. Ermini, "La poesia enigmistica e faceta di Paolo Diacono," *Medio Evo latino* (Modena, 1938), pp. 137–40.

114. J. P. Bonnes, "Une lettre du xe siècle," *Revue Mabillon* (1943) 23–48.

115. "Études sur S. Bernard," 143–47, 79–80, and *passim*.

116. "S. Bernard et la devotion joyeuse," *S. Bernard homme d'Eglise* (La Pierre qui Vire 1953), pp. 237–47. *Bernhard von Clairvaux. Die Botschaft der Freude* (2nd ed.; Einsiedeln, 1954), pp. 30–33. "De l'humour à l'amour," *La vie spirituelle* (1959) 182–203.

117. "Les paraboles de Galland de Rigny," *Analecta monastica* I 167–80. J. Chatillon, "Galland de Rigny, Libellus Proverbiorum," *Revue du moyen âge latin* 9 (1953) 1–152.

118. E. P. Goldschmidt, *Burchardus de Bellevaux, Apologia de barbis* (Cambridge, 1935) sermo III c. 8 and 39, pp. 38 and 77.

119. Ibid. Sermon III, c. 47, p. 85. As proof of this Cistercian brand of humor, on which a fine study could be made, we may cite the dialogue which I presented under the title "Textes sur S. Bernard et Gilbert de la Porrée," *Mediaeval Studies* (1952) 111–28, which has been identified as the work of Evrard of Ypres by N. M. Haring, ibid. (1955) 143–72.

120. See Appendix II, and "Grammaire et humour dans les textes du moyen âge," *Convivium* (1959) 270–76.

121. The classical sources of very many proverbs have been pointed out by W. Heraeus, "Zu Werners Sammlung lateinischen Sprichwörter des Mittelalters," *Studien zur lateinischen Dichtung des Mittelalters: Ehrengabe K. Strecker* (Dresden, 1931), pp. 84–85.

122. A. Wilmart, "Une riposte de l'ancien monachisme au manifeste de S. Bernard," RB (1934) 296–344.

123. A. Wilmart, "Le dialogue apologétique du moine Guillaume," *Revue Mabillon* (1942) 80–118.

124. In spite of the impression one might take from its title there is no discussion of humanism in the well-documented biography by N. Scivoletto, "Angilberto abate di S. Riquier et l' 'humanitas' carolingia," *Giornale italiano di filologia* (1952) 289–313.

125. S. Hilpisch, "Günther und das Mönchtum seiner Zeit," *Tausend Jahre St. Günther, Festschrift zum Jahre 1955* (Cologne, 1955), pp. 57–61.

126. "This thesis is no longer tenable," writes H. Woltjer, *Ordericus Vitalis*, 5.

127. "Y a-t-il une culture monastique?" in *Il monachesimo nell'alto medioevo e la formazione delle civiltà occidentale* (Spoleto, 1956). "Cluny fut-il ennemi de la culture?" in *Revue Mabillon* (1957). The same idea is to be found in H. Rupp, *Deutsche religiöse Dichtungen des 11. und 12. Jahrhunderts* (Freiburg, 1958), pp. 284–94.

128. L. Th. A. Lorié, *Spiritual Terminology in the Latin Translations of the Vita*

Antonii (Utrecht–Nijmegen, 1954), pp. 164–71: "Monastic Latin and Primitive Western Monasticism."

129. "L'humanisme bénédictin du VIIIe au XIIe siècle," *Analecta monastica* I 1–20.

130. M. Hubert, "Aspects du latin philosophique aux XIIe et XIIIe siècles," *Revue des études latines* 27 (1949) 227–31.

131. As to such authors, cf. E. de Bruyne, *Études d'esthétique médiévale* (Bruges, 1946) II 160–63.

132. A. H. Thompson, "Classical Echoes in Mediaeval Authors," *History* (1948) 38.

133. *Historia pontificalis*, c. 9–11 (ed. R. L. Poole, 21–29). "S. Bernard et la théologie monastique du XIIe siècle," *S. Bernard théologien: Anal. S. Ord. Cist.* 3–4 (1953) 17.

134. *The Letters of John of Salisbury* I (edd. Millor, Butler, Brooke [London, 1955]) lvii–lxi.

135. C. Mohrmann, "Le dualisme de la latinité médiévale," *Revue des études latines*, 29 (1952) 344–47. Reprinted in *Latin vulgaire, Latin des chrétiens, Latin médiéval* (Paris, 1955), pp. 50–53. R. R. Bolgar, *The Classical Heritage*, p. 117, has pointed out that this dualism had existed since the ninth century.

136. H. Woltjer, *Ordericus Vitalis.*

137. For example *Un humaniste ermite: Le B. Paul Giustiniani (1476–1528),* "Le Stoïcien," pp. 17–40 (Rome, 1951).

THE FRUITS OF
MONASTIC CULTURE

8

Literary Genres

In the Middle Ages, as in antiquity, no writing is done without "composition": the stylistic material is arranged in a certain order. Authors conform to ways of writing and types of composition, each of which has its own rules. No doubt the idea of "literary genre" is difficult to define, since it is seldom formulated in a theoretical manner; but it is a fact that the genres exist. Often at the beginning of a piece of writing, it is explained to which category it is to belong, whether it is to be, for example, a sermon, an epistle, a treatise, or a gloss.[1] Certain of these genres were codified: this was to be particularly true of the sermons in the *Artes praedicandi* from the second half of the twelfth century on, and outside of monastic circles. The work of Guibert of Nogent († 1124), *On the Manner of Making a Sermon*, does not treat specifically of preaching, but of the share every explanation of the Scripture should allot to moral exhortation.[2] But the *Artes dictandi* or *dictamina* had already prescribed rules for the composition of letters. The monks' letters are rare and very short. Before they were codified, the different genres were differentiated and briefly defined by Isidore of Seville in terms used later by Conrad of Hirsau.[3] Above all, classical and patristic tradition furnishes examples of certain literary genres, and they are the ones that are used by the monks. We must point out their general characteristics and then describe more fully the ones most frequently cultivated.

The monks prefer the genres which might be called concrete. Differing from the scholastics whose interest goes chiefly to the *quaestio*, the *disputatio*, or the *lectio* taken as a basis for formulating *quaestiones*, the monks prefer writings dealing with actual happenings and experiences rather than with ideas, and which, instead of being a teacher's instruction for a universal and anonymous public, are addressed to a specific audience, to a public chosen by and known to the author. Thus, whatever form they may take, monastic writings are generally preceded by a letter of dedication, and the treatises themselves often appear to be expanded letters. The monks prefer to cultivate genres like the letter, the dialogue, and history in all its forms from short chronicles and accounts of individual events to long annals.[4]

Then secondly, genres which are pastoral in nature occupy a large place in monastic literature. Sermons abound, and the commentaries themselves, instead of being a continuous and uninterrupted explanation of a text, written in the impersonal tone of research divorced from all preoccupation with edification, often take on the form of sermons. They are more like exhortations than explanations. This concern with the practical and moral aspect results in the complete or virtually complete exclusion of genres widely found in classical tradition. They are those which are considered futile, like comedies, *fabliaux*, or satirical poems.[5] This "edifying" characteristic of monastic literature is the more striking because of the contrast between most monastic poems and many written by worldly clerics anxious to entertain and amuse, sometimes at any price. The monastic writings are directed to the practice of the Christian life.

THE LITERATURE OF SILENCE

Another of their characteristics is that of being very often exchanges between monks, between men, one of whose principal obligations is silence. They are perfected in the school of silence: *silentium loquendi magister*,[6] and they are destined to give it preference. Their literature of silence is therefore expressed in a written rather than an oral style. This is another way in which it differs from scholastic literature: in ancient and medieval schools, dialogue was the rule, the exchange of views between master and pupils, the alternation of question and answer. In the schools there is much talking, much "disputation"; work is essentially oral—"in large part improvised."[7] If they write to each other it is generally after having talked together; they write down what has been said or heard, and as it was remembered. In the monastery, on the contrary, they write because they do not talk, they write to avoid speaking. Their works accordingly take on a more highly fashioned and literary quality. They take time to express themselves in verse. If discourses or sermons are composed, they are often works of "written rhetoric." These sermons, which were not delivered and never would be, were intended for public or private reading, aloud in both cases. The ancients had cultivated rhetoric because of its effectiveness in public life; classical authors had used it mostly in politics. Christian orators—who were bishops or else spoke in their name—had employed it for the instruction of the faithful. Monks, in a milieu where silence reigns, continue to practice the same genres because of the literary resources they offer. Consequently the art of speaking is applied to the writing of letters or sermons. It derives nonetheless from an authentic rhetoric, one made known to them by the classical authors and the Fathers who had themselves been influenced by the classics.[8] No doubt the monks rarely studied it as theory. It is mostly in scholasticism that, under the influence of Aristotle's logic, they came to develop a speculative rhetoric as they did a speculative grammar.[9] In this domain also, the *lectio divina* was the monks' school.

Finally, the monastic literary genres are marked by a certain immutability: from the eighth to the twelfth century, they evolved hardly at all. By this characteristic, monastic milieux are again revealed as conservative, faithful to the ancient tradition of the classics and the Fathers. In the schools, the genres never stop evolving and becoming diversified: the *quaestio* will give birth to the *quaestio disputata*, the *quaestiuncula*, the *articulus*, and the *quodlibet*; to the *lectio* will be added a *reportatio*, and each of these genres, as well as the sermon itself, will obey a more and more precise plan and a more and more complicated technique. Monastic literature always retains the same liberty, the same absence of complexity. Its motto remains *sancta simplicitas*.

Let us now attempt to describe in greater detail the literary genres the monks preferred to cultivate: history, the sermon, the letter, and the *florilegium*.

History

The monks loved history very much. More than any other writers, they concentrated on it, and sometimes they were almost the only ones to do so. That is a fact which students of medieval literature have noted and which, once more, distinguishes monasticism from scholasticism. "In France, not one of the masters of the schools of Chartres, Poitiers, Tours, Rheims, Laon, or Paris, in spite of the renown of their teaching, had any concern for historical work."[10] In England also, the historians are almost always monks, and certain monasteries like Bury and St. Albans had, over successive generations, real schools of historians. Doubtless some hagiographical texts were occasionally composed by seculars, members of the clergy of churches which wished their patron saints extolled. Still, it is revealing that the church of Le Mans, for example, should have commissioned the monk Letaldus to write up the legend of St. Julian. This interest in history even seems proportionate to the degree of monastic fervor. At Cluny and its dependencies, a line of historiographers connects St. Odo with Ralph Glaber and Ordericus Vitalis, by way of the Fleury and

Flavigny chroniclers.[11] The Cistercian Order was not to be outdone in this connection. Otto of Freising, Helinand of Froidmont, Gunther of Pairis, Ralph of Coggeshall, and Aubrey of Trois-Fontaines compete with many authors of anonymous chronicles.[12] In 1161, a monastery was founded in Denmark and one of its tasks was to write the annals of the kingdom.[13] This interest in history appears not only in the monks' writings but also in their reading matter. In the one year for which we have any information as to the Cluny monks' Lenten reading, we know that six of the sixty-four members of the community were given works on history to read: Josephus, Orosius, Bede's *Chronicle*, and even Livy.[14]

What explains the monks' interest in history? Two reasons may perhaps account for it. The first is that the historical genre had been in existence since classical antiquity and had left models. The monks had become acquainted with them in school and, later on, sought inspiration in them. Grammar was the art of "interpreting the poets and the historians."[15] To the reading of the ancient annalists was added that of historians like Sozomen, chroniclers like Isidore, and bibliographers like Jerome and Gennadius.[16] Sallust, in the words of Rupert of Deutz, "is the greatest of the historiographers, as Virgil is the greatest of poets, and Cicero the greatest of orators."[17] William of Poitiers praises Ordericus Vitalis for having "imitated Sallust."[18] And Livy also had imitators of his own.[19]

The other explanation of this attraction to history is the conservative tendency which is congenital, so to speak, in monasticism. There was a predisposition toward the traditional and also a concern for the preservation of contemporary gains. Many monastic historians, in the prologues to their chronicles, have acknowledged this love of the past, and their desire to see it committed to writing so that it should not be forgotten and that others might benefit from all the lessons it held for the future. Ordericus Vitalis, for example, has related how eagerly his fellow monks "read about the deeds of their predecessors"; they exhorted each other to write their story, but since that was a very onerous task, *opus arduum*, no one ventured to undertake it.[20] More enthusiastically than anyone else, Peter the Venerable chanted history's praises and lauded historians who transmit to future generations the things their own has witnessed:

> It makes me very sad, more so perhaps than many people will believe, yes, and I am often angered by the laziness of a great number of men who, though distinguished for their knowledge, love of learning, and eloquence, are yet so sluggish that they do not hand down in writing to those who are to come after them the marvelous works the Almighty repeatedly accomplishes in different parts of the world to

strengthen His Church. It was an ancient custom, not only with the first fathers of the Christian faith but even with the gentiles, to consign to writing every undertaking, good or evil; but our contemporaries, the ones of whom I am speaking, less zealous than these Christians and pagans, nonchalantly allow to die out the memory of everything that is happening in their times and which could be so useful to those who might come after them. The inspired Psalmist said to God: "Let all Thy works praise Thee, O Lord!"[21] which is to say, may Thou be praised in all Thy works; but how can God be praised by works that remain unknown? How will they be known to those who have not seen them, if they are not related to them? How are they to persist in the memory of ages far distant from ours which will replace us, if they are not written down? All the good or bad works performed in the world by the will or the permission of God ought to serve for the glory and edification of the Church; but if men are ignorant of them, how can they contribute to glorify God or to edify the Church? This apathy which encloses itself in a sterile silence has reached the point where everything that has happened for four or five hundred years, whether in the Church of God or in the kingdoms of Christendom, is practically unknown to us as to everyone else. In fact our times are so different from former times that, while we are perfectly informed about everything that happened five hundred or a thousand years ago, we know nothing about later events or even what has taken place during our own lifetime. Thus we have a great number of ancient histories, ecclesiastical acts, and great doctrinal books containing the Fathers' precepts and examples; but as for the events which have occurred in periods closer to our own, I am not at all certain that we possess even one book which treats of them. The ancient historians, eagerly searching for anything they could make use of, took from far distant nations and from foreign tongues whatever these peoples and languages had to offer that was worthy of interest and that could benefit humanity. The Egyptians ardently embraced the language and learning of the Greeks; the Greeks, those of the Latins; the Latins, those of the Greeks, the Hebrews, and many other peoples, and whatever they found eminently useful, they spread abroad in various kinds of written works and translations of every description. In our times, those who know Latin act very differently; not only do they take no interest in anything outside their own native land but they will not condescend to find out what is happening only two steps away, or inform the public about it in either the spoken or the written word.[22]

This text reveals the monks' conception of history which, in turn, explains their manner of recording it. Their works differ, depending upon whether they are narrating history in general or the lives of the saints. These two types of writing have certain characteristics which are common to both, although there is very little uniformity to be found within either category, particularly in the first. Style and method vary from one historian to another as well as between the various poets and different theologians. But within this diversity itself, two features are apparent in every historiographer. The first might be called the edifying character of this literature —which connects it with the pastoral genre. "Edifying" in this context is close to the meaning it had in St. Paul: to edify means "to construct" the Church, the body of Christ. This historiography is edifying in intention, in method, and in subject matter. Its purpose is not purely scientific or intellectual, as if knowledge of the past were an end in itself. Its purpose is a practical one: to instruct, in order to do good, and to do this in two ways. The first way is by praising God; one writes for the glory of God and in order to stimulate the reader to praise the Lord. Ordericus Vitalis, without any hesitation, says several times that one must "sing" history like a hymn in honor of Him who created the world and governs it with justice.[23] Moreover they wanted to propose examples to be imitated if good, to be avoided if bad. Ordericus foresees that some day readers will scrutinize his text seeking useful lessons for their contemporaries.[24] If the monks care little for the progress of speculative thought they are nonetheless far from indifferent to the future.

Their Purpose in Writing

The manner of presentation is determined by the end in view; to incite to the practice of virtue and promote praise of God, the events once recorded must, to a certain extent, be interpreted. Above all they must be situated in a vast context; the individual story is always inserted in the history of salvation. Events are directed by God who desires the salvation of the elect. The monks devote to the interests of this conviction a comprehension of the Church which was developed in them by the reading of the Fathers and the observance of the liturgy. They feel they are members of a universal communion. The saints, whose cult they celebrate, are, for them, intimate friends and living examples. In similar fashion, thinking about the angels comes naturally to them. Liturgical themes permeate their entire conception of what takes place in time. Consequently, Otto of Freising's historical writings are dominated by broad theological concepts: the mystery of the Epiphany where Christ appears as Priest and King, the meaning of eschatology, and the description of the heavenly Jerusalem and of the Last Judgment. Throughout, the entire vocabulary of the martyrology is very prominent.²⁵ In any case, when dealing with concrete events, their intention is to serve the Church, to penetrate more deeply the mystery of the Christian vocation, and to perceive how humanity's salvation is realized in the fabric of time. Correspondences with sacred history, especially with the narratives of the Old Testament, are therefore both frequent and legitimate. To begin with, we find the word *historia* used for the passage from the Bible in the office, in the atmosphere of prayer.²⁶ All narration is conceived, more or less, in accordance with this model, and the biblical, patristic, and liturgical stamp evident in their ideas as well as in their vocabulary has made it possible to speak of a "monastic" historiography, that is, a monastic way of writing history.²⁷ The classical authors, moreover, such as Cicero, "had acquired a very liberal notion of the way history should be recorded,"²⁸ and this is another point on which the medieval monks felt no obligation to repudiate them.

Finally, history thus conceived as a religious teaching concentrates on the religious rather than the economic or social factors. The economic phenomena—poor harvests, famines, rises in prices—are mentioned only in relation to the charity of virtuous men. Political events are considered from the viewpoint of their religious implications, mainly those involving relations between princes and Church authority. On the other hand, the monks pay a great deal of attention to the manifestations of liturgical life: processions, the transferral of relics, dedications of churches, and coronations of kings and emperors. Suger elected to compose a whole treatise to tell about the construction and dedication of St. Denis, and many others devote considerable space in their chronicles to events like these, as if they had universal historical repercussions or as if they deserved to be remembered forever. The monks have described fewer battles than ceremonies.

CRITICAL JUDGMENT

Does that mean that in the interests of edification their critical judgment had to be sacrificed? This was not the case by any means, and the second characteristic of monastic historiography is precisely its scientific aspect. In this realm, no doubt, we must not expect medieval men to employ the critical methods of our day. And, likewise, some allowance must be made for variations due to differing times and places. From the Carolingian renaissance on, the liberal arts remained the basis for historiography. But these historians and their milieux were, possibly, more or less inclined to give credence to the marvelous. Perhaps because sensibility had gained ground, even in the realm of devotion, credulity is greater in the twelfth than in the eleventh century.[29] The Evolution taking place moved, not toward skepticism as in modern times, but toward credulousness. Yet, in every period the monk–historians gave proof of the scientific spirit. In the middle of the tenth century, Letaldus of Micy "for the good of religion," as he says, attacks the legend according to which St. Julian, a contemporary of the Apostles, is supposed to have been sent by St. Clement to Gaul where he founded the church of Le Mans; his position was destined to encounter serious opposition for ten successive centuries.[30] He sets forth excellent principles for the verification of facts: "I have omitted the things which seemed to me less probable. On the other hand, I did not think I ought to pass over in silence what I have learned from the authentic testimony of some of the ancients, convinced, as I was, that if miracles are indeed rare today, there are, nevertheless, in the Church many Christians who are not inferior in the holiness of their lives to the makers of miracles."[31] Later, Guibert of Nogent, in his treatise *On the Saints and their Relics*,[32] raises his voice against veneration being prematurely paid certain people who perform miracles or who are credited with so doing;[33] he protests against those who venerate false relics, in particular against the monks of St. Médard who pretended to have one of the Lord's teeth,[34] and he warns against dubious marvels.[35] Ordericus Vitalis also uses a vigorous method in seeking out and interpreting original documents. After listing a series of sources, he makes this statement: "I have taken pleasure in inserting these texts here, so that readers may search avidly for documents such as these: they contain great wisdom and yet they are hard to find."[36] And, again, in the twelfth century, Goscelin of St. Bertin recasts the lives of the Anglo-Saxon saints "in a new style"—and with a more critical approach.[37] He deliberately eschews the method used by writers who know nothing whatever of the person they are talking about and resort to attributing commonplaces to him—when they do not simply invent the story out of whole cloth.[38] To avoid this drawback, he consults the ancient chronicles written in Old English, and other reliable sources.[39]

The critical sense is not altogether inoperative even when the monks are making things up. For, it must be frankly admitted and sincerely regretted, there are in their writings cases of pure and simple fabrication and even of falsification. Their relative proportion, however, must not be exaggerated. Monastic historiography does not consist entirely in forging false documents and creating legends: far from it. However, such cases do exist. At San Millan all the documents are predated; at Monte Cassino Peter the Deacon writes his own version of history; at St. Laurent of

Liège, facts and texts are altered; at Cîteaux, interpolations are made in the authentic account of the Order's origins. Sometimes there are excuses for such procedures. No doubt, under the cover of legends or spurious stories they were, in certain cases, only protecting their material interests.[40] Elsewhere, attempts were made to win acceptance for dubious relics.[41] Often also it was the edification of the people that was hoped for, or else the protection of the monastery against the incursions of neighboring feudal lords. These men, although eager for plunder, were timorous when it came to profaning a place hallowed by miracles or saintly visitation. To claim that the church of Einsiedeln or of St. Denis had been consecrated by Christ in person was to ensure respect for these churches and for their possessions. And furthermore, even in cases like these, the monks sometimes forestalled future criticism by multiplying their precautions and preparing refutations in advance. This has been found to be true, for example, of the tales that were invented at St. Denis in the eleventh century.[42] If they are indeed lies, they are more than just clever lies. Consequently, the untangling of these snarled skeins of truth and falsehood has had to await the acumen of a scholar of our own time.[43]

The Lives of the Saints

Hagiography is one branch of this historiography whose methods it applies to a special domain. It also demands an appreciation of the truth and a critical approach. But, in its case, attention is even more sharply focused on the aim to edify, which is indeed often its sole aim. The reason for recording a saint's life is not always, as we might believe at first thought, to tell the story of his life. For what is being dealt with is the existence not of just any outstanding personality—even one who had played a role in political life—but of a Christian who has achieved sanctity. What matters is less the circumstances of his existence than the opportunities they afforded him to practice virtue. Hippolyte Delehaye has pointed out that what defines a document as hagiographical is not its being the account of a life, but the fact that the narrative is intended to edify.[44] This intent, generally stated in the prologue, determines the structure, the methods of composition—laudatory or doctrinal digressions—and the style itself as well as the themes and reminiscences.

There are various kinds of lives of the saints.[45] At times, particularly when they are "metrical," they are nothing more than school exercises.[46] But, for the most part, they are written for devotional purposes either to promote the veneration of a saint or to provide texts for reading (*legenda*) during the divine office. These lessons, or legends, are collected in a volume called the *legendarium*.[47] The liturgy does not offer a theoretical program for the Christian life; it illustrates the Lord's teaching with examples selected to fill the psychological needs of each generation. In these legends can be seen, more clearly than anywhere else, the twofold aim of historical narration: not only to instruct and exhort through the recollection of great Christian deeds, but to glorify God in the devotional exercise itself in which the text is to be read. For this reason, sometimes, the only events of a whole lifetime that are retained are those which are suitably edifying or are worthy of being read aloud at divine office, without, at the same time, unduly prolonging it.[48] The desire to praise God in His saints is conducive to exaggeration: everything becomes admirable, and the narrative turns into a panegyric. And the desire to make use of the acts of the saints as a basis for instruction encourages the finding of the meaning desired—even if violence has to be done to the facts.[49] For real personages and concrete examples supply the pretext for the exposition of ideas. In the lives of the bishops, for example, a certain conception of the episcopal function and the rapport between the Church and temporal authority are often highlighted. The bishop is a prince of the King of Heaven; his attitude furnishes an opportunity for passing judgment on persons taking part in the conflicts between the episcopate and the empire.[50] In the lives of the abbots a conception of monastic life and abbatial dignity is emphasized.[51] Likewise, in the lives of princes, what was edifying, "imitable," or of such nature as to manifest the power of God was given primary consideration.[52]

Hagiography is distinct from biography, and the latter was a literary form that had been practiced since antiquity. In Plutarch's work it consisted in relating the existence—virtuous or otherwise—of an individual. His life, with its sum total of contingent happenings, gave the impression of being the result of circumstances, environment, and destiny.[53] Hagiographical legend advances a moral thesis and a religious idea. No interest is taken in the individual as such, in the memory he has left behind him and which history will record. Not the things he did, only the ideal he illustrated will be remembered. The saint, therefore, is considered above all as a model, a Christian personality who should be imitated. Today, we like a life of a saint to be, first of all, a biography. In this respect the Middle Ages were less demanding than we. From their point of view, the less edifying facts should be passed over in silence—or altered. If someone had left no fine examples, or very few, it was better his life were not written down. This is, no doubt, the reason why there are so few medieval biographies in existence.

LEGENDS

But for all examples to be good examples, is it not possible that medieval authors were likely to be tempted to manufacture some? They did not hesitate to add on to real miracles, or those considered as such, marvelous doings whose authenticity, no doubt, they would not have guaranteed with the same conviction. The confidence they had in the intercession of a saint, and which they wished to communicate, prompted them to accept cures and visions very readily and on the grounds of insufficiently controlled testimony. Nobody lends except to the rich; it was even more reasonable to extend credit to the saints. Their authentic miracles seemed to justify imagining others, guaranteed by the first. Their unquestioned acts of virtue authorized the most edifying interpretation of all their other actions and, when there was no information as to other acts, the reconstruction of what these might have been. Records did not always correspond with the event which had taken place, but they were always a means for recommending to all both protectors to invoke and models to imitate. Moreover, a state of things which had existed in the sixth and seventh centuries must have re-occurred; later on the necessity of having a legend for the office led, in some localities, to the composition of a *vita*, many of whose elements were either borrowed from other texts or simply invented.[54]

CONVENTIONAL THEMES

Since the resources of the human imagination are limited, writers resorted to conventional hagiographical themes. Between the prophecies which customarily foretold the birth of the person in question and his posthumous apparitions, they interposed a whole series of actions, words, and miracles which could, with little if any change, serve as well for one legend as for another. Finding them was no problem. Tradition offered many models: the *Lives* of Anthony and of Hilarion, the *Historia monachorum*, the *Dialogues* of St. Gregory, the *Life* of St. Martin by Sulpicius Severus, and the writings of Gregory of Tours. The life of St. Willibrord by Alcuin was also widely known and served as a model.[55] These texts had, in some cases, been read and studied in school. Writers referred to them spontaneously when called upon to produce the same kind of composition. At the time of the Carolingian restoration, the renascent monasteries needed to have the great deeds of their founders recorded. But, during the period lacking in culture which had preceded theirs, the necessary information had not been written down or preserved. Hence they had no choice but to invent, select, or even falsify with the avowed intention of encouraging their contemporaries and posterity to emulate the good examples attributed to the saints of earlier days. If, for this reason, one is led to question the veracity of authors, whose "piety" notwithstanding "is manifest in every line,"[56] he can, at least, have no reservations as to their integrity. Their design was not to relate true stories, but to expound a moral doctrine which itself is always true.

Some monks, no doubt, were cautious about hagiographical themes. We have already seen what Goscelin of St. Bertin thought of them.[57] Letaldus also denounces them: "In the life of our saint," he declares, "one can discover much that had already been said, and in practically the same words, about St. Clement, St. Denis, and St. Furse."[58]

> Whatever is to be read in the presence of the Truth must be written with great reverence and seriousness, since without them, in spite of one's desire to please God, one would risk provoking Him. There is nothing so pleasing to Him as the truth. And yet there are some who, in their desire to exalt the saints, offend truth; as if falsehood could possibly contribute to the glory of saints who, had they lied, would never have attained to sanctity. What the Truth has accomplished must be told in truth. If a miracle is attributed to one of our Fathers, it was not the man who performed it but God who acts in and through the men He chooses.[59]

All did not share Letaldus' scruples and, on this point, medieval historiographers may well be criticized for a certain monotony. These themes, however, were not always simple edifying features; they could be reminiscences of classical literature—like the symbolism of Y, "the letter of Pythagoras"[60] —or a theological formula: just as the idea of the *regio dissimilitudinis*, which St. Bernard had elaborated on several occasions, was incorporated at Clairvaux in a *Life* of St. Mary Magdalen.[61]

THE TRUTH OF HAGIOGRAPHY

Moreover, the genre itself evolved from one period to another. As a consequence of the devotion paid to relics, miracles had, for a long time, been considered as manifestations of a saint's personal power. But, little by little, they appeared to be intended more to enhance the reputation of the just or to bring sinners back to righteousness.[62] A liking for extraordinary phenomena persisted but more and more emphasis was placed on the reliable criteria of sanctity, particularly on humility. Considered in this light, the hagiographical legends remain an important, and too little exploited, source: for if they tell us little of the history of the saints—which, as we have seen, was only partially the intention of the authors—they do give us abundant information on the milieux in which they were written, what idea these circles had of the monastic vocation and of sanctity, and on the kind of life that was led there.

Lives of saints, of a different sort, were composed with the more or less conscious design of laying the groundwork for their canonization, particularly from the beginning of the second half of the twelfth century. Before this time, some of these lives go on the assumption that the canonization has already taken place or that they themselves are its equivalent; they validate the cult and give it its expression. This seems to apply to the life of St. Odilo which St. Hugh of Cluny commissioned St. Peter Damian to write although other versions were already extant. But sometimes the account is intended to obtain a bishop's recognition of a cult, the "elevation" of the saint's relics, or the pope's proclamation of his sancity, that is, his canonization. The text in this case is presented in the form traditionally required for an investigation of this kind, which should—as indeed it still does today—bear on the life, virtues, and miracles of the saint and whatever writings he may have left. This is true of the *First Life* of St. Bernard and of several other texts of the same description.[63] And again, even during the lifetime of a virtuous monk, testimonials of those who lived with him were collected so that his memory might be preserved with accuracy. It hardly seems likely that the honors of the altars were contemplated for simple lay monks such as Christian the Almoner who had played no important role either in his Order or in the Church.[64] More probably the monks wished to gather together materials for a menology which took the form of compilations like the *Great Exordium of Cîteaux* and the *Book of Miracles* by Caesarius of Heisterbach. These are concerned, for the greater part, with the marvelous which is still very important in the Cistercian hagiography of the thirteenth century.[65] Through these often charming accounts, in which imagination has been given freer play than we could wish for, we obtain a vivid picture of many real details and insights into many true ideas.

One must, therefore, know how to read medieval hagiographical texts. One may wonder if their authors were the dupes of the themes they used; if they allowed themselves to be deluded, and if they themselves intended to deceive. Since some of them could see that it is better to refrain from such inventions, that one should be critical, not overcredulous, why could not all, or at least many of them, have shared the same skepticism? Were they in error or suffering from a collective illusion? Or is it not, rather, a question of a literary genre whose laws have to be known and understood? Isidore had distinguished two types of the narrative genre: the *historia* and the *fabulae*.[66] Yet in many of these collections, purely historical chronicles are found in juxtaposition with definitely legendary "visions." These texts, whose characteristics were known to be different, were intermingled because they possessed the common advantage of providing instruction on the way life should be led. Narration was not always, any more than in our times, necessarily "historical" in our sense of the word. In the account of the past, we must distinguish between what is relevant to historical accuracy and what is attributable to the desire to exhort. The ancients, before us, were aware of this distinction. But in order to edify, some used means we, today, would rather avoid. We shall not expect their biblical commentaries to provide the same kind of explication as found in the works of Father Lagrange but a different sort which is still valuable in its own way. Consequently, critical information which modern requirements have made into a law for this type of writing must not be sought in the ancient lives of the saints. The *Analecta Bollandiana* correspond to one literary genre, the *Vitae sanctorum* to another. From the latter we must expect to learn, not historical facts, but ideas on monastic life and on sanctity as illustrated in non-historical themes. These texts must be approached according to form criticism (*Formgeschichte*): besides the actions of the personages they are dealing with, these texts also reveal to us something of their authors, the readers who liked them—in brief, something of a whole civilization. And, in addition, we can still find in them a few chronologically accurate facts.

Every age has its own set of values. When we admire a Renaissance palace we do not condemn it because living in it may have been uncomfortable. We acknowledge a successful artistic achievement, and we accept the fact that the men of the time may have had a different concept of daily living from ours. In like manner, medieval men took more interest in permanent and universal ideas than in specific events transitory in nature. To understand them, one must adopt their point of view. Once this is done, legend becomes, in a sense they themselves would have approved, truer than history. It brings to us another aspect of indivisible truth, one which belongs to the realm of the ideal rather than to its passing materializations.[67]

The Sermon

In monastic literature, the sermon is the genre most copiously represented, and with good reason: on the one hand, it is patristic—this is attested by all ancient homiletic tradition; on the other, it is monastic, essentially pastoral in character. But it differs from the sermons of the patristic age and from those which the regular clerics of medieval times preached to the secular clergy or, as appears to have been a more frequent practice, to other clerics regular, in so much as the sermon constitutes a part of monastic observance. The sermon is itself one of the observances. That there did exist a specifically monastic form of preaching is attested by the ancient customaries. Whatever time of the day was set aside for it, it never failed to be given, and we know how this rite, at once solemn and intimate, was performed in the great abbeys and in the monasteries which adopted their usages. These details amply explain the literary genre in which the spiritual conference most often appears: the commentary.

At Cluny, at Farfa, and at still other abbeys, the "sermon" took place twice a day and in two different locations: the first time in the morning, in the cloister before the beginning of the manual work of the day—then, the sermon would at times have as its topic the book which was being read in the refectory; the second, in the evening when the work was over, at the very place where the work was being done, for example under a tree or some other spot where all could sit around the superior. This talk or *collatio* often had as its theme a text from Scripture, or from the *Rule*, or some patristic writing. In any case, the appointed reader—a monk or a child—first of all shows the passage he is going to read to his superior so that the latter can read it and prepare his commentary. Then he reads two or three lines until the superior stops him with the *Tu autem*, after which the superior, or the one he has asked to do so, explains the reading.[68]

Preaching was, then, an institution and was widely practiced. There is no evidence to show that it was always done by the abbot; at least, most texts say nothing about this. We do have examples of sermons which were preached and later put into written form by ordinary religious like Julian of Vézelay or William or Merlehaut who dedicated his collected sermons to a person who appears to have been the abbot of his monastery.[69] There is nothing at all irregular in this since the customaries made provision for such cases.

However, all the sermons that were preached were not put into writing any more than all that were written were delivered. Thus we must differentiate between different kinds of sermons. Some have come down to us as single units, others in collections. The first are rare; there are few authors represented by only one sermon. Most sermons have reached us in the form of collections compiled either by the author himself or by his auditors and disciples. Julian of Vézelay, dedicating his collection to his abbot, writes: "At the request of many people, your charity constrained me to revise, and then to assemble in book form, the little sermons which I had delivered in chapter and had put into writing; they had been snatched from me and had become scattered."[70] In this case, as in several others, it is the author himself who first writes and then revises and assembles isolated texts which through dissemination had passed beyond his control. In other cases, auditors write up another's sermons, sometimes without his knowledge, or even after his death. This was done by the disciples of Odo of Morimond.[71] This leads us to the principal distinction which must be made between monastic sermons: those which were delivered and those which were not.

Sententiae

In reality, the sermons which were actually preached were greatest in number; however, these are, without a doubt, the rarest among those we now have in written form. There was no stenography, no system of abbreviations making it possible to take down the words as they were uttered.[72] We can, nevertheless, get an idea of what oral preaching was like from two kinds of texts. Some are actual transcripts; in this case they are relatively well developed and fairly long redactions. Thanks to this procedure, we possess a few of St. Bernard's sermons "reported" by his auditors.[73] They are most revealing: certain—in fact, some of the most important—aspects of Bernard's psychology are known only through texts of this kind. In similar fashion, toward the middle of the twelfth century, the sermons of an abbot of Admont were taken down in notes, unknown to him, by a cloistered nun and, rare enough in that period, fairly accurately.[74] The sermons that were preached, however, are most frequently found to have been transmitted in the form of *sententiae*, or even sometimes in what the manuscripts call *sententiolae*. These are brief texts which give a résumé or simply an outline, written either by the author himself before or after the sermon or, more often, by auditors during or after the sermon. These texts constitute what are sometimes called *exceptiones*—the word meaning at that time not excerpts but texts "seized" in flight (*excipere*)—or, as is more frequently the case, *sententiae* in a sense proper to the monastic vocabulary. In scholasticism, the *sententia* is the text itself under discussion, or else the result of the *quaestio* and the *disputatio*, that is to say, the *determinatio* of the master. In monastic tradition, however, the primitive meaning of *sententia* is also the text being commented. Therefore, in Cistercian manuscripts, facing passages of the *Rule* concerning the divine office which consist merely of enumerations of Psalms, we read this notice: *Haec sententia non exponitur*.[75] But very shortly, and in a more generally accepted sense, the *sententia* is the exposition itself reported in résumé. Since these résumés are dealing with "outlines" of sermons, exhortations which are, in a sense, meditations spoken aloud, they are generally clear. Many appear in the form of numerically divided parts: "The community has two walls: an inner wall and an outer wall. . . . Three goods preserve unity: patience, humility, and charity. . . ."[76] There are three kinds of penitence. . . . Four things confer true humility. . . ."[77] There are thus two Advents, two loves, two spurs, two feet of God, three degrees of obedience, three kinds of chalices, horses, and lights, four animals, four loaves, four impediments to confession, and so on. In this framework, imagination was disciplined. An example, quoted in its entirety, will show the sense of what is fitting, the good nature and the power of observation that Bernard employed daily in his commentaries on the *Rule*. In reference to the first chapter, he said:

> In every monastery can be found the four kinds of monks enumerated by St. Benedict. First, the cenobites, under obedience according to the common rule of the monastery and the rule of the communal life. Then, the anchorites: it is of them that the Book of Job says, "They have built for themselves solitudes";[78] though living in community, they devote themselves, with the most honorable intentions, to meditation in private. Then come the spiritual gyrovagues: their inconstancy carries them from reading to prayer, from prayer to work, preventing them from obtaining the benefits of their undertakings: stability in effort and perseverance in devotion. Victims of *acedia*, they think it better at one moment to do one thing, and, at another, something else; they begin everything and finish nothing. Finally there are the Sarabites: loving only themselves, pursuing only their own interests, they go about in groups of two, three, or four, forging opinions and devising observances contrary to the common rule of the monastery, creating cliques and divisions, never ceasing to sow unrest in the flock of the Lord through the obstinacy with which they defend their egos and their individuality.[79]

This way of numbering the different "points" of the sermon makes its memorization easier for the author who is going to speak—and, if the points are written down in advance, for the auditor who is supposed to take notes; or, if they are written afterward, for those later on who will wish to reflect on them. These will find in them "points for meditation."

Collections of sentences of this kind are numerous, and sometimes voluminous. Occasionally all the sentences in a single collection come from the same author. St. Bernard's, for example, are combined with long sermons[80] or assembled in separate series.[81] Other sentences from the same collection may emanate from different preachers; among them, moreover, may be found sentences by Origen, Cassian, and the Fathers, that is to say, résumés set up in the form of "points" from passages of theirs that had been read. Many of these collections are anonymous: they represent common—that is to say, typical of the average monk—monastic wisdom and are the ones, without a doubt, which give us the most faithful account of the topics which were treated daily in lectures at innumerable abbeys where the abbots were by no means on a level with the outstanding orators whose discourses were normally worth publishing.[82] The dominant characteristic of all these sentences is that they are hardly, if at all, speculative; they are eminently practical. In them can be glimpsed monastic good sense, which is spontaneous and unaffected and which is transmitted with a minimum of literary effect. These medieval monastic *sententiae* are very reminiscent of the *Verba seniorum* of ancient monasticism. They resemble them and in reality are continuations of them.

Among these sermons, barely influenced by the laws of writing, we can easily distinguish those which were composed without having been delivered, at least not in the form in which we have received them. Here again they fall into two categories. The first are sermons which have no connection with real preaching. They were composed to be sent like a letter or else inserted in a letter.[83] Accordingly, a monk will address an exhortation to an abbess who will pronounce it before her nuns, or St. Anselm will compose a sermon for a recluse so he can recite it in the presence of the faithful who come to see him. Occasionally, one monk will ask another for a sermon, a request that is never denied. Writing it gives both pleasure to another and an opportunity to exhort oneself through preaching to another. Works of this description belong, from a certain point of view, to the epistolary genre. They are nevertheless sermons, and in harmony with this literary form. On all points they resemble the second category of sermons, themselves also written sermons. The latter may have some connection with actual preaching, but because of the form in which they have been preserved they are "literary" sermons.

From the eighth century on, we have examples of sermons written to be read in a community,[84] although often they were intended for a larger public. In this case they are more markedly doctrinal in nature. While the sentences give us the daily, familiar teaching of the abbots, it is the literary sermons we must consult for the theology of those who may have had one. The fact that St. Bernard, for example, did the major part of his teaching in the form of sermons does not exclude his having proposed a theology. He expressed his ideas very fully, but as a monk–theologian who is addressing monks, and not as a teacher resolving problems in the presence of pupils. The "written" character of the sermons stems from the fact that they generally form collections, some of which are liturgical collections. Just as was done by many of the clergy, Maurice of Sully and others composed sermons for the priests to read to the faithful; so in the monasteries, sermons are composed which are intended to be read privately or else publicly in the chapter or the refectory. An example can be found in St. Bernard's four homilies on the *Missus est*, which are one of the masterpieces of Christian eloquence—one is even tempted to say of the "Christian pulpit," were it not that they begin with these very characteristic words: *Scribere me aliquid et devotio iubet. . . .*[85] It is precisely because St. Bernard, for reasons of health, is separated for a time from communal life that he chooses to take advantage of this leisure to talk about the Virgin, *loqui videlicet*; not being able to preach, he will speak through the written word. The result was to be what he himself calls "an opuscule" composed of sermons, and which probably appeared in two successive editions, the first including only a part of the initial three sermons.

Other collections of sermons form biblical commentaries. This is eminently true of the *Sermons on the Canticle by St. Bernard*.[86] This lengthy doctrinal treatise has come down to us in a form obviously quite different from a version to be delivered before an assemblage of monks. While most of their subjects are monastic in tone, there are some that are clearly not— as, for example, an invective against ambition in prelates. Two of them are a detailed answer to a doctrinal inquiry he had received from outside the monastery. In them St. Bernard refutes, point by point, the Rhineland heretics whom Eberwin of Steinfeld had denounced to him,[87] while at the same time there were, close at hand, heretics just as dangerous whom he does not even mention. This is not to imply that St. Bernard did no preaching whatever on the Canticle; he had, and often. But it is not the *Sermons on the Canticle* that tell us how he did this. Neither can it be learned from the *Brief Commentary* whose style is that of a résumé of real sermons, whereas the *Sermons on the Canticle* are the development of this résumé.[88] Similarly, when Gilbert of Hoyland undertook to continue St. Bernard's incomplete commentary on the Canticle he started by rewriting and putting to further use sermons he had already composed for some nuns. The succeeding part is an original composition which has nothing in common with actual preaching.[89] Between the sermons orally delivered and those that were composed, and have come down to us, there is, therefore, an intermediate step: writing. Sometimes, moreover, there may even be two steps because sermons were not always edited by the author himself. In St. Bernard's case, for instance, we must differentiate between those entirely composed by him and those composed by his "notaries" and later submitted, more or less, for his correction. Several series of "Bernardine sermons" belong therefore to what might be called "the school of St. Bernard." The work of disciples written during Bernard's lifetime or after his death, these texts bring us his teaching and, in this sense, they are authentically Bernardine—though they reveal his style only to a certain degree. His thought can be found in them but not his way of expressing himself.[90]

St. Bernard and his "Secretaries"

Some of Bernard's notaries, moreover, imitated him closely enough so that their writings, within a very short time, came to be confused with his.[91] This intervention by notaries also explains why some sermons have come down to us in two or more different versions.[92] To understand this, one must recall the medieval meaning of the word *dictare*; it did not mean "to dictate" in the sense given to this word today and which it still had during the patristic age.[93] It means to compose, to draw up, to write a literary work. Often, they used to write aloud, just as they read aloud; the author therefore dictated to himself what he was writing. He would enunciate it as his hand was writing the words. As Alcuin once put it, "the tongue dictated to the hand."[94] To "dictate" could thus refer to the successive stages of composition.[95] First came the impressing on wax tablets of the first draft of a work; this was reread, corrected, and only then was the definitive version "noted" either by the author himself or, more frequently, by a professional "notary" who copied it over or took it down from dictation.

Dictare is therefore the author's own work. He is the *dictator*, the creator, the poet, and, as they still say in German, the *Dichter*.[96] Consequently *dictator* is occasionally a synonym for *versificator*.[97] As for the copyist, he is the one who "notes," the *notarius* who puts into writing the work of the author.[98] Hence, we can understand how the word *dictamen*, which, beginning with the second half of the twelfth century, was to be used more and more to designate the art of letter writing, had at first been applied to the art of composing literary works of every description. The *Breviarium de dictamine* or the *Dictaminum radii* by Alberic of Monte Cassino has also the title of *Flores rhetorici*. It illustrates by means of examples taken from St. Augustine and Boethius, but mainly from the classical authors, the *figurae verborum et sententiarum* (figures of speech), sometimes also referred to as *proprietates* or *colores rhetorici*: that is to say, all the rules and devices which can be employed to "ornament" a piece of writing.[99] It is these rules which govern all literary genres, including the sermon.

RHETORIC AND SINCERITY

These observations bring up a problem which is really the most serious of all those that arise in monastic literature. If all these sermons are written according to the literary conventions, if all is "literature," is there anything left that is spontaneous, living, and really sincere? Are they all worth the time spent in reading them? Assuredly, they should be read, but one must know how to read them. If, like the author, one can accept its demands, rhetoric only adds to beauty. And, there is a true beauty in the mastery, in the total liberty with which the best monastic preachers manipulate these devices and were not enslaved by them. In so doing, the monks made their own times the last great classical period of the Middle Ages. Outside the monastic world, and in later times, preaching came to be governed as much by dialectics as by rhetoric. Sermons were composed which were rigidly logical, but which bear a much closer resemblance to *quaestiones disputatae* than they do to homilies, and the laws which govern them are codified in the vast literature of the *artes praedicandi*. In scholasticism, the technique of the sermon becomes more and more subtle and complicated: one manual on the art of preaching teaches, for example, eighteen ways to "lengthen a sermon."[100] The end result is a very clear, very logical oration which may be doctrinal and occasionally not devoid of stylistic or theological merit; but from this category, there is not in existence today one work of genius still worth reading.[101] One of the best informed authorities wrote: "The scholastics are professors. . . . Their sermons, like St. Thomas', will themselves be scholastic. And the Church will consider the greatest of them as its 'doctors,' no longer as its 'Fathers.' "[102] Consequently, to say the least, it was not in their sermons that they gave the best they had to offer.

The transition from the traditional and monastic sermon to this technical sermon takes place in the second half of the twelfth century. Even after this date, it is true that many monks remained faithful to the monastic manner of preaching. But from then on the contrast between the two methods—which reveal two different conceptions of preaching—becomes very evident from a comparison between a monastic preacher such as Geoffrey Babio and a scholastic preacher like Peter Comestor.[103]

> Toward the end of the twelfth century, although allegory was still far from approaching the end of its reign, the reading of the Bible tended to look for support to a more literal exegesis. At the same time, moreover, allegory was losing its purely mystical character in order to appeal more directly to the senses and the imagination. And so, there came about a merging of two tendencies, one due to the development of public preaching, the other to the expansion of the schools. The latter gave preaching a more abstract character, so abstract indeed, that at times spirituality seems to retreat before speculative thought; and upon occasion, the preacher, leaving the *terra firma* of reality, engages in futile word-juggling.[104]

In monasticism, they were content to imitate the models of genius that the Fathers of the Church had been, particularly St. Augustine, and to follow their suggestions, especially those St. Gregory had made in his *Pastoral Rule*, and, to an even greater degree, those of St. Augustine in book four of his great work on Christian education, the *De doctrina christiana*. Artifice is reduced to the minimum; it plays no greater part than that accorded it in ancient rhetoric where eloquence makes sport of eloquence, and where technique was never a substitute for inspiration.

Monastic sermons are then pieces of written rhetoric. The readers for whom they were written were also auditors. For their sake attention is given the elegant style which is of the essence, and the very definition, of eloquence. The writer keeps his hearers in mind and is stimulated by them. He aims to satisfy this demanding audience, and therefore he conforms to its taste and to its literary training in order to instruct, exhort, and even, what never does any harm, to please his audience, as St. Augustine as well as Cicero had recommended.[105] Monastic authors spontaneously give their writings an oratorical character. This determines, as if by the very nature of things, the devices they choose to use: rhymes, parallelisms, apostrophes, and even continuous verses. St. Bernard habitually writes artistic, rhythmical prose; at times, overcome with intense enthusiasm and great spiritual ardor, he will sing a hymn or a doxology similar to those found in the Epistles of St. Paul or the *Confessions* of St. Augustine.[106] When he writes —for he is essentially a writer and in this sense a man of letters—he always writes for someone, he is always addressing someone, and it is just as if he were speaking. His talent for oratory is given free rein. In any literary work, he remains an orator, and, to be more precise, a Christian orator; he is a preacher and he needs an audience. He needs to express himself in order to find an outlet for his inner fervor, he has to communicate his love, and, in expressing it, he feels it still more intensely. His style is always oratorical but especially so when he composes sermons. Bernard never thinks of his audience in the abstract. It is, he knows, far greater in number than if it were limited to a single community of the Clairvaux chapter. But Bernard is a universal doctor because of the fact that he is an orator; his message, though addressed to all, still retains its personal quality. He is a man with a human heart who thinks, prays, suffers, and yearns, and who wants to tell all men how they too should love God. In his letters and treatises as well as his sermons, his written style remains an oral one because Bernard cannot cease being an orator.

And yet he serves as merely one example to illustrate a psychology shared by many others. For others besides Bernard, art is reconciled with sincerity. The portion allotted to art consists of the legitimate, even necessary devices for which tradition furnished perfect models. These become conventional in scholasticism, but in monasticism they are still spontaneous thanks to an intensity of culture which was derived from the classics and the Fathers. Reminiscences of the ancient oratorical art are as spontaneous for the monks as biblical reminiscences. And because they are spontaneous and not the result of any "research," they can be taken lightly and quite for granted. As has been said,

> we admire the humanism of these churchmen who were so very learned, but what is no less remarkable is that some of them could prune from their style the artificial beauties which were inherent in their culture and which were even, at times, imposed by their own memory. . . . Their piety could effectively mitigate the demands of their own imperious natures.[107]

In their sermons, therefore, the artistic element poses no threat to sincerity. The element of sincerity accounts for the simplicity which makes these texts so easy, and even agreeable, to read. We feel that their authors are still free of the bonds of the rigid laws which were to govern scholastic preaching. The monastic preachers' modes of expression are the same as those of the rhetoric of all times in its essentials; they are not the product of a refined but soon outmoded rhetoric of any single milieu or any one period.

> The psychological demands of the present, and the necessity, experienced by many, of attaining the truth or of expressing it in the language of the moment, have no power over contemplatives who have withdrawn

from the world. Consequently, the spirituality which animates the patristic sermons seems less remote from our times than the spirituality of
the sermons of the High Middle Ages.[108]

In the same period when the technique of scholastic sermons had already
become complicated, the monks remained simple. They are "unified." They
used to like to say that the word monk expresses the unity (*monas*) they
realize within themselves.[109] This simplicity of the soul whose sole desire
is for God is apparent in their style. They feel no real conflict between the
pursuit of art and the search for God, between rhetoric and the transcendence which is the essence of their vocation, between grammar and the
desire for practice. Rhetoric has become a part of them; and without becoming dual personalities, but remaining wholly and uniquely monks,
they are able to use it to give expression to their sincerity.

Monastic Letter Writing

The letter was another literary form that the monks prized very much.
This way of conversing through the written word harmonized with the
silence enjoined by the *Rule*, with the vow of stability, and with cloistered
life. It had, besides, the authority of a long tradition. St. Benedict seems
to have foreseen that monks of the same monastery would write letters to
each other; he prescribes only that they should be sent to the addressee
through the abbot. The classical authors, and later the Fathers, had left
numerous examples of this genre. Among the former, Cicero and Seneca,
and among the latter, St. Jerome, continued to be the great masters of the
art. A postal service which operated between abbeys, particularly at times
when a death occurred, made it possible for the monks to carry on correspondence with each other. On these occasions, announcements, called
rolls (*rotuli*), would be sent to other religious houses. At the various stops
on his journey, the roll-carrier (*rolliger*) would report the news vocally
and also deliver business correspondence.[110] The announcement was copied
on a strip of parchment at the end of which a large space was left blank.
Then the whole was rolled up and the "roll" entrusted to a special carrier
who went off to display it at all the religious houses associated in the
same compact of sharing in prayer, which were often quite numerous. The
roll-carrier would start off with the letter announcing a death, enclosed in
a wooden or metal cylinder hanging at his side. One after the other he
would visit the appointed addresses. There, bells were rung to announce
his visit, and the monks would gather in the cloister, the chapter, or, more
customarily, in the church. We have information as to the ritual which

accompanied his reccption in several of the monasteries: first, he would bow before the altar, greet the community, and then unfurl his roll in the middle of the choir. A young religious would take it up and present it to the cantor who would read it aloud. Then the prayers requested in the announcement would begin.

Before the carrier was allowed to go on his way, he would be provided with food and an opportunity to rest. On the blank space at the end of the letter, a sort of receipt, a message of condolence, or the news of the monastery would be written. When the parchment strip became entirely filled with writing, an additional piece was sewed to it and later others as the document made the rounds, and its travels often covered quite a distance. An ancient roll from the Abbey of St. Peter of Ghent measures almost 70 feet in length and this is in proportion to the distance traveled, for the carrier visited as many as 524 religious houses and the additions made to the document required 28 extra pieces of parchment. The carrier was almost 16 months on his journey. A roll from St. Bavo is almost 100 feet long. It consists of fifty pieces of parchment and represents a twenty-month journey. Hence, with good reason, we can visualize medieval Europe as being crisscrossed in every direction by countless monastic couriers.

To understand the content of the letters, one must also recall what they were like even in their material aspect.[111] To write a letter, especially if one were not a trained copyist and had no secretary, no *notarius*, always cost time and effort. The very terms which serve to describe the writing of a letter tell us what time and resolution had to be devoted to it: one "engraved" a letter or "sculptured" it, as if by striking (*cudere*) the parchment from which the letter was extricated as if by plowing or digging (*exarare*); the parchment, even after careful preparation, always offered a certain resistance to the goose quill or the pen. The pieces of parchment (*schedulae*) used for personal letters must often have been only scraps; they were inferior in quality to the skillfully prepared skins reserved for the books copied in the scriptoria or for charters and public acts. Consequently the dimensions of the *schedula* might determine the size of the letter itself: running out of parchment curtailed any effusions. A letter could not be too verbose or too short; nevertheless the epistolary genre (*modus epistolaris*) retained its character of brevity in which it differed from books. This, no doubt, was one of the requirements of literary tradition but it may also have been a practical necessity; the raw material being scarce and costly, it was used with the greatest economy.

Writing a letter involved both expense and fatigue. It was always something of an event, as was receiving one. A letter was a gift whose value was appreciated because everyone knew just how much it entailed. Even personal letters therefore are almost always somewhat public in quality. It is generally taken for granted that the letter's contents will fall under the eyes, or reach the ears, of several others, and that the receiver will take pains to see that it is available. This explains how it can happen that the writer will tell his correspondent things that both already know; he is taking into consideration the fact that others will read what he has written. Whenever a member of a religious community received a letter from a friend, everyone was immediately informed. It was passed from one to another or even read in community and admired by all. The writer of a letter took great pains with it because he knew it would be brought to the attention of a more or less extensive audience. He was, therefore, almost always motivated by concern for public opinion. Many letters, on this account, have a quality that is literary and real at the same time. The laws which governed the *modus epistolaris* were observed in the composition of the most ordinary letters.[112] They called for a special form of composition. To conform to the tradition handed down from antiquity, a letter had to include the following: a salutation, an introduction, a narrative, a petition, and finally a conclusion,[113] the whole ornamented with rhetorical figures and expressed in a more or less rhythmical style.

During the second half of the twelfth century, the art of letter writing was to be codified with greater and greater precision in the *artes dictandi* whose technicality was soon to become as complex as that of the *artes praedicandi*. Here again, monasticism was to retain greater simplicity, and the monastic writers were guided almost exclusively by the ancient tradition. The general norms it had established were followed, the different types of letters it had distinguished were respected (*genera epistolarum*), and inspiration was found in the models it had bequeathed. The *dictamen* consisted in formula-models rather than in numerous and precise rules. Literary technique exacted a certain conformity, but in this case more than in others, it was more easily reconciled with the spontaneity of the spiritual life. The truth of this fact becomes apparent when one examines these documents: there is more élan, more of the interior life in most monastic letters, even those written by anonymous monks and secondary authors, than in those of the greatest letter writers who were not monks, like Yves of Chartres, Peter of Blois, and John of Salisbury. If there is art, or even artifice, in monastic letters just as in the others, they are in no way fictitious. They are merely fine letters in which spontaneous feelings are expressed in the forms fixed by literature. In reading them we must always make allowance for the part played by this literary attitude. Once again, we must repeat that taking a medieval text seriously does not necessarily mean taking all its expressions literally.

Monastic milieux, their intense life, and their psychology could not be really understood if their epistolary literature were not taken into account. St. Bernard reveals as much of himself in his letters as in his sermons. Letters were very numerous, and these writings which can be called "minor" (since they are neither long treatises nor solemn sermons) are, no doubt, the very ones which best enable us to penetrate into the atmosphere of the cloister. It is true that many letters have been lost, and many are unedited or have been but recently published, and we must not delude ourselves into thinking that we are well acquainted with the average monastic milieu. Most sources of information still elude us. But at least when a literary genre is as copiously represented as the monastic letter—and this is true for all observances, as much for the Cistercian as for any other Order —we can presume that it was practiced to a much greater degree than the extant examples would lead us to believe. They enable us, however, to picture almost every aspect of monastic life; indeed, some aspects are known to us only through letters.

Vocation Letters

At this point it is necessary to describe briefly the principal types of letters, of which there is quite a variety. "Vocation letters,"[114] in which a monk, sometimes a young monk, full of admiration for his new state, urges his former fellow-students to follow his example: "If you only knew how content I am in the monastery," he tells them in substance, "you would immediately come and share this same existence." A novice of Clairvaux, in St. Bernard's time, reminds a cleric he had known in the schools of their old-time friendship: "When we were students, you never left my side. Do you still feel the same way?" And he ends his note with these words: "If I had become Archbishop of Rheims, you would already have joined me. What are you waiting for to come and join the novice of Clairvaux?" It is possible that some of these writings are not real letters, for, just as there are sermons which were not delivered, there are, no doubt, letters which were not sent. But even these are sincere. They may have been composed by someone for his own sake, to define or recall the motives for his vocation in the way one meditates by writing. Or perhaps they may have been school or novitiate exercises, which a schoolmaster or the master of novices had proposed as a theme for composition: "Write a letter to a friend encouraging him to enter monastic life." In any case this kind of writing shows us the monks' conception of their vocation and of their life itself.

Letters of exhortation, of consolation, of "direction" as we would say today: many such are found in the correspondence of Elmer,[115] St. Bernard, Peter the Venerable, Adam of Perseigne, and many other abbots.

Doctrinal consultations exist; exchanges of answers to points of controversy, as in the correspondence of William of Auberive with the abbot of Lieu-Dieu.[116]

Business letters may be found, like those in which the Fécamp monks dealt with their properties located in England, but in which considerations of a personal, even of an intimate, nature are interspersed with the financial problems.[117]

Letters of recommendation are at times very brief like the phrases we jot down on a postcard or a calling card, but they are nonetheless charming for their brevity. Many of them have disappeared because of the small dimensions of the *chartula* on which they were written. An exquisite little note of this description, written by St. Bernard, has been recovered, addressed to Pope Eugene III, consisting of but a single line. These few words tell everything: the youth of the candidate, his moral character, intellectual gifts and good reputation: "*Mittimus ad te iuvenem pudicum, ut aiunt, litteratum pro aetate. Cetera sunt in spe.*"[118] What charity, what confidence in the final insinuation!

Letters may be seen exhorting the dying to make a good death, of congratulation to the fortunate monk who is finally about to enter the heavenly Jerusalem. An admirable missive of Peter of Celle to the dying Alvisus of Anchin inspired his successor to provide us with an equally fine description of this abbot's last moments.[119] There are other letters which are death-announcements and in which the whole doctrine on the death of a monk is transmitted.[120]

Finally, for every stage of monastic life, there are letters of friendship in abundance whose sole purpose was to give pleasure to the recipient. Sometimes they coincide with genres already enumerated, but in the main, they have no ulterior purpose or any precise end in view. They are sent to relatives, to friends who have remained in the world; these are called "epistolary visits." Formularies furnish models for them at Cîteaux as elsewhere.[121] But, for the most part, these friendly letters are exchanged between monks;[122] they are addressed to confrères either in the same monastery or at a distance, to childhood friends, former classmates, intimates from whom one is separated by the circumstances of life. And when they want to write to each other without having anything in particular to say, they send one another prayers, edifying thoughts,[123] or dissertations. On two occasions Peter Damian felt like writing to Abbot Desiderius and the monks of Monte Cassino. Casting around for something to say, he got the idea, as he admits in the preamble to the first of these letters, to examine the question as to why, in the representations of the Apostles, St. Peter is placed on the left, St. Paul on the right. . . .[124] In his second letter, he was to adapt the symbolic significance of various animals to monks.[125] However, most of the time there is no lack of inspiration. With no feeling of constraint, the monks give vent to effusions and elevations which express communion in a common ideal, an identical desire for God.

Of course, in these demonstrations of affection, rhetoric does play a part. Still, a more disinterested kind of friendship appears in them than is to be found in friendly letters composed in a non-monastic environment. This contrast becomes apparent when the entire epistolary literature of a given period is examined. The great importance given to friendship in the monks' letters shows how considerable a part it played in monastic life itself. There is no need at this point to retrace the history of friendship from antiquity to the Middle Ages and to show the relation of monastic friendship to the tradition.[126] It is enough to point out that it was the monks who contributed most to the rediscovery of a type of friendship which had almost disappeared from literature after the invasions: pure, disinterested friendship which solicits no favors. The expansion of feudal relationships had encouraged the appearance of a form of *amicitia* which was merely a juridical bond. In many formularies, the numerous kinds of friends are differentiated according to the services each could be expected to perform. People had to relearn to love one another without ulterior motives, to write to each other to give pleasure, or to do another good without seeking material advantages. From the Carolingian period on, many monks excelled in this. If, during the great monastic expansion of the twelfth century, the greatest number of letters attesting this type of friendship were the work of Benedictine and Cistercian letter writers, is it not because the love of God and of one's neighbor was the very core of their lives? It was also the heart of their doctrine and the subject of their most revealing treatises from St. Benedict of Aniane[127] to Aelred of Rievaulx.[128] Thus literature is the reflection of what is most profound in the monastic soul.

Florilegia

Finally there is a genre which monasticism did not invent but upon which it impressed, as on others, its own stamp: the *florilegium*. The monks did not invent this genre, since it had been practiced for didactic purposes in Greek and Latin antiquity.[129] The monks often used it, however, in a way that differed from that of the schools. In the monasteries and the towns, the grammar schools had collections of examples taken from the authors. These collections of excerpts, either from the classics or, more frequently, from the Fathers and the councils, were used by the urban schools in particular as a veritable arsenal of *auctoritates*. They were seeking important, concise, and interesting extracts for doctrinal studies, something of value for the *quaestio* and the *disputatio*. In this way the master or student acquired a capital of arguments and proofs always conveniently ready for use. As with Denzinger or Rouet de Journel in our age, these collections facilitated research; they eliminated the necessity of handling numbers of manuscripts. Consequently, they were primarily working tools for the intellectuals.

The monastic *florilegium*, on the other hand, grew out of spiritual reading. The monk would copy out texts he had enjoyed so as to savor them at leisure and use them anew as subjects for private meditation. The monastic *florilegium* not only originated in the monk's spiritual reading but always remained closely associated with it. For this reason the texts selected were different from those required in the schools,[130] and we have manuscripts offering collections of monastic *florilegia*. Many monks, from Defensor of Ligugé in the seventh century to Helinand of Froidmont in the beginning of the thirteenth, compiled them either for their own use or for community reading in the refectory or at the *collatio*,[131] and some of them were very widely disseminated.

These collections are sometimes entitled *Sententiae* or Extracts: *Excerptiones, Excerpta*, or even, through derivation, *Scarapsus*. But more often they were given poetic titles: "Book of Sparklets" or, again, *Florilegia*: *Flores, Deflorationes, Defloratiunculae*. The colors of these choice flowers depict good conduct.[132] Like bees, we sip from them what is most nutritious,[133] and, in his own way, each author develops this flower symbolism. There are different kinds of these bouquets. In medieval metaphor, the perfume they exude and the honey that can be extracted from them vary according to the flower-bed where these writings were culled and collected. The *florilegia* are divided according to their general design, but particularly with reference to sources and objectives. The source could be a single author: for instance, collections of excerpts from St. Gregory the Great were very numerous, beyond any doubt the most numerous of all, because the Gregorian texts were eminently conducive to contemplative prayer. But collections were also made of texts by St. Jerome, St. Anthony, St. Nilus, and St. Isidore. Sometimes, they are followed by a series of excerpts from several authors. The compiler may also add some more or less original contribution of his own: between patristic texts, the subject of the *lectio*, he will intersperse thoughts and aspirations which have been suggested by his own *meditatio*. The structure is as free as the outline for meditation. To emphasize that there is nothing systematic about it, many an author will choose an entirely conventional number of chapters: one hundred. Maximus the Confessor and Diadochus of Photike had written *Centuries*. Smaragdus in his *Diadem*[134] and Walter Daniel[135] restrict themselves to the same figure. Even in this manner of choosing another's texts, there is an element of fantasy that defies logic.

The monks, at the same time, did not refuse to own or transcribe collections of sentences created by scholasticism. In these they could find patristic texts and doctrine based on them as interpreted by the masters. But on this point, as well, they preferred, as if instinctively, the sentences which issued from the schools whose teaching was most definitely traditional. The scholastic texts are most fully represented in monastic libraries of the twelfth century by the works of Anselm of Laon, William of Champeaux, and Hugh of St. Victor.[136] These masters are regular canons whose cloistered existence is like that of the monks, and whose doctrine is "strictly patristic." In contrast, the monks' position is one of "silent opposition" in regard to Abailard, Gilbert of la Porée and even Anselm of Canterbury; to any, in short, whose writings betray a greater preoccupation with the dialectical method of intellectual research. The monks hardly ever contend with them but abstain from reading them or having them copied. Their decision reveals to us a deep-rooted tendency. If they do use writings from the school of Laon, if Benedictine or Cistercian copyists intermingle sentences from the Laon school with works by William of Saint Thierry or St. Bernard—whose excerpts sometimes bear an astonishing resemblance to the Laon sentences—it is because all these texts are equally dependent upon patristic sources.

Some monks devoted their attention to the needs of the secular clergy. In the twelfth century, Werner of St. Blaise, preoccupied, as it were, with the liturgical pastoral sermon, offers parish priests a vast choice of texts from the Fathers and a few recent authors to be used in their preaching.[137] But most monastic *florilegia* would, today, be considered as being ascetic and mystical in nature: ascetic *florilegia* which remind the conscience of its obligations, mystical florilegia which promote prayer, sustain attentiveness to the presence of God, and foster contemplation. To this last genre are due some of the most beautiful texts produced by the monastic Middle Ages: the "little prayer books" by John of Fécamp in which it is difficult to detect what is original and what comes from the Fathers. The truth is that everything is his and, at one and the same time, everything is the Fathers'. He said himself: *Dicta mea, dicta Patrum.* But before the Fathers' texts were passed on to us they had been appreciated through being read with a love and devotion that made reading a prayer.[138] From this fervent reading—*lectionis igne*—nurtured by desire for God, and savored *in palato cordis*, these texts have emerged refined, polished, and enriched with new sweetness. They have become immediately assimilable; they no longer demand any effort, merely consent. They can, henceforth, be used as the basis for the kind of reading which produced them and which shares the same characteristics of fervent love, persistence, and even repetition: *Saepius relegere*, as Alcuin had recommended.[139] *Cotidie lectitare et lecta frequenter in corde revolvere* advises John of Fécamp.[140] The monks, trained to the life of prayer by the liturgy in which the Church tirelessly repeats the same formulas, the same one hundred and fifty Psalms, could, without taking them for granted, read and reread the most beautiful pages of the Bible and of the Fathers. The *florilegia*, in which reading and prayer become as one, provided the best possible means for the kind of meditation closest to their hearts, a means completely devoid of any method. Consequently it is understandable that generations of contemplatives looked upon them as their staff of life, and copied them over endlessly, scarcely ever knowing whose writings they were. They were no longer the sayings of this or that author; they were the anonymous pronouncements of the Fathers of the Church: *dicta Patrum.* And soon, especially in Cistercian monasteries, to these were to be appended excerpts from the "last of the Fathers," St. Bernard. They also are in perfect harmony with the title given to this type of *florilegium*: "Booklets assembled from the Scripture and the words of the Fathers, intended mainly for those who love the contemplative life."[141]

NOTES

1. "Recherches sur les Sermons sur les cantiques de S. Bernard," RB (1955) 80–81.
2. *Liber quo ordine sermo fieri debeat*, PL 156.21–52.
3. *Dialogus super auctores* (ed. Huygens, pp. 17–18).
4. The dialogues sometimes treat of real persons, but more often of fictitious characters. "La vêture 'ad succurrendum,' d'après le moine Raoul," *Analecta monastica* III 158–65. C. H. Talbot, *Aelred of Rievaulx, De Anima* (London, 1952).

5. G. Cohen, *La comédie latine en France au XIIe siècle* (Paris, 1931) I xxxix, writes that the comedies edited in the volume originated in the "monastic schools"; as a matter of fact, he realized elsewhere (p. xxviii) that their authors belonged to the scholastic milieux of the second half of the twelfth century. The edition of the *Historia septem sapientium* of the Cistercian John of Haute Seille, at the beginning of the thirteenth century (ed. A. Hilka; Heidelberg, 1913), is the work of a discontented monk, as he himself says in the preface, p. 1; on this piece, cf. E. K. Rand, "The Mediaeval Virgil," *Studi Medievali* (1932) 437. This sort of pedagogical riddle, to which has been given the name of *joca monachorum*, often takes the form of a dialogue between Epictetus and the Emperor Hadrian, and depends in large part on the Bible; see the edition of W. Suchier, *Das mittellateinische Gespräch Adrian und Epictetus nebst verwandten Texten (Joca monachorum)* (Tübingen, 1955).

6. St. Peter Damian, *De perfecta monachi informatione* 4 (PL 145.724).

7. M. Hubert, "Aspects du latin philosophique aux xiie et xiiie siècles," *Rev. d' ét. latines* 27 (1949) 217.

8. R. McKeon, "Rhetoricism in the Middle Ages," *Speculum* (1942) 1–8.

9. "Un traité de fallaciis in theologia," *Revue de moyen âge latin* 1 (1945) 43–46. M.-D. Chenu, "Grammaire et théologie aux xiie et xiiie siècles," *Arch. d'hist. doct. et litt. du moyen âge* (1936) 5–28.

10. J. de Ghellinck, *L'essor de la littérature latine au XIIe siècle* II 10.

11. There is a list of Benedictine historians in Germany in *Münchener theologische Zeitschrift* (1953) 242.

12. Cf. J. M. Canivez, art. "Cîteaux (Ordre)" in DHGE XII (1953) 914.

13. "Ut in eo viri eruditione praestantes alerentur, qui regni annales resque posterorum memoria dignas cartis quotannis mandarent," quoted by Canivez, ibid. 915.

14. A. Wilmart, "Le couvent et la bibliothèque de Cluny," *Revue Mabillon* (1921) 113–15.

15. "Scientia interpretandi poetas et historicos," *De clericorum institutione* III (PL 107.395). See p. 17, *supra*.

16. A. Viscardi, "La cultura nonantonala nei sec. xi–xii," *Disputazione di storia patria per le antiche provincie Modenesi* (Ser. VIII, 5 [Modena, 1953] 349–51).

17. *In Matt.* V (PL 168.1424).

18. H. Woltjer, *Ordericus Vitalis*, p. 195.

19. L. Sorrento, "Tito Livio dal Medio Evo al Rinascimento," *Medievalia* (Brescia, 1944), pp. 410–12. G. Billanovich, *Lamperto di Hersfeld e Tito Livio* (Padua, 1945), p. 47 could speak of the "religious Livy" conceived of by medieval monks: he shows how Lambert of Hersfeld applied to the history of a monastery the same formulas Livy had used in speaking of the political and military history of Rome (p. 33 and *passim*). Also, Thierry of St. Trond († 1107), in order to exalt the virtues of Landradus of Münster–Bilsen, took as his model the portrait Livy drew of Hannibal, without once succumbing to bathos. Ibid. 39.

20. Woltjer, *Ordericus Vitalis*, p. 195.

21. Ps. 144.10.

22. *De miraculis*, Prol. (PL 189.907–909).

23. "Ad laudem Creatoris et omnium rerum iusti Gubernatoris chronographia pangenda est"; this text, among others, is quoted by Woltjer (n. 20), p. 73 and notes.

24. Ibid., p. 204*n*56.

25. L. Arbusow, *Liturgie und Geschichtsschreibung im Mittelalter* (Bonn, 1951).

26. P. Lehmann, "Mittelalterliche Büchertitel," *Sb. d. Bay. Akad. d. Wiss.* (1953) Heft 3, 20–24.

27. Woltjer (n. 20), p. 71.

28. H. L. Mikoletzky, "Sinn und Art der Heiligung im frühen Mittelalter," *Mitt. des Instit. f. Österr. Geschichtsforsch.* (1949) 105.

29. We have evidence for this fact, in the diocese of Liège, in H. Silvestre, "Renier de S. Laurent et le declin des écoles liégeoises au xiie siècle," *Annales du Congrès archéologique et historique de Tournai* (1949), p. 122.

30. J. P. Bonnes, "Un lettré du xe siècle. Introduction au poème de Létald," *Revue Mabillon* (1943) 29–33: "L'historien et l'écrivain," and 24n2.

31. *Vita S. Juliani, Epist. dedic.* 4 (PL 137.784).

32. *De sanctis et eorum pignoribus* I, 1 (PL 156.615).

33. This is the point of Book I of the same treatise (PL 156.607–30).

34. Book V (ibid. 649–66).

35. Book I, II, 5 (ibid. 620 and *passim*). G. Monod, *De la méthode historique chez Guibert de Nogent* (Paris, 1904).

36. *Hist. Eccles.* II 161, cited by Woltjer (n. 20), p. 204n71.

37. C. H. Talbot, "The liber confortatorius of Goscelin of St. Bertin," *Analecta monastica* III 11–22: "Goscelin as Hagiographer."

38. "Nescit adeo recens scriptor, omni probamento desertus, quid eius vita terris ignota astruat, nisi quod illi communes aliorum sanctorum virtutes aggerat," quoted ibid. 17n83.

39. Texts will be found ibid. 17–18.

40. B. de Gaiffier, "Les revendications de biens dans quelques documents hagiographiques du xie siècle," *Analecta bollandiana* (1932) 123–38, quotes examples taken from monastic literature. N. Huyghebaert quotes a similar example, *Sacris Erudiri* 7 (1955) 165.

41. Thus in the stories as to the finding of the tooth of Our Lord at St. Médard; cf. B. de Gaiffier, "La source latine du miracle Dou sainct dent Nostre Seigneur," *Neuphilologische Mitteilungen* 54 (Helsinki, 1953) 195–201.

42. "La consécration légendaire de la basilique de Saint-Denis et la question des indulgences," *Revue Mabillon* (1943) 74–84.

43. H. Silvestre, *Le Chronicon S. Laurentii Leodiensis dit de Rupert de Deutz* (Louvain, 1952).

44. H. Delehaye, *The Legends of the Saints*, tr. D. Attwater (New York, 1962), p. 3.

45. W. Lampen, "Mittelalterliche Heiligenlegenden und die lateinische Philologie des Mittelalters," *Liber Floridus: Festschrift P. Lehmann*, p. 122. R. Aigrain, *L'Hagiographie* (Paris, 1953) 305–12, gives some examples from monastic literature in the judicious pages he devotes to the history of hagiography from the end of the patristic era to the twelfth century.

46. These metrical lives can be compared with the legends composed in dramatic form by Hrotswitha, in the tenth century. Cf. E. Franceschini, "Il teatro postcarolingio," *I problemi comuni dell' Europa post–carolingia* (Spoleto, 1955) 307.

47. B. de Gaiffier, "L'Hagiographie et son public au xie siècle," *Miscellanea L. van der Essen* (1947) 135–66.

48. "Compendioso magis quam compto sermone aliquanta discerpere, ut in vigiliis videlicet sollemnitatis ipsius habeant fideles populi . . . ut possint in laudibus omni-

potentis Dei eiusdemque pretiosi martyris largius devotiusque vacare." Prologue of Leo Ostiensis to his *De origine beati Clementis*, edd. P. Meyvaert and P. Deos, *Analecta Bollandiana* 73 (1955) 417.

49. There is a curious example taken from Book III of the *Vita prima* of St. Bernard which is quoted by A. de Meyer and J. M. De Smet, RHE (1953) 190–93.

50. O. Köhler, *Das Bild des geistlichen Fürsten in den Viten des 10. und 12. Jahrhunderts* (Berlin, 1935).

51. St. Gregory the Great followed a model of this kind in his life of St. Benedict, in Book II of his *Dialogues*. It has been studied from this point of view in a study by A. Sapin, *Le moine d'après Les Dialogues de S. Grégoire le Grand* (Grenoble, 1953). Since then, B. Steidle has shown that many of the themes used by Gregory were to be found in the oldest monastic literature, especially in the *Vita Antonii*: "Homo Dei Antonius: Zum Bild des 'Mannes Gottes' im alten Mönchtum," *Studia Anselmiana* 38 (1956) 149–95.

52. H. Baumann, "Die Historiographie des Mittelalters als Quelle für die Ideengeschichte des Königstums," *Historische Zeitschrift* (1955); 458–72: "Heiligengeschichte und Profanhistorie."

53. W. Lampen (n. 45), p. 127.

54. B. de Gaiffier, "La lecture des actes des martyrs dans la prière liturgique en Occident," *Analecta Bollandiana* 72 (1954) 161.

55. W. Lampen (n. 45), p. 122.

56. B. Krusch, "La falsification des vies de Saints burgondes," *Mélanges J. Havet* (Paris, 1895) 38.

57. See *supra*, note 38.

58. PL 137.785.

59. Ibid. 781–82.

60. M. A. Dimier, "La lettre de Pythagore et les hagiographes médiévaux," *Le moyen âge* (1954) 403–18.

61. V. Saxer, "La 'Vie de Sainte Marie Madeleine' attribuée au pseudo-Rhaban Maur, œuvre claravallienne du XIIe siècle," *Mélanges S. Bernard* (Dijon, 1954) 408–21, and "La Crypte et les sarcophages de Saint-Maximin dans la littérature latine du moyen âge," *Provence historique* (1955) 203.

62. S. Roisin, "Réflexions sur la culture intellectuelle en nos abbayes cisterciennes médiévales," *Miscellanea L. van der Essen* (1947) 247.

63. "S. Bernard docteur," *Coll. Ord. Cist. Ref.* (1954) 284.

64. "Le texte complet de la vie de Christian de l'Aumône," *Analecta Bollandiana* 73 (1953) 21–52.

65. P. Roisin, *L'hagiographie cistercienne dans le diocèse de Liège au XIIIe siècle* (1947). Similar studies for different times and regions are very much needed.

66. *Etymologiae* I 40–41.

67. A similar point of view is adopted by P. Landsberg, "Le Moyen âge et nous," cited by J. M. Oesterreicher, *Septs philosophes Juifs devant le Christ* (Paris, 1955), p. 333. Also, W. von den Steinen, in *Historische Zeitschrift* (1931) 256.

68. "Recherches sur d'anciens sermons monastiques," *Revue Mabillon* (1946) 1–12.

69. "Predicateurs bénédictins aux XIe et XIIIe siècles," *Revue Mabillon* (1943) 48–73.

70. M. M. Lebreton, "Les sermons de Julien de Vézelay," *Analecta monastica* III 118. Similar expressions are used by Guerric d'Igny. *Exordium magnum Cisterciense*, d. 3, c. 8 (PL 185.1059).

71. *Études sur S. Bernard*, 81.

72. Ibid. 34–37.

73. Ibid. 45–83.

74. R. Bauerreiss, "St. Georgen im Schwarzwald," *Studien und Mitteilungen z. Gesch. des Bened. Ordens* (1934) 50.

75. "Manuscrits cisterciens à la Bibliothèque Vaticane," *Anal. S. Ord. Cist.*

76. PL 183.573n26; 754n32.

77. PL 184.1145n71; 1146n88.

78. Job 3.14.

79. "Inédits bernardins dans un MS d'Orval," *Analecta monastica* I 151.

80. Ibid. I 142–60. "Inédits bernardins dans un MS d'Engelberg," *Revue Mabillon* (1947) 1–16.

81. PL 183.747–58; 184.1135–56.

82. "Anciennes sentences monastiques," *Coll. Ord. Cist. Ref.* (1952) 117–24.

83. "Textes et mss. cisterciens dans diverses bibliothèques," *Anal. S. Ord. Cist.* (1956) 292.

84. P. David, "Recueil de conférences monastiques irlandaises du viiie siècle," RB 49 (1937) 62–89.

85. PL 183.55.

86. "Recherches sur les Sermons sur les Cantiques de S. Bernard, III: Les sermons sur les cantiques ont-ils été prononcés?" RB 65 (1955) 71–89. IV: "Les étapes de la rédaction," 228–58.

87. *Sermones* 65–66.

88. "Le commentaire bref du Cantique attribué à S. Bernard," *Études sur S. Bernard*, 105–24. J. Hourlier, "Guillaume de Saint Thierry et la Brevis commentatio in Cantica," *Analecta S. Ord. Cist.* (1956) 105–14.

89. "La première rédaction des Sermons in Cantica de Gilbert de Hoyland," RB 62 (1952) 289–90.

90. "Les sermons synodaux attribués à S. Bernard," RB 63 (1953) 292–309. "Sermons de l'école de S. Bernard dans un ms. d'Hauterive," *Anal. S. Ord. Cist.* (1955) 3–26.

91. "Les collections de sermons de Nicolas de Clairvaux," RB 66 (1956) 269–302.

92. "Sur la genèse des sermons de S. Bernard," *Études sur S. Bernard*, 45–83. "S. Bernard et ses secrétaires," RB 62 (1952) 208–29.

93. E. Dekkers, "Les autographes des Pères Latins," *Colligere fragmenta. Festschrift Alban Dold* (Beuron, 1952), pp. 127–39.

94. "Cur non movebis linguam ad dictandum, manum ad scribendum?" Epist. 191 (MGH, *Epp. kar. aevi* II 319.8).

95. E. Lesne, *Histoire de la propriété ecclésiastique en France*, IV Les Livres, Scriptoria et bibliothèques (Lille, 1938), p. 354.

96. On the semantic evolution which brought the word to its present meaning in German, cf. A. Ernout, "Dictare, 'dicter,' allem. 'Dichter,'" *Revue des études latines*, 29 (1951) 155–61.

97. As, for example, in the text edited by A. Boutemy, "Notice sur le recueil poétique du ms. Cotton Vitellius A XII du British Museum," *Latomus* (1937) 313.

98. *Études sur S. Bernard*, 34–36 and 226. Here, by way of illustration, the distich from MS 18 of Engelberg, will suffice:

Hic Augustini est opus ac Froeuuini
Alter dictavit, alter scribendo notavit.

99. Edd. M. Inguanez–H. M. Willard (Monte Cassino, 1938).

100. T. M. Charland, *Artes praedicandi* (Paris–Ottawa, 1936) 99 and *passim*. "This 'modern' rhetoric has become simply an exercise of pure dialectics. . . . The *Artes praedicandi* are one of the clearest proofs of the invasion of medieval thought and its various literary forms by dialectics." Ibid. 9.

101. "Le sermon sur la royauté du Christ au xiiie siècle," *Archives d'histoire doctrinale et littéraire du moyen âge* (1943–45) 143–80. "Le magistère du prédicateur au xiiie siècle," ibid. (1946) 105–147.

102. M.-D. Chenu, *Introduction à l'étude de S. Thomas d'Aquin* (Paris–Montreal, 1950), p. 53.

103. J. P. Bonnes, "Un des plus grands prédicateurs du xiiie siècle, Geoffroy du Lauroux dit Babion," RB (1945–46) 184 and 109.

104. Ibid. 210.

105. "Le sermon, acte liturgique," *La Maison Dieu* 8 (1946) 32–35.

106. C. Mohrmann, "Le style de S. Bernard," *San Bernardo* (Milan, 1954), pp. 172–84; "Le style des œuvres mariales de S. Bernard," *Marie* (Nicolet–Quebec, 1954), pp. 26–30.

107. J. P. Bonnes (n. 103), 190.

108. J. P. Bonnes, 200.

109. "Ab hoc uno et ab hac monade monachorum appellatio et professio ducit originem. Hoc unum necessarium." "Le témoignage de Geoffroy d'Auxerre sur la vie cistercienne." *Analecta monastica* II 176.

110. "La poste des moines," *Cahiers de Saint André* (1955) 74–77. L. Vailhé, *Histoire générale des postes françaises*, I (Paris, 1945) 206–19.

111. "Commerce Epistolaire," *Analecta monastica* II 145–50. On the role of the *notarii*, cf. "S. Bernard et ses secrétaires," RB (1951) 208–29. "L'écrivain," *S. Pierre Damien ermite et homme d'Église* (Rome, 1959), pp. 161–75.

112. 'Le genre epistolaire au moyen âge," *Rev. du moyen âge latin* 2 (1946) 63–70.

113. Salutatio, exordium, narratio, petitio, conclusio.

114. "Lettres de vocation à la vie monastique," *Analecta monastica* III 169–97.

115. "Écrits spirituels d'Elmer de Cantorbéry," *Analecta monastica* II 45–117.

116. "Manuscrits cisterciens dans les bibliothèques d'Italie," *Anal. S. Ord. Cist.* (1949) 105.

117. J. Laporte, "Epistulae Fiscamnenses. Lettres d'amitié, de gouvernement et d'affaires (xie–xiie siècles)," *Revue Mabillon* (1953) 5–31.

118. *Études sur S. Bernard*, 96.

119. Ed. R. Gibbon, *B. Goswini vita* (Douai, 1620), pp. 267–73.

120. "Documents sur les morts des moines," *Revue Mabillon* (1955) 167–80.

121. MS Vat. lat. 7528, pp. 244–45: a letter to a sick friend when one cannot visit him; 247–48: "Quando visitat aliquem de parentibus suis per litteram suam"; cf. "Textes et manuscrits cisterciens dans diverses bibliothèques," *Anal. S. Ord. Cist.* (1956) 295–96. There is another letter of this kind in the formulary of Tromond, a Cistercian of the end of the twelfth century, PL 204.232; in the MS Montpellier, Médecine, H. 302, this letter is entitled *Ad socium amicabilis epistola*.

122. *La spiritualité de Pierre de Celle*, pp. 14–23. "Lettres d'amitié," *Pierre le*

Vénérable, pp. 53–59. "Amitié par correspondance; la conversation par écrit," *Analecta monastica* II 145–50.

123. "Lettres spirituelles," *Analecta monastica* I 115–19.

124. *Opusculum* 25 (PL 145.589).

125. *Opusculum* 42 (PL 145.763).

126. "L'amitié dans les lettres au moyen âge," *Rev. du moyen âge latin* 1 (1945) 391–410.

127. See p. 42 *supra*.

128. PL 195.659–702. Trans. J. Dubois (Bruges–Paris, 1948). The expression *spiritualis amicitia* is found as early as St. Boniface to some nuns; MGH, *Scr. rer. germ.* N.s. I (Berlin, 1955), *S. Bonifatii et Lullii epist.* 221.5. Friendship in the poetic and epistolary literature of the Carolingian era would be a fruitful field of study. Bolgar, *The Classical Heritage*, p. 184 makes reference to this.

129. H. Rochais, "Contribution à l'histoire des florilèges ascétiques du moyen âge," RB 63 (1953) 246–91; an excellent study.

130. R. W. Southern, *The Making of the Middle Ages* (London, 1953), p. 207.

131. This aim is specifically mentioned by Defensor, Alcuin, and Smaragdus. Cf. H. Rochais (n. 129), 264*nn*1&2.

132. "Hic carpat flores, quis depingat sibi mores," we read at the head of *Testimonia de libris Gregorii magni* by Paterius, in a manuscript of the tenth century. Ed. P. Lehmann, *Mitteilungen aus Handschriften, Sb. Bay. Akad.* IV (1938) 35.

133. PL 194.1540.

134. *Smaragde et son œuvre*, p. 5.

135. F. M. Powicke, *Ailred of Rievaulx and his Biographer, Walter Daniel* (Manchester, 1922), pp. 10–18.

136. H. Weisweiler, *Das Schrifttum der Schule Anselms von Laon und Wilhelms von Champeaux in deutschen Bibliotheken* (Münster, 1936), pp. 244–47.

137. P. Glorieux, "Les deflorations de Werner de Saint-Basile," *Mélanges J. de Ghellinck* (Gembloux, 1951) II 699–721.

138. *Un maître*, pp. 37, 97.

139. Cited by H. Rochais, in RB (1953) 264*n*2.

140. *Un maître*, p. 97.

141. "Jean de Fécamp et S. Bernard dans les florilèges anciens," *Analecta Monastica* I 94–108.

9

Monastic Theology

ALL THE MONKS were readers. A certain number of them also wrote. Several of the latter proposed a doctrine which the others accepted, and it is this doctrine which we must now attempt to determine. Not that all the writings of the monks were, as with the scholastics, theological in nature; nor that all the monks who wrote or those who read their writings were theologians. But all together, they created an environment which made the appearance of a "theology," which was the work of one of their own, both possible and necessary. There were among them theologians whose works contained a theology intended for a monastic audience for whom it had been conceived and composed. Since it answered their needs and filled their requirements, it has been called "monastic theology."

Its existence is a fact which was admitted by medieval men and is winning recognition from present-day historians;[1] more and more it appears to be a prolongation of patristic theology.[2] We know that as early as the ninth century Benedict of Aniane had assembled traditional documents with the intention of "giving a form to the faith."[3] In 806, Regimbert of Reichenau got together a corpus of commentaries on the Lord's Prayer and Apostles' Creed, thus constituting what has been called "a manual of dogmatics," the Reichenau manual of theological studies."[4] During the same period, Rhabanus Maurus, Regino of Prüm, and Williram of Ebersberg are among those considered today as "Benedictine theologians,"[5] and, in later times, it developed considerably. We shall inquire into its nature, to learn if it differs from non-monastic theology, and in what respects.

These questions can receive no precise or definitive answer until the various representatives of this doctrinal current have been studied in detail, and thus far, only a partial and provisional answer can be offered. It is not easy even to frame the question without the risk of falsifying historical perspectives and, consequently, jeopardizing the objectivity of research itself. In fact, we are always tempted to compare theology at a certain stage, that of the ninth or of the twelfth century, with that of other periods, the tenth or the sixteenth, for example, or even our own century, and to base our appraisal of ancient times on the evolution which occurred later. But this method would result in every period of theology's being considered as a preparation for another. However, the patristic age or the early Middle Ages did not engage in theology for the purpose of laying a foundation for a future theology; they did so because it was essential to the life of the Church and to their own lives and times, and the theology they devised was commensurate with their powers and with their sense of dedication.

DEFINITION OF THEOLOGY

At the outset, we would do well to avoid any speculation as to the scientific nature of the monks' theology: whether it was and to what extent a science, or rather a wisdom. Such a problem had practically never arisen before the start of the thirteenth century. During the thirteenth and fourteenth centuries, it caused continuous division among theologians,[6] and no agreement can be claimed to have been reached as yet. Moreover the discussion very soon grew into a quarrel over terminology, and since then, the strictly Aristotelian idea of science has ceased to be considered applicable to certain sciences. Science, furthermore, can be defined by its method, which varies according to the potentialities of each period or by the degree of certitude attained. But the very idea of what science itself is has likewise evolved. It seems more fitting consequently, before beginning this examination, to dispense with a concept borrowed from the vocabulary of another age and to proceed with a very general definition of theology. Theology may be taken as a "discipline in which the truths of the Christian religion, based on and illuminated by revelation, are interpreted, developed, and ordered into a body of doctrine."[7] We shall not consider as theology anything which does not comply with all the essential yet adequate terms of this definition. And all the requirements are fulfilled in the monastic doctrine. Here we find not merely a religious empiricism or a simple description of the monastic states of soul or forms of prayer; nor is it concerned only with suggestions for asceticism, practical directives for daily living, "pastoral teaching,"[8] or the "proclamation of the truth."[9] Monastic doctrine shows genuine reflection on the facts of faith and the pursuit of an organic general conception of these principles. Monastic doctrine, therefore, truly deserves to be called a theology. What remains to be learned is to what extent it differs, at any given period, from another theology in the Church. Before any attempt is made to answer this precise question, its significance should be properly stressed.

THE UNITY OF THEOLOGY

To determine the characteristics of a theology—in the present case monastic theology—does not mean isolating it from the whole doctrinal current of a given period. Fundamentally, as there is but one Church, one faith, one Scripture, one tradition, and one authority, there is but one theology. Theology cannot be the specialty of any one milieu, where it would be, as it were, imprisoned. Like every great personality, every culture, and even more, necessarily, every reflection on the Catholic faith, every theology is, by its essence, universal and overflows the confines of specialization. It is only within the great cultural entities which have succeeded one another in the life of the Church that different currents can be observed; but they cannot be separated.

These differences became more or less marked according to the times. As a culture evolves and becomes richer, it becomes diversified without endangering its unity. It is during the twelfth century that monastic theology emerges with all its distinguishing characteristics clearly delineated. This individualization was already in germ in the preceding century but was much more difficult to discern. From the sixth to the eleventh century, monasteries were not the only cultural centers since schools also existed in the towns. Yet, as a matter of fact, it is particularly the theology which flourished in the monasteries which provided the substance for preaching and the religious instruction of the people. Many bishops were monks and it can be maintained that the spirituality of the Western Church, its "piety," in every domain of its activity, was completely impregnated with monastic doctrine.

Within this doctrine, especially at its height in the twelfth century when it differs from non-monastic theology, there still persists a certain inherent diversity. As we shall see, the very notion of a "school" of monastic theology is a contradiction in terms. There were, so to speak, during a given period several different monastic theologies; they had in common, however, the fact that their authors were monks. We must therefore inquire what makes the monks' theology so distinctively their own.

TWO CULTURAL MILIEUX

To do this, we must recognize an established sociological fact: the existence in the Middle Ages of at least two different milieux where Christian reflection was operative—the town schools and the monasteries.[10] Here any ambiguity about the meaning of schools is to be avoided. The study of the history of the monastic schools gives rise to the temptation to exaggerate their importance, since only monastic schools are under consideration. But when schools in general are studied, and the monastic schools and the conceptions they imply are compared with non-monastic schools and their underlying philosophy, the lines of demarcation are clearly perceived; they have recently been stressed by several historians.[11] Nothing, of course, should be over-simplified, but there was, as has already been mentioned, a certain diversity in monasticism itself. In particular, it is important to differentiate between the Anglo-Saxon monasteries—that is to say, those of England proper and those of English affiliation later founded in the countries of the Western Empire—and those of France, Italy, and their neighboring regions. On the Continent, these two domains of Western monasticism may be symbolized by the names of Gorze and Cluny.[12] The monasteries of the first group were a part of the hierarchy of the Church. In England particularly, several were cathedral monasteries that had played a part in the conversion of England. Since every church had its school, they also had schools which at times bore as great a resemblance to secular as to cloister schools. They had theologians who must have been working with the same theological problems as were being studied in non-monastic milieux. A case in point is that of Senatus of Worcester in the twelfth century.[13] Even so he is against "disputing on God without reverence," directing attacks "by means of subtle objections," against the ineffable secret of the divinity.[14] He does not head the theological movement but keeps himself informed about it, and consents to contribute to it but does not seek to become its leader. In so doing, he remains a monk. For, to the degree that monasticism is faithful to its original orientation and is directed toward the search for God in a certain detachment from the world, the fewer reasons it has to become involved with secular schools and the problems debated there, even if they are theological problems. This attitude was adopted with the utmost logic by Cluny and later by Cîteaux which, on this point as well as on many others—however paradoxical that may seem—followed Cluny's reasoning.[15]

TWO KINDS OF SCHOOLS

With these nuances in mind we should also distinguish the existence throughout the Middle Ages of two kinds of schools: the monks' schools and the clerical schools. The monks' schools are "internal" schools, that is, open to children who are preparing for monastic life and to them alone,

or "external" schools to which other children are admitted, and the latter
are sometimes located outside the cloister. Cluny, for instance, had an external school in the market town next to the cloister. It was not unusual
in such external schools for the teaching to be entrusted to the secular
clergy. Indeed, it was often felt that schools had many disadvantages and
were hard to reconcile with monastic observance. Consequently efforts
were made progressively to limit their size and even to eliminate them.
In the internal school the liberal arts were taught in a liturgical setting
to prepare the future monk for the *lectio divina*, and the young religious
thereby acquired a liberal culture, "contemplative" in tendency. On the
contrary, the clerical schools, situated near the cathedrals in the cities, are
attended by men who, either in parochial or in monastic external schools,
have already received a liberal arts training.[16] They are at this point preparing for pastoral activity, for the "active life," and it is in these urban
schools that scholastic theology is born and develops. The syllabus of what
a secular priest must learn and know in order to exercise his pastoral functions was clearly defined by the bishop of Paris, Maurice of Sully. The
priest must know everything needful for the liturgical celebration, the
administration of the sacraments, particularly penance, and, finally, for
preaching. He must know this not for his personal sanctification but for
the sake of the faithful confided to his care. In this matter, Maurice of
Sully admits that he is echoing ecclesiastical tradition.[17] But the readings
and the studies toward which the monks are oriented by St. Benedict and
monastic tradition are of an entirely different kind.

The proof that there was indeed a difference between the two types of
schools and between what was taught in them lies in the fact that, beginning with the ninth century, some abbots felt the need of sending some
of their monks to study for some length of time in the towns.[18] For exchanges did take place between these two different academic milieux and
they were not entirely closed to each other. At times, secular clerics would
come to study under an outstanding monk at Bec, for instance, in St.
Anselm's time. He himself had had as a schoolmaster Lanfranc, who
himself had been trained by St. Fulbert at Chartres; St. Anselm, in turn,
had disciples in his own monastery. Most of those whose names or works
are known are Anglo-Norman monks, and they did not do any scholastic
theology with him. These facts help us understand in what sense it is
possible to speak of a "school of Bec."[19] Eadmer himself, moreover, made
this quite clear. His somewhat inflated way of writing, which is characteristic of hagiography, nonetheless reveals a profound truth: "From every
country, many noble personages, well-informed clerics, and brave knights

came to him in droves. . . . In this same monastery they consecrated to God's service their persons and their wealth. The monastery grew. . . ."[20] Thus Bec remained a monastery, a school for the service of God.

Sometimes—and in fact more frequently—it was the monks who kept themselves informed about the activity of the schools. Some had attended them before their conversion, or even afterward if they had been sent there to complete their education. Others took adcantage of the fact that their abbey was near a town where schools were active: this was the case with Rupert of Deutz during his years of instruction at St. Lawrence of Liège. And finally many kept up friendly relations with scholastic masters: all these contacts have been stressed by several modern historians.[21] But monastic schools retained their own individuality which was determined by the tendencies of their environment and, in the final analysis, by the very exigencies monastic life imposed. The difference between scholastic theology and monastic theology corresponds to the differences between the two states of life: the state of Christian life in the world and the state of Christian life in the religious life. The latter was what was, in fact, until the end of the twelfth century, unanimously called the "contemplative life."[22] It was contemplative because of its organization and orientation, even if some of those who led it also took part—to a greater or lesser extent depending on the time and the region—in some active service for the Church. Ordinarily the monks did not have to abandon their state of life in order to assume that of the urban schools.

SCHOOLMASTERS BECOME MONKS

On the other hand, many students and even schoolmasters were converted to the monastic life. Among the students can be noted Goswin of Anchino who had been taught by Abailard. Geoffroy of Auxerre, also a pupil of Abailard's, was converted by St. Bernard, as were so many to whom the Abbot of Clairvaux had in 1140 addressed his sermon *On Conversion.*[23] Having gone to study in Paris, Odo of Austria and his companions stop off on the return trip at the Cistercian abbey of Morimond. They remain and make their profession in the expectation of taking home soon with them the Cistercian way of life.[24] Among the masters, Alger, Hezelon, and Tézelin, all three canons of Liège, enter Cluny at the beginning of the twelfth century, there to become "disciples of humility."[25] Later a constellation of famous masters become Cistercians. Odo of Ourscamp, for instance, who, having been made a cardinal at a later date, considered this promotion as a punishment for his past school-life, of which he says: "I chose, despite divine prohibition, to eat of the tree of knowledge of good and evil."[26] Another was Thierry of Chartres who, his epitaph tells us, moved by love for the religious life (*religionis amor*) left the city (*cedens urbe*) to hide away in solitude (*in latebris heremi*) so as to lead an austere life and, master that he was, to seek knowledge:

Dedidicit "doctor" dici voluitque doceri.[27]

Many others did likewise, and of these, Adam of Perseigne, Gauthier of Cîteaux, Serlo of Wilton, Evrard of Ypres, and Alan of Lille have left works and their names. And they cannot make us forget the throngs of masters and students who have voluntarily remained in obscurity. Many clerics, noticing that several who had given up the professorship in the schools were assigned to the same position in the abbey, hid the fact, Caesarius of Heisterbach says, that they possessed literary learning and had received holy orders. In their humility they preferred to pass for laymen and tend flocks instead of reading books and giving commands to others.[28] What is involved for all of them is a real change not only in their state in life but in their spiritual orientation—in other words, a true conversion like St. Benedict's. Accordingly, the biographer of Blessed David of Himmerod can write in words in which we recognize two reminiscences from the *Dialogues* of St. Gregory:

> From Italy he had come to study in France. During his stay in this country, he heard about the Cistercian Order, that new religious institution. Immediately, under the impulse of the Spirit of God, he drew back the foot he had just put down in the world. Giving up the studies he had already begun, he chose in preference to be instructed in the disciplines of the *Rule*; he would rather be ignorant of certain things in complete security than learn them at the risk of his soul.[29]

St. Peter Damian also refers to St. Benedict's conversion before recalling a cleric's entrance into monastic life.[30]

This conversion was sometimes a slow and painful process. The temptations that had to be overcome in passing from the life of a studious cleric to that of a monk have sometimes been recorded and analyzed with great penetration, as for example in the case of Goswin of Anchino.[31] Elsewhere more or less precise allusions have been made to them,[32] but everyone was acutely aware of a profound difference between scholastic and monastic milieux, and, consequently, between the kinds of religious knowledge to be acquired in each. Monastic knowledge is determined by the end of monastic life: the search for God. Of course, just as a monk may, for the needs of the Church, engage in occupations not implicit in the monastic state, so he may undertake intellectual researches not required in the search for God. But, insofar as he remains a monk, his theology is marked by a certain monastic cast.

THE CLOISTER AND THE SCHOOLS

This is the source of the fervent tone, the mystical vocabulary, the urgings to transcend the self that are found even in the most speculative writings of St. Anselm and are not to be found in those of the scholastics. This contrast makes the difference the more noticeable. Their contemporaries perceived it, and many, irrespective of their state in life, have drawn a parallel between the cloister and the schools. One of the canons regular, Philip of Harvengt, expresses himself in this fashion:

> In the cloister there is hardly any room for vanity: sanctity alone is sought for. There, day and night, the just man submits to the divine will, devotes himself to hymns, prayer, silence, tears, and reading. There, I say, the sincerity for a purified life cleanses the intelligence which then makes it possible to acquire knowledge more easily and efficaciously. In your eyes no knowledge is commendable which has not been forged in the tumult of the secular schools as if it were a certainty that among those who have been receiving instruction in them for a long time there could be found no error or heresy. You are indignant because I mentioned that you had learned sacred letters in a cloister, as if in doing so I had insulted you. You consider that what you have learned in the school of Laon in the famous lecture hall of Master Anselm does you greater honor. And yet, blessed is he, not he who has heard Master Anselm, not he who went off to pursue knowledge in Laon or Paris, but "blessed," it is written, "is he whom you instruct, Lord, he to whom you teach your Law."[33] And again, it is said: "I shall listen to what the Lord my God says within me."[34] I would that it had pleased God for me to have been taught sacred letters in a cloister from childhood so that henceforth I might have consecrated my whole life to sacred studies; raised from childhood in the house of God in imitation of Samuel, I would have burned with the desire to know like a Daniel. To have been educated from childhood in the school of the religious life seemed to me an honor: therefore I had no intention of offending you when, praising your knowledge, I mentioned the cloister and not the secular schools.[35]

Another non-monastic source, Peter Comestor, likewise emphasized the contrast between two categories of Christians: "There are some who do more praying than reading: they are the cloister dwellers; there are others who spend all their time reading and rarely pray: they are the schoolmen."[36]

It is, however, particularly "with the monks" that "the opposition between cloister and school" became a literary theme.[37] St. Bernard enlarged on it in his letters to Henry Murdach[38] and to Aelred,[39] and Rupert of Deutz in his Commentary on the *Rule*.[40] Peter of Celle makes it the subject of several of his letters,[41] St. Peter Damian also spoke of it,[42] and anonymous writers often stressed it.[43] All concur that once one has centered upon monastic life, he should not wish to leave it to study in a different way from that in the cloister. St. Peter Damian raises his voice clearly in a work *Against Monks who Contemplate Studying Grammar*: although already settled in their vocation they wish to leave and join the turbulent crowds of the students of letters.[44] On another occasion, in his treatise *On Holy Simplicity*, he addresses a hermit undergoing the temptation to go and exercise his fine intelligence in the study of the liberal arts.[45] Such prohibitions are not the equivalent of a condemnation of the schools on the part of the monks: they recognize their usefulness on the whole, encourage their teachers, and sometimes assist the students; but they do feel that the schools are full of dangers for all: the life led there is incompatible with the cloistered life whose spiritual orientation is different.

Thus in the opinion of medieval men, monks or not, a contrast exists between the two milieux where Christian thought flourishes. In the cloister, theology is studied in relation to monastic experience, a life of faith led in the monastery where religious thought and spiritual life, the pursuit of truth and the quest for perfection, must go hand in hand and permeate each other. This orientation, proper to the cloistered life, was to affect the methodology used in Christian reflection and the subject matter of this reflection. Each of these two points requires closer examination.

Differences in Method

In the domain of method, the difference between monastic and scholastic theology of the same period appears in both the modes of expression and the processes of thought. The former, as we have already had occasion to emphasize, are linked with a style and with literary genres which conform to the classical and patristic tradition. John of Salisbury characterized—and caricatured, for there is a dash of exaggeration and consequently of injustice—the schoolmasters such as Adam of Petit Pont, Robert of Melun, Aubrey of Rheims, and Abailard; he sees them as innovators, "moderns" in opposition to the ancients—*veteres*—to the upholders of the tradition:

Formerly everything the ancients had put well found favor.

Today, novelties alone give pleasure. . . .

He who studies the arts and the written texts is thought a poor debater, for an ally of the past cannot be a logician. . . .

Aristotle is extolled but there is nothing but scorn for Cicero and for all that vanquished Greece gave the Romans.

Law, physics, all literature are derided: logic wins the approbation of all.[46]

Littera sordescit, logica sola placet: the entire conflict is rooted in this antithesis. The new style results from the predominance accorded certain disciplines: the accent is no longer placed on grammar, the *littera*, but on logic. Just as they are no longer satisfied with the *auctoritas* of Holy Scripture and the Fathers and invoke that of the philosophers, so clarity is what is sought in everything. Hence the fundamental difference between scholastic style and monastic style. The monks speak in images and comparisons borrowed from the Bible and possessing both a richness and an obscurity in keeping with the mystery to be expressed. St. Bernard has described this mode of expression excellently:

> As for us, in the commentary of mystical and sacred words, let us proceed with caution and simplicity. Let us model ourselves on Scripture which expresses the wisdom hidden in mystery in our own words: when Scripture portrays God for us it suggests Him in terms of our own feelings. The invisible and hidden realities of God which are of such great price are rendered accessible to human minds, vessels, as it were, of little worth, by means of comparisons taken from the realities we know through our senses. Let us also adopt the usage of this chaste language.[47]

St. Bernard sees in the biblical tongue a certain modesty which respects God's mysteries; he admires the tact and discretion God used in speaking to men. Hence, he says: *Geramus morem Scripturae.*

The scholastics are concerned with achieving clarity; consequently they readily make use of abstract terms, and they never hesitate to forge new words, the *profanae vocum novitates* which St. Bernard, for his part, avoids.[48] Not that he refuses to use the usual philosophical terminology which through Boethius had come down from Aristotle: on occasion he will use *forma, materia, causa efficiens* or *esse materiale*; he does not recoil from the concepts current in the schools, as for example that of *satisfactio*. But, for him, this terminology is never more than a vocabulary for emergency use and it does not supplant the biblical vocabulary. The one he customarily uses remains, like the Bible's, essentially poetic; his language is consistently more literary than that of the School. It has been remarked that in answering doctrinal questions put to him by Hugh of St. Victor he uses different terms in dealing with the same realities; he transposes into the biblical mode what his correspondent had said to him in the school language.[49]

This does not imply that Bernard himself did not possess a technical language. There are terms which he and other monastic authors use, as the Fathers formerly before them, to describe with precision experiences and realities for which ordinary language has no exact equivalent.[50] But —and this is one of the difficulties connected with monastic theology— these terms, instead of being borrowed from an abstract language forged for the need of the case, are drawn from the language in general use and from a book intended for all: the Bible. There are other known examples of technical languages' taking their vocabulary from current usage—for instance, the language of physicists in speaking of "mass," "speed," and "force." In St. Bernard we find the same kind of technical language. It has been said that "the element of such very appealing images and descriptives" ought not take anyone in: "In the case of masters like these it is erroneous to draw any premature conclusions as to literary fantasy or stylistic artifices; here we are dealing with a real technique, a rigorous technique which has nothing to do with the mystico-lyrical elucubrations of medieval decadence."[51] And in the use of this traditional technical vocabulary there also exists a certain diversity: each monastic author chooses from the Bible and the Fathers his favorite expressions and gives them the shade of meaning he prefers. Within the overall unity there remains a variety which is characteristic of a living culture.[52]

As the monks' language differs from that of the schools, so also do their thought processes differ from those of scholasticism. Of course, there can be no essential difference since the thought and language of both are men's thought and language. It is therefore difficult to define what distinguishes these two manners of thinking. First of all, it must be understood, the monks were, as if by instinct, oriented toward tradition rather than toward the pursuit of problems and new solutions, and two reasons account for this. The first lies in the antiquity of the monastic life, its sources, its *Rule*, and its models. This attachment to the past and to the Fathers of the Church—many of whom were as well Fathers of monasticism—was, so to speak, congenital in the monks. Moreover, they considered this submission to the Fathers a form of humility, the humility which St. Benedict had established as the first degree of obedience. References have often been made to St. Bernard's declarations that he does not

wish to add anything to what the Fathers had taught.[53] Others spoke in
the same sense, using expressions that are no less definite. Isaac of Stella
considers tradition a walled cloister it is forbidden to leave.[54] When the
scholastics wished to describe their dependence on the thinkers of antiquity they compared themselves with dwarfs perched on the shoulders
of giants: smaller than their predecessors they nevertheless see farther
ahead. St. Bernard uses a different image, inspired by the Book of Ruth,
to explain his still more modest attitude toward the Fathers of the Church:
in the wake of these great harvesters we are but lowly gleaners. He who
has given himself up entirely to "Christian discipline" should seek all his
grain in Holy Scripture as in the field of Boaz; he should have no longing
to reap a foreign field, by immersing himself in secular studies. The great
reapers are St. Augustine, St. Jerome, and St. Gregory, and those who
come after them should remain in the ranks of the poor and the servants:
in the Church they should number themelves humbly amongst the least.[55]

The Need for Dialectics

All theology, however, necessarily involves some reflection on the content
transmitted by tradition. How did the monks carry out this reflection? It
is clear that they did not refuse to use dialectics. This they could not refuse
since the use of dialectics in theology is a necessity and had become traditional.[56] Consequently dialectics, in monastic education, was the usual
complement to grammar. We are told, for example, that Jerome of Pomposa, "having learned in childhood to live according to the monastic rule,
then studied grammar as the basic branch of learning, after which he exercised his mind for a time in dialectics."[57]

Furthermore, the monks did not show any reluctance to using the other
liberal arts. Aelred is not alone in enlisting the aid of mathematical figures,
perhaps under the influence of Boethius and the school of Chartres.[58]
William of Auberive, Geoffrey of Auxerre, and Odo of Morimond also
compose treatises on the meaning of numbers.[59] And yet they do so in
their own way, which is not the way of a scholastic such as Thibaut of
Langres.[60]

Indeed if they do not, and cannot in principle, have any objection to
dialectics, they feel a certain instinctive distrust for the too frequent use
made of it in the schools. This accounts for certain contradictory statements encountered at times even in the same author on the subject of
dialectics.[61] Wariness with regard to dialectics—as well as the classics—
forms, in the monastic milieu, a literary theme that was inherited from

the past. Scholasticism's essential method of procedure had been fixed since the ninth century, and it consisted in "disputing"; a dialogue took place between master and pupils: *quaeritur, respondendum est,* and the main feature of the liberal arts was what was called *disputare liberaliter, disputare scolastice,* or even *scolasticissime.*[62] If disputing did happen to take place in the monastic schools, it was almost always on the subject of the liberal arts.[63] But in the town schools the same procedure was applied to sacred doctrine. As it was, discussion in this domain often degenerated into what St. Bernard and others, using one of St. Paul's expressions, called mere verbal battles, *pugnae verborum.*[64] The best historian of twelfth-century scholasticism admits that there was something "tormented" about it and that, inevitably, it had to lead to the dangerous doctrines of Abailard or Gilbert of la Porrée.[65] Grabmann had already acknowledged that a "hyperdialectic" had been introduced into sacred doctrine: it is against this, and this alone, that there arose the "mystical" current represented by a Rupert of Deutz.[66]

Commenting on the words of St. Paul *et pugnas verborum,* Peter Cantor interprets them as a reproof to the theologians of his times who discuss for the pleasure of discussing, not in order to arrive at truth, and accept it when it is known, but in order to set traps for each other. They have so little respect for God's word that they treat it as if it were just any one of the liberal arts or even a mechanical art: *ac si ars liberalis esset vel mecanica.*[67] In order to appreciate the full pejorative connotation of the last word, one must remember that the "mechanical" arts included the whole range of "servile works." The "liberal" disciplines were proper to free men and were supposed to free the spirit from its inclination to matter; but the mechanical arts were trades for serfs. Hugh of St. Victor defined them as being stained with "adultery," "as if the spirit engaging in them were soiled by an immoral contact with something degrading."[68]

Respect for Mystery

But sacred doctrine must remain something other than and more than a liberal discipline. This is all the more reason why it cannot be reduced to being nothing more than a profession. According to the testimony of a scholastic like Peter Cantor, however, theology did come to be considered as merely one technique among the others. And it was against this sort of degradation and profanation of God's mysteries that the monks reacted. They were afraid that some might become completely absorbed by the procedures of the disputation, which began to assume a value of its own, for in it each individual could show off his own personality to advantage by bringing forth new arguments. On this account they preferred to limit themselves to tradition, which itself is essentially religious. They felt that research through discussion could be carried out independently of any religious experience—whether this were a personal experience or the experience of a whole group living in conformity with the demands of religious truth. The monastery was for them a "school of charity," a school for the service of God. They maintained a certain reserve toward any intellectual research carried on outside of this setting and without the guarantees it offers of sincerity and humility. They feared it would be wanting in respect for divine truth to attempt to penetrate it as if by forcible entry after breaking the seal of mystery; one should not, as St. Bernard says, be an *effractor, scrutator maiestatis*.[69] And he says again: "This sacrament is great; it must be venerated, not scrutinized."[70] Protest against this form of "curiosity" came also from Rupert of Deutz,[71] Baldwin of Ford,[72] and Alexander of Jumièges. The title attributed to Alexander's treatise is significant: *De praescientia Dei, contra curiosos*.[73]

The monks' attitude toward the philosophers is dictated by their distrust of the abuses of dialectics. They are not against philosophers as such; they ask only that they be adapted to fit the Christian message as the classical authors had been. William of St. Thierry, who owes so much to Plato, disapproves of those who resort to the philosophers without having previously expurgated them and, as it were, baptized them: *intonsos et illotos*.[74] For the *Hortus deliciarum*, Herrad of Landsberg had the two philosophers, Plato and Socrates, painted in the center of the liberal arts. An inscription identifies them: "The philosophers, those sages of the pagan world, were clerici." And Philosophy herself holds in her hands these words from Scripture: "All wisdom is from God."[75] It is also very revealing that the two sages illustrated should be Socrates and Plato.[76] The latter, more than others, was considered a religious man. The few writings of his they possessed and those which showed his influence were represented in monastic libraries.[77] More than one monastic author felt a sort of secret sympathy for what Plato, in their belief, said about God and the good.[78] Aristotle, on the other hand, who was known only through his works on logic, passed for being the master *par excellence* of the very dialectics whose abuses they feared.[79]

HOLY SIMPLICITY

Thus, on both sides, in the cloister as well as in the school, "the intelligence of faith" was being pursued; but it does not have the same meaning for both centers nor is it attained by wholly identical methods. No doubt the portion allotted to faith could not be less than equal; the enterprise for both is a theological activity, and the application of the intelligence to the task cannot be essentially different; it relies, for both parties, on the use of dialectics. The psychological content, though, is different. The abuse of dialectics engenders a form of curiosity that the monks reject since it appears contrary to the humility upon which St. Benedict had founded monastic life. The monks were fond of quoting St. Paul's words: *Scientia inflat.*[80] They counteracted this vain knowledge with "simplicity."[81] But the meaning of the latter should not be misunderstood. To begin with, it is neither ignorance nor rusticity, not even the *sancta rusticitas* that St. Jerome had introduced into literary tradition.[82] All agreed that knowledge is better than ignorance: "Holy simplicity is good, but holy knowledge is better."[83] And St. Bernard was to say that the spouse of the Lord should not be a simpleton.[84] Simplicity should go hand in hand with learning but not with the self-inflation that a certain kind of learning produces. What is this inflation like? It can be said to be both psychological and moral. In the domain of psychology, it is that complexity which is the characteristic of a mind attracted to multiple and varied objects. It incurs the risk of giving rise to a sort of agitation hardly compatible with "contemplative repose" or pure prayer. It also risks distracting the spirit from the undivided search for God and diverting its attention to numerous and superfluous problems. Questions, objections, argumentations rapidly lead into an inextricable forest: *nemus aristotelicum*; like a deer, one laboriously makes one's way through it.[85] To offset these undesirable effects, the mind must be brought back to a single occupation and preoccupation. A single quest and a single search must be substituted for all these questions. To seek God, not to discuss Him, to avoid the inner turmoil of overly subtle investigations and disputes, the manifold arguments, to flee from the outer noise of controversies and to eliminate futile problems—such is the foremost role of simplicity.[86]

But psychological complexity, besides distracting one's attention from God, also jeopardizes humility. It is simplicity's function to lead the spirit back to them. William of St. Thierry, among others, said:

> Holy simplicity is an unchanging will in the pursuit of a changeless good. Such was Job, "a simple, direct, and God-fearing man."[87] Simplicity, in fact, is properly the will fundamentally turned toward God, asking of the Lord only one thing, seeking it with fervor, with no ambition to multiply itself by becoming dispersed in this world. Simplicity is also, in the conduct of life, the true humility which has the virtue of

attaching more importance to the evidence of the conscience than to reputation.[88]

In the Cistercian tradition Guerric of Igny praised "the simplicity of Christian humility."[89] In all eyes, "holy simplicity" is the humility which safeguards the integrity of the mind, which ensures the search for God alone. All else, including intellectual pursuits, should remain subordinate to the search for God. Nothing should interfere with the monk's living in the presence of God, that is to say, with humility as St. Benedict conceives it. This insistence on humility is a spontaneous reaction of the monastic soul. Accordingly it is very often expressed in terms which St. Benedict, in his chapter *On the Degrees of Humility*, had taken from the Psalmist.[90] "Neither have I walked in great matters, nor in wonderful things above me."[91] St. Bernard applies this text to those who, having had knowledge of God, have not served or loved Him: "They have contented themselves with the learning which puffs up."[92] He likewise applies to Abailard: if the latter is lacking in simplicity and moderation in the disputes, it is because he is trying to go beyond his capacities, because he is great in his own eyes.[93]

We might well ask if such fear of the self-inflation which is induced by excesses in learning is a literary theme, or a lesson taught by actual experience. It partakes, no doubt, of both, and so has lent itself to certain literary treatments which we may find somewhat facile but which must be taken seriously because of their sources and context. There is no lack of statements denouncing the pride of the scholastics as a reality that was both too universal and a very real danger. At the end of the twelfth century Stephen of Tournai felt justified in writing the pope: "Students no longer take any interest in anything except novelties; masters who cherish their own popularity above all else are daily composing new *Summae* and new works on theology which entertain their readers and lead them astray as if the writings of the Fathers, they who have explained the Scriptures, did not suffice."[94]

Still later, in the middle of the thirteenth century, the abbot of Villers opposed the founding of a Cistercian college near the University of Paris. He feared that the impetus thus given to scholastic studies might become an obstacle to that "great simplicity" of the Order which he identified with "humility" and "purity." The danger, he says, is first that the monks may abandon the practices of the cloistered life which are eminently suited to their profession, in favor of devoting themselves to literary studies. At this point he refers to the words of St. Jerome which he attributes to St. Bernard and which the latter, as a matter of fact, had quoted: "The work of the monk is to weep, not to teach."[95] Furthermore he is afraid that members of the Order, because of their studies, will become more insolent and proud than in the past, according to St. Paul's expression: *scientia inflat.*[96] A little later, Arnoul of Villers was to be held up as an example of one who, "while still young, did not choose to be sent to do his studies in Paris, aspiring rather to the charity which edifies than to the learning which puffs up, in imitation of St. Benedict who, abandoning school, consecrated himself entirely to the religious life."[97]

As witness to this opposition to "science," other authorities might be quoted, although their testimony is not always equally unimpeachable. Of course, there are some who protest sincerely against a method which, not without foundation, appears to them vainglorious, because of the kind of curiosity it arouses and fosters. But there are also some for whom any effort at investigation is pride of intellect and who would be inclined to view laziness of the intelligence as a form of faith. These two attitudes have, without doubt, had their representatives among those who opposed the rising scholasticism; and later on the scholastics were occasionally found complaining in the same way about anyone who attempted to rouse them from their accustomed routine. These more or less unconscious deviations are, however, not the main issue. But what is clear is that lucid minds perceived distinctly that there was occasion to combat, not "knowledge," but a certain form of learning felt to be scarcely compatible with the contemplative life.

LEARNING AND LOVE

For the Cistercians of the great scholastic period the danger, we imagine, does not arise exclusively from the psychological and moral effects of study; the observance itself is threatened. University studies are, in fact, rewarded with titles and honors which entitle the holder to preferment and give him access to functions scarcely compatible with a cloistered existence,[98] and this fear was by no means unwarranted. In the fourteenth century, Richard Rolle and a monk of Farne continue to react against the excessive intellectualism of the schools whose effects appear in the conduct of certain "graduate monks" endowed with privileges, prebends, and high functions. The unnamed monk of Farne had himself received a scholastic formation: he uses definitions and distinctions. But he turns his back on learning like St. Benedict who was "learnedly ignorant and wisely unlearned." He echoes Richard Rolle's protests against "these doctors all blown up with complicated arguments." He counsels rather the kind of learning which is love, as St. Gregory had said in this connection: Love itself is knowledge: the more one loves, the more one knows.[99]

Thus the ancient theme of the opposition between knowledge and faith was applied to new conditions by the medieval monks. It had been initiated by the Fathers to emphasize the contrast between the Christian faith and pagan wisdom: "God has not chosen to make the salvation of His people depend on dialectics. . . ."[100] Thus St. Ambrose had said, and further: "It is not in the philosopher that we place our faith, it is not in the dialecticians. . . .[101] In the twelfth century, this literary theme was used in connection with the difference which distinguishes simple faith or mystical experience from the subtlety of the schools. Does that mean that this theme was without any real foundation in the doctrinal movement of those times? Did the abuse of dialectics present danger only to the monks' spirit of recollection and not to doctrine itself? And they, in reacting against the intellectual extravagance which could lead to verbalism, verbal duels, and a certain pride, did they neglect to take an interest in the progress of theology? It would not seem so. Still they did perceive that the doctrine itself could not help but suffer some disadvantages from the abuse that some were making of the scholastic method. Theological research was approaching the dangerous point at which it might escape the limits set by faith. In trying to submit God's mysteries to reason, one could be tempted to forget their transcendency and yield to a kind of naturalism.[102] In the effort to explain the realities of religion would they not reduce these realities to something which reason could understand? The monk William of St. James of Liège, speaking before the monks of Liessies, put into words their common apprehensions in regard to "these innovators who apply to faith the yardstick of reason" and who, turning St. Anselm's formula upside down, "make faith derive from intelligence rather than intelligence from faith."[103] St. Bernard's controversy with Abailard was one of those occasions when monastic milieux suspected that this peril was no mere chimera. For not only the method was at stake but the doctrine as well. William of St. Thierry and St. Bernard denounce both a certain use of dialectics and certain erroneous or dangerous conclusions to which Abailard was led through this use. According to a certain nineteenth-century historian, "to men like St. Bernard the *Summa Theologiae* of St. Thomas, with its objections and its free discussions, would have seemed a display of human pride, of intellectual presumption as shocking as Abailard's *Theology*."[104] But today, many historians do justice to Bernard's clairvoyance:[105] he perceived in Abailard deviations which St. Thomas, although he inherited his method, was to avoid a century later.

As has been said, dialectics had a tendency to impose itself as a "panacea."[106] The monks' reaction against the excessive confidence placed in dialectics was not conditioned by St. Bernard's conflict with Abailard. When they confronted each other in 1140, monasticism, in the persons of Peter Damian, Rupert of Deutz, and others, had already taken a stand along the same lines as Bernard.[107] The latter was simply defending a traditional attitude, and this took courage. David Knowles has brought out this point very well:

> . . . to us, wise after the event, Bernard appears as the aggressor, the man with the big stick; it was in fact he, in at least two of the controversies, who more resembled the boy David. . . . When he attacked Abelard he came forward as one who had come to challenge on his own ground the most brilliant and adored master of his age. Even later, when, now venerated, he joined issue with the bishop of Poitiers, he had an opponent who was intellectually his equal, technically his superior, and inferior, if at all, only in the deepest spiritual qualities of a theologian.[108]

These words describe very exactly the significance of the reserve the monks observed with regard to scholasticism. Except in exceptional cases like those just recalled, they were not in conflict with it. They held it in esteem and practiced its method. But they held that technique was not all-sufficient, that it had to be completed and transcended for the good of theology itself, and occasionally they were able to prove it.

Tradition and Progress

In fact, their vigilance in safeguarding tradition, their care to draw on Christian sources rather than the philosophers' doctrine, did not merely enable them to prevent deviations. Rather, these qualities helped them discover new treasures in revelation itself. An outstanding example of the progress that monastic theology is capable of instigating is found in the treatise composed by Eadmer, a disciple of St. Anselm's, on the subject of the Conception of the Virgin. The latest Dominican historian to treat this question felt justified in calling Eadmer, in the title of the study consecrated to the subject, "the first theologian of the Immaculate Conception."[109] Here we find it essential to quote the pages where he describes Eadmer's attitude.

> It is not without a modicum of irony that the learned theologian contrasts the "simplicity of the ancients" with "the sublimity of the genius

of these new doctors" who, "full of a learning that is without charity, have been inflated by this knowledge rather than established on the solid foundations of the true good." They pride themselves immoderately on their own perspicacity. In their astuteness they are willing to destroy what the simplicity and love of the ancients for the Queen of the Universe had built up. They seem to base their case on the arguments of reason but "a purely human reason," the opposite of the "celestial point of view" through which other conclusions are reached. Furthermore, they have not understood the point.

It is against these people then that Eadmer is to write "In defense of Mary" as much as in the interests of "those whose purity of devotion to God is attested by their simplicity and humility." He will "introduce a few words from the sacred books; and the authority of the divine word will decide . . . what, for his contemporaries, is the safest path to follow." Eadmer asks "those who are not afraid to judge impartially to tell him which group is in the right: those who adhere to the divine word, or those who pride themselves inordinately on their own perspicacity. He submits beforehand to the judgment of God and of Mary. He in no way wishes to affirm anything contrary to the doctrine of the Catholic Church, but he is convinced that his assertions are neither improbable nor contrary to faith, for he will propose nothing unreasonable. Everything he says will be the fruit of the esteem which pure simplicity and the simple purity of love for God and for His very sweet Mother are not afraid to feel for her Conception." Still, he must confess that "he is incapable of penetrating these mysteries he desires to consider with pious intention"; however, "the ultimate possession of benefits of such magnitude as those the Lord's Mother procures for every creature seems to invite the human mind to the pious consideration of the origins of his Benefactress." Against the subtle arguments of those who reject the doctrine, the pious monk will therefore use "superior reasons." He has no wish to impose his personal opinions; he asks only that attention be given to the doctrine he is going to expose "from God's point of view." As for himself, "as long as God does not bestow on me the power of speaking more worthily of my sovereign Lady's excellence, at least what I have said, I shall say again and shall always say; what I have written, I will not change. As for the rest, I entrust myself and my intention to her son and to Her, my Queen, Mother of my Lord, Mother also of my heart's illumination." And the monk repeats: "I myself believe and profess that Mary is conceived immaculate, and that she is likewise free from the slightest stain."[110]

The historians of dogma describe a similar attitude on the part of another theologian who belongs to the Anglo-Norman monasticism of Eadmer's period, the pseudo-Augustine, whose treatise caused decisive progress to be made in the understanding of the dogma of the Assumption of the Virgin Mary. He also presented his assertions as "the fruit of his contemplation." In his case, too, there was no lack of reasons, but they were "veiled by piety and the literary form he used."[111] Likewise, the author of a recent study on Isaac of Stella stresses the contribution this "Cistercian theologian" made to the progress of theology.[112] Justice would not be done the monks' theological method if it were seen only as a warning against the abuse of dialectics. It possesses a positive, constructive factor which must now be examined.

Personal Experience

St. Bernard has stated in a few words that "We search in a worthier manner, we discover with greater facility through prayer than through disputation [*orando quam disputando*]."[113] The reverence for God's mysteries which characterizes the monks' theology devolves from what St. Benedict calls the "reverence of prayer."[114] This is the additional value which is superimposed on the scientific method; it is the source of all understanding and all love. It is what will always distinguish the work of the spiritual man from that of the intellectual. In the ninth century Ratramnus of Corbie, in his treatise on the Eucharist, makes allowance for speculation,[115] but his speculation bears no resemblance to that of the later scholastics. And when Baldwin of Ford at the end of the twelfth century spoke at length on the mystery of the altar,[116] he did not dwell on the "scientific" questions which the Berengarian controversy had made the principal topic of scholastic discussions on the Eucharist: the separation of substance from accidents, the role of "quantity," the multiplication of the real presence and its relation to place. What interests Baldwin primarily is not the way in which the Eucharistic mystery takes place; it is the mystery itself and its connection with the other mysteries in the totality of the Christian Mystery. Someone has added, in an appendix, as a concession to the learning of the times, some speculative questions. The monks kept themselves informed as to these problems and the solutions which were proposed for them, but these were considered as secondary matters in relation to the content of Revelation itself and the illumination which was obtained through contemplation, just as, in Christology, St. Bernard and Peter the Venerable place little emphasis on the speculative problems which might arise on the subject of the hypostatic union: the idea of "nature" and of "person," their inter-relationship and the consequences of their union in regard to the psychology of Christ. But St. Bernard and Peter the Venerable show the bond between successive phases of the mystery of the Redemption: the Incarnation, the Baptism of the Lord, the Transfiguration, the Passion, the Ascension, and Pentecost.[117]

KNOWLEDGE THROUGH LOVE

They are, no doubt, not the only ones to unite speculation with a certain experience of love, and so, the difference between the scholastic and monastic milieux must not be too sharply opposed. As later with St. Thomas, St. Bonaventure, and with the greatest of the twelfth-century masters, a significant role is played by religious experience and knowledge through love, sometimes referred to as wisdom or "philosophy." "The latter," writes Thierry of Chartres, for instance, "is the love of wisdom, and wisdom is the integral comprehension of the truth: without love it cannot be attained, or at best it is barely attained."[118] But altogether the great difference between the theology of the schools and that of the monasteries resides in the importance which the latter accord the experience of union with God. This experience in the cloister is both the principle and the aim of the quest. It can be said of St. Bernard that his watchword was not *Credo ut intelligam*, but *Credo ut experiar*.[119] Still, this way of emphazising experience is not exclusive with St. Bernard. The word and the idea are found, for example, in Rupert:

> This knowledge does not come from an outer, as if foreign, document, it comes from an inner and personal experience. Those who are puffed up with learning, let them increase their knowledge—or at least what they think is knowledge—as much as they will, as much as they can, they will never acquire that particular comprehension.[120]

What he is talking about is receiving a visitation from the Lord like those Bernard describes. "The Lord," Rupert goes on, "is a more effective teacher than all the others. I myself have had several fathers in the scholarly disciplines. But I must affirm that a visitation from the All-High is of greater value than ten of their type."[121] The word "visitation" is a biblical term enriched by the monks with psychological overtones; but for them as for Scripture it means an intervention of the Lord.

A certain experience of the realities of faith, a certain "lived faith," is at one and the same time the condition for and the result of monastic theology. The word "experience," which has become equivocal in meaning because it has been abused in a certain recent period, should not, in this context, imply anything esoteric. It simply means that, in study and in reflection, importance was granted to the inner illumination of which Origen and St. Gregory spoke so often,[122] to that grace of intimate prayer, that *affectus* as it is called by St. Benedict,[123] that manner of savoring and relishing the Divine realities which is constantly taught in the patristic tradition.[124] This means a Christian thought perpetually residing in the interior of faith, never going beyond faith, never losing sight of faith, never departing from the practice of faith and at every level remaining an act of faith. This personal experience is closely linked with a whole environment; it is conditioned and promoted by the conventual experience of a community and it flourishes in the midst of this common fervor. As we have seen, monastic speculation is the outgrowth of the practice of monastic life, the living of the spiritual life which is the meditation on Holy Scripture. It is a biblical experience inseparable from liturgical experience. It is experiencing the Church, an experience undergone *in medio Ecclesiae*, since it is nourished by the texts inherited from tradition. It is the Fathers who teach the monks to read Holy Scripture as they themselves read it. This experience presupposes nothing more than the pursuit of the spiritual life led in a community whose essential aim is the search for God.[125] It presupposes the grace necessary for one who desires to increase his faith through living the spiritual life, or, as we would say today: through spirituality. On the part of the abbots, or those who are to teach spiritual living, it assumes the grace of being able to communicate its ineffable quality. It is charismatic in nature. St. Bernard and Rupert ask for prayers that they may receive from God what they are called upon to give.[126] This experience promotes the presence in the Church of spiritual men rather than of intellectual masters, and history has shown that the former are also capable of being guardians of the faith; we have only to recall the part that St. Anselm and St. Bernard played in the Church in their time. These doctors were abbots, spiritual fathers, and in this sense also pastors, as were almost all the monastic writers.[127] They watched over the monks entrusted to their care, and when the need arose, they extended the same pastoral solicitude to the entire Church of God.

This common inspiration gave rise to the varied—and in the proper use of the term, analogous—manifestations of monastic wisdom: such as the teachings of St. Gregory, St. Peter Damian, and Rupert, those also of the theologians of the Carolingian period, and those of Cluny and Cîteaux. Among the Cistercians further diversity is found in St. Bernard, Aelred, William of St. Thierry, Isaac of Stella, Guerric of Igny, and so many more. They stress more than do the scholastic doctors the fact that theology belongs to a mode of understanding of a higher order than the one which can be reached through reason. Hence their anxiety not to allow theology to be reduced to nothing more than a rational science like any other: "The reasoning of faith," says St. Bernard, "should not be the object of petty human rationalizations."[128]

On the whole, the monastic approach to theology, the kind of religious understanding the monks are trying to attain, might better be described by reviving the word gnosis—on condition naturally that no heterodox nuance be given it. The Christian gnosis, the "true gnosis" in its original, fundamental, and orthodox meaning, is that kind of higher knowledge which is the complement, the fruition of faith, and which reaches completion in prayer and contemplation.[129] Gilson once cited the gnosis of Clement of Alexandria to explain the complexity and richness of St. Anselm's *Proslogion*.[130] And, beyond a doubt, it is this comparison which gives the closest idea of St. Anselm's intellectual research, his applied dialectics, and mystical transcendence. Through many aspects of his work, St. Anselm belongs to scholasticism; but an authentic monastic doctrine can also be found in his work. In similar fashion, learning and mysticism, or more precisely what he himself describes as "the two sciences," are combined in St. Bernard.[131] This differentiation also recalls to mind the higher degree of faith that constitutes gnosis. In this connection a very important text by the Abbot of Clairvaux must be consulted. In explaining a verse from a Psalm in which the "fear of God"—in the deeply religious sense this expression is given in the Old Testament—is called the "beginning of wisdom," Bernard shows that, here, fear and wisdom represent, so to speak, speculative knowledge and knowledge through contact, the *affectus*:

> There we hear Wisdom teaching, here we welcome it within us. There we are instructed, here touched: instruction makes learned men, contact makes wise men. The sun does not warm all those on whom it shines: many of those who are taught what they must do by Wisdom are not equally inspired to do it. It is one thing to know many enriching truths, another to possess them. Likewise, knowledge of God is one thing and fear of God, another; what confers wisdom is not knowledge but fear that touches the heart. He who is puffed up because of his learning, by what right can he be called a wise man? One would have to be entirely lacking in wisdom to call those wise who, having acquired knowledge of God, have not honored Him as God, and have not rendered Him thanks. As for myself, I am in accord with the Apostle to whose judgment their heart was insensible. Truly, the beginning of wisdom is the fear of God; the soul does not begin to enjoy God until God touches it

to give it this fear, not when He teaches it in order to become known by it. Are you in fear of God's justice, of His power? If you are, you are experiencing the delectability of a just and powerful God, for this fear is delectable. And this is what makes the wise man, as knowledge makes the learned and wealth makes the rich. Fear comes first: it is only a preparation for wisdom. With the former you receive a preparation, with the latter a beginning. The preparation is knowledge: it easily engenders presumptuousness unless fear represses it. He who combats this lack of wisdom from the very start possesses in truth the beginning of wisdom. In the first step one arrives at the threshold of wisdom, in the second one enters upon it.[132]

In this page St. Bernard is merely expressing in a masterly fashion what was felt by all the others. There is an objective knowledge of God but it is no more than the preparation for a subjective, personal (a "committed," we might say) knowledge, and these are not two antagonistic knowledges but two degrees of the one and the same search for God: *ibi accessus—hic ingressus.* Monastic theology is a *confessio*; it is an act of faith and of recognition; it involves a "re-cognition" in a deep and living manner by means of prayer and the *lectio divina* of mysteries which are known in a conceptual way; explicit perhaps, but superficial. "To understand" is not necessarily "to explain" through causality; it can also mean the acquiring of a general view: *comprehendere.* For this reason it can mean "to compare." In order to bring the mysteries close together, grasp their coherence, and acquire a synthetic view, there is no need to resort to any ideas gleaned from extraneous sources. Soliciting aid from sources which are foreign to revelation is certainly legitimate, often useful, and occasionally necessary, particularly in matters of controversy "against the Gentiles"; it makes it possible to defend divine Truth, demonstrate its agreement with human truth, and draw up an exposé which is satisfying to reason. The monks preferred to reduce this procedure to the minimum, and they were within their rights. Thus they sought for and obtained a type of theology, "an understanding of the faith" in which the intelligence draws sustenance almost exclusively from the content of the faith itself. Instead of proceeding by rational conclusions and demonstrative reasoning, it questions, in order to understand one aspect of God's mysteries, all other aspects as revealed in Christian sources. Eadmer's example has shown how fruitful this method could be.[133] It fully justifies the assertions made by a present-day theologian:

> Theology brings to this effort at explication the force and logic of reason enlightened by faith. Contemplation contributes to the project the

penetration born of love. The theologian reasons, makes deductions, and
expresses concepts in precise terms; the contemplative scrutinizes the
living depths of truth. Both serve the same cause. It appears to us, however, that the theologian's reasoning excels in organizing already established points of doctrine while the contemplative's love, possessing greater
penetration, makes him a bold, avant-garde scout. . . . We owe to contemplatives the explication of most dogmas, particularly those concerning
Mary's privileges.[134]

St. Bernard, like all monks, stresses the essentially *religious* character that
knowledge of God should retain: it should be a knowledge which unites
and joins one to God. It utilizes the intelligence, dialectics, and learning,
but infinitely surpasses them. It transcends them as God's mystery transcends nature. "He who has set limits to all things," writes Nicholas of
Clairvaux, "cannot be imprisoned within the limits of dialectics."[135] God's
mysteries are "incomprehensible."[136] But they can at least in a sense and
to a certain degree be "comprehended" or embraced in the enveloping
glance of understanding; but for this, learning does not suffice. Let us listen once more to St. Bernard:

> It is not disputation, it is sanctity which comprehends if the incom-
> prehensible can, after a certain fashion, be understood at all. And what
> is this fashion? If you are a saint, you have already understood, you
> know; if you are not, become one, and you will learn through your own
> experience.[137]

To speak of gnosis and to differentiate between two knowledges or two
degrees in the understanding of faith by no means implies echoing the
difference which certain gnostics of antiquity or certain heretics of the
twelfth centnry found between the simple believers—*credentes*—and the
"perfect" who receive a different teaching: this meant in those times a
secret esoteric doctrine reserved for the initiate. The monastic theologians
are speaking of two different ways of knowing the same mysteries. We
must reiterate that here is but one theology. For all, there is the one faith
laboring upon the same truths and in the same Church. But those who
are by profession spiritual men, oriented by their vocation exclusively
toward the search for God, can, in the exercise of this faith, in the practice
of equally religious reflection, reach a higher mode. Accordingly St. Bernard begins his sermons on the Canticle with these words: "To you,
brothers, I must say something different from what I say to others, or,
in any case, I must say it in a different way."[138]

Another Cistercian, Baldwin of Ford, expressed the same idea. In Christian society, he finds two degrees. In each, the level of faith corresponds to the level of moral perfection reached: most of the faithful are satisfied with the "simplicity of faith," and consequently live "in the mediocrity of an inferior life"; others seek "the depth of the mysteries" and live therefore "in the sublimity of a more perfect life."[139] As, under the Old Covenant, the "simple" limited themselves "to venerating the signs" whose meaning was known to the "perfect," so, under the New Covenant, the faithful adhere simply to the faith of the Church, receive the sacraments, and participate in their sanctifying power; but those who are to instruct them, and those whose life is devoted to contemplation, need a certain spiritual intelligence.[140] It is for these that Baldwin wrote.

The emphasis the monastic authors placed on the experience in which their understanding through faith should culminate is the crowning characteristic of their theological method. As can be seen, if it is distinguished from the scholastic method, it is not essentially different. Thus, highlighting the monastic method does not cast the slightest discredit on the scholastic method. But since these authors, belonging to a certain time and place, shared common and sharply defined tendencies, it is necessary, in order to understand them, to compare them with contemporaries in whom the same tendencies were not so explicit. To compare does not mean to separate. The differences between the monks and the scholastics lie less in the doctrinal than in the psychological domain. They are the result of two different states of life, both of which are lawful in the Church.

Theology and Contemplation

Finally the fundamental characteristics of monastic theology determine the objective they deliberately chose to set for it. Since this knowledge of God, which is part of a life of prayer, is a religious knowledge, the two areas of predilection to which effort is devoted are those in which man's relation to God are most immediately apparent. They are, on the one hand, the history of salvation itself; on the other, the presence of God in man and man's presence before God. The mystery of salvation—the mystery of union with God. The first of these domains represents, as it were, the objective aspect of man's relations with God: it is the οἰκονομία as related by Holy Scripture and as it is lived in the liturgy; the second is to a greater degree the subjective element. The first was studied particularly by the Benedictines, the second by the Cistercians. Clearly this is only a question of accent: each of these two aspects of the same Christian life implies the other, so that these two groups of authors complement one another: each takes for granted the object of the other's study.

There is, besides, a sort of connecting link between these two domains, that is to say, the two objectives of their theology. They correspond to two successive moments of the "intelligence" of Scripture as schematized by traditional definition. After the "allegorical" or "mystical" meaning, the one which provides the substance of the mystery, the objective realities of the οἰκονομία, comes the spiritual meaning properly speaking, the one which interiorizes the mystery in the soul of each of the faithful. It is then entirely natural that the emphasis placed on the first of these two "senses" should be the specialty of the Benedictines since they are chronologically earlier; later, the Cistercians garner in this inheritance and assist monasticism as a whole to take possession of it more fully and to assimilate it increasingly in its inner life. There is a kind of logical development, a homogeneous evolution taking place throughout monastic history itself.

The Benedictine who has left us the broadest synthesis is Rupert of Deutz. He is the source *par excellence* for traditional monastic theology, and almost all his work consists of biblical commentaries. He does not attempt to find a basic idea from which everything devolves as from a first principle: even the idea of God cannot be elaborated if we prescind from Christ. Rupert follows the order according to which the revelation of God took place during the course of sacred history. His *De Trinitate* is not composed according to a speculative, abstract plan but according to an historical development. No doubt, if Rupert's teaching is reduced to its main points, the conclusion might be drawn that he is advancing only commonplaces. As a matter of fact, he is simply handing on the traditional teaching, the classical Christianity. But he does so with such a deeply religious feeling and such a rich poetic orchestration that he awakens in his reader new conceptions of mysteries which are not familiar to him; he never ceases wondering over them. Another eminent representative of this Benedictine theology is Eadmer of Canterbury. This too-little-known disciple of St. Anselm deserves wider recognition for the profundity of his insight on the subject of the Immaculate Conception. Once more let us listen to his latest historian:

> He often invokes "higher reasons," that is to say, the "heavenly point of view" which is none other than "God's point of view," on Mary. It happens that for Eadmer, this truly "theological" point of view had solid dogmatic bases, that is, the ancient Church liturgy founded on the doctrine of Mary's intimate association with the Son of God, and on her

mediation with God. Eadmer inquired into the meaning of this belief. It was the *"fides quaerens intellectum"* of St. Anselm's *Proslogion* which guided him far along on the path which by the very nature of things could lead only to the secret known to God alone. He did however perceive the existence of this mystery and the reasons for its existence; he was almost able to put his finger on it. And in any case he demonstrated that it was not contrary to the faith to hold that this mystery was included in "God's point of view" on His Mother.

On two occasions Eadmer tells us expressly how and why he undertook his task: he wanted to meditate on the Virgin's excellence by going back to the "origins of all her privileges," and in order to do so "he let himself be guided by the Holy Scriptures." In his "contemplation" he adopted "God's viewpoint" rather than allowing himself to be carried away by "human reasons" as did the *summi viri,* the *philosophantes.* It was the right method for doing good work in theology. Let us investigate its principles and sources.

When research is carried out down to details, it must be confessed that the numerous texts of the Scripture, with which the author had familiarized himself to the extent of making them his own personal vocabulary, are almost invariably texts which have no strict relation to the doctrine under consideration. On the contrary, the so-called classical "Marian texts" are not found in this treatise. The Scriptural texts served to orient his research and his method and to provide food for his contemplation rather than to bring any influence to bear on the doctrine itself. The most one could claim is that they are quotations which embellish or confirm his own theological thought. Moreover, it is true that under his pen these texts were sometimes given an interpretation *sui generis.* We must therefore conclude that his doctrine draws upon other sources.

The author, as we have already said, does not expressly quote any of the patristic authorities. If he did read texts or works by certain Latin Fathers, as is proved by one implicit quotation or another, it is certainly not for the purpose of using them in the exposition of his thought, properly speaking. In addition, one wonders really in which Latin Fathers the English monk could have found texts and reasons in support of his own doctrine. His knowledge of the documentary material in Greek patristics—taking into consideration the fact of his personal contact with the Greek world as well as the Greco-Byzantine influence which before this had already made itself felt through the intermediary of the first missionaries, and later on through men such as Anselm the Younger in the twelfth century—is surely no adequate reason, either, to explain the clarity and solidity of the doctrine of his treatise.

There is one historical and doctrinal source of the highest value which without any possible doubt inspired our monk, and whose defense he undertook at the same time: to wit, the liturgy of the Church. Eadmer reflected and meditated on the liturgical cult. And he did so with a "feeling for the faith" evident throughout his treatise. He contemplated the object of this liturgical worship in order to grasp its true dogmatic meaning. It is true that the liturgical celebration of the Conception of our Lady in Eadmer's milieu and time did not necessarily imply that this conception had been "immaculate"; but, it is likewise true that the Greco-Byzantine world whose influence is found in twelfth century England, venerated the Virgin's conception because that conception was "holy, and without sin." Thus the liturgy of the Church and the sense of the faith were the two great sources of Eadmer's doctrine. The monk who had meditated and contemplated the teaching of the liturgy, found in it "the sense" it suggested to him. And he tried to develop and give currency to the "theology" that it possessed in actuality.[141]

Thus Eadmer antedated the efforts of Scotus and the greatest theologians of the high scholastic era, and "it is Eadmer's doctrine which triumphed on December 8, 1854."[142]

The importance the monks attribute to history also explains the great weight they give to considerations of eschatology: for the work of salvation, begun in the Old Testament and realized in the New, is brought to completion only in the next world. Christian knowledge here below is only the first step toward the knowledge that belongs to the life of beatitude. Theology, here below, demands that we be detached from it, that we remain oriented toward something else beyond it, toward a fulfillment of which it is merely the beginning. This is yet another of the differences which distinguish the monks' intellectual attitude from that of the scholastics. As has been correctly observed, eschatology occupies practically no place in the teaching of Abailard.[143]

The second doctrinal current, not separate from but parallel to the preceding, and rather Cistercian, is more closely connected with what might be called Christian anthropology. St. Bernard and his disciples are less concerned with the acquisition of an explicit knowledge of God's salvific plan than with the consent to this plan. Everything comes back finally to a problem of spirituality; what is important is the way in which the work of salvation becomes man's possession in his interior life. Everything can be reduced to the two correlative aspects of one and the same religious knowledge: knowledge of the self and knowledge of God. The end in view is not knowledge of God for its own sake alone; the knowledge of the self has its own value. One is the necessary complement of the other;

it leads to the other and cannot be separated from it: *Noverim te—noverim me.*

Here we discern one of the points on which the influence of St. Augustine was predominant. His conception of the inner illumination, which penetrates us from the light which the Word Incarnate brought into the world, had a powerful guiding influence on the orientation of the spiritual doctrine of monasticism in the Middle Ages. In this domain, which is identified more with mysticism than with speculation, the monks are Augustinian. This is at times less true of their way of conceiving or explaining man's relations with God. The idea of grace held by Rupert or Bernard seems to depend very little upon the Augustinian theological synthesis. To tell the truth, the orientation of their mystical doctrine is that of the whole tradition upon which monasticism depends. Origen had accentuated the spirituality of the Christian life, Cassian had stressed purity of heart, and Gregory the Great had described all the consequences and all the manifestations of this life of God in the soul. These authors, perhaps as much as St. Augustine, had laid the foundations for that doctrine of the image which was so important in the thought of Peter of Celle, St. Bernard, or William of St. Thierry. The last, in his *Enigma fidei* and the *Speculum fidei*, evolved explicitly, almost systematically, a whole psychology of faith and of dogmatic development. These are the same problems which preoccupy the other writers and on which they express their thought throughout their various works.

Fundamentally, because of their concern for it, the reality which ensures the unity of all their theology is the mystery of love: the "economy" is the manifestation of God's love for us and the "anthropology" is the realization in us, the application to each of us, of this love. St. Bernard has left us definite statements: God's love for us is the source of all the knowledge we have of God and, for our part, there is no religious knowledge of God without love. "The Father is never fully known if He is not loved perfectly."[144] To know God in a salutary manner, which is both the outcome and the means to salvation, is to love Him; it means willing that His mystery may be accomplished in us. The two lips required for the kiss of the soul are reason and will:[145] the one understands and the other gives consent.

This mystery of love itself becomes a matter for reflection; its accomplishment demands our understanding its exigencies and its foundations. Thus it is the whole work of grace in us that we must consider. This opens up perspectives on the whole domain of what we must do for God; in

other words, the domain of morality. When St. Bernard says, toward the
end of his *Sermons on the Canticles,* that henceforth he is going to treat
of Christian morals—*mores*—he does not confine himself to counsels on
asceticism. Rather, he elaborates a doctrine on union with the Word and
on the restoration within us of God's image which had been distorted by
sin. The question then becomes less one of sins than of sin, less one of
virtues than of the deep-seated disposition which makes the soul the spouse
of God.[146]

In dogmatic theology there are questions, such as those relating to marriage, which were much discussed in the theological schools of the times
but which the monks spoke of but little. In general, however, the object
of their theology is the object of all theology. The only difference lies in the
viewpoint from which they regarded it, and this was determined by the
profound exigencies of their cloistered life entirely consecrated to the search
for God. When Arnold of Bonneval, Peter the Venerable, William of St.
Thierry, and Baldwin of Ford speak of the Eucharist, they do not do so in
the same way as do the scholastics of their times:[147] what occupies them
is less the mode according to which the mysteries are accomplished and
made known to us than their end, which is the loving union with the
Lord in this life and in the hereafter.

A SPIRITUAL THEOLOGY

Since we have dwelt at some length on the differences between the two
theologies, that of the schools and that of the monasteries, we must remember their unity. There exists and must exist only one theology in the
unity of the Church. To speak of two theologies merely means calling
attention to the fact that a certain group of Christian thinkers laid more
stress on a given aspect of the unique mystery of salvation or on some
one of the components of Christian reflection. Accordingly, the two methods
which have been described here by means of contrast are merely two
complementary aspects of theological method. Once the monks have demonstrated that prayer and humility are necessary conditions for any religious knowledge that purports to be a lived theology, a theology to live
by, they can indulge as much as others in speculation. This they did not
fail to do. No doubt they have not left many great works. But the admirable
writings of St. Bernard or William of Saint Thierry all presuppose that
they had a public, a milieu which demanded them, made them possible,
and lived by them. Similarly, in scholasticism, for Gilbert of la Porrée,

Abailard, and a few others, there are many schoolmen and clerics of lesser distinction who nonetheless also constitute a public. These milieux, these parallel currents, if you will, must be studied without separating them, so that their individual characteristics may be perceived.

The two theologies draw in common on Christian sources and both enlist the aid of reason. Scholastic theology has recourse more frequently to the philosophers; monastic theology contents itself more generally with the authority of Scripture and the Fathers. But the fundamental sources in both cases are the same. Theology is a method for reflecting on the mysteries revealed in Christian origins. The question now before us is to learn if there are several ways in which this reflection may be practiced and if amongst them there is a mode of reflection more appropriate to the monks. The texts themselves have led us to confirm that what individualizes monastic thought is a certain dependence on experience. Scholastic theology, on the other hand, puts experience aside. It can subsequently hark back to experience, observe that it agrees with its own reasonings, and that it can even receive nourishment from them; but its reflection is not rooted in experience and is not necessarily directed toward it. It is placed, deliberately, on the plane of metaphysics; it is impersonal and universal. In that very fact reside both its difficulty and its grandeur. It seeks in secular learning and philosophy for analogies capable of expressing religious realities. Its purpose is to organize Christian erudition by means of removing any subjective material so as to make it purely scientific.

As for the monks, they call as if spontaneously upon the testimony of the conscience, upon the presence within them of God's mysteries. Their principal purpose is not to reveal the mysteries of God, to explicate them or derive from them any speculative conclusions, but to impregnate their whole lives with them and to order their entire existence to contemplation. Hence, it is quite natural for their spiritual experience to affect their mode of reflecting and for this experience itself to become in large measure the matter of their meditation. These two modes of religious understanding are, in the original meaning of the word, complementary. Monastic theology is, in a way, a spiritual theology which completes speculative theology; it is the latter's completion, and fulfillment. It is the added something, the *sursum* in which speculative theology tends to transcend itself and become what St. Bernard calls an integral knowledge of God: *integre cognoscere*.[148]

This is what endows monastic theology with both its limitations and its lasting value. The effort it represents is always necessary if theology, while remaining scientific, is to avoid becoming purely abstract (one might venture to say: devitalized); and, as Peter the Cantor expresses it, sacred doctrine is not to be manufactured like machinery. The scholastic endeavor is to a greater degree occasioned by the need for action in the Church: controversy, pastoral administration, or, again, the solution of new questions. Monastic thought is less affected by the concerns of the moment: rather it is governed only by the enduring necessities of the search for God. And for this reason, no doubt, it remains more timely than pre-scholasticism. In preparing the ground for the great scholastic era, pre-scholasticism played an important historical role. But monastic theology was not just a sort of gap between two theological periods, the patristic age of which it was a prolongation and the scholastic age during which it recalled the importance of the life of faith. Monastic theology no more belongs to the life of the past than does the theology of the Fathers. It is not a stage which is now over, and its role is not ended. An historian has pointed this out in connection with Alexander and with William of Jumièges:

> This "monastic theology," however, is certainly not an outmoded, devaluated commodity as the radical evolutionism, to which some had already succumbed in Alexander's time, would have us believe. In exactly the same way as the *Ordo monasticus* itself, it expresses permanent values both for the Church and for humanity.
>
> The continuing presence of the text of the Scriptures, the absolute value of faith for its own sake with its accompanying silent adoration; the perception of mystery which, despite its excesses, was legitimately championed by St. Bernard against Abailard's extravagant attacks; the contempt for dialectics the moment it becomes self-complacent; the transcendency of wisdom, in respect to both understanding and knowledge, to any mere scientific learning, even sacred learning; the inferiority of the "theologian" who is nothing more than a professor: all these are permanently valid, and the *schola Christi*, which the monastery truly is, is their essential and enduring expression.
>
> Humane culture, moreover, flourishes in the monastery, because the wholesomeness of this faith gives rise to a humanism which was, alas, to be lost by the scholastic method. Jumièges, like the other monastic centers, remains faithful to tradition, and the name of William of Jumièges alone is enough to win a place of honor for the abbey in the process of history which has remained one of twelfth-century monasticism's lasting glories in opposition to all the scholastics who were eventually to lose, along with the sense of mystery, the sense of history itself,

including even the history of the earthly economy of the kingdom of God.[149]

The sixteenth- and seventeenth-century editors, who were great Christian humanists, were clearly aware of which authors' writings deserved publication. As well as the scholastic masters of the thirteenth century, they brought out editions of the monastic theologians of earlier times; they did not, however, edit any twelfth-century, prescholastic manuscripts. The work of these doctors had been useful at a given moment in history, but their role had ended with their times. To be sure, modern scholars are justified in making known the most typical of their texts or utilizing excerpts from them as footnotes in their works on doctrinal history. But these authors, while they shed light on the past, contributed hardly anything at all to the enrichment of religious reflection of later periods although they had laid the groundwork. In contrast, there are always reasons for reading Rupert or William of Saint Thierry: spiritual and intellectual research can, at any period, benefit substantially from consulting them.

A Theology of "Admiration"

The latter authors have in common the fact that they were monks—that is to say, essentially religious men preoccupied with union with God. This is, in fact, as we have seen, the only feature they had in common. It is what gives their doctrine a value not only enduring but universal. St. Bernard addressed his teaching particularly to the monks of his abbey, to his friends, most of whom were monks, and to the whole Order which owed its expansion to him. His doctrine is, therefore, closely related to Cistercian life. But precisely because that is one authentic way of life within the Church, its riches belong to all the members of the Church. For this reason, St. Bernard, a monastic doctor, and primarily because he was a monastic doctor, is also a doctor of the universal Church. He himself said that he belonged to all the Orders through charity: *Unum opere teneo, ceteros caritate.*[150] This is likewise true of his work and that of the other monastic authors. Their role is to recall to all that the word "theology" has not entirely lost the traditional meaning associated with it up to Abailard's time: according to tradition, theology is praise of God,[151] and the theologian is a man who speaks to God. Evagrius' saying is valid at any period: "If you are a theologian you will pray in truth, and if you pray in truth, you are a theologian."[152] The theologian is a man who, so to speak, prays over truth, whose prayer is a tissue of truth. He ponders the greatness of God and His works in order to admire them. St. Bernard confirmed this very clearly,[153] and the exclamations scattered throughout the work of Rupert prove that he too is in a state of prayer and admiration.

Baldwin of Ford often describes his attitude in the presence of the Eucharist by these two words: *stupor et admiratio*.[154] He is surprised, rapt, as in an ecstasy, in a state which partakes both of the immobility caused by astonishment and the spontaneous élan provoked by enthusiasm; he never grows accustomed to the sublime realities on which his glance lingers; his wonder never diminishes; he marvels at the mystery Revelation proposes for contemplation, and he also marvels at the fact that men believe in it in the Church: he marvels at the faith. His admiration rewards and, at the same time, stimulates his faith, and these two dispositions of the soul augment each other mutually. They awaken the intelligence and all the other faculties of man: reflection and understanding are benefited by admiration and, in turn, foster charity and all the other virtues, and mystical experience and asceticism flow from them. The thought of Christ, His words, His works, and His sacraments may produce two reactions in man: either we understand the truth, or by the infusion of a higher grace, we experience something sweet: in either case, we are admiring and astounded, *admirantes et stupentes*;[155] through the process of understanding or through some higher perception, we feel something of God's sweetness and we delight in and long for the full manifestation of the reality which is given us under the veil of faith and the sacraments, and we long for our true homeland.

THE KISS

Monastic theology is a theology of admiration and therefore greater than a theology of speculation. Admiration, speculation: both words describe the act of looking. But the gaze of admiration adds something to the gaze of speculation. It does not necessarily see any farther, but the little it does perceive is enough to fill the whole soul of the contemplative with joy and thanksgiving.

A seventeenth-century Cistercian published a summa of "speculative theology" in two columns. Facing an abstract exposition whose matter is taken from St. Thomas, he placed texts taken from St. Bernard. Although his intent in quoting them was to provide a spiritual complement for the doctrine of St. Thomas, he did not in any way misrepresent the meaning of St. Bernard's teaching.[156] Still, the philosophical problems he treats are by no means the ones which excited Bernard.[157] "Can the existence of God and each of His perfections be proved by the demonstrative method?" Bernard is preoccupied by questions of a totally different nature. His aim is to know something other than this about God and in a different fashion. A final text will illustrate how exacting his theology is, all that it wishes to attain, and everything this endeavor demands. God makes a total gift of Himself: in order to receive it, the Christian must make the commitment of his whole life.

The revelation which is made by the Holy Spirit gives light so that we may understand, and fire so that we may love, according to the words of the Apostle: "The charity of God is poured forth in our hearts by the Holy Spirit who has been given us."[158] For this reason, no doubt, those who have known God but who have not honored Him as God, of them we do not read that they have known Him through the revelation of the Holy-Spirit: knowing Him, they have not loved Him. What we read is: "God revealed it to them";[159] they do not add: through the Holy Spirit. These irreverent spirits cannot enjoy the kiss of the spouse; satisfied with the knowledge which puffs up, they have ignored the knowledge which truly edifies. And the Apostle himself tells us how their knowledge was acquired: "By the reflection of the intelligence on created things."[160] Therefore, they have not known Him perfectly whom they have not in the least loved. If they had known Him totally, they would not have been blind to the goodness which made Him, for their redemption, become flesh and die. And what has been revealed to them of God? "His eternal power and His divinity," it is said.[161] As you see, relying on their own intellect, and not on God's spirit, they have thought of what is sublime in Him and full of majesty; but they have not comprehended that He is gentle and humble in heart. And this is not astonishing, for their leader, Behemoth, is he of whom it is written "that he sees everything that is sublime."[162] David, on the contrary, did not walk amid great things and marvels far above his station, so that he should not, by attempting to gaze on majesty, be struck down by its glory.[163]

Do you also, therefore, walk with prudence into the hidden realities. Remember the sage who gives this warning: "Seek not the things that are too high for thee and inquire not into things above thy ability."[164] Walk in the spirit of these directives, and not in accordance with your own understanding. The doctrine of the Spirit does not whet curiosity; it enkindles charity. In like fashion, the spouse seeking the one she loves does not rely on her own bodily instinct, neither does she assent to the vain reasonings of human curiosity. She begs for the kiss; in other words, she invokes the Holy Spirit from whom she will receive, at one and the same time, the favor of knowledge and the seasoning of grace. The knowledge given in the form of a kiss is received with love; the kiss is the sign of love. The knowledge which is vain, being without charity, does not come from a kiss. Even those who are eager for God but not for knowledge cannot claim it as theirs. The kiss, therefore, confers at once a double gift: an enlightened knowledge and a fruitful devotion. It is the soul of intelligence and wisdom; as the bee provides both wax and honey, so it furnishes that which kindles the flame of knowledge and pours out the perfume of grace. He who understands truth without loving it, or loves without understanding, possesses neither one nor the other. Thus this kiss leaves no room for error or for lukewarm feelings. To receive the holy kiss of this two-fold grace, the spouse must prepare two lips: reason for intelligence, will for wisdom. And this total kiss will win for her the reward of hearing: "Grace has been poured upon thy lips; for its sake, God has blessed thee for all eternity."[165]

For St. Bernard then, the integral knowledge of the Trinity should lead to a certain experience of divine sonship. This he says in a few concluding phrases in which we find a synthesis of the expressions he had previously introduced: complete understanding, supernatural sensibility, contact with God in faith, trust, and love:

Blessed is the kiss by which not only God is recognized but the Father is loved who is never known fully if He is not loved perfectly. Which among you is the soul who has not at some time or other felt, in the depths of his conscience, the Spirit of the Son crying: *Abba, Father?* That soul, beyond any doubt, can believe itself beloved of the Father since it feels touched by the same Spirit as the Son. Have confidence, then, you who are this soul, have confidence and do not falter. Know that in the Spirit of the Son you are the Father's daughter and at the same time, sister and spouse of the Son.[166]

NOTES

1. "S. Bernard et la théologie monastique du xiie siècle," *Anal. S. Ord. Cist. 9,* iii–iv (1953) 8.

2. Archbishop Landgraf was good enough to write me about monastic theology: "Sie ist die traditionelle Theologie, von der sich die Frühscholastik losgelöst hat." I want to thank the eminent theologian for letting me quote this highly authoritative judgment.

3. See above, p. 42.

4. K. Künstle, "Die Theologie der Reichenau," *Die Kultur der Reichenau* (Munich, 1925), pp. 704–705.

5. F. Zoepfl, "Die Grundlegung der deutschen Kultur durch die Benediktiner," *Münchener theologische Zeitschrift,* 242–43.

6. "La théologie comme science d'après la littérature quodlibétique," RTAM

(1939) 351–74. Beumer, "Die Kritik des Johannes von Neapel, o.p. an der Subalternationslehre des hl. Thomas von Aquin," *Gregorianum* (1956) 261–70.

7. Y. Congar, "Théologie," *Dict. de théol. cathol.* XV.I.341 (Paris, 1946).

8. "Seelsorgstheorie."

9. "Théologie kérygmatique."

10. "At least two," so that the question of the canons regular, especially those of the school of Saint-Victor, could be reserved for the specialists.

11. M. van Assche, "Divinae vacare lectioni," *Sacris erudiri* I (1948) 13–21. Especially P. Delhaye, "L'Organisation scolaire au xiie siècle," *Traditio* 5 (1947) 211–68. Simultaneously with the appearance of this well-documented study, I arrived at similar results—and not only on the subject of the 12th century—in my "L'humanisme bénédictin du viiie au xiie s.," *Analecta monastica* I 120. Cf. also R. Bolgar, *The Classical Heritage*, pp. 117–18.

12. K. Hallinger, *Gorze-Kluny* (Rome, 1950–1951), has studied these two centers from the monastic point of view; here they are seen from the cultural point of view.

13. P. Delhaye, "Deux textes de Senatus de Worcester sur la pénitence," RTAM (1952) 203–24.

14. Quoted in R. W. Hunt, "English Learning in the Late Twelfth Century," *Transactions of the Royal Historical Society*, 4th Series, 19 (1936) 30.

15. "Pierre le Vénérable et les limites du programme clunisien," *Coll. Ord. Cist. Ref.* (1956) 84–87.

16. On the episcopal schools cf. J. Fleckenstein, "Königshof und Bischofsschule unter Otto dem Grossen," *Arch. f. Kulturgeschichte* 38 (1956) 38–62, and J. Autenrieth, "Die Domschule von Konstanz zur Zeit des Investiturstreits," *Forsch. zur Kirchen- und Geistesgeschichte*, n.f. 3 (Stuttgart, 1956).

17. "Determinant igitur sancti patres et ecclesiastici doctores, quae sunt quae necessario presbyteros scire oportet, scilicet librum sacramentorum, lectionarium, baptisterium, compotum, canonem paenitentialem, psalterium, homilias per circulum anni . . ." *Sermo ad sacerdotes*, ed. C. A. Robson, *Maurice of Sully and the Medieval Vernacular Homily* (Oxford, 1952), p. 56; the continuation of the text, which serves as an introduction to the collection of Maurice's sermons, develops that program and details everything which has to be known about the different kinds of sin so that the sacrament of penance can be well administered.

18. *L'humanisme bénédictin* (n. 11). Cf. E. Lesne, *Les écoles de la fin du XIIe s.* (Lille, 1940), *passim*.

19. See above, p. 115.

20. *Vita* I 32 (PL 158.69).

21. E. Kleineidam, *Wissen, Wissenschaft und Theologie bei Bernhard von Clairvaux* (Leipzig, 1955), pp. 11–13; notations of several medievalists in *Jumièges, Congrès scientifique du XIIIe centenaire* (Rouen, 1955), pp. 604, 775ff.; 783ff.

22. "Contemplation et vie contemplative du vie au xiie siècle," *Dict. de spiritualité* II (Paris, 1953) 1929–48. It will be sufficient to note here this traditional and unanimous designation.

23. *Études sur S. Bernard*, p. 152.

24. L. Grill, *Bernard de Clairvaux* (Paris, 1953), pp. 143–44.

25. The expression is from Peter the Venerable, *Epist.* III 2 (PL 189.279). See on these persons, S. Balau, *Étude critique des sources d'histoire du pays de Liège au moyen âge* (Brussels, 1903), pp. 304–307.

26. "Lettres d'Odon d'Ourscamp, cardinal cistercien," *Analecta monastica* III 156.

27. A. Vernet, "Une épitaphe inédite de Thierry de Chartres," *Recueil de travaux offerts à M. Clovis Brunel* (Paris, 1955), p. 666.

28. Caesarius of Heisterbach, *Dialogus miraculorum*, Dist. 1, De conversione, xxxix: "Tanta est virtus humilitatis, ut eius amore saepe ad ordinem venientes clerici, laicos se simulaverint, malentes pecora pascere, quam libros legere, satius ducentes Deo in humilitate servire, quam propter sacros ordines vel literaturam ceteris praeesse." Ed. J. Strange (Cologne, 1851), pp. 46–47.

29. A. Schneider, "Vita B. Davidis monachi Hemmerodensis," *Analecta S. Ord. Cist.* (1955) 33.

30. *De sancta simplicitate* V (PL 145.699).

31. "L'humanisme bénédictin," *Analecta monastica* I 18–20.

32. "Lettres de vocation à la vie monastique," *Analecta monastica* III 196.

33. Ps. 93.12.

34. Ps. 88.9.

35. *Epist.* 7 (PL 203.58).

36. *Sermo* IX (PL 198.1747); the same theme is treated in Serm. VII of Comestor (PL 171.412D–413A (ps.-Hildebert, XIV; cf. PL 198.1741D).

37. Delhaye, "L'organisation scolaire" (n. 11) 228.

38. *Epist.* 106.2 (PL 182.242).

39. Ed. Wilmart in *Revue d'ascétique et de mystique* (1933) 389–90.

40. *In Reg. S. Ben.* I (PL 170.480).

41. *La spiritualité de Pierre de Celle*, pp. 92–93. See especially letter 73 (PL 202.519).

42. *De sancta simplicitate* V (PL 145.699).

43. "Textes sur St. Bernard et Gilbert de la Porrée," *Mediaeval Studies* 14 (1952) 111–28.

44. "Post acceptum sacrum ordinem . . . grammaticorum vulgus adeunt . . . , exteriorum artium nugis insudant . . . , theatralia grammaticorum gymnasia insolenter irrumpere." *De perfectione monachi* II (PL 145.306–307).

45. *Prol.* PL 145.695.

46. *Entheticus* 59–60, 93–94, 111–14 (PL 199.966–67).

47. *Serm. sup. Cant.* 74.2.

48. *De baptismo, Praef.* (PL 182.1031).

49. Kleineidam (n. 21), 147, 153, 156.

50. J. Vendryès, *Le langage* (Paris, 1921), pp. 294–95.

51. M. Hubert, "Aspects du latin philosophique aux xiie et xiiie s.," *Revue des études latines* 27 (1949) 212.

52. Examples in E. von Ivanka, "La structure de l'âme selon S. Bernard," *S. Bernard théologien*, pp. 202–208.

53. Texts in *S. Bernard théologien*, pp. 16n5, 101n1, 108, 304–305.

54. "We are enclosed by the boundaries set down by the Fathers, which we may not transgress." PL 194.1862.

55. "Inédits bernardins dans un ms. d'Orval," *Analecta monastica* I 157 (for "Christian discipline" see above, pp. 101–102). A commentary on this page by St. Bernard can be found in M. Dumontier, *S. Bernard et la Bible* (Paris, 1953), p. 67.

56. A. Landgraf, *Dogmengeschichte der Frühscholastik* II (Regensburg, 1953)

57–60. "Der heilige Bernhard in seinem Verhältnis zur Theologie des zwölften

Jahrhunderts," *Bernhard von Clairvaux, Mönch und Mystiker* (Wiesbaden, 1955), p. 46.

57. "A puero advectus sufficienter didicit monasticam normam; deinde in grammaticae studuit fundamento, sed et dialecticae litavit aliquando acumina," ed. G. Mercati, *Opere minore* (Vatican City, 1937) I 372.

58. C. H. Talbot, *Sermones inediti B. Aelredi* (Rome, 1952), p. 40.

59. "L'arithmétique de Guillaume d'Auberive," *Analecta monastica* I 181–204. Therefore the "animosity" of the monks toward scholasticism, of which H. Weisweiler speaks in *Scholastik* (1955) 407, should not be attributed to the use of mathematical figures more than to any other causes. Tannery and Clerval, "Une correspondance d'écolâtres au XIe s.," in *Notices et extraits des mss. de la Bibl. nationale* 36.2 (1899) 533–36, have published a letter from a monk to a teacher of arithmetic which shows the good relations which the monks maintained with the scholastics and the interest they had in arithmetic.

60. Ibid. 195–96.

61. J. Beumer, s.j., "Rupert von Deutz und seine Vermittlungstheologie," *Münchener theologische Zeitschrift* (1953) 257ff. quotes Rupert's texts and presents a much more comprehensive appreciation than that of many a less informed historian.

62. Landgraf, "Zum Begriff der Scholastik," *Collectanea Franciscana* (1941) 487–90, quotes texts, particularly the commentary on the Epistle to the Hebrews which came from the school of Auxerre in the 9th century. PL 117.858. In his "Probleme um den hl. Bernhard von Clairvaux," *Cistericenser-Chronik* (1954) 3–7, the same author shows that the dialectical method of the *sic et non* had been in use well before the time of Abailard, who was not the inventor of this technique. Nor can the "reconciliation" between dialectic and theology be ascribed to Peter Lombard, a theory advanced by Bolgar in *The Classical Heritage*, pp. 205–206 and 578.

63. Hartig, *Die Kultur der Reichenau*, p. 643.

64. 1 Tim. 6.4. Esp. St. Bernard, *De baptismo*, Praef. (PL 182.1031), and *Super Cant.* 16.9, in a context where he cites the mistakes committed by the monks before their conversion.

65. Landgraf, "Zum Begriff" (n. 62) 352.

66. *Geschichte der scholastischen Methode* (Freiburg, 1911), pp. 98–100. The same contrast between "mystical" and "rationalistic tendencies" is pointed out by Michel in his article "Trinité" in *Dict. de théol. cathol.* XV (1947) 1713 and 1717.

67. "Et pugnas verborum. Ecce quia modernorum theologorum arguit disputationem, qui pugnas verborum et quasdam cavillationes quaerunt, veritate Dei etiam manifesta, qui disputant ut illaqueant potius quam discernant et inquirant. Et sic reverenter fructus et ramos huius arboris, scil. sacrae paginae, cuius radices fixae sunt in caelis, tractant et carpunt ac si ars liberalis esset mecanica." Quoted by Landgraf in *Theologische Revue* (1955) 350.

68. M.-D. Chenu, "Arts 'mécaniques' et œuvres serviles," *Rev. des sc. philos. et théol.* (1940) 314.

69. *De consideratione* 5.6.

70. "Sacramentum hoc magnum est, et quidem venerandum, non scrutandum," *De consideratione* 5.18.

71. "Scrupuli quidam curiosorum, qui Deum malum velle argutantur," *De voluntate Dei* 5 (PL 170.440); cf. *De omnipotentia Dei*, 23 (ibid. 473).

72. *De sacram. altaris*, PL 204.703; cf. ibid. 679D.

73. Chenu, "Culture et théologie à Jumièges après l'âge féodal," *Jumièges, Congrès*, p. 780.

74. *Disputatio altera adv. Abael.*, PL 180.321.

75. Eccli. 1.1.

76. Reproduced in the Straub–Keller edition (Strasburg, 1899) pl. xi bis.

77. M.-T. d'Alverny, "Le cosmos symbolique du xii⁰ s.," *Arch. d'hist. doct. et litt. du moyen âge* (1953) 81.

78. Beumer (n. 61), 263–64.

79. *La spiritualité de Pierre de Celle*, p. 92.

80. 1 Cor. 8.1.

81. "De sancta simplicitate scientiae inflanti anteponenda," PL 145.695.

82. "Holy rusticity is profitable only to oneself." *Epist.* 53, 3 (CSEL 64.447). This exhortation, addressed, in addition, to a priest, contained simultaneously praise (sancta) and a reservation (solum sibi).

83. *In Eccles.* 18–21 (PL 168.1218). "Immoderata, sanctam rusticitatem repellit." *In Ioannem* 8 (PL 169.77).

84. "The spouse of the Lord must not be stupid." *Sup. Cant.* 69.2. Also ibid. 76.10: "How can an ignorant shepherd lead his flock into the pastures of divine teaching?"

85. Texts in *Pierre le Vénérable*, pp. 282–83. *La spiritualité de Pierre de Celle*, p. 92.

86. Ibid. 95. Cf. P. Lehmann, "Die heilige Einfaltigkeit," *Historisches Jahrbuch* 58 (1938) 305-16. The biblical and patristic quotations are indicated in the Index of the *Liber scintillarum*, ed. H. M. Rochais (Turnhout, 1957), p. 300, at the words "simplex" and "simplicitas."

87. Job 1.1.

88. *Epist. ad Fr. de Monte Dei* I 13, trans. J. M. Déchanet, *Lettre d'or* (Paris, 1956), p. 54. In a sweeping synthesis so characteristic of him, William of Saint-Thierry inserts this common notion of simplicity. The history and significance of *sancta simplicitas* would deserve further study.

89. "Christianae simplicitas humilitas," *Exord. magn. Cist.*, d. 3, c. 8 (PL 185.1059).

90. *Rule*, ch. 7.

91. Ps. 130.2.

92. *Sup. Cant.* 85.9.7.

93. *Epist.* 188.1 (PL 182.353); *Epist.* 191.1 (ibid. 357); *Epist.* 189.2 (ibid. 355); *Epist.* 330 (ibid. 535).

94. *Epist.* 251 (PL 211.517).

95. This formula is inspired by St. Jerome, *Contra Vigilantium* 15 (PL 23.351), who in turn is cited by St. Bernard, *Epist.* 89.2 (PL 182.221); *Sup. Cant.* 64.3 (PL 183.1085).

96. *Chronicon Villar* 25 (MGH 208.25).

97. Ibid. 210*n*6.

98. Referring to the schools of Paris in the 13th century, Chenu says, quite rightly: "We are far from the monastic schools where teachers prepared the young monk for Bible reading and for divine service without haste, without ambition, and without worry for the morrow, purely for the love of God." *Introduction a l'étude de S. Thomas d'Aquin* (Montreal–Paris, 1950), p. 16.

99. "Inflated with knowledge: the psalmist has not said 'I went to school,' or, 'I was taught by the learned,' but '*I have sought thy commandments.*' There is a knowledge which is called love or charity, because, according to Gregory the Great, love itself is knowledge of him in whom it is directed, because in proportion as we love, to that extent we know." Quoted by W. A. Pantin, "The Monk-solitary of Farne," *Eng. Hist. Rev.* (1944) 178.

100. *De fide* I 5 (PL 16.537).

101. Ibid. I 13 (548).

102. Pantin (n. 99), 177.

103. "Novi commentatores . . . fidem potius ex intellectu quam intellectus ex fide consequi speraverunt. . . . Qui fidem sola ratione metiuntur." "Le traité de Guillaume de Saint-Jacques sur la trinité," *Arch. d'hist. et litt. du moyen âge,* 18 (1950–1951) 94.

104. H. Rashdall, *Doctrine and development* (London, 1898), p. 143, quoted without reservation by G. G. Coulton, *Five Centuries of Religion* (Cambridge, 1923) 1.238.

105. To the testimony quoted in *S. Bernard mystique* (1948) 162, 169–75, and by M. Bernards, "Stand der Bernhardforschung," *Bernhard von Clairvaux, Mönch und Mystiker* (Wiesbaden, 1955), pp. 8 and 29, add: A. Landgraf, "Probleme um den heiligen Bernhard von Clairvaux," *Cistercienser-Chronik* (1954) 1–3, 6–7; D. Knowles, "St. Bernard of Clairvaux: 1090–1153," *Dublin Review* (1953) 118, and, above all, the precise, detailed, and documented rectification by J. Chatillon, "L'influence de S. Bernard sur la pensée scolastique au xiie et au xiiie siècle," *S. Bernard théologien,* pp. 284–87. On the clever but hazardous character of Abailard's teaching, see the suggestive pages of Bolgar, *The Classical Heritage,* pp. 158–61.

106. Bolgar, p. 158.

107. On St. Peter Damian, see the excellent clarification provided by J. Gonsette, s.j., *S. Pierre Damien et la culture profane* (Louvain–Paris, 1956), especially "Pierre Damien et les excès de la culture profane," pp. 8–15.

108. (N. 105), 117.

109. G. Geenen, o.p., *Virgo Immaculata, Acta congressus mariologici* 5 (Rome, 1955), pp. 90–136.

110. Ibid. 100–101.

111. Ibid. 101n18.

112. J. Beumer, s.j., "Mariologie und Ekklesiologie bei Isaac von Stella," *Münchener theologische Zeitschrift* (1954) 48–49.

113. *De consideratione* V 32 (PL 182.808).

114. *De reverentia orationis. Rule,* ch. 20.

115. *De corpore et sanguine Domini,* PL 121.125–70.

116. *De sacramento altaris,* PL 204.770–74.

117. *Pierre la Vénérable,* pp. 325–40: "Mort et Transfiguration"; C. Bodard, "Christus–Spiritus. Incarnation et résurrection dans la théologie de S. Bernard," *Saint Bernardus van Clairvaux* (1953) 89–104. "Le mystère du corps du Seigneur. Quelques aspects de la christologie de Pierre le Vénérable," *Coll. Ord. Cist. Ref.* (1956) 100–31.

118. "Philosophia autem est amor sapientiae; sapientia autem est integra comprehensio veritatis eorum quae sunt, quam nullus vel parum adipiscitur nisi amaverit,"

E. Jouneau, ed. "Le 'Prologus in Eptateuchon' de Thierry de Chartres," *Mediaeval Studies* 16 (1954) 174. Similar definitions can be found in R. Baron, "Hugonis de Sancto Victore epitome Dindimi in Philosophiam," *Traditio* 11 (1955) 130.

119. J. Schuck, *Das Hohelied des hl. Bernhard von Clairvaux* (Paderborn, 1926), p. 11.

120. *In Apoc.* 2.2 (PL 169.881).

121. *In Matth.* XII (PL 168.1604).

122. See above, p. 25. "Voce sua foris etiam per apostolos insonat, sed corda audientium per se ipsum interius illustrat," *Mor.* 27.43 (PL 78.424).

123. "Ex affectu inspirationis divinae gratiae," *Rule*, ch. 20.

124. P. Delfgaauw, "La lumière de la charité chez S. Bernard," *Coll. Ord. Cist. Ref.* 18 (1956) 42–61. This significant formula can also be found in St. Boniface: "Illumined not only by the exterior study of literature, but by the interior light of divine science." *S. Bonifatii et Lullii epist.* MGH, *Scriptor. rer. germanicar.* n.s. I 221.5.

125. J. Mouroux, "Sur les critères de l'expérience spirituelle d'après les Sermons sur le Cantique des cantiques," *S. Bernard théologien*, pp. 253–67, and especially 256, "L'expérience en Église."

126. Texts by Rupert are indicated by J. Beumer, *Rupert von Deutz* (n. 61), 261*nn*26–27. For Bernard, see above, p. 4 and *Super Cant.* 3.6, 7.8, 11.8, 14.8, etc.

127. See above, page 153.

128. "Rationem fidei humanis committi ratiunculis agitandam," *Epist.* 189–94 (PL 182.355).

129. See the penetrating analyses by T. Camelot, *Foi et gnose. Introduction à l'étude de la connaissance mystique chez Clément d'Alexandrie* (Paris, 1945), particularly pp. 58, 99, 123. Cf. also L. Bouyer, *Le sens de la vie monastique* (Paris, 1950), pp. 300–13: "Sagesse et Gnose."

130. E. Gilson, "Sens et nature de l'argument de S. Anselme," *Arch. d'hist. doct. et litt. du moyen âge* (1934) 49ff. See also the interesting remarks by J. B. Bonnes, RB (1945) 184–88.

131. Kleineidam (n. 21), pp. 30–64.

132. *Sup. Cant.* 23.14.

133. Would it be permissible to point out here how much this manner of seeking an understanding of the faith is in line with what the Vatican Council I was to indicate? Thus, we read in *Sessio* 3, c.4: "If human reason, with faith as its guiding light, inquires earnestly, devoutly and circumspectly, it attains, by God's help, to some understanding of mysteries, and that a most profitable one. It achieves this by the similarity with truths which it knows naturally and also from the interrelationship of mysteries with one another and with man's final end . . ." (Denzinger–Rahner ed., 1896) The tenor of this declaration seemed to be in contrast with the schemas which were proposed when it was being prepared.

134. Eugène de l'Enfant Jésus, O. Carm., *Je veux voir Dieu* (Tarascon, 1949), p. 428. If St. Bernard, in the case of the Immaculate Conception, appealed to theological reasoning rather than to the intuition of the contemplative as Eadmer had done, by that very fact he retarded the development of dogma; but, at the same time, his opposition and the researches which they provoked were the occasion of an advance in the explication and the rational justification of truths which, in the case of others, were perceived by "the sense of faith." Cf. A. Fracheboud, "La lettre 174 de S.

Bernard et les divers facteurs du développement dogmatique," *Coll. Ord. Cist. Ref.* 17 (1955) 193–95.

135. *Sermo in Nativ.* 2.7 (PL 184.837).

136. "Peter Abailard seeks to deprive Christian faith of all merit, when he imagines that the nature of God can be understood by human reason." St. Bernard, *Epist.* 191 (PL 182.357).

137. *De consideratione* 5.30. Cf. Guerrie d'Igny, *Rogat* 4 (PL 185.153).

138. Cf. above, p. 4.

139. *De sacram. alt.* PL 204.758.

140. Ibid. 713.

141. Geenen (n. 109), pp. 122–24.

142. Ibid., p. 133.

143. Kleineidam (n. 21), p. 44.

144. *Sup. Cant.* 8.9; see p. 227.

145. *Sup. Cant.* 8.7.

146. *Sup. Cant.* 80. I: "redeamus ad indaganda moralia"; there follows a treatise on the soul as God's image; 86. I: "quae ad mores spectant" introduces a treatise on prayer and the union with the Word.

147. These suggestions are developed in the Introduction to the edition, with a translation of the tract, *Sur le sacrement de l'autel de Baudouin de Ford*, in the collection *Textes monastiques d'Occident* (Sources chrétiennes; Paris, 1957).

148. *Sup. Cant.* 8.5.

149. Chenu, "Culture et théologie à Jumièges après l'ère féodale," *Jumièges*, 781.

150. *Apologia*, 8 (PL 182.903).

151. *Un maître*, p. 77.

152. *De oratione*, 60 (PL 79.1179). Cf. I. Hausherr, "Le traité de l'oraison d'Evagre le Pontique," *Revue d'ascétique et de mystique* (1934) 90.

153. "Intendere audet, sed quasi admirans, non quasi scrutans," *Sup. Cant.* 62.4.

154. *De sacram. alt.*, PL 204.655, 685.

155. Ibid. 749.

156. On the "double loyalty" which is due to St. Bernard and to St. Thomas whose "doctrines surpass each other at different points," see the discerning pages by A. Forest, "S. Bernard et S. Thomas," *S. Bernard théologien*, pp. 308–11.

157. See Appendix III.

158. Rom. 5.5.

159. Rom. 1.19.

160. Rom. 1.20.

161. Ibid.

162. Job 41.25.

163. On these texts, cf. above, p. 203.

164. Ecclus. 3.22.

165. *Sup. Cant.* 8.5–6.

166. *Sup. Cant.* 8.9.

10

The Poem of the Liturgy

THE SENSE OF THE MAJESTY OF THE LORD was one of the salient characteristics of the monks' religious reflection, and it was expressed, even more
than in their theological writings, in their liturgical production. The latter
merits consideration and should be reserved to the last because it is linked
with all other aspects of monastic life: with its practice, since it is connected
with one of its principal observances, that is, the celebration of the cult;
and with its culture for which it is both the stimulus and the outcome.
There is no doubt that liturgy constitutes one of the sources of this culture: it is partly through it and in it that the monks made contact with
Scripture and the Fathers and were permeated by the great traditional
religious themes. But it was equally in the liturgy that their culture found
one of its chosen fields for expression: for it, and in connection with it,
they composed the greatest number of texts. These have almost been forgotten by now with the exception of a few masterpieces whose monastic
origin is mostly unknown because they have been absorbed into the common treasury of Western liturgy. But these choice examples are part of
a very large collection, without which we could have no complete idea of
monastic literature.

LITURGY: SYNTHESIS OF THE ARTS

The word "liturgy" in this study is used in the broad sense to mean all
the activities involved in prayer. In the Middle Ages the public celebration
of the divine office represents their perfect expression and synthesis. This
cannot be said of every period, since the first generations of monks had
either privately or together recited the Psalms, and occasionally large numbers participated; but in their life of retirement from the world, little attention was given to the Church's public worship.[1] St. Benedict, on this point
as well as on others, stood for moderation: twelve Psalms a night, and the
whole Psalter each week. He had enriched the monastic office with non-
biblical texts which some churches were using in the celebration of the
liturgy, like the hymns he called "Ambrosian." He had emphasized the
great value of this common prayer, the details of which were almost en-

tirely determined by St. Benedict in his *Rule*. Yet in his *Rule*, the divine office is not among the occupations requiring the most time. However, under the influence of circumstances he could not have foreseen,[2] the role played by the liturgy in the monastic life tended to grow, and Benedict of Aniane ratified this evolution. From then on, the monks' life, in this respect, bore a great resemblance to that of canons who performed the services of worship in the cathedral churches. From the ninth to the twelfth century, monastic liturgy continued to grow richer and developed to the point where, in certain localities, it accounted for almost the entire day. In this domain, beginning in particular with the middle of the tenth century, a difference in practice grew up and was maintained between the two regions whose predominating points of view are symbolized by the names of Gorze and Cluny. In the beginning, less time was allotted to the office. But monastic life everywhere remained marked by its great esteem for public worship. The monks' entire life was led under the sign of the liturgy, in rhythm with its hours, its seasons, and its feasts; it was dominated by the desire to glorify God in everything, and first of all, by celebrating His mysteries.

The literary productions which resulted from this preoccupation were extremely varied. For our purposes they can be grouped under three headings: those which treat of the liturgy, those which constitute texts for use in the service itself, and those which describe the characteristics which the liturgy conferred on the monks' religion.

The monks wrote little about their attitude toward the liturgy: its importance was quite taken for granted; for men who were living constantly under its influence, it hardly needed any commentary. Rather, it was the liturgy itself which formed the usual and ordinary commentary on Holy Scripture and the Fathers. This is true especially of Cluny where liturgy occupied such an important place. St. Odo in his *Conferences* and his poem on the *Occupation*, St. Odilo in his sermons, Peter the Venerable in his various writings do not explain the liturgy and they rarely mention it. No doubt texts were written that were intended for reading at Cluny: legends of the Saints, solemn sermons like those of Peter the Venerable on St. Marcellus or on the relics of a saint,[3] or those of St. Bernard on St. Victor. Treatises on the *computus* were composed in which all the resources of arithmetic and astronomy were enlisted in calculating the dates of movable feasts.[4] The liturgy was called upon to supply themes for sermons even when the latter consisted in the interpretation of Scripture; thus St. Bernard's sermons on the Psalm *Qui habitat* abound in allusions to Lent during which verses of this Psalm are often sung. Still it remains true that we possess few monastic writings on the liturgy,[5] although some do exist; the most outstanding have been published, while others are as yet unpublished.[6] In general—and here again we encounter one of the constants of monastic culture—the rites are sanctioned on historical grounds as in the "manual of liturgy" in which Walafrid Strabo made a study of the origins and growth of certain ecclesiastical observances.[7] But these treatises, practical or scholarly in nature, are not eulogies of the divine office, its beauty, or its pedagogical merit; nor are they exhortations to reserve a position of preference for it in religious life. Literary works of the latter type become necessary only in periods when the liturgical sense must be reanimated and the liturgy restored. The monks themselves are unanimously convinced of the primary importance which belongs by right to the activity in which they proclaim the glory of God. Belief in the Lord's majesty directs and dominates all their expository works, such as Rupert of Deutz' treatise *On the Divine Offices*. In its prologue he asserts very forcibly that

> The rites which, following the yearly cycle, are performed at the divine office are symbols of the highest realities; they embrace the greatest sacraments and all the majesty of the heavenly mysteries. They were instituted for the glory of the head of the Church, Our Lord Jesus Christ, by men who understood all the sublimity of the mysteries of His Incarnation, His Nativity, His Passion, His Resurrection, and His Ascension, and who had the ability to proclaim it in the spoken word, the written word, and in the rites. . . . But celebrating the rites without understanding them is like speaking without interpreting what is being said. The Apostle St. Paul counsels him who has the gift of speaking to pray that he may receive the ability to interpret what he says.[8] Among the spiritual gifts with which the Holy Spirit enriches His Church, we should lovingly cultivate the one which consists in the power to understand what we say in prayer and in psalmody: this is no less than a manner of prophesying.[9]

All the liturgical literature of the monks consisted in similarly commenting, "with the voice and the written word," the content of the rites. Rather than treatises on the rites, their commentary took the form of texts for use in conjunction with the celebration and which displayed its riches.

The liturgical texts consist of written formulas to be used in the various exercises of the liturgy. Before describing them we should recognize the fact that additional texts were constantly being composed. For the liturgy was not considered as a complete and final whole to which nothing could be added. In this realm St. Benedict was an innovator since he had introduced into monastic liturgy the "Ambrosian hymns," amongst others. The tendency to embellish the divine service with new texts, and especially poetic texts, continued to manifest itself everywhere.

NOTKER AND THE SEQUENCE

First of all, new offices had to be composed as new feasts were added to the Church's calendar. But above all, the texts already in existence soon became a subject for amplifications. The origin of this practice is well known, thanks to the account Notker of St. Gall gives of it in the preface to his collected sequences.[10] He tells us how difficult it was to remember, so as to sing them correctly, "the very long melodies" which prolonged the final *a* of the *alleluia* at the Gradual. But one day around the year 860, a monk of Jumièges, fleeing before the Normans, arrived at St. Gall with an antiphonary in which each note of the Alleluia corresponded to a syllable, and all were in great admiration of this mnemonic device for preserving the melodies. Now, at St. Gall there was a real poet, Notker, and around him a whole school of disciples and successors to perfect the technique which had come to them from Jumièges. This was the origin of *prosae*.

Thereafter, these compositions never ceased being multiplied, amplified, and diversified; meters, *versus, versiculi*, tropes, sequences, *prosulae*, motets, *organa*:[11] each of these forms had its own laws and its own history. Over the centuries all were transformed and corrupted: out of dialogued tropes grew the *ludi*, and the latter contributed, to a great extent, to the origin of liturgical drama.[12] We need not describe here these different literary forms nor relate the evolution of each since this obviously could not be done in a few pages with the precision the subject demands. It is enough for us to record the fact that during the entire Middle Ages throughout the West, men continually composed literary texts that were intended to be sung in the divine service.

These texts form the largest part of the forty-two thousand pieces of verse mentioned in the *Repertorium hymnologicum* by Ulysse Chevalier, and of the fifty-five volumes of the *Analecta Hymnica* published by Dreves and Blume. These are texts one seldom has occasion to read today; they were written not to be read but to be chanted during the divine office. We would, however, have only an inadequate idea of the life led by the monks and of their literary activity if we lost sight of the place these compositions held in their schedule and in their preoccupations.

For these texts were loved. Those who had a reason and the talent for doing so, loved to compose them.

> And all loved to sing
> The delightful kyrielles
> The sweet and lovely sequences
> With full voice and in rich tones.[13]

It happened that certain communities would inaugurate a feast or add to
its solemnity in order to have the joy of singing or reading beautiful texts.
It has been remarked that "some feasts have a strictly literary origin. It
is quite possible that the celebration of the feast of a certain saint may
have been initiated in a monastery because its library had a marvelous
Life which had guaranteed him a local celebrity."[14] At St. Bertin, in the
eleventh century, St. Vincent was celebrated with only three lessons and
three *responsoria*. But, one fine day, some brethren who had come from
other parts brought along a greater number of *responsoria*. These were
written down and delighted the monks and especially the young oblates.
Hence, it was decided to adopt them; to carry this out, St. Vincent's feast
became a twelve-lesson feast. "And," adds the chronicler, "the devotion of
the brethren to God and the holy martyr increased from day to day."[15]

No doubt many of these literary and musical compositions would no
longer be to our taste, and to us their length might well seem tiresome.
We wonder if they were equally so for the great many who sang, heard,
or copied them? They may very well correspond to a taste whose criteria
are not ours and exemplify a different concept of time and a different
internal rhythm. The verve of primitive, original, and youthfully exuberant spirits is often combined in these authors with a curious need for
purely conventional artifices. They are willing slaves of the *clausulae*; they
overexaggerate the use of diminutives and superlatives, unusual words and
Greek expressions. Mythological allusions betray the pedantry and preciosity of some of them. But side by side with these defects, this literature
has real qualities which it has been claimed make it "often lofty and
grand, with at times the majesty of a romanesque cathedral."[16] In these
productions are to be found many examples of true poetry, more than
they are sometimes believed to have. Literary historians—Léon Gauthier,
Rémy de Gourmont, W. von den Steinen—are the ones who have brought
this home to us. The *Alma Redemptoris mater*, the *Veni Creator*, and
other jewels of the liturgy were born of the medieval monks' intensely felt
need to versify for God.

Almost everything in this material, as the historians admit, is of monastic origin.[17] It is true that some of the manuscripts in which these texts
have been preserved have come from cathedrals; still it is true that almost
all the known authors were monks. Their poems became the common

fund of the universal liturgy, but they had arisen in monastic milieux and expressed the aspirations of monks everywhere. St. Gall, Fleury, Monte Cassino, St. Martial of Limoges are only the most renowned of the abbeys to which we are indebted for them. For the list to be complete many other abbeys would have to be mentioned in the countries of the Empire as well as in England,[18] France, and Italy. This proliferation of texts whose purpose was to embellish other texts could, of course, give rise to dangers, and abuses did occur. The Cistercians inaugurated a reaction, almost a revolution, when they reinstated the pure and simple liturgy in which biblical texts play the predominant part. Still, not a few of their number prefer solemn Masses to austere psalmody.[19] The Order as a whole, finally, although tardily, like the others adopted the votive office of the Blessed Virgin. St. Bernard was to compose a hymn in honor of St. Malachy and —for the Benedictines, to be sure—an office in honor of St. Victor.

The fact, then, is that whereas the essential elements of the missal and even of the divine office had been settled before the monastic revival of the Carolingian period, it was during the great monastic centuries, from the ninth to the twelfth, that the minor texts were established, such as the formulas for the benedictions of the lessons, the absolutions, and all the accessory pieces which enriched the primary texts of the liturgy.

As for characteristics of these productions, they are precisely those which our knowledge of monastic culture would lead us to expect, and all the elements of this culture as present. The most important are highly traditional; meter alone was to evolve and take a new direction.

Sources of Inspiration

The traditional bases were primarily the Bible and the Fathers. If all these compositions are essentially poetic in character, they owe it to minds which had been fashioned by Holy Scripture. Their modes of expression are concrete and rich in images. The value of their words lies more in what they mean than in what they actually say: their evocative power is greater than their precision; each of them is like a note which awakens harmonics. All the delicacy of liturgical poetry comes from the free and harmonious use it makes of the sacred words: the groups of versicles, each of which, because of its origin and own particular meaning, has special significance and whose combination produces a more complex and a newer whole; they are daring in juxtaposing two texts, one of which throws light upon the other, thereby forming, because it is so different, a contrast with it which makes each one's individual light more intense; their way of lending a wide range of different colors to the same unchanging texts by, for example, incorporating verses of the Psalms within the antiphons; the continual passage from fact to allegory, from event to idea; the alternation of formulas, each of which evokes a different reality, which complete each other within a whole that is richer still, as the facets of a diamond permit us to see all its fires asparkle. All this art—and how much it recalls Claudel and Péguy—belongs to the great traditional liturgy. This is the style in which the *responsoria* are generally composed. The antiphons and versicles composed for new offices and other developments added to the ancient forms all derive from the same inspiration. Their authors know how to make use of the Old Testament as the liturgy had done in its great creative period; they introduced into the cult, services with exquisite taste, all the imagery of the Canticle of Canticles which was so well suited to singing the joys of the Church, of Mary, and of every Christian soul. At the height of the Middle Ages in the West, they were able to maintain in the liturgy the biblical spirit and a whole glowing play of oriental colors.

This biblical sense was authentic and vouched for by the tradition of the Fathers who had known how to make the sacred works sparkle with the same purity and the same freedom in the service of the Church's great dogmas. All the doctrinal advances of centuries during which incomparable doctors had sought to explain the faith or fight for its truth were reflected in the ancient liturgy, and in the writings of the Latin and Greek Fathers as well. Constant association with such teachers made it possible for the monks to safeguard the hierarchy of religious values. They knew enough not to allow devotions to triumph over *devotio*.[20] The great realities of salvation remained the core of their piety, their thought, and the greater number of their texts. Their worship celebrated the mysteries of Redemption, the saints who had lived by them, and the Virgin Mary in whom these mysteries found their perfect fulfillment. The result is triumphant devotion brimming with enthusiasm, animated with intense joy, and with the confidence of the children of God. This vigor, this joy, and this craving for a life in God explain, and to some extent justify, the occasionally strained epithets and the preciosity of certain images. They had to sing, accentuate, proclaim, and reiterate their happiness at what God was doing for man. "Joy," says Léon Gauthier, "is the 'dominant' in all that poetry: *Dominum veneremur, eia et eia, laudes persolvemus, canentes, eia.* This cry *eia* rings out a thousand times in each of our tropers; it is, somehow, both their résumé and their essence."[21] And this faith in the Redemption, this confidence in Christ's victory are the special mark of the religion of the patristic centuries and the writings which gave it expression. So long as it was maintained, contact with these sources prevented the liveliest imaginations from getting lost in pious fantasies. The piety expressed in these poems owes its vitality to doctrine. "Our monks," Léon Gauthier goes on to say, "are those rare theologians whose enthusiasm is not wanting in exactness."[22] Furthermore, the same historian was able to distill from their poems what he describes as "an exposition of Catholic doctrine."[23] Moreover, he has offered us nothing more than an outline; the tropes and sequences of the ninth to the twelfth centuries present on a great many points a reflection of doctrinal progress, and their evidence is well worth compiling.

To be sure, all excesses were not avoided. In this immense production, naïvetés, lapses from good taste, and gross exaggerations can be found. But, almost always, these have to do with the details of the mode of expression. On the whole, it can be maintained that the religious sense was unerring. It accorded less importance to intense feeling than to precise ideas. The emotions intervened only in the orchestration of the ideas; they were not the source from which the poetry sprang. This religion made no pretense of remaining an "interior religion." It engendered an uncontrollable need to speak of God and to God; for it is He, His grandeur, and His mysteries that were sung, more often than man and his lowliness. Above all, the poets loved to exalt the royalty of Jesus Christ. A special type of trope called the *Regnum* commented, in a sort of royal litany of the Incarnate Word, on the words of the *Gloria*: *Quoniam tu solus altissimus, Iesu Christe*.[24] This was at first done briefly in the form of a decade of profound and sonorous acclamations; then, on this theme which they knew was inexhaustible, they would yield to the universal tendency to protract, which often resulted in a real "debauchery of interior vocalisation." This trope almost always began with the words from which it took its name; *Regnum tuum solidum . . .* , and after the identical beginning, the theme was played upon with an endless number of variations. This trope, remarks Léon Gauthier, "fills up our tropers. . . . There are as many as seventeen in a single troper."[25] It can be said to have set the tone of monastic religion, nurtured as it was on the religion of the Apostles and the Fathers.

In the interests of this biblical and patristic inspiration they marshaled all the resources of their literary culture. This culture had shaped and set free talents which could henceforth realize their full potential and fulfill their highest ambitions. Worship, since the time of St. Benedict, had been the culmination of their culture. Literary experience was necessary to understand and sing the Psalms and to take part in the reading of the offices.

In the Carolingian era, culture had been still more explicitly oriented to divine worship; the revival of studies was intended to teach the monks and the clerics the right way to live, and at the same time how to speak well and write well in order to pray well: "For many desired to pray to God properly but prayed to Him poorly because of books full of mistakes."[26] Consequently, in teaching grammar, they were very careful not to forget the liturgical texts: Abbo of Fleury, in his *Grammatical Questions*,[27] takes examples from the *Te Deum* and the "Ambrosian hymns";[28] he explains at length an article of the Athanasian Creed, exactness in expression being important for doctrinal precision.[29] And Conrad of Hirsau praised secular literature which, through the beauty of its words and phrases, can become an ornament for the divine service. "When you offer God your person and your possessions, everything that remains in you from your education is lawful if you order it, as you should, to the divine service."[30] The composition of a new office—like those of St. Philibert and St. Aycardus at Jumièges—was a work of art with which they took great pains. The task required the writing of a kind of long poem, each division of which had to be made to conform with the laws governing meter.[31] They preferred the expression not to be unworthy of the beauty and truth of the mystery they were singing or the examples they were extolling.

Thus, Peter the Venerable entirely recomposed a hymn to St. Benedict because the one they had been singing at Cluny seemed to him to run counter to metrical laws, and was, besides, full of empty phrases: "You know how distasteful it is to me to sing things in church which do not ring true, and how odious I find melodious nonsense"—the *canorae nugae* of which Horace spoke.[32] Talent, however, was not always able to live up to such expectations; yet they always made every effort to use in the divine service everything they knew about literature.

Sacred Music

In any other type of literary production whatever, the style itself was sufficient. But in composing for the liturgy, a new and different element intervened: music. Actually almost everything in the divine office was chanted; the text was obliged to conform to the laws of a special rhythm which is not like that of ordinary or even artistic prose, nor yet that of recited poetry. Not that the divine office was a concert: it was not an aesthetic activity. And many a monk would have subscribed to the opinion of the anonymous author of the *Speculum virginum*: it is better to sing in a hoarse voice than to be bored in choir.[33] But if the composer knew beforehand that his text was to be chanted, and in what manner and at what moment in the liturgy, it was his duty to cast it in a literary form which made this possible. Thus the Venerable Bede in his treatise on meter proposes a special rule for hymns to be sung by two alternating choirs.[34] Music theorists were then called upon to supplement the work of the metrical experts. St. Odo of Cluny is only one of the monks who had to study both literature and chant.[35]

The monks did even this in their own way. For example, neither arithmetic nor astronomy was studied for its own sake. Through the *Computus*, those disciplines which served to determine the dates of coming feasts became auxiliary sciences for the liturgy. In the same fashion the monks took an interest in "speculative music" insofar as it was necessary for the particular ends of monastic life. Guido of Arezzo, the greatest among them, said quite definitely, in proposing his new notation, that his intention was to do so "as a monk for monks": *me monachum monachis praestare*.[36] And in order to give him a title, one of the plays on words the Middle Ages liked so well was used uniting his two functions as if they were indivisible: *musicus et monachus*.[37] Many others were, like him, monk–musicians, and they were musicians because they were monks. Among their writings on music, there are good reasons for studying not only their theories on the modes and tones but what they have to say about their ideas on the liturgy and monastic life.[38] We can discern in the general intent of their study—and sometimes even in the prologues to their treatises —their awareness of the majesty of God.[39] Their purpose is to help their brethren by means of ordered, unanimous song to join in the praise which the universe and the angels render to God, to sing in anticipation on earth the song they will continue in Heaven,[40] and the means they worked out to attain this eschatological end are an outgrowth of Christian grammar. The task called for illustrating in melodies the words of God as transmitted by the traditional liturgy and the Bible even when the language these use is not that of the secular authors.[41] Accents had to be found in which to express redeemed man's consent to the mysteries he is celebrating and whose benefits he receives. The few capitals from Cluny that have been preserved show, not the chimeras which St. Bernard deprecated, but the Christological symbols for the different tones of the chant. The third tone, for example, like compunction, moves the soul deeply and causes it, as it were, to experience Christ's Resurrection.[42] It is hard to conceive vocal prayer more efficaciously transformed into mental prayer, in conformity with St. Benedict's desire.[43]

The Cistercians had the same end in view as the earlier tradition, and used similar methods in prefacing their reformed antiphonary with a long explanatory introduction. In it, ideas on musical techniques were adapted to spiritual considerations. One of these concepts is explained by the theme of the "region of dissimilarity," so dear to St. Bernard: in this context, the *regio dissimilitudinis* is the confusion of poorly organized chant.[44] The remedy is found in Scripture: the authority of the Psalter restores dignity to each note by suggesting the use of the ten-note scale.[45] This biblical norm, unknown to pure musical science in combination with the laws established by Guido of Arezzo,[46] was to make it possible for the Cistercians as well as all the other monk–musicians to achieve their ends: to add to the holy words of the gospel the color and beauty of song.[47]

The latter had extremely complex repercussions in the field of versification that have been analyzed in great detail by philologists. It will be sufficient, at this point, to state that from that time on, poetic compositions conformed to one or the other of two different techniques. One was in the classical poetic tradition based on the quantity of the syllables, long or short. This method of versification continued in use, as, in the twelfth century at the abbey of Tegernsee, Metellus was to compose poems in the Horatian meters in honor of St. Quirinus. We know even the copy of Horace which provided his inspiration for these *Odae Quirinales*.[48] But most of the liturgical compositions were in a different style—that of syllabic poetry whose rhythm is determined by the stress of the accents. Each of these two techniques evolved, influenced in part by the pronunciation proper to the varying regions. No particular one grew into a set of laws fixed for all time and beyond the possibility of variation. Authors were not condemned to the pastiche, to the artificial imitation of verses which had themselves already been written in accordance with the dictates of an outdated phonetics. Each poet, provided he deserved the name, retained a certain liberty in regard to the disposition of his verbal material; medieval meter remained a living art form and an art practiced by the living.

This, no doubt, accounts for the number and variety of liturgical poems. In this respect we can offer no more telling example than the "poetic school" of Nonantola of the eleventh and twelfth centuries.[49] There, toward the middle of the eleventh century, we can follow a growing preference for the Leonine hexameter. This technique came to be widely used, but, at the same time, rhythmical pieces of various other structures were also being composed. And not one of these genres was limited in practice to a small number of formulas. They were, on the contrary, multiplied; there are twenty-three *benedictiones De sancta Maria* and as many as fifty-five *benedictiones* for Pentecost.[50] A like profusion is seen in many other cases whether they concern *benedictiones* or other parts of the office. The present-day Roman liturgy has kept only fifteen or so of these *benedictiones*, but each of them is a little masterpiece. Their very existence presupposes an unlimited inspiration. Innumerable texts bear out this supposition although among them there are some texts which are less felicitous. But all testify to the fact that the milieux which produced them were animated by an intense vitality.

To these texts which were used in the conventual celebration of the liturgy may be added all those which fostered private devotion. These are not always easy to distinguish from the former since they often take the form of offices or liturgical prayers.[51] And many of them eventually found a place in public worship, such as the *Rythmus de nomine Jesu* which so richly deserved it. Gilson remarked that one would have to have "a manuscript in place of a heart" not to recognize in this admirable poem a masterpiece inspired by St. Bernard's sermons.[52] Its vast dissemination proves that it corresponded to the aspirations of many fervent souls who continued to copy it, to sing it, and to transform it.[53] For, in medieval times, texts like these are living texts. They are not confined within the perfection of an established critical edition *ne varietur*. Dom Wilmart has shown how the *Adoro te* had experienced similar vicissitudes.[54] St. Bernard's ardent prose would undoubtedly inspire some talented unknown to write verses which in turn belong to anyone since they belong to all. Many other pseudo-Bernards furnish proof that the great movement of piety given impetus by the abbot of Clairvaux tended spontaneously to find expression in verse as if to complete and set off the great poem of the liturgy.

The Mystery of the Liturgy

The non-liturgical texts of the monks were not written for purposes of formal worship. But they would not be what they are if their authors had not lived in the light of the liturgy. Consequently we must now point out what monastic literature as a whole owes to the liturgy.

It is, to begin with, the general atmosphere this literature breathed, the atmosphere of Christian optimism, of faith in the Redemption, which makes Christ's victory a constant and personal cause for hope. If each author, each reader, in a word each monk, believes he can attain to a certain experience of God, it is because he knows that this union between himself and the Lord is realized primarily in the mystery of the liturgy. It only remains to secure for this effective sharing in salvation certain further psychological effects in the areas of reflection, of the attachment of the heart to God, the *affectus*. Thus one of the Christian realities the monks speak of most readily, even apart from the works consecrated to it, is the world of the sacraments. In them is accomplished the most positive contact of man with God since it is the basis for all other encounters. Attention has been drawn to the great degree of preoccupation with baptism demonstrated by the Carolingian authors. They also wrote a great deal on the eucharist,[55] and the latter remained the focal point of interest in monastic circles. We know the importance given it in the work of John of Fécamp.[56] In the twelfth century, Peter of Celle,[57] Peter the Venerable,[58] St. Bernard,[59] Senatus of Worcester,[60] and many others[61] allude to it frequently. Arnaud of Bonneval,[62] William of St. Thierry, and Baldwin of Ford wrote treatises on the sacrament of the altar. However, they never regard these as opportunities for debating abstract problems. They speak of the sacrament as a living reality which the Church in its liturgy daily proposes for their adoration, in the words of the Bible.

In the same way, the monastic authors' emphasis on frequent confession followed by absolution[63] comes from an absolute faith in the sacrament which anticipates God's judgment. In the numerous texts where Cistercian and other authors recommend confession and define the requisite conditions for its being followed by pardon, they usually do not mention the simple manifestation of conscience that the religious make to their spiritual father in accordance with a tradition which goes back to ancient monasticism. The confession they are discussing is that sure means given by God to man on earth for doing penance in the fullest sense of the term by admitting he is a sinner and professing his faith in the power given by Christ to the Church to pardon, to purify the conscience, and to prepare it to appear without spot at the Last Judgment. All these attitudes can be understood only in the light of a living conception of the Church. Many authors like Rupert of Deutz have dispersed through their writings the elements of a very rich ecclesiology. But all of them live and write with the same conviction that the meeting between the monk and God, the intimate union which all literature has the mission to prepare, is accomplished in the bosom of the Church. The Spouse who will be revealed in all her glory, the Jerusalem which is the goal of monastic effort, is already given by faith to men on this earth; it is only in union with the Church that each of us receives the kiss of the Bridegroom. Devotion to the Church, which is only another aspect of devotion to Heaven, a form of the desire for God, is already a participation in the mystery of God which is celebrated in the liturgy and communicated by the sacraments. Ecclesiology and eschatology unite, consequently, as the two dominating themes of a literature born in the atmosphere of the liturgy.

LITURGY AND CULTURE

Liturgy has marked with its imprint the whole of monastic culture, first and foremost the language of its writers who abound in reminiscences of liturgical expressions. This conclusion has already been noted with regard to John of Fécamp but it would be no less convincing were it advanced in connection with St. Bernard.[64] The rhythm of the monks' life is also marked by the liturgy and its feasts. A number of their writings have contributed to the introduction of new feasts and the addition of splendor to others recently established; we have only to think of the office of the Transfiguration and the treatise on it, both of which were composed by Peter the Venerable when he instituted this brilliant solemnity[65] at Cluny. Or we may recall the treatise written by William of Saint Jacques on the Trinity as a brief directed against some theologians of his time, and, in reaction to whose rationalistic tendencies, he asked that a feast be inaugurated to proclaim very resoundingly the Church's belief in the Trinity.[66] The whole monastic economy was organized around a life in which leisure for praising God absorbed a great amount of time.[67] Their art, in sum, was the reflection of the whole monastic existence and the habitual thoughts of the monks. Just as the cathedrals of the thirteenth cenutry have been compared to theological summas, monastic writings of the Romanesque period may be likened to the abbey churches of the period: the same simplicity, the same solidity, the same vivacity of biblical imagination. It is known that Rupert of Deutz' treatises influenced Rhenish enamel work and, through the intermediary of St. Denis, the art of many other regions; the Cathedral of Cologne may even, possibly, have been designed after a plan found in Rupert's writings.

No one has better described the bond which unites monastic liturgy and spirituality than Suger in his treatise *On the Consecration of the Church of St. Denis,* where the account of its construction and dedication is inserted in a vast exhortation to peace, the whole of which is climaxed by an allusion to the Most Holy Eucharist: in this mystery, Christ reconciles men here below with each other, with the Angels and with God, and unites in one kingdom this redeemed world which He will offer His Father when He returns.[68] And in the report *On his Abbatial Administration,* Suger defends his having done so much to beautify his basilica. The testimony he gave in his own behalf could be applied to all who represent monastic culture. What Suger did in the field of architecture and the decorative arts, others did in the realm of literature; all tried to use the resources of culture in the service of prayer and divine praise.

As for me [concludes Suger], I confess that I took great pleasure in devoting all the costliest and most precious things I could find to the service of the administration of the Most Holy Eucharist. If, to fulfill an order from God manifested through the mouth of the Prophets, golden chalices, vases, and cups were used to receive the blood of goats, calves, and the red cow of the expiation,[69] how much greater is our obligation to use, in order to receive the blood of Jesus Christ, in perpetual service and with the utmost devotion, vases of gold, gems, and everything that is considered most precious. Surely neither we nor our worldly goods can suffice such great mysteries. Even if, in a new creation, our substance were changed into that of Seraphim and Cherubim, it would still be unworthy to serve the ineffable Host. We can, however, offer propitiation for our sins. Some, no doubt, would, in contradiction, tell us that all that is necessary is to bring to the cult a pure heart, a holy soul, and true intentions; we also think that these conditions are a prime necessity and have a very special importance. But we likewise affirm that the ornamentation of the sacred vessels used for the Holy Sacrifice should possess an outer magnificence which, so far as is possible, equals our inner purity. We must serve in every way and with the utmost circumspection our Redeemer, Him from whom we receive everything without exception, and who has united His nature with ours in a Person who, placing us at His right hand, has promised us that we should truly possess His kingdom, Our Lord who lives and reigns world without end.[70]

LITURGY AND THE DESIRE FOR GOD

The liturgy is at once the mirror of a culture and its culmination. Just as the office of Corpus Christi, in the composition of which St. Thomas surely participated, crowns his doctrinal work, so the hymns, sequences, and innumerable poems written by the monks are the culmination of their theology. The liturgy had been the motive for the renewal of monastic culture in the Carolingian period, and was also its fruit. During the following centuries, it is in the atmosphere of the liturgy and amid the poems composed for it, *in hymnis et canticis*, that the synthesis of all the *artes* was effected, of the literary techniques, religious reflection, and all sources of information whether biblical, patristic, or classical. In the liturgy, all these resources fully attained their final potentiality; they were restored to God in a homage which recognized that they had come from Him. Thanksgiving, eucharist, theology, *confessio fidei*—all these expressions, in monastic tradition, expressed only slightly differing aspects of a single reality. In the liturgy, grammar was elevated to the rank of an eschatological fact. It participated in the eternal praise that the monks, in unison with the angels, began offering God in the abbey choir, and which will be perpetuated in Heaven. In the liturgy, love of learning and desire for God find perfect reconciliation.

NOTES

1. E. Dekkers, "Les anciens moines cultivaient-ils la liturgie?" in *Vom christlichen Mysterium: Gesammelte Arbeiten zum Gedächtnis von Odo Casel* (Düsseldorf, 1951), pp. 97–114.

2. J. Winandy, "Les moines et le sacerdoce," *La vie spirituelle* (1949) 23–32.

3. G. Constable, ed. "Petri Venerabilis sermones tres," RB (1954) 255–77.

4. A. van de Vyver, in his article "Les œuvres inédites d'Abbon de Fleury," RB (1935) 139–50, gives several examples.

5. U. Berlière, in *L'ascèse bénédictine des origines à la fin du XIIe siècle* (Maredsous, 1927) Part II, ch. III, "L'Œuvre de Dieu: Messe, office divin," 150–168, quotes only Rupert of Deutz, *De divinis officiis*, PL 170.11–532, as an example of a work treating the liturgy explicitly.

6. "Dévotion privée, piété populaire et liturgie au moyen âge," *Études de pastorale liturgique* (Coll. *Lex orandi*, I; Paris, 1944) 171; the list of manuscripts given there could well be lengthened, since many of the fragments seem to be addressed to secular priests rather than to monks.

7. "De exordiis et incrementis quorundam in observantiis ecclesiasticis rerum," MGH II.471; this text is adapted from the *Lehrbuch der Liturgik* by K. Künstle, "Die Theologie der Reichenau," *Die Kultur der Abtei Reichenau* (Munich, 1925), p. 709.

8. 1 Cor. 14.5.

9. PL 170.11–12.

10. PL 137.1003. Critical text in L. Gautier, *Histoire de la poésie liturgique au moyen âge. Les tropes* (Paris, 1886), pp. 20–21. According to this source, the facts have been noted many times, for instance by W. Meyer, *Gesammelte Abhandlungen zur mittelalterlichen Rhythmik*, I (Berlin, 1905) 37, 304.

11. On the medieval use of *metrum, tropus, sequentia*, see P. Lehmann, "Mittelalterliche Büchertitel," *Sb. Bay. Akad.* (1948) fasc. 4, 50–54.

12. "Dévotion privée, piété populaire" (n. 6), 156–69. K. Young, *The Drama of the Mediaeval Church* I (Oxford, 1933) 576. P. Alfonso, "Sulle origini del dramma sacro," *Annuario del Pontificio Istituto di Musica Sacra* (Rome, 1942) 19–26, shows that even the plays that have no liturgical origin are really from the monasteries.

13. "Walter of Coincy, Monk of St. Médard († 1236)," *Le livre de la Vierge*, ed. B. Guégan (Paris, 1943) p. 172.

14. B. de Gaiffier, "L'hagiographe et son public au xie siècle," *Misc. L. van der Essen* (Brussels, 1947), p. 139.

15. *Miracula S. Bertini*, MGH SS, XV.517.

16. L. Gautier, *La poésie religieuse dans les cloîtres des IXe–XIe siècles* (Paris, 1887), p. 45.

17. Gautier, *Hist. de la poésie*, Part I, 28; W. Meyer (n. 10), 2.307. V. Sesini, *Poesia e musica nella latinità cristiana dal III al X secolo* (Turin, 1949), pp. 200–42: "Monaci artisti."

18. J. Handshin, "The Two Winchester Tropers," *The Journal of Theological Studies* (1936) 34–49, 156–72.

19. "Anciennes sentences monastiques," *Coll. Ord. Cist. Ref.* 14 (1952) 120*n*viii.

20. Monastic tradition has reserved the ancient meaning of "service of God" for this word and has at the same time enriched it with a new, psychological nuance. *Pierre le Vénérable*, pp. 331, 332; *S. Bernard mystique*, p. 113; J. Chatillon, article "Devotio" in *Dict. de spiritualité*, 710–12.

21. *Hist. de la poésie*, pp. 124—27.

22. *La poésie réligieuse*, p. 11.

23. Ibid., p. 32.

24. Gautier, *Hist. de la poésie*, pp. 270–78.

25. Ibid., 271.

26. Cf. *supra* Ch. 3. The religious aim, which gave impact to Carolingian studies, was recalled with particular emphasis by P. Lehmann, "Das Problem der karolingischen Renaissance," *I problemi sulla civiltà post-carolingia* (Spoleto, 1954), pp. 330–33.

27. PL 139.532*n*18.

28. Ibid., 526*n*6.

29. Ibid., 532–33*n*21.

30. *Dialogus super auctores*, ed. Huygens, 65.

31. R. Derivière, "La composition littéraire à Jumièges: Les offices de S. Philibert et de S. Aycarde," *Jumièges* (Rouen, 1955), pp. 969–76.

32. *Pierre le Vénérable*, p. 272.

33. *Speculum viginum* (1955), ed. M. Bernards, 201*n*366.

34. *De arte metrica*, quoted by W. Meyer (n. 10), 2.120.

35. P. Thomas, "S. Odon de Cluny et son œuvre musicale," *A Cluny: Congrès scientifique* (Dijon, 1950), pp. 171–80.

36. Letter to Michael of Pomposa, at the beginning of the *De ignoto cantu*, ed. M. Gerbert, *Scriptores ecclesiastici de musica* (Saint-Blaise, 1784) II 44.

37. Donizo of Canossa, *Vita Mathildis*, quoted by Mabillon, *Annales O.S.B.* (1739) 4.301.

38. E. de Bruyne, in the chapter on "L'ésthétique musicale" in his *Études d'ésthétique médiévale* (Bruges, 1946) I 306–38, has shown that in these treatises considerations referring to the moral life were mixed with the technical details on music.

39. For example Ps.-Hucbald, *Commemoratio de tonis et psalmis modulandis*, ed. M. Gerbert (n. 36), I 213.

40. For instance, Berno of Reichenau, *Prologus in tonarium*, ed. Gerbert (n. 36),

II 62–63; Guy d'Arezzo, *De ignoto cantu*, ibid., II 35; Regino of Prüm, *De harmonica institutione*, ibid., I 234–35.

41. For example, Berno of Reichenau, *De varia psalmorum atque cantuum modulatione*, ibid., II 105: "The works of Terence, Virgil, Cicero, and other practitioners of the Liberal Arts have been transmitted to us exactly as they wrote them. . . . Is it not even more fitting that the words of divine revelation should come to us in their own grammatical form?" Cf. also 106 and *passim*.

42. "Teritus impingit Christumque resurgere fingit," text in *Pierre le Vénérable*, p. 275. Cf. Evans, *Monastic life at Cluny (910–1157)* (Oxford, 1931), pp. 122–25.

43. "Mens nostra concordet voci nostrae," *Rule*, ch. 19.

44. PL 182.1128A.

45. Ibid., 1128C.

46. Ibid., 1128C-D.

47. "Litteram ut sanctam et evangelicam retinentes, honestate et pulchritudine cantus supercoloravimus," ibid., 1123B.

48. L. Sorrento, *Medievalia* (Brescia, 1944), p. 148.

49. G. Vecchi, "Metri, ritmi nonantolani. Una scuola poetica monastica medievale (sec. XI–XII)," *Deputazione di storia patria per le antiche provincie Modenesi, Atti e memori*, ser. 8, 6 (Modena, 1954) 220–57.

50. "Bénédictions pour les lectures de l'office de Noël," *Misc. G. Mercati* (Studi e Testi; 1946) II 477–83.

51. F. X. Haimerl, *Mittelalterliche Frömmigkeit im Spiegel der Gebetbuchliteratur Süddeutschlands* (Munich, 1952), especially the first part: "Benediktinisches Mönchtum als Hauptträger des Gebetsfrömmigkeit im Frühmittelalter," 5–19; the list given there should be completed; cf. "Dévotion privée" (n. 6), 151–56; *Un maître*, pp. 37–44, 60–62; "Écrits spirituels de l'école de Jean de Fécamp," *Analecta monastica* I 91–114.

52. *Les idées et les lettres* (Paris, 1932), p. 47.

53. Wilmart, "Le 'Jubilus' sur le nom de Jésus dit de S. Bernard," *Ephemerides liturgicae* 68 (1943).

54. Wilmart, *Auteurs spirituels et textes dévôts du moyen âge latin* (Paris, 1932), pp. 361–414.

55. Künstle, "Die Theologie der Reichenau," 707–709. Gautier, *La poésie religieuse*, p. 20.

56. *Un maître*, pp. 33–34, 44.

57. *La spiritualité de Pierre de Celle*, Ch. VI: "La confession fréquente et la communion quotidienne," pp. 124–26.

58. *Pierre le Vénérable*, pp. 310–11, 360–64.

59. R. J. Hesbert, "S. Bernard et l'eucharistie," *Mél. S. Bernard* (Dijon, 1954), pp. 156–76; C. Hontoir, "La dévotion au Saint-Sacrement chez les premiers cisterciens (XII–XIIIᵉ s.)," *Studia Eucharistica* (Antwerp, 1946), 132–56.

60. P. Delhaye, "Deux textes de Senatus de Worcester sur la pénitence," RTAM (1952) 205, Letters 4 and 5.

61. Bernards, *Speculum virginum*, pp. 117–18.

62. "Les méditations eucharistiques d'Arnauld de Bonneval," RTAM (1946) 40–56.

63. *La Spiritualité de Pierre de Celle*, pp. 121–24; *Pierre le Vénérable*, pp. 134, 311–17; Bernards, pp. 113–17. "Sic confitere ut absolvi merearis," ibid. 113*n*266.

64. "Recherches sur les Sermons sur les Cantiques de S. Bernard: Aux sources des sermons sur les Cantiques," RB (1959) 237–57.

65. *Pierre le Vénérable*, pp. 326–90.

66. "Le traité de Guillaume de Saint-Jacques sur la Trinité," *Arch. d'hist. doct. et litt. du moyen âge* (1950–51) 89–102.

67. "La vie économique des monastères au moyen âge," *Inspiration religieuse et structures doctrinales* (Paris, 1948), pp. 211–59.

68. Suger, *Comment fut construit Saint-Denis* (Paris, 1945): "Suger, grand bâtisseur," pp. 5–26.

69. Num. 19.2.

70. PL 186.1234. Suger (n. 68), pp. 25–26.

Literature and the Mystical Life

Protestations of modesty at the beginning of a work and the offering in conclusion of excuses for its shortcomings were once popular literary themes. But, even today, without any literary implication, any exposé which deals with a long cultural period must, of necessity, be submitted as provisional and incomplete; its lacunae are all too evident. This work, then, will be in keeping with its nature as an "essay," if it is brought to a close with the formulation of the two major problems which arise from the findings presented in the preceding pages. One is concerned with history; the other with spirituality. The first has to do, we might say, with the objective aspect of monastic tradition, the other with the subjective element, with the personal mystery which emanates from the texts. We shall try to see, on the one hand, which were the dominant characteristics of medieval monastic culture, and, on the other, how mysticism was brought into harmony with literary forms.

A Culture of a Group

Monastic culture is the culture of a milieu; it is not merely the privilege of a few great minds. The life of a milieu depends on its élite; but without it, an élite could not exist. It also makes possible the maintenance of a tradition despite changing circumstances determined by the turn of political events. The economic life of the medieval monasteries reveals alternating periods of poverty and prosperity during which the institution remained unchanged. In the realm of study and of observance there also appeared what historians customarily call peak moments, followed by declines and even decadence, and finally, revival; these are dated according to their great names and are judged in the light of a few exceptional documents. In reality, there was a general level of virtue amongst the average monks which enabled the abbeys on the whole to remain centers of religious vitality and spreading influence in the midst of so many upheavals. The researcher can occasionally perceive, through a few anonymous texts, the existence of obscure but zealous religious of whom the chronicles have nothing to say, but who, like invisible columns, supported the whole edifice.

Medieval monasticism possessed a common homogeneous culture insofar as it kept alive ways of life and institutions which other milieux had failed to produce. Without a doubt, the monasteries had at times exerted such great influence that all Christian society lived, more or less, in the light they diffused. Curtius' conclusion is as true of the Middle Ages as of the patristic period: "Much of what we call Christian is purely and simply monastic."[1] Nonetheless, wherever monastic life was lived to its fullest capacity, it produced works which were most distinctly marked by its own character. As we have seen, the whole difference between scholastic and monastic theology lies in the fact that the same religious reflection was exercised in two places and two environments which were not the same. In either case, those who had no personal contribution to make could at least enrich themselves by association with more gifted minds. In the schools they acquired a taste for intellectual pursuits, a certain aptitude for speculation, and the doctrinal learning useful in the pastoral life. In the cloisters they participated in an atmosphere where spiritual preoccupations received greater attention and culture, for its own sake, could develop more freely. The soldiers who came to follow St. Anselm's teaching and the adults who entered the twelfth-century Cluny or the Cistercian abbeys were not all, beyond any doubt, equipped with a classical education. But they profited from all those whose literary and spiritual culture made the environment productive. With this in mind, we feel justified, in the sketch we are attempting here, in not positing any fundamental difference between the Cistercians and monastic tradition in general. Tendencies were basically the same everywhere and differences in color were only varieties of shading. The cultural contributions of the white monks and that of the monks who were called, not "black," but "gray," has its roots within a living whole whose composition becomes evident through contrast with everything non-monastic.

Together, all the monks played a role in the Middle Ages not played by others or at least not to the same extent. They formed the link between two cultural periods, between the Fathers and the "moderns." They preserved nothing just for the pleasure of preserving, but did so in order to live by the texts and to unify in the interests of their religious life the cult and the culture. This is the reason why they were induced to keep alive and transmit the treasures of beauty which had been accumulated over the centuries of antiquity. Romanesque monastic art preceded and paved the way for the flowering of the Gothic; so also, monastic culture was the necessary precondition for the scholastic Golden Age and the short period which has since been called the Renaissance. The greatest cultural periods are not the most productive so far as literary output is concerned. Activity always entails dispersion. But there are always periods when people lived more intensely. The thirteenth century, for example, produced the greatest number of works and in that sense is the greatest century of the Middle Ages. But on the whole, minds were less cultivated then than in earlier centuries, centuries so happy that no need to produce was felt; it was enough to be alive.

Yet, the expansion of the classical thirteenth and fourteenth centuries became possible because, in preceding centuries, the treasures of culture had been possessed in tranquillity. In periods of great production, technique tends to triumph over spontaneity. How far La Bruyère seems from Montaigne! The same distance separates the masters of scholasticism from the monks who embodied the humanism of the preceding centuries. What the monks did for Christian culture must be measured not only by what they produced but by what was produced by the non-monastic centuries which came after them and which owe to them not only the transmission of the texts but, what is more important, a spiritual tradition and the life of the spirit itself.

LITERARY STYLE: AN ACT OF HOMAGE TO GOD

This culture, which belonged to a whole milieu, bears the stamp of certain constant characteristics which, at this point, we need merely recall. This culture is primarily literary and traditional or, more precisely, literary because it is traditional. It was profoundly marked by the literary tradition of antiquity. The latter, particularly in Rome, was the property of an élite who used, in writing, a language that was not the everyday language or entirely like the spoken tongue, the *elocutio vulgaris*. Every piece of writing was artistic, "technical"; none was altogether devoid of art ($\check{\alpha}\tau\epsilon\chi\nu o\nu$).[2] Christian writers had even fewer reasons to abandon this procedure since it had been adopted by God's spokesmen themselves. The word of God is a book written with art. Inspired authors, even when writing in the "vulgar tongue" like those who wrote the New Testament, respect and employ literary genres and rhetorical procedures. The Prophets are poets, and each one of Christ's witnesses added to the message he had received the accent of his own eloquence. Rhetoric appears in the Lord's discourses as recorded by the Evangelists, and in St. Paul's epistles as well. Nor were the Fathers of the Church to initiate any departures from this attitude. They proclaimed that eloquence is only a means and cannot lawfully be pursued as an end in itself. Once these reservations had been made, however, the Fathers felt the obligation to use its resources. Their testimony had to retain the same literary character as the word of God in order not to be unworthy of it. In their eyes, "elegant style" was homage rendered to God.[3]

An ascetic like St. Jerome is a professional writer. He knows that the efficacy of his teaching depends in part upon the quality of his language. Consequently, he takes great pains not only with his style but also with his reputation. His prologues are full of oratorical precautions intended to prevent the reader's failure to appreciate the literary genre chosen for each work.[4] These prologues present the usual themes of the traditional exordium: his incapacity for writing, reasons which constrain him to do so, his desire for brevity; in sum, the things everyone felt obliged to say under the same circumstances.[5] And one sometimes gets the impression that St. Jerome is really himself only afterward when, in the course of his exposition, to some extent he shakes off these literary shackles. But, to tell the truth, he is also being himself in the prologues and epilogues to which he gives such complete submission, for he is a man of letters and his culture is so much a part of him that he cannot express himself without consciously reverting to it. He wishes to be respected as the disciple of the Word that has become writing. By His Incarnation, the Word deposited His eternal truth in vessels which history fashions in every period for men who must keep it in their hearts and then hand it down in the words their own civilization has taught them.

A mystic like St. Gregory also betrays the learned man's preoccupations and the author's mentality. Having learned that commentaries on Holy Scripture which he had given before the monks of Monte Celio had been written up by a monk after his own fashion, Gregory has them read to him and finds that his statements have been modified "in a very childish manner." Accordingly, he censures this way of proceeding and firmly orders all the notes taken during his lectures to be located and returned to him.[6] Yet the infidelity of the composition was "quite relative" since the editor had "had at hand the stenographic record of the homilies."[7] But Gregory was concerned with expression as well as with doctrine.

In the Latin world, the ancient monastic milieux shared in the literary atmosphere of Christian society as a whole. They were, perhaps, more closely connected with the hierarchy and its cultural élites than were the Eastern monks. However that may be, it has been claimed that "Western monastic life, from its origins, has been literary in character."[8] Neither St. Benedict nor the renovators of the Carolingian period could break with so established a tradition; on the contrary, they strengthened it. They not only required the monks to be literate, but by founding and organizing schools, they gave them the means to become so. Along with the obligation to study they inculcated the love of study. The joy study afforded them shines through many a poem:

Audite pueri, quam sunt dulces litterae. . . .

And the refrain, like an echo, takes up the theme and enlarges upon it:

Et nos felices, qui studemus litteras.[9]

The tenth to the twelfth century in the West witnessed the continuous expansion of monastic literature whose form derived from classical tradition but whose inspiration was exclusively Christian. Grace elevates the soul and enriches it with divine capacities. Still, culture also refines and embellishes it, thereby increasing its ability to receive and to tell of the gifts of God. St. Bernard in a few words, *scientia litterarum, quae ornat animam*,[10] has very accurately described the role of learning in the history of Christian culture.

Mea grammatica Christus est

Monastic culture, however, is not merely that of learned Christians. Among the Christians, even the erudite, the monks' orientation is theirs alone and can be described as mystical. To an extent not attained by others, they feel and express the great difference which exists between the two orders of realities which they are, nevertheless, willing to unite since God Himself has not separated them: the Christian life and culture. More than any other Christians and men of letters, they feel a constant inner urge to transcend belles-lettres in order to safeguard the primacy of the spiritual domain. St. Bernard has declared that the Jews are merely "literary," because they gnaw as on a dry crust the letter of the divine writings.[11] But all monastic authors pass the same judgment on those who would derive all their nourishment from literature alone. If *grammatica* were to occupy in their hearts the place which belongs to Christ, they would reject it. And sometimes, indeed, they appear to, so intense is their obsession with the one sole necessity: *Mea grammatica Christus est,* affirms St. Peter Damian with the vehemence of love.[12]

Fortunately these men of God, the word-possessed, know that they do not have to make a choice. Having renounced everything which could be the result of strictly human agency, they are free to accept everything God gives them: His truth under beauty's fairest guise. As the truth is revealed to the eyes of their sensitive souls, the brilliance of its splendor increasingly pervades them. In Heaven, they will be totally penetrated with light. The rays which can be glimpsed here below, any one of which might interfere with the perception of another, will then be blended into a whole. The word of God and culture together give the soul an appetite for a happiness which will be fully satisfied only in eternity. Faith and literature, instead of satiating the Christian, stimulate his thirst for God, his eschatological desire. Grammar's role is to create in him an urgent need for total beauty; eschatology's role is to indicate the direction in which to look for its fulfillment. There is a book which the finger of God writes in the heart of each monk; no other can substitute for it. No written literature, even sacred literature, can dispense with the state of recollection essential for hearing God's word within one's self: "We read today in the book of experience," said St. Bernard.[13] And one of his disciples adds even more plainly: "I think, brothers, that you have read in the book of your experience, in your heart rather than in a manuscript": *et in corde magis quam in omni codice.*[14]

LEARNING AND CONSCIENCE

The corrective for literature is the experience of God, the devotion to Heaven which St. Benedict and St. Gregory had helped so much to inculcate in the monks. Monastic theology and liturgical poetry reaped the benefits of these efforts. All trditional asceticism had served to pave the way for this conciliation between spiritual life and cultural values. Peter of Celle and others have spoken of the conflict which may arise between "learning" and "conscience" but, at the same time, proved by their own example that this conflict can be resolved. *To combine a patiently acquired culture with a simplicity won through the power of fervent love, to keep simplicity of soul in the midst of the diverse attractions of the intellectual life and, in order to accomplish this, to place oneself and remain firmly on the plane of the conscience, to raise knowledge to its level and never let it fall below: this is what the cultivated monk succeeds in doing. He is a scholar, he is versed in letters, but he is not merely a man of science or a man of letters or an intellectual: he is a spiritual man.*

Its greatest representatives have shown how the culture of the monastic milieux can lead to the highest manifestations of Christian experience, those pertaining to the mystical life. St. Bernard elicits our admiration as the supreme example of the way in which, under the action of God, literature and the mystical life become one, to the point of being inseparable.

St. Bernard is highly literary and makes little effort to disguise it. His prologues, like those of other writers, reveal the fact that his is an author's mentality. Not only does he take every ordinary precautionary measure to disarm criticism; he frankly admits to being afraid of it.[15] Even in the main body of his works he takes care to comply with the literary forms.[16] Comparison between the successive editions he prepared of some of his writings proves that he corrected his style down to the smallest details.[17] Rhetorical figures abound in his treatises as well as in his sermons. In the *Apology*, for example, he presents as an "omission" what is, in reality, a long enumeration of things he wishes to denounce as abuses;[18] that is what Cicero called the *praetermissio*.[19] Elsewhere, Bernard uses the device recognized by one of his contemporaries as the rhetorician's *insinuatio*.[20] In the face of this evidence one may well wonder if St. Bernard, after having attained to sanctity, would still have allowed himself, as in his literary youth, the same ingenuous concessions to oratorical art.[21] But in the *De Consideratione* and the last *Sermons on the Canticles*, works of Bernard's old age, rhetoric still holds a place of honor.[22] On this point, seemingly, no evolution took place in his life, nothing resembling a second conversion. Conversion to God came, in his case, before any literary production; the latter was never anything other than a manifestation of the former. From his arrival at Clairvaux to his entry into Heaven, the real, the only Bernard was, indissolubly and simultaneously, a learned man and a man of God, a thinker and a saint, a humanist and a mystic.

It would be wonderful to acquire some idea of the kind of purification which enabled him to achieve this synthesis. If literature occupies such an important place in his writing we would like to know how great a part can be ascribed to spontaneous ardor, actually lived experience—in brief, to sincerity. The problem is a delicate one. The analyses of modern psychologists shed but little light on it, for their phenomenology was elaborated to deal with "complex" personalities.[23] But the medieval mystics, like their contemporaries, are simple and "primitive" in the sense we have stipulated in this book.[24] Furthermore, no man, and still less so St. Bernard since he is a great man, can be reduced to a solution which takes no account of the mystery within him. We must respect the secret of God's action in his soul. Our concern, after all, is with the work he has left us.[25] Perhaps it will tell us something of the inner victory he won over literature for the cause of the love of God.

What criterion distinguishes pure literature, cultivated for its own sake —as we speak of "art for art's sake"—from spiritual literature? In what does a writer, who is a literary man and nothing else, or, in any case, practically nothing but a literary man, differ from one who is not a literary but a spiritual man, uniquely or at least primarily spiritual? *Spiritualibus spiritualia comparantes*, St. Bernard likes to repeat, in referring to the doctrine he espouses in his written sermons. This criterion is the complacency one feels for himself and for what he has written. One can be complacent about his writing because it expresses or extends the self. Or one can also be pleased with the self and write because of that, to communicate and prolong the beloved self, seeking, more or less consciously, to have it admired, to make it "interesting," which is the same as making sure others will take an interest in it.

This complacency is actually a turning in upon the self or egotism. It is therefore the opposite of spiritual experience which is a pure gift to God, forgetfulness of the self, humility, consent to God alone, and, to say all in one word, love. Self-interest and interest in God or in what one has written about God are mutually exclusive. No one can go off in two different directions at the same time. As P. Petit humorously put it, "if one absolutely insists on looking at himself in the mirror, it is altogether useless to kneel at a prie-Dieu."[26]

DETACHMENT

The criterion of the true mystic, the proof that, even though he is a literary man, he is inspired, is his detachment. If he is detached from himself, he can have no complacency for what he writes. But if one gathers that the desire to write is of prime importance to him, if an artist's stylistic preoccupation can be discerned in his writing, then he is nothing more than a man of letters. A certain artistic elegance is justifiable in his writing but it should never seek after admiration for itself. If anyone listens to himself talk, if he pays less attention to what he is saying than to how he says it, we are annoyed by the intrusion of his ego which he erects as a barrier between us and Truth. An author of this type does not possess simplicity. He is a double personality; he is a literary man and, at one and the same time, something else even when he is writing about the realities of the spiritual life. The sign of an exclusively spiritual piece of writing is its simplicity: a simplicty of soul which is reflected in a certain simplicity of artistry. The latter will be spontaneous, though not necessarily stripped of ornamentation when the whole cultural formation of a period makes it a desirable and necessary feature. It can be a studied work, the product of considerable literary effort, but the predominant concern will be for what is said and not for the artistic way of saying it. When a man is impressed by a truth or by an experience, his major concern is to express it, not the form the ideas take. If the experience is truly spiritual even the first draft will be lofty, beautiful, and naturally artistic. *A literary revision may perfect it, but artistry alone can never produce the experience. Art can be but the reflection of spiritual experience, never a means for provoking it in the writer or in the reader. Sought after for its own sake, it forms a screen between the author and ourselves; the author becomes an aesthete, we are spectators, and there is no longer any communion in love of Truth.*

St. Bernard often speaks of the "ministry of the word," *ministerium verbi.* Every thought that comes to him is intended for God's service. If he chose to keep it for himself, it would lose all its value; it belongs to the Spirit whose nature it is to communicate Himself. Bernard, in expressing it, is in a certain way prolonging the Incarnation of the Word. And just as Christ was humble and gentle in order to make Himself accessible to all, so everything said of Him should be able to be of service to all and should be attractive to all. Man should not appropriate God's word and make it his own and use it for his own personal ends. Man's word must remain an instrument if it is not to betray God's word. Literature must be a means of serving charity, not an obstacle or an impediment. It cannot become an end, even a secondary end. It must be placed at God's service alone, not that of an author's reputation.

Yet the problem is not so simple. For the author's reputation is, in itself, a means for procuring God's glory, which to a certain extent depends upon the author's personal glory, provided he is working for God. If he performs his task poorly, he compromises his reputation and also the cause he serves, the truth he should manifest, and the Church whose honor he hopes to enhance. It is therefore quite usual and permissible for an author to be concerned about his reputation insofar as it depends on him. To the extent that it depends upon others, he must place it in God's hands and submit to criticism. And this will never be lacking. The writer must renounce his reputation; anyone who writes exposes himself to a thousand judgments which do not always represent the opinion of the most competent critics. For example, Peter Berengarius criticized St. Bernard[27] without rallying any supporters, and yet Bernard may have been wounded by his reproaches. To the degree that an author's reputation depends on his conscientious attitude toward his work, he should feel a sense of responsibility. He must not consciously court failure or purposely write poorly. If certain enterprises result in a failure which was not of his own doing, he cannot fail to reap benefit from this. He will see it as an authentic way for imitating Jesus Christ. When the second Crusade resulted in failure, St. Bernard could say: "I accept being deprived of glory provided the glory of God suffers no outrage." [28] But when he writes, he cannot be indifferent to his responsibility for the success or failure of his message. He feels the obligation to give it an expression worthy of his subject matter. He must create a fine piece of work knowing all the while that God's glory alone must be his sole source of satisfaction. Accordingly, to the extent that Bernard succumbed to self-complacency, to that same extent he was more a man of letters and less a mystic. And this is known only to God. In his Prologues, Bernard assures us, in the customary literary forms, that he is mindful of his reputation only so far as he must, if he is to serve and honor God. What reasons have we for doubting his sincerity? Are his statements borne out in the works which follow the Prologues? Let us attempt to discover what effect the spiritual principles just reviewed had in the domain of literature.

Just as dialectics are used in theology, but, without Revelation, would be powerless to originate any religious reflection, so, too, literature may be the vehicle chosen by the spiritual man to express his experience. Two major observations must be made at this point: one has to do with literature's incapacity to awaken experience; the other, the effect in turn of all experience on the domain of literature.

There is no spiritual literature without spiritual experience: it is the experience which gives rise to literature, not the reverse. Had he depended on the resources of literature alone, St. Bernard could not have spoken as he did of the spiritual life; he would not have been able to describe its realities had he not lived them. Spiritual experience alone enabled him to transcend literature, to use it, certainly, but never to become its slave. He was able to remain free, undivided and uncomplicated, and to produce literature as if he were not trying to do so. The difference between those who are merely literary men and those who are saints at the same time can be seen in the contrast between Bernard and Nicholas of Clairvaux. This gifted notary, devoid of personality though full of talents, full of "having" but low in "being," carries out his functions as a writer very ably but his writings reveal no personal experience whatsoever. Because he could imitate to perfection, he could compose business letters for Bernard who had given him the outline. Left to his own devices, however, he could never have composed even one of the *Sermons on the Canticles.* Unless St. Bernard dictates to him, he succeeds when reduced to his own resources in producing only an inflated rhetoric whose artifices make every sentence a stumbling block. The complacency he derives in the process and the effort it costs him are very obvious. Moreover, he talks a great deal about himself and his style.[29]

St. Bernard, on the contrary, is self-effacing before the truth to which he is to testify. He never mentions his style; he seems to forget he is writing. Entirely absorbed in the experience of God, he receives from it an inexhaustible spontaneity and "invention." He is a poet, a creator. In a language which is his alone he makes his own spiritual universe come alive for us. He invents language and words as his thought progresses. The greater interiority, intensity of experience, and reflection he attains, the loftier his style becomes. He manipulates language at will, molds it with utmost freedom, and transforms it into a flexible and docile instrument. In the hands of a genius or a saint, or, even more so, a man who, like Bernard, is both, the artificial, the factitious, and art become natural, or, rather, nature yields itself unrestrainedly to art and its laws; the latter are forgotten, and eloquence is totally unconcerned with eloquence. The mystical writer achieves the utmost simplicity in his mode of expression. Within the limitations imposed by art, he can use artifice to dazzle, eliminate it entirely, or reduce it to what is hardly noticeable.

Thus experience transforms literature. Many twelfth-century scholars were equipped to produce literature. But how else can we explain the fact that Bernard did so in writing the sublime pages we owe to him unless what he wrote in them represented his vision of reality? Let us assume, for the sake of argument, that the literary pieces which make up his work were written by someone else or by secretaries; in that case we should have to credit them with his genius, his holiness, and consequently with his perfection of style. Neither a mystic without literary ability nor a man of letters without spiritual experience will ever, even in collaboration, write a great spiritual work. Literary genius without holiness, holiness without literary genius, will never adequately explain the writings which result from the union of these two gifts of God. Literature alone could not give these texts their religious intensity; holiness would not be sufficient to give them the beauty which is one of the reasons for their permanent value. Yet this meeting of holiness and literary genius is by no means extraordinary. When God chooses, fashions, and enriches a privileged soul, He gives it a human quality to conform to the heavenly grace He bestows on it. There is a gift for writing, a charism of style which makes of Ruysbroeck, St. John of the Cross, St. Teresa of Avila, St. Francis de Sales, and many others besides St. Bernard literary classics of their times and their countries. A mystical language is thus created through the association of talent and experience. No doubt one may think that, in the various parts of a long work, one or the other of these is receiving the greater emphasis; but both are present throughout.

Style becomes loftier as life becomes more spiritual. The gift of God does not eliminate human effort in the domain of literature any more than it does in asceticism or in prayer itself. Mystical writers try to improve their already noble style in the proportion that they cultivate the gifts of God in their souls. More precisely, God, working in them, augments their talent and their means for expression. But they possess and retain this charism or ability to write well only when they are speaking of Him. It is this charism alone which is responsible for their being not simply literary writers. If St. Teresa had written letters on any other subject than God, if she had talked about the flowers in her garden or what was being said in the drawing-rooms in Seville, she would have been only a Marquise de Sévigné. But she was speaking of God, and God who gave her the power to love Him also gave her the ability to write well. There is a story that St. Thomas Aquinas, as death was drawing near, heard the Lord ask: "You have spoken well of Me; what reward would you like?"—"Nothing but Yourself, Lord," he answered. He was able, at that moment, to make such a reply since he had previously, in his mortal life when speaking and writing of God, desired nothing but God alone. It is for that very reason that he spoke of Him well.

Experience does not issue from literature. It neither imposes nor necessarily gives rise to it, and need not be expressed in writing. But if it is to be written down, its own inner insistence on beauty confers the means. Whatever literature is needed, experience raises to its own level. Consequently, a higher type of sincerity is apparent in the writings of the mystic even amid the forms appropriate to the various periods, sometimes to our confusion. We are so prone to judge the ancients by the standards of today. One historian has noted that "There is a prejudice against rhetoric; people are disposed to judge it, wherever it is encountered, as unworthy of consideration and lacking in sincerity. But it is an art just as poetry is an art, and in antiquity a *true* sentiment could, without losing its integrity, use it as an instrument." [30]

Since rhetoric appears under different guises, we can occasionally be duped; we think it has disappeared and that only sincerity still survives. Ours is the day of sincerity in literature. People write diaries of private thoughts with a very casual air, whereas in former times no attempt was made to disguise the great pains which had been taken to write well. Both methods are compatible with the type of sincerity which is the author's sincerity. An author's complete and fundamental sincerity must be judged not by the stylistic methods he employs but by his soul. Not according to the way he expresses himself but by what he says: whether he actually experienced it, or whether he could have said it without having experienced it. There are at least two kinds of literary sincerity. A certain writer of today may, in all sincerity, try to give the impression that he is not writing literature; St. Bernard will admit with sincerity that he is. In both cases we can perceive the same urge to write and to express oneself, arising from the conviction that one's message is true and may do some good. In either case, the author needs a public and is sincere toward it when he is speaking of God. The difference between them lies entirely in the manner used to put things. But because of this fundamental sincerity, a saint like Bernard can achieve in a period when rhetoric holds sway a perfect literary mortification which mirrors his own inner detachment. His mystical style attains a purity and an intensity worthy of his simplicity and purity of heart.

He is able consequently both to submit to the laws of rhetoric and to free himself from them through the spontaneous ardor which carries him beyond the scope of his own faculties. Literature is to a large extent an imitation; it lays down laws which have been illustrated by examples. But mysticism is creation, a renewal. Literature forms the beauty of a written work, mysticism gives it its grandeur. Literature's portion is the literary genre and style which have been adopted; sincerity contributes the experience these devices are to express: it finds them essential and they do it no injury. Amid genres and literary conventions, the mystic can be recognized by the extreme simplicity of the means he uses. His style becomes as limpid as his soul is pure. And the more elevated his thought, the less contrived is his expression. Pages can be found in the treatise *On the Degrees of Humility*, in the *Apology*, or in the *De Consideratione*, and at every stage of Bernard's life where the use of literary devices is quite evident; in these places, he is saying things others might well have said. But when he is most completely himself, that is to say, most absorbed with God, as he is for example in many passages of the *Sermons on the Canticles*, he is much simpler but no less the artist. Now, art resides solely in the rhythm of the sentences which is attuned to an inner rhythm born of the possession of God. Articulation in words adds only sound to the ideas, the echo that was lacking in the word as pure thought; the accent of sincerity qualifies the message to be received, and therein is contained the whole of rhetoric.

Freedom of the spirit alone enables the mystical author to use his literary gifts with this degree of liberty. Carried to the extreme, this freedom and this austerity would result in silence, for experience is a form of intimate love exchanged between the soul and God; insofar as it is personal and incommunicable, it is predisposed to silence. But this very charity assumes another aspect in that it includes, besides the mystic, his neighbor. Should the mystic be a shepherd of souls, a doctor and a writer of the Church, he has the duty to communicate to others what he knows of God. And when he speaks of this, he must do it well since whatever he says must always be imperfect. St. Bernard thinks the angels will help him since they also are servants of the word.[31] They "administer" to the mind beautiful conceptions and the images which make them perceptible. But while images express God they likewise conceal Him. This radical defect in every thing the mystic tries to express succeeds in detaching him from his literary pursuits and in removing any self-satisfaction he might take in what he writes. Literature, he knows, with all its formalities and necessary laws, is an example of the impotence of our condition, its limitations, and of the inadequacy of what we say to represent what gives us our life. To become aware of this lack and this impediment is to intensify one's desire to possess God fully in eternity.

The extreme frontiers of literature, therefore, open into the whole realm of the ineffable. At this point the word must yield before the inexpressible gifts which are granted through the liberty and the liberality of God. In the last of his completed sermons on the Canticle, St. Bernard stressed this truth in a text which could serve as his literary testament:

> And now someone may perhaps ask me what it is like to enjoy the Word. And I shall answer him: "Seek out, rather, someone who has had the experience and ask him. For if it had been given to me, even to such as me, to have that experience, do you think that I could express the inexpressible?" Hearken to the Apostle St. Paul who did have this experience: "For whether we be transported in mind, it is to God; or whether we be sober, it is for you."[32] In other words: "It is very different when I am all alone with God, and when I am with you. What takes place between God and me, I can feel, but not express; when with you, on the contrary, I try to speak in a way that you will understand." Oh

you who are anxious to learn what it is to enjoy the Word, prepare not your ear but your soul; for it is grace that teaches it and not language. This secret remains hidden from the wise and the cautious, and is revealed to the little ones. Yes, my brothers, it is great, it is great and sublime, the virtue of humility which obtains the reality of what cannot be expressed, which alone teaches what cannot be taught. It alone is worthy to receive from the Word and to conceive through the Word what it cannot explain in words. And why is that? Surely not because it deserves it but because such is the will of Him who is the Father of the Word, the bridegroom of the soul, Jesus Christ the Lord who is God blessed above all for ever and ever. Amen.[33]

NOTES

1. E. R. Curtius, *European Literature and the Latin Middle Ages*, p. 515.

2. C. Mohrmann, "Problèmes stylistiques de la littérature chrétienne," *Vigiliae christianae* (1955) 222. *Latin vulgaire, latin médiéval, latin chrétien* (Paris, 1955), p. 1.

3. "Problèmes stylistiques," 234.

4. Cf. L. Stade, *Hieronymus in prooemiis quid tractaverit* (Rostock, 1925).

5. Cf. L. Arbusow, *Colores rhetorici* (Göttingen, 1948), pp. 97–103: "Topik des Exordiums."

6. *Epist.* XII 6 (MGH, *Epist.* II 351–53).

7. B. Capelle, "Les homélies de S. Grégoire sur le Cantique," *Revue bénédictine* (1929) 205. In his thesis, "Le commentaire de S. Grégoire au premier livre des Rois" (Louvain, 1956) 126, P. Verbraken arrives at the same conclusion: that the editing had "shown relatively few traces of the personal intervention of the Abbé Claude. The pope had yielded to a most superficial impression. . . . This might well be the reason for the annoyed tone of his letter to the subdeacon John."

8. Mohrmann, *Latin vulgaire* (n. 2), 2.

9. L. Traube, *Vorlesungen und Abhandlungen* III (Munich, 1920) 193, and MGH, *PLAC* IV, ii, 657.

10. *Sup. Cant.* 37.2. A similar form by Conrad of Hirsau was quoted *supra*, p. 118.

11. *Epist.* 106.2 (PL 182.242).

12. *Epist.* VIII, 8 (PL 144.476).

13. *Sup. Cant.* 3.1.

14. MS. Auxerre 50 (13th cent., Pontigny, O. Cist.) fol. 139ᵛ: "In libro propriae experientiae et in corde magis quam in omni codice, fratres, puto vos legisse satis."

15. "Les prologues de S. Bernard et sa psychologie d'auteur," *Cahiers de civilisation médiévale* 1 (1958) 425–36.

16. *Apologia* 15: "In fact, this letter, if it is really to be a letter, should come to a [formal] conclusion."

17. "Les sermons de Bernard sur le Ps. *Qui habitat*," *Bernard de Clairvaux* (Paris, 1953), pp. 435–46. "Formes successives de l'Apologie," RB (1955) 257–58. "S. Bernard écrivain," in RB.

18. "Omitto oratoriorum immensas altitudines, immoderatas longitudines . . ." *Apol.* 28.

19. Martianus Capella, *De nuptiis philolog.* 5.523, *praeteritio*; *Ad Herenn.* 4.27.37: *occultatio.*

20. Concerning the first part of the *Apologia*: Quid est illud genus . . .? Rhetores appellant illud insinuationem . . .: tunc enim advocatus accusati in principio orationis cum detestantibus detestatur . . ., postea vero, mira verborum arte, quae firmaverat infirmat, quae accusaverat, excusat." *Dialogus inter Cluniacensem et Cisterciensem,* ed. Martène, *Thes. nov. anecd.* (Paris, 1717), 1577. On *insinuatio*: *Ad Herenn.* 1.6.9.

21. Reasonable doubt is expressed by Knowles, *Cistercians and Cluniacs* (Oxford, 1955), p. 14.

22. Lehmann, "Die Vielgestalt des zwölften Jahrhunderts," *Hist. Zeitschr.* (1954) 323–33, has stressed the admirable points of this rhetoric. L. Negri "Appunti nella personalità letteraria di S. Bernardo," *Humanitas* (1954) 625–37, has illustrated with examples drawn from different writings of St. Bernard the perfection of his "stylistic technique."

23. From H. Bremond, *La poésie pure* (1926) and *Prière et poésie* (1926) to J. Monchanin, *De l'ésthétique à la mystique* (1955), as well as J. Rivière, *Rimbaud* (1930), H. Lavelle, *La parole et l'écriture* (1947), and H. v. Balthasar, *Phénoménologie de la vérité* (1955).

24. See above, p. 131. This was an entirely different problem from the one studied in the writings of St. Teresa by M. Florisoone, *Esthétique et mystique d'après Sainte Thérèse d'Avila et St. Jean de la Croix* (Paris, 1956).

25. Mohrmann, "Le style de S. Bernard," *S. Bernardo* (Milan, 1954), pp. 177–84, remains the most suggestive study on the relationship between St. Bernard's language and his spirituality.

26. P. Petit, Preface to the French translation of Kierkegaard's *Postscriptum*, viii.

27. *Apologeticus pro Abaelardo*, PL 178.1863.

28. *De consideratione* II 4.

29. "Les collections de sermons de Nicolas de Clairvaux," RB (1956) 269–302.

30. A. v. Harnack, quoted by P. Duployé, *Rhétorique et parole de Dieu* (Paris, 1955), p. 108n7.

31. *Sup. Cant.* 41.3–4. Other texts indicated by E. Boissard, "La doctrine des anges chez S. Bernard," *S. Bernard théologien*, p. 128

32. 2 Cor. 5.13.

33. *Sup. Cant.* 85.14.

APPENDICES

APPENDICES.

I

The *Rule*
of St. Benedict
and the Canticle of Canticles

A MANUSCRIPT OF AUXERRE (no. 50, 13th century) from the Cistercian
Abbey of Pontigny contains an anonymous and unpublished commentary
on the *Rule* of St. Benedict. In explaining the words of the last chapter
of the *Rule*—"Is there a page, is there one word of divine authority in the
Old and the New Testament, which is not a very reliable rule for leading
our life?"—the author refers to the Canticle of Canticles (see above, p. 86).
His text is as follows:

> Quas nimirum aversiones atque conversiones Novi Testamenti paginae,
> denique sanctorum omnes tibi resonant libri catholicorum patrum, sed prae
> ceteris dulcius illa Testamenti Veteris pagina quae dicitur Canticum canti-
> corum. Spirituales iucundaeque admodum Patris nostri illius Salomonis col-
> lationes, adeo ut sub colloquiis privatisque confabulationibus negotium hoc
> deprompserit totum. Regulam ipse descripsit bene viventium et legitime
> amantium animarum, non novitiarum quidem, sed quae ad perfectionem con-
> versationis et amoris a suae conversionis initio festinarunt; non quae aliqua-
> tenus, sed omnino plenius iam se demonstrent habere honestatem morum, et
> quarum, in quantum possibile est, perfectus sit ornatus omnis. Quid enim sibi
> volunt huiuscemodi ut et nos demonstremus ea, scilicet murenulae aureae
> vermiculatae argento? Morum honestas omnia ista, colli monilia denique talis
> animae varietates omnes. Ibi igitur vita et instituta, regula et rectissima vivendi
> norma talium animarum, denique et quae comparari debeant spiritualibus
> spirituales collationes. Sint autem huiusmodi: *Veni, electa mea. . . . Veni,*
> *dilecte mi. . . . Surge, surge, egredere in campum*, in locum illum vel illum.
> Faciamus haec vel illa. Quid? Huiusmodi collationes liber ille resonat per
> totum. Ha quam dulce ibi resonat illud: *Quae habitas in hortis, amici auscul-*
> *tant te, sonet vox tua in auribus nostris; fac me audire vocem tuam! Qualis*
> *dilectus, talis et dilecta*: candidus et rubicundus ille, candida et rubicunda illa.
> Videte igitur, fratres, si nobis desidiosis et male viventibus talis inest, et non
> magis merito confusionis rubor, quod in illo certe et ipso Veteris Testamenti
> nondum invenimur libro de conversionis et conversationis perfectione?

II

The Monk
who Slept during the Office

THIS POEM, translated above on page 137, is found in a manuscript of
Montpellier (Med. 35, 12th century, fol. 12). M. A. Vernet has kindly informed me that it very probably comes from Pontigny; in any case, it was
there in the seventeenth century (cf. C. H. Talbot, "Notes on the Library
of Pontigny," *Analecta S. Ord. Cist.* [1955] 166n289). The Latin text of
the poem given below follows this manuscript (P). The same text is found
with but a single variant in MS Montpellier, Med. H. 294 (12th–13th
century, Clairvaux), fol. 138 (C). It has been published after a manuscript
of the 12th–13th century coming from the Cistercian Abbey of Villers-en-
Brabant, in J. Martini, *A Catalogue of Manuscripts, Early Printed and
Rare Books*, 28 (Lugano, 1938) 15. The variant readings in this edition
are given below under the symbol M. Finally A. Wilmart pointed out that
the text is to be found in Berlin Phill. 1685, fol. 175 (14th century, Collège
de Clermont) in the *Revue bénédictine* (1936) 167.

DE MONACHO DORMIENTE[1] AD VIGILIAS.[2]
ABBAS: Flecte caput, fili, quia dicunt:[3] *Gloria Patri.*
DIABOLUS: Non flectet, triplicem nisi ruperit antea funem.[4]
ABBAS: Ne perdamus ovem, funem Deus, aufer et hostem.
DEUS: Libero captivum; tu corripe, desidiosum.[5]
MONACHUS: Ante caput perdam, quam deinceps lumina claudam.

1. dormiente *om.* C.
2. qui dormiebat in choro M.
3. Dicitur M.

4. Cf. Eccles., 4.12.
5. desiosum M.

III

The *Speculative Theology* of Dom Bertrand

UNDER THE TITLE *Divi Bernardi . . . theologia speculativa, ex sparsis per illius opera sententiis collecta . . .*, *opus tam theologiae lectoribus quam concionatoribus et devotione* [sic] *studentibus perutile ac necessarium*, Laurent Bertrand, Cistercian of Pignerol, in Piedmont, published at Asti, between 1675 and 1678, a work in four volumes (complete title and information on the author in L. Janauschek, *Bibliographia Bernardina* [Vienna, 1891], ns. 1213, 1220, 1234). The work is divided into treatises according to the following outline: *De Deo* (existence, attributes, etc.), *De creatione*, *De Trinitate, De distinctione rerum creatarum, De angelis et eorum cultu, tam activo quam passivo, De Incarnatione*. The end of the work, which was almost completed, was to have included the treatises *De sacramentis* and *De justitia et jure*. Death prevented the author from making the final draft and publishing it. Each *tractatus* is divided into *quaestiones*, each *quaestio* into *articuli*. Accordingly *Quaestio* I^a, *De Dei existentia*, contains Art. 1. *An Deum esse sit per se notum*, Art. 2. *An Deum esse possit demonstrari*, to Art. 6. *An rationes praemissae probent divinam existentiam et perfectiones demonstrative*. Each article includes *Textus, Conclusiones, Resolutiones*. Article 1 of the *De Incarnatione* is entitled *An Incarnatio sit possibilis*; the last article, *Quinam defectus fuerint in anima Christi*. As an example of the way the questions are put, one might quote the beginning of art., vol. I, p. 82: "*An Deus communicetur, quot et quibus modis?* Difficultas procedit ex sententia divi Thomae docentis rationem boni non esse formaliter constitutam in relatione . . .*" (see above, p. 220).

IV

Monastic Theology

ON A NUMBER OF OCCASIONS in the course of this study we have been at pains to point out the limitations of monastic theology; it should be repeated here that our appreciation for monastic theology should in no sense lessen the esteem which is due to that form of theology which developed after the monastic period. In this connection I should like to reproduce here some remarks on this topic which I made in a conference to young monks with regard to the monastic orders.[1]

> There are certain things which the Church wishes us to know and which we will not learn from our monastic authors. We will not find in them all of theology. We speak, quite legitimately, of monastic theology; but this attractive new formula should not become for us the excuse for a new form of laziness which would consist in studying only the monastic authors. In order that we might become capable of assimilating the theological contribution of the centuries which followed the epoch of our Fathers, it is most important that we have clear ideas on the problems which had not arisen in their times. We have need of a terminology that will be precise and sure, proved by experience, and approved by authority. We need concepts. . . . We should not succumb to the temptation of believing that fervor, religious ardor, and, still less, religious sentiment will ever take the place of the knowledge and the methodical study of the traditional scholastic philosophy and theology.

It is also fitting that we should recall the words of Father Alszeghy, S.J., Dean of the Faculty of Theology of the Gregorian University:

> The works of St. Bernard offer to us a religious thought which has a high value in itself, and not merely as a preparation for scholastic theories. In his works we find a theology which differs from scholastic theology less by the diversity of opinions than by a difference in the forms of thought. . . . The present-day theologian realizes that he cannot fulfill his function without a systematic theology and a rational method; at the same time, however, he is aware how much he needs, in order to succeed in his task, the theology of St. Bernard which will provide him with a necessary complement.[2]

---

1. A conference given to the students at the house of the General of the Reformed Cistercians and published in *Collectanea Ord. Cist. Ref.* 19 (1957) 238–48.
2. "Contributi alla teologia bernardina," *Gregorianum* 38 (1957) 340.

V

St. Anselm

IN THIS PRESENT WORK I had avoided situating St. Anselm in relation either to monastic theology or to scholastic theology. But the felicitous way in which S. Vanni Rovighi, Professor at the Catholic University of Milan, has spoken of this Doctor would have no other result than to stimulate an interest which he so richly deserves.[1] In the chapter devoted to "the Bene- dictine tradition" in the *Histoire de Spiritualité* (Paris: Aubier), there is an evaluation of St. Anselm along those lines of which the following re- marks will suffice:

> Above and beyond all the representatives of ancient monasticism there stands the figure of St. Anselm. In all truth, it is difficult to place him in any particular category; he is a genius and is therefore beyond classification. He is a monk and clings with every fiber of his being to the patristic tradition which gives life to monasticism. At the same time, he is passionately devoted to formal logic. At times, in his reflections on the data of revelation, he is inclined to use more the light of reason than the weight of authority; as a consequence, he elaborated a provisional and incomplete synthesis which fell short of his expectations, but it was a bold endeavor and one that proves that he had a beautiful confidence in the resources of nature. His influence was to make itself felt particularly in the thirteenth century. Even in the seventeenth cen- tury his influence on certain minds such as Isaac of Stella, Aelred of Rievaulx, and Richard of St. Victor cannot be entirely discounted. It is precisely because he belongs in no category, since he is an exception, that he confirms the normal standards for differentiating between monks and scholastics.[2]

1. S. Vanni Rovighi, "Questo mirabili secolo XII," *Studium* 54 (1958) 423–24. Similarly we find a good deal of information on St. Anselm in the very substantial volume entitled: *Spicilegium Beccense*. I. *Congrès international du IXᵉ centenaire de l'arrivée d'Anselme au Bec* (Paris: Vrin, 1959).

2. These are extracts from a lecture given at the Collegio Angelico in Rome, the text of which has been published under the title of "Richesses spirituelles du XIIᵉ siècle," *La vie spirituelle* 100 (1959) 298–306.

Index